COLLEGE BASKETBALL, U.S.A.

BOOKS BY JOHN D. McCALLUM

Ivy League Football: Since 1872
Big Ten Football: Since 1895
College Football, U.S.A.
This Was Football
We Remember Rockne
The World Heavyweight Boxing Championship: A History
The Encyclopedia of World Boxing Champions
Dumb Dan
Boxing Fans' Almanac
Ty Cobb
The Tiger Wore Spikes
Everest Diary
That Kelley Family
Six Roads From Abilene
Going Their Way
How You Can Play Little League Baseball
The Crime Doctor

JOHN D. McCALLUM

ennis

, 1924-

COLLEGE BASKETBALL, U.S.A.

SINCE 1892

5D STEIN AND DAY/Publishers/New York

PHOTO CREDITS: Princeton, Texas Western, La Salle College, St. John's U., West Virginia U., U. of Kansas, U.C.L.A., Indiana U., Duke U., Loyola (of Chicago), U. of Wyoming, U. of North Carolina, Louisiana State U., North Carolina State U., Seattle *Post-Intelligencer*, U. of Washington, Seattle U., Memphis State U., Holy Cross, Oklahoma State U., Stanford U., Washington State U., City College of New York, U. of Cincinnati, Marquette U., U. of Oregon, Ohio State U., U. of Michigan, U. of Wisconsin, St. Louis U., Phil Woolpert, John D. McCallum, Dr. Marvin (Tom) Tommervik, Ken Dunmire, Jim Ennis, Dave Stidolph.

Printed in the United States of America
Stein and Day/*Publishers*/Scarborough House,
Briarcliff Manor, N.Y. 10510

Library of Congress Cataloging in Publication Data

McCallum, John Dennis, 1924–
    College basketball, U.S.A., since 1892.

    Includes index.
    1. Basketball—United States—History.
2. College sports.   I. Title.
GV883.M3   796.32′363′0973   78-7466
ISBN 0-8128-2503-9

To
my old coach,
Jack Friel,
who took Washington State
to the 1941 NCAA finals—
a Hall of Famer
in every way

MEMORABLE QUOTES FROM AL McGUIRE

"Basketball is a veritable ballet—most people don't realize what tremendous athletes basketball players are."

"To me, the four most important things that make a team a winner are scheduling, referees, coaching and material—in that order."

"I never thought referees were dishonest. I just did my thing [protest fouls] and they did theirs [call fouls]."

"There are games so tense, so dramatic, that I don't think anyone but God can referee them."

"What do I think of the way coaches conduct themselves on the sideline during games? Now that I am retired and have time to reflect, I never realized I was so obnoxious."

"It would be nice to be remembered in the same breath with John Wooden. But if I'd won as often as he did, you'd need four guys to carry my head around."

CONTENTS

"It doesn't look to me like the pros have as much fun. It doesn't seem as exciting as playing college basketball."

David Thompson, North Carolina State, 1974

THE SAGES

A New Era

It would be, John Wooden said, a new era in college basketball. Get rid of the jump ball—legislate it out of the rules.

"The jump ball isn't fair, it's tough to administer," Wooden said. "I'd like to see the game started by the visiting team taking the ball out at midcourt, with an unmolested throw-in to the backcourt only. Then after that, in every jump ball situation, the teams would take turns taking it out of bounds."

The former UCLA coach said he was also in favor of two other major changes in the college rules.

"One is a 30-second clock. I wasn't for it until I served on the rules committee for five years and we did a study on one of Hank Iba's teams. Almost every time, they got shots off in less than 30 seconds. I was convinced that if Iba, the foremost advocate of ball-control basketball, didn't need 30 seconds to shoot, the clock wouldn't hurt the ball-control coach. But it would prevent the farcical games that no one, not even the home fans, want to see. Games are scheduled to be *played* and I'd like to see them be played every minute. I tried to show how foolish stalling is when we played Villanova for the NCAA championship in 1971—but few people seemed to get the point."

What's the other change he'd like to see?

"The end to offensive-rebound baskets," he said. "If a shot is missed, the offensive team may not put it back in the basket until *after* it throws at least one pass. This would cut down on fouls because defensive men wouldn't block out as viciously, and offensive men wouldn't go over the backs and shove as much. It would also make for better in-close passing—better finesse."

Wooden made it clear that he did not like to see the game's growing trend toward roughness.

"I saw the trend developing the last several years I was in coaching," he said. "It's mainly the result of what some choose to call the passing game, where the emphasis is on screens, especially away from the ball. The game has tended to be more physical. It's taken away finesse—and I don't want to see basketball stop being a game of finesse. The more screens there are, the more defenders subconsciously may think they have to use their hands. All of this contact is covered in the rules, but officials are looser in their calls lately. It handicaps the defense. The rules are there, they just have to be better enforced. I remember in the old pro league, back when I was just getting out of Purdue, it was too rough and there was public reaction to it. Whether that will be true today or not, I'm not sure. I'm not for banning all physical contact, but if you want a boxing match, go to the prizefights, not a college basketball game.

"Basketball is a great game, but that doesn't mean we should stand still. Progress comes from change. Where we see there are ways and means that we can improve it, we should improve it and not say, 'No, we won't do it because the pros do it.' But we can't always copy the pros, either. They have a new statistic now, for steals. But I bet you'll find that the top stealers in the NBA aren't good defensive players because they gamble too much. The colleges have a great game and it will continue to get better."

In writing the words "John Wooden," I was

John Wooden. His UCLA Bruins won 10 NCAA championships in 12 years.

impelled to call Marv Harshman by telephone to settle a point. Harshman is the head basketball coach at the University of Washington and a vice-president of the National Association of Basketball Coaches. In 33 years of college coaching, he started the 1977-78 season as the second biggest winner in the U.S. among active coaches, with more than 500. In 1975, he led

the United States to the Pan American Games Gold Medal. I've known him for more than 30 years. He is a walking encyclopedia of facts, figures and anecdotes.

"I'm writing about John Wooden," I told him.

Harshman started to chuckle.

"Well, put this down," he said. "It's an historical fact that my career against him reads like bookends."

"Bookends?"

"I mean," he explained, "I beat him the first time I opposed him; and then, 17 years later, I beat him the last time we met. Victories at both ends. But in between I think I beat John only twice. Still, that's probably more wins over UCLA and Wooden than anyone else in the Pac-8 can claim."

"Let's see," I said, getting out a record book, "you beat the Bruins in 1959, your first season at Washington State. And then you came to Washington in 1971 and beat Wooden again four years later, before he retired. I'll bet you Pac-8 coaches were glad to see him go."

Harshman grew serious.

"A lot of people didn't understand Wooden. Perhaps he won too much. I didn't resent him. He was always honest with me. A great competitor, you knew he'd try to beat you any way he could, but that's the name of the game. Not once in the 19 years I've known John have I ever heard him berate a player or a coach. I appreciate that.

"John was one of the enigmas of coaching. I mean, I don't believe he was a great coach when he started. Like so many All-American players fresh out of college, he had to teach himself how to coach, because playing and coaching are not necessarily analogous. The first time I beat him I remember saying to myself, 'So this is the great Pac-8—the great UCLA—the great John Wooden, huh?' Of course, I soon returned to earth and was made to eat those words many times afterwards. At that time, Pete Newell was the epitome of coaching, and after beating Wooden and then Stanford I ran into Pete's California Bears, who literally pulverized us. I felt lower than a snake's belly. I remember I was sitting on the stairs going down to the dressing rooms and Pete came by and said to me, 'Hey, Marv, don't do anything differently. Let me tell you a story. When I left San Francisco University and went to Michigan State I thought I knew all the answers to coaching. But then I took my lumps in the Big Ten and I wanted to quit coaching, I wanted to get out of East Lansing. But some old geezer who'd been in the game a long time told me that there was nothing wrong with what I was doing. He said to keep at it, to do what I understood best and the result would be that my kids would play better.' I often think of Pete's words. Wooden's greatest asset was his ability to make adjustments. He was great because he was able to take great players and make great teams. Many other coaches in college basketball—all of us, I think— have had a clutch of great athletes but have somehow failed to mold them into great teams. It's very difficult to take great players and make them into a great team. Wooden's greatest teams occurred when he had seven very good players and five guys who didn't care if they got off the bench. In fact, John once told me that his most trying times were during his last several years at UCLA, when he had to deal with a collection of his greatest players, 10 or 11 of them, and there was so much discontent and backbiting because some didn't get enough playing time. I can understand that. That's the problem a lot of us have when we get more than our share of outstanding recruits."

Harshman, a member of the old *New York Sun*'s All-America football team in 1940 as an all-purpose fullback at tiny Pacific Lutheran University, was later drafted by the Chicago Cardinals. He has seen a lot of basketballs drop through the hoop since beginning his coaching career in 1946. Like Wooden, he has passed through quite a few eras, and witnessed some of the more important changes in the way the game is played.

"The most revolutionary change," he attests, "has been the jump shot, because that brought offense to a new level, and then out of necessity defense had to change. There's been so much specialization. I've often felt that basketball sort of followed on the coattail of football. That is, defense gets ahead of offense; offense makes quick changes, such as team alignments and men in motion. In basketball, all of a sudden, there was the full-court press. Now we get full-court offenses, we get many more screening

Marv Harshman, former All-America football fullback turned major college basketball coach.

situations, we get a variety of alignments of high-low posts, double-low posts. Then came the pressure defenses where everybody overplayed and denied you the ball. People then took people away from the basket so that there was no defensive support and moved them upcourt, daring people now to overplay. If they did, they threw over the top."

The classic example, Harshman feels, was UCLA vs. Houston in the 1967 NCAA semifinals. "That was after Houston had beaten the Bruins in the Astrodome earlier in the season, the only game Wooden lost with that crew. The game was played in Los Angeles and Houston came out and tried to pressure and front UCLA. So Wooden took Alcindor off the baseline and moved him out to high post; still Houston tried to front him. The result was that the Bruins threw over the top, made several easy layups, completely shattered the Houston defense, and went on to win in a breeze.

"The coaching is better today. Everybody has more systems. But there's only so many plays in any sport. What has happened is that there's a big facade, a big camouflage of action. A lot of people call it false motion. What it is is a lot of action to make the defense *think* you're going to do something when what you're actually doing is something entirely different. An early example was Pete Newell's California Reverse Action. The Bears would start penetration on one side of the court, forcing the defense to concentrate there, and then reverse the ball around where the defense could make only one defensive play without supporting players. If you had a good player it was one-on-one and you were going to beat the defense because your man was better. This was an early illustration of camouflage, of taking advantage of inequality. What you try to do is find the weak link in the defense and then attack that, but you can't attack it directly, because the defense will rush help to it. In other words, there's a lot of smokescreening going on out there. Basketball is one gigantic game of chess.

"Now, I love football," Harshman admits, "it was always my great love, for playing and coaching, but it's become a coaches' game. Basketball is still a players' game. And what I love about it is that you must do your coaching during the week."

Marv doesn't believe players will be getting much taller and heavier. "They're about as big as they are going to get. Equipment, training, coaches, athletes—all these parts have gone nearly as far as they can. Weight-training equipment, for example, has probably reached its maximum. The problem now is that some of our physical attributes may have outstripped

our facilities. In my day, which wasn't all that long ago, a center who stood 6' 3" or 6' 4" was considered huge, but now they stretch 7' 4" and are as capable and agile as the shorter players. One of the best things that could happen to basketball would be to put the basket at 11 feet. In three different years we ran experimental games with the higher basket in the NCAA tournament, and they worked out well. I've been on the National Board for eight years now, and most of the people serving with me really believe it would be to the advantage of the game to up the baskets to 11 feet. What it does, we've found, is help the shorter player. There are less blocked shots in the medium-range, inside-range area because it forces a player to shoot the ball at a higher trajectory. That opens up the basket area; now instead of shooting at about 60 per cent of the area, you're going to shoot at 80 or 90 percent because of the arc of the ball. Statistically, we felt it proved that it dispersed rebounding so that the big 7-footer guarding the basket lost some of his advantage. When it dispersed rebounding it also cleared the congestion and there were fewer fouls in the basket area. The proposed rule is an excellent one, but it has been held up because of cost—the added cost of all those high school gyms where the roof isn't very high.

"I've often thought that our elementary schools should have a 9-foot basket, so that they don't learn bad habits by trying to force the ball; perhaps nine at the intermediate schools, 10 at the high schools, and go to 11 at the colleges. In our experimental games we discovered that the players, after only one season of practice, without exception had better field goal shooting percentages at 11 feet than they did at 10. That truly surprised us. We thought it would be the other way around. The only shot they missed more frequently was the layup. Of course, the layup is a habit shot at 10 feet, so for 11 the players had to relearn it."

Harshman foresees some continued experimentation and rules changes. But he's not in favor of wholesale changes.

"I'm not sure I like the dunk coming back in. I have a 7-footer now and he dunks the ball, but I still think we should have learned our lesson during the Chamberlain and Alcindor eras.

Wilt, playing with the dunk, was never a good shooter away from the basket; neither was George Mikan. They played in the days when you could stand right next to the basket and drop it in. Alcindor had to change his style in his sophomore season and play without the dunk. That made him the greatest shooting big man we've ever had. A player's skill should be what's important, not his physical strength. We've copied the pros too much in that regard. Neither do I like the proposed 30-second clock. The clock legislates strategy. The college game, the amateur game, should be kept different from the pros. Pro basketball has become boring, stereotyped; we shouldn't change the college rules to mimic them.

"If we're going to change college basketball, let's borrow from the International rulebook. A bigger lane, for example, similar to the International lane, definitely would be a plus. It spreads out the game. The less the officials handle the ball, the less attention they call to themselves, the better the game will be for both the players and spectators. In other words, some combination of International rules and our own present rules might be progressive.

"I'd love to see three officials assigned to a game instead of the present two. With the players so big and fast now, the game is most difficult to officiate. It's impossible for two referees to cover everything. In my career, we've played 10 games using three officials. There were some mistakes, sure, but with the extra ref it was like having a speed cop stationed alongside the highway; you knew there was an official watching. The result was that the players were less apt to try to get away with something."

Seven-footers may seem to be dominating college basketball, but Harshman is still a believer in the value of the smaller player.

"In my coaching career, I've probably played with more little guards than anyone else in the Pac-8. The best team I ever had was at Washington State in the Lew Alcindor years, when we were second in the league to UCLA. My guards were 5' 9" Lenny Allen and 5' 11" Ray Stein and I well remember traveling down to Los Angeles to play USC and then UCLA. We beat the Trojans to cinch second place and then got ready for the Bruins. With all candor, I told my guys that we weren't going to beat

UCLA and Alcindor, but the plain truth was that UCLA was nothing but a myth; without Alcindor their guys were no better than the rest of us. 'But Alcindor's presence makes them appear better,' I said. 'So tonight we're going to play one-on-one against Alcindor.' Jim McKean, a scrawny, 6' 8" kid from Tacoma, was my center. I said, 'Jim, you're probably going to go down in history as the guy who held Alcindor to maybe 50 points, and I'll go down in history as the coach who was dumb enough to match you one-on-one with him.' Then I went to the other four starters and gave them their assignments. I put Stein on Lucius Allen, I put 6' 5" Gary Elliott on Lynn Shackleford, and so forth. And what happened? Allen didn't make a field goal, Shackleford didn't make a field goal— but Alcindor got 61 points! Still it proved my point: sometimes the presence of a great player, if you're concentrating your defense around him, thus leaving several of his teammates relatively free, makes them appear much better than they really are.

"I've always believed that the excitement of basketball is in the little men. I love the 5' 10", the 5' 11" player. He creates situations, which is another reason I'd like to see the basket raised. Everything has tended to help the big guys, who are not necessarily that skilled—and Dr. Naismith invented basketball as a game of skill. That's why I'm going to continue to work through the National Association of Basketball Coaches to keep the little man in the game; in fact, to get him back in it even more. John Wooden always believed a team should not be allowed to shoot the offensive rebound. I like that. You'd have to bring the ball down, throw it out and initiate again. That'd make the little guy all the more important.

"The hardest guy to recruit right now is what we call the lead guard; the little man who can handle the ball and get it into play. Because with the jump shot, everybody's thinking one or two or three bounces; get in the air and he can get a shot on anybody. Of course, we're all statistically oriented, and shooting and point-making is important. They're already thinking of their name in the paper, all-star teams, the NBA draft, so they don't work and polish up the rest of their game. But I repeat, for the last 10 years the hardest player to recruit is the lead guard, the little guy who runs the show. He is very, very scarce.

"The best lead guard I've seen in years was Seattle University's Carl Ervin. He had an innate ability to get the ball, find where his people were, and then get the ball to one of them; that's the greatest trait in basketball.

"If I were putting together a 'dream team,' I'd start with a player like Ervin, anywhere from 5′ 10″ to 6′ 2″. You say I could find a 6′ 4″ guy to do the same job. Maybe so, but I haven't found him yet. It's just not that simple, because the 6′ 4″ guys in high school generally play forward or even center. To be a good lead guard you need experience in constant ballhandling, the instinct of what to do with the ball. It's something you must grow up with. That's why the better guards usually come out of the big-city playgrounds of the East, where, if you lose the ball, you don't get a shot. Those kids know the value of controlling the ball. They can handle the ball, fool around with it. When they get a chance to play with better players, if they can show they are able to handle the ball competently and move it around and get it to the stars, then the stars choose them for their pickup team. That's the way those good guards from the ghetto get started.

"The lead guard and the 7-foot center are the two most important people on your team; the 7-foot center not so much because he's going to be so dominant offensively, but because of his value in the domination of the defensive end of the floor. And then you must have a shooter on your dream team. Generally he'll be your second guard. We look for a bigger guard here because of potential matchups in defense. You can hide one little guy, and you can play pressure and he can go out and fight anybody away from the basket, but your second guard should be 6′ 3″ to 6′ 5″, with the ability to hit from outside. His other skills are not so important. Of course, the better he is in all phases the better the team is going to be.

"I try to have one power forward. He might be like the young man I had at Washington in 1977-78, Tim Stewart, a 6′ 7″, 225-pound bruising rebounder, physical. He'd fight anybody, any hour. He could do all the skill things reasonably well. Your second forward should be quick, someone who can attack the basket with the ball; you need him both offensively and

defensively. You're going to find someone on the other side, on the front line, who's going to have a bit more quickness than probably your big guy, or maybe your power guy, so you must have somebody up front with the ability to take the ball to the basket, to press the defense. The ideal combination, I think, is the 7-foot pivot man, with his various skills; the power forward, who's going to be able to go to the boards and give added support to the center; the quick forward who can shoot the ball and take it to the basket, too; the shooting guard; and then, of course, the guy I especially love, the little guard who can handle the ball and get it downcourt to people and make things happen and blast open the defense."

To fully appreciate Marv Harshman the coach, you must know something about Marv Harshman the athlete. Actually, he made his national reputation in football. As a fullback and Pacific Lutheran College's play-caller, he was a gambler, a risk-taker, a bulldog. He met all the requirements of a super fullback: he was big enough (6′ 1″, 215 lbs.) to make all the tough yardage, had enough speed (9.9 in the 100) to go the distance when his blockers broke him into the clear and he had, as all backs should have, that really quick start. He was a Vince Lombardi-style player—powerful, all football player, all desire. He had good enough hands to run pass routes, too, because if he hadn't it wouldn't have been long before enemy defenses learned to ignore him as they did some other fullbacks. But no one ignored Harshman. Giving him the ball was like giving him a shot of adrenalin. He had that good secondary speed, a fine change of pace, and he mastered the art of working with his interference, and once out in the open he had those great head, shoulder and hip feints.

Harshman played a lot of games for tiny Pacific Lutheran in 1939-40-41; his quickness, combined with his awesome underpinnings and tremendous balance, made him a very difficult runner to bring down. Few fullbacks have had his balance, because he'd stumble and stagger and still hold his feet, and where some runners will give you that leg and then take it away from you, Harshman would give it to you and then ram it through your chest. Some claimed that he ran best when somebody was hanging onto him, but he was so shifty he seldom gave tacklers their best shot at him. He was as good as they come at running inside or outside his blockers.

In an open field Harshman was something else again. When he saw a clear field ahead he hunted down somebody to run into, and while you have to enjoy body contact to play football, Harshman exulted in it. He was fond of saying, "You gotta sting 'em a little out there. You've gotta make those tacklers respect you." Opponents respected him, all right. In fact, every time he carried the ball there were 11 of them, all of whom wanted to pay their respects to him personally.

Harshman, who was also a star basketball playmaker at PLU, and in 1940 led the Gladiators to a stunning upset over University of Washington, brought his rugged spirit to coaching; first at Pacific Lutheran as one of the country's most successful small-college coaches, then at Washington State, and now at Washington.

Reminded that he'd been coaching college basketball for 32 years, but that he still displays the zealous enthusiasm of a sophomore breaking in, Harshman explains it this way. "We all coach much differently from the way we did 10 years ago, or we wouldn't be in coaching. When I began it was all blind faith. You'd say to a player, 'Hey, do it this way,' and the boy didn't even question you. He did what he was told. *Blind faith.* He never stopped to ask himself if you even knew what you were talking about. Nowadays, you don't expect your players to do what you say without them asking questions— but now you anticipate their questions and are ready with the answers. You try to hypothetically frame in your mind everything that may happen, then show the player what his options are. As coach, I'm not saying, 'Hey, do it this way because I say so.' What I'm saying is, 'If this occurs, this is what's going to happen; and if we do this, they're probably going to have to do this.' It used to be, the play went A to B to C, and you went from this point to that point. But that's passé now. Now you must give your players at least two, possibly three alternatives, because the defense is often damn sharp and forces your people to make split-second decisions without looking to the bench for help. For example, you give your lead guard, the workhorse, a point of penetration with the ball. He dribbles past, creates a defensive reaction,

and then, based on what the defense does, he chooses what is best. As coach, you can point out, 'Hey, maybe that wasn't the best choice after all, because this is what the defense did. If you would have gone the other way, this would have opened up for you.' So many of us, in our present society, are afraid to fail. But failure is what you build success on. You have to understand that things don't always go right, and if you work harder you can find the solution. All great champions know that you learn more from your defeats than from your victories. Losing requires some soul-searching, some humility, because human nature is such that too much success makes us believe we are better than we really are, to become overconfident. Then some obscure opponent flattens us, knocks us out of basketball's Top Ten, and we go back to our corners and admit, 'Hey, as an individual I'm dependent on all these other guys, and I'm not carrying my share of the load; gotta go back and start over and find out some better answers.'

"Now, let's get down to the bottom line: The future of college basketball is unlimited. Several summers ago, I got involved internationally in the game. I went for our national organization and the State Department to Iceland, of all places, where they have great knowledge of basketball. On TV, they see our Eastern pro games and the Eastern college games. I also went to Denmark where, like many European nations, they are trying to develop a sound sports program. They even have sports colleges, where we put on two weeks of clinics for their national basketball teams and coaches. We tutored the 200 best men and women basketball players in Denmark, drawn from a base of 50,000 candidates. This sports college had 12 gyms and 12 stadiums; outside fields with tracks, and soccer fields. Then I went over to Sweden and discovered more of the same. If anything, the Swedes are even more advanced, because they've hired American coaches to teach them and they've imported Americans to play in their National Basketball League.

"Then I went to Ireland for a series of basketball clinics. The game is still new there.

"A Father Herron was head of Irish basketball while I was there. He belonged to a very small Catholic diocese, which had the best gym in Ireland. Actually, it was nothing more than a crackerbox, about like our old grammar school gyms of 40 years ago, with no seats and low ceiling. Everybody stood as I talked, but no matter, they were very attentive, very enthusiastic. They were quick to learn, quick to adapt, and worked their tails off. And so sincerely appreciative. When I left Europe I was convinced basketball had replaced soccer as the most international sport in the world."

A Man You Listen To—Phil Woolpert

In this business you are always hearing about people like the late Hirsch Jacobs, who trained pigeons and horses; and people like the late Clyde Beatty, who trained lions; people like my old boss in New York, the late NEA Sports Editor Harry Grayson, who thought Beatty was "the greatest guy in America," because when Harry took his little kid to the circus years ago, "Beatty let him go into the cage with the lions"; people like Raul Vasquez, of Key West, who trained fish to climb up on his lap, eat out of his hands, and then lie there, content, until he put them back in the water; and people like Phil Woolpert, who trained men.

Recently, I got to thinking about Woolpert—you know, where did he go after he quit coaching? What is he doing today? Does he still stay close to basketball? And all those things a writer thinks about. I questioned some of the other coaches about him and got the grand total I already knew—left the University of San Francisco in 1959 and then disappeared. That was all they knew. He just dropped out of sight.

Then, one day, I was having lunch with John Owen, Sports Editor of the Seattle *Post-Intelligencer*, and John said, why, didn't I know, Phil Woolpert and his wife had settled down up at Sequim, Washington, on the Olympic Peninsula, about 100 miles northwest of Seattle.

Later, I got to thinking hard about Woolpert again and I went down to the local newspaper and dug up the old files on him. That was when I first felt a little jerk around my heart when I suddenly realized that this fine man and great coach retired at the peak of his career because he had positively soured on the pressures of the business.

I read this on Woolpert and then, because everything that meant something was missing, I grabbed my hat and went after him. The route to Sequim by car is neither a straight nor a narrow path, but pleasantly meandering. Once past Bremerton, the big naval shipyard where the *U.S.S. Missouri* is permanently anchored, the drive is steeped in beauty and the smell of salt air. Twenty miles north of Bremerton you cross the Hood's Canal pontoon bridge, climb into the rugged, snow-capped Olympic Mountains. This is deep woods country, lumberjack country—remote, wild, breathtaking. This is the country that Phil Woolpert has chosen to make his home—far from the tumult of noisy crowds, ticket hustlers, college alumni, zone defenses, and the daily pressures of big-time recruiting.

As I headed into the rolling wooded hills, the tops of the Olympics up ahead were now obscured by formations of angry gray thunderheads advancing east from the Pacific Ocean. A heavy rain fell for the next hour. But then, about 45 miles up the highway the rain softened to a drifting mist. Suddenly, as I approached a rise in the road, even the slow rain began to give way to a bright clearing in the sky, and now the only clouds that could be seen were toward Port Angeles 20 miles north of Sequim. All else was a fluorescent blue.

As I wound my way down out of the mountains, I could see Sequim basking in the sunshine, a picture right out of the pages of Hilton's "Lost Horizon." You leave the bottom end of the Peninsula in heavy downpour, fight it for 100 miles, until you get to Sequim, where the clouds part and you suddenly find yourself in sunshine. The valley spreads out for about 10 miles under an enormous blue sky, cloudless,

Phil Woolpert, builder of national champions at University of San Francisco (1955-56), retired at peak of his coaching career.

The population of Sequim is about 2,700. In 1977, its chief claim to fame was the fact it was the home of the Olympic Game Farm which supplies all those talented animals for the Walt Disney movies and for TV's "Grizzly Adams," featuring Ben the amiable bear.

While I waited for Woolpert, I reviewed my notes. In 1955 and 1956, he'd been one of the country's true success stories in college basketball, climaxing both seasons with the NCAA championship. He was voted Coach of the Year in '56, and was elected president of the National Association of Basketball Coaches. The 60 wins in a row his University of San Francisco Dons rolled up in the mid-1950s stood as an NCAA record until John Wooden's Walton Gang shattered it in the early 1970s. But perhaps his greatest personal achievement in basketball was the job he did in the development of Bill Russell, whom Red Auerbach of the Boston Celtics rates as "the greatest player ever to play basketball." Russell was the perfect machine at blocking shots and dominating opponents defensively. "He could play a whole team defensively," Auerbach was quoted in the papers as saying. "He could hold any one player scoreless, but he was more interested in stopping five. He could get anything within 15 feet of the basket, blocking as many as four separate shots on one play. No other big man ever had his lateral quickness, or his perfect timing to block shots." Because of Bill Russell, defense in general became a more important part of basketball.

I made a special notation to myself to ask Woolpert about Russell.

Marv Harshman told me I would like Phil Woolpert, and I did. The last time I had seen him was at Madison Square Garden in New York 20 years earlier. Now, seeing him there across a table from me in Sequim, Washington, was like mislaying several decades. The feeling that he was still in the business of training young men to do more than just stand bonily around with their knees sticking out was understandable, because as time is measured for college coaches, 20 years isn't a great deal short of always. Smooth-shaven and casually dressy in slacks, sports shirt and golf sweater, he looked ageless, lean, and pleasant.

I asked him all the conventional, preliminary questions—How'd he like living in Sequim after

like a biblical miracle, a Shangri-la, though Sequim, Washington, is no imaginary place, it's real. Sequim Valley receives only 11 inches of rain annually; the famous Rain Forest, about 90 miles northwest of the town, boasts 144 inches. For native Californians like Phil Woolpert, with their inherited love affair with the sun, Sequim is the place to escape to.

On the edge of town I came to a full stop in front of a modern restaurant, found a phone booth, and after looking up his name in the local directory, called Woolpert. There was a country friendliness about his telephone manner. Yes, he said, he could see me. "Wait right there," he said. "I'll be right down. But I can talk to you only for two hours. At 3 p.m. I have to pick up my bus."

"Bus?"

"Yes," he said. "I drive a school bus for the local district."

big-city life in San Francisco? How was he feeling? He warmed up slowly, but eventually got to talking, softly and pleasantly, rubbing his forehead and squinting a little into the slanting sunlight that filtered through the window as he talked.

"In 1956," I said to him, "you were fighting for your second straight NCAA title. You and Bill Russell and K.C. Jones and all that group were sitting on top of the world. Now here you are, retired from coaching and driving a school bus in this little town." I wanted to know if it all seemed a long time ago.

He smiled.

"I don't miss it," he said. "This is a good life, no pressures."

"When you look back over your career, what do you remember? What games? What fun? What frustrations?"

Again that smile.

"I don't know," he said. "Not the games so much. The practice gym, I guess. Things that happened."

Now he grinned.

"Meeting Bill Russell for the first time," he said. "I can still see him. He was all skin and bones, only 6' 7" and 185 pounds, a freshman just out of McClymonds High School in Oakland. On the strength of a scouting report from Hal DeJulio, a respected USF alumnus, I had given Bill a full ride: room and board, books, tuition, the works. Personally, I'd never seen him play a minute of basketball, understand, but DeJulio had been very impressed with Bill's defensive and ball-blocking ability and urged me to get him. It was the only college offer Bill received, which tells you what kind of an athlete he had been in high school. So Bill reported to my office his first day on campus. Pete Rozelle was then our publicity man and joined Bill and me, and during a break in the conversation Bill gazed through the window, across the campus, and said to no one in particular, 'I'm going to be the first All-American ever to play at USF.' Historically, he was wrong, of course, because there had already been several All-Americans at the school, including Don Lofgran. Still, Pete and I were very impressed with Bill's determination.

"Then came the moment of truth. At his first practice, he was all arms and legs, terribly uncoordinated. I was so disappointed, so flab-bergasted, at his performance that I said to Rozelle, 'Golly, Pete, have we blown it; the scholarship, I mean. He's going to need a lot of enthusiasm just to make the traveling squad.' My spirits were really low. But then I felt much better the next afternoon when he dropped the pose and started pushing the varsity around more than somewhat. He showed me then and there he very definitely had some genuine physical skills. Being a defense-minded type, I saw he was going to fit in very well with my plans.

"As a sophomore, Bill attained his full height of 6' 9" and was devastating. A lot of credit for his development goes to K. C. Jones, his roommate in college. Bill never had any money, but he used to go everywhere K. C. went. If Bill needed a new pair of shoes, K. C. bought them for him. If Bill wanted to go to a movie, K. C. took him. Whatever Bill asked for, K. C. saw he got it. But K. C. never talked much. He was a perfect balance for Bill's ebullience.

"K. C. Jones is probably one of the most underrated players in the history of basketball. When he first came to me he had no left hand whatsoever. Unlike Russell, he'd played high school football; in fact, was All-City. He was also All-City in basketball. I'd seen him play basketball in high school and he had absolutely no left hand. I could have tied it behind his back and he never would have missed it. He came to me while the Korean War was on and I started him as a freshman, because frosh were eligible to play varsity under the war rules; but I recall telling him when he made the team that 'it's positively necessary for you to develop your left hand' I told him, 'If you don't, smart teams are going to force you to the sidelines; force you into situations where you'll have to rear turn and then they'll take the ball away from you.' On his own, after regular practice, K. C. worked and worked on his left hand until he became one of the greatest dribblers in history. I remember in his senior year we played Stanford in the Cow Palace and really pounced on them. K. C. had one of his usual, excellent nights. Later, after the game, we were in our dressing room and an old gentleman walked in. He had to be in his 80s, and he came up to K. C., introduced himself, and said he'd been watching basketball since before the turn of the century. He said, 'K. C., I've seen all the greats, but I have never seen a player with the ability you have to make moves—moves that to anybody else would be a full commitment—and then recover so fast.'

"I had never thought of K. C. in those terms, but in watching him carefully after that, it was positively true. He'd let you assume you could make a certain move and that he was totally committed, completely faked out of the play, and so you'd go ahead and make the move the other way—and there was K. C. waiting for you. He had as great a pair of hands as I've ever seen, was an incredible dribbler, passer, all-around ballhandler, and take-charge guy. Most important was his defensive play. He was fantastic on defense. But to get back to his dribbling, we were matched against a very good Wichita State team one time. Ralph Miller was the coach. The game was played on their court. It was a plywood floor, quite dead and most difficult to dribble on. Miller used at least seven or eight different types of full-court, half-court, three-quarter-court presses to try to stop us, yet K. C. tore them apart. He dribbled the ball in, out, through and around them, he brought the ball upcourt by himself the entire game—and not once did he lose the ball. We beat them easily, but K. C. did it on his own. He never talked much, but you knew he was our leader, a guy who did his job.

"Hal Perry was K. C.'s running mate. Extremely quick, Hal was an excellent outside shooter, a great passer and a fine dribbler. He was not big, 5′ 11″, two inches shorter than K. C., but when they were out there together they gave us the two best defensive guards I have ever seen. They seemed to get into one another's head. They anticipated the other's moves; would set opposing players up and take the ball away.

"At one forward we had 6′ 5″ Jerry Mullen, a tremendous player, a fine jumper, excellent outside shooter, very strong off the board, with a great natural sense for the game. At the other forward was 6′ 2″ Stan Buchanen, who got the job quite by accident when the top candidate broke a shoulder in preseason competition. So Stan won the position by default. He couldn't jump, he was slow, a poor shooter with very little all-around skill, but he had heart, determination, and a tremendous attitude. He was also very smart. Stan started every game for us, including the championship contests, and did

everything I asked of him. Basically, he did it with determination, a big heart. We pitted him against 6′ 8″ forwards and he still got the job done. He typified our team spirit—one-for-all and all-for-one. That team spirit carried us all the way to two straight national championships."

One of his most uplifting experiences in his career, Woolpert said, was the night USF opposed St. Mary's in the Cow Palace. It was K. C.'s last college game. More than 16,000 Bay Area fans were there, the biggest crowd in the history of Pacific Coast basketball. With nine minutes left in the contest, the Dons led by a wide margin and Woolpert, not wanting to pour it on, turned to his bench.

"I sent in reserves for K. C. and Russell and Perry, intending to put them back if St. Mary's closed the gap," Woolpert said. "But then a strange thing happened. The crowd, all 16,000 of them, thinking K. C. and Bill and Hal were through for the night, rose to their feet and started applauding. Even the hard-bitten reporters at the press table stood and joined in. The game stopped. For five minutes the cheers and hand-clapping rocked the Cow Palace. I could feel the chills down my back. Members of the press told me later it was the most moving experience they'd ever witnessed. It was San Francisco's way of saying to K. C. on his final night: Thank you, K. C.; thank you, an unheralded athlete at the start, for helping so much to put our area on the national basketball map."

A similar incident happened in New Orleans one December. The Dons were headed for New York and the Holiday Festival at old Madison Square Garden. En route they played three games. Following a win over Wichita State, Woolpert received a call from Pete Rozelle, back home. In a game between Loyola of New Orleans, their next opponent, and Bradley University there had been a riot, provoked by a fistfight on the floor between one of Bradley's two black players and a white from Loyola. Tempers spilled over into the stands and some of the hometown partisans got very nasty, indeed. Now, back at USF some of the officials were apprehensive about letting blacks go on to New Orleans. "It might inflame the situation," Rozelle told Woolpert. "With five blacks on the squad, perhaps you should by-pass New Orleans. The decision is yours." Without hesitation, Woolpert made his decision: his team would play.

"When we arrived a black restaurateur hosted a big welcome-to-New Orleans banquet for us and invited all the Loyola players and coaches, the local press, and many of the city's dignitaries," Woolpert recalled. "I was asked to be the master of ceremonies. So I got up and the first thing I did was to introduce the members of our team, all sitting at the head table. Bill Russell was to my left, and saving him for last I asked each player to rise and say a few words. As each one told of what it meant to be there, I noted that Russell had his head down feverishly scribbling notes. This was of some concern to me because Bill was even then known for his strong views and wasn't particular about where he expressed them. Finally, I came to Bill, and reluctantly gave him the floor. He stood up, paused for effect, and said, 'Ladies and gentlemen, the greatest place to be from on earth is New Orleans.' I died. There was a tone of sarcasm in his voice. I wanted the floor to open up and let me escape. But my fears were exaggerated. Suddenly Bill reversed direction and went on to give a warm, courteous speech—a beautiful, beautiful presentation. The audience ate it up. And when we played the game the following night, to an integrated crowd, the place was packed. Loyola had a fine team, but they were nervous and couldn't handle the ball. The pressure, with its racial overtones, had gotten to them. Midway in the first half there was a scramble for the ball—Russell vs. two of their whites—and when they came down they hit the floor with a thud. Russell, with the ball, suddenly stopped. He put the ball down, then helped both players to their feet. The crowd did not miss the sportsmanship. They exploded, went utterly insane. The whole crowd was on its feet, applauding Russell. Toward the end of the game I sent my subs in, and as the USF blacks trotted off the floor, one at a time, the New Orleans fans greeted each with a standing ovation."

"Heart and desire," Woolpert said, "was what made Russell a superstar; that was what distinguished him from most athletes. There is no question but that many athletes have come along with skills as good as Bill's, or maybe even better, but you haven't seen any team, college or pro, dominate as much as the Russell teams. Why? Because Bill hated to lose, he felt nobody could beat his team. Bill Russell was a classic example of positive thinking.

"Listen, it wasn't always so. Frankly, Bill made my practices pure hell when he was a sophomore. He hadn't yet developed the team attitude, the right approach toward winning. He had some psychological problems to overcome first: you know, his poor background, the fact he was a black man living in a white man's world; the fact he was 6' 9" and was expected to produce more for the team than he felt he could. Consequently, he was a very poor practice player. I booted him out of the gym, I don't know how many times. We argued, we fought. But Bill overcame. As a junior he became a great team leader, and as a senior the finest college basketball player in America."

The Woolpert teams of the Bill Russell/ K. C. Jones era did everything asked of them, including successive NCAA championships, and then embarked on a 30-game barnstorming tour throughout South America, which resulted in an unprecedented clean sweep.

"Playing in foreign countries is really tough," Woolpert acknowledges. "You're forced to play under so many adverse conditions, it's a tremendous challenge. The team we took to South America wasn't the same as the one we had in the NCAA tournament, because we were limited to only our seniors down there. But we were unique when we played at full strength. The thing that distinguished our championship unit was the strength of the first team. They'd run up big leads and I'd take them out; then the substitutes would go in and oftentimes lose the lead. Then the first-stringers would go back in and run the lead back up again. I always marveled at their recuperative powers. With the average team you generally lose momentum when you substitute too freely; the momentum changes hands. The opponent catches up and sometimes you lose the ball game. But that wasn't the case with my 1954-55 and 1955-56 teams."

Woolpert took great pride in the fact that the personnel on his national champions were home grown. They all came from the Bay Area, with the exception of Perry, who came from a little town 200 miles north of San Francisco. Racially, the team was half black and half white. It was the first college team, to Woolpert's knowledge, to play five blacks at one time on the court in NCAA championship competition.

"Certain alumni beefed because I played so many blacks," Woolpert said. "I received a lot of flak, some of it downright nasty. In 1953, when Russell was a sophomore, we suffered some serious injuries early in the year, including the loss of our captain and K. C. Jones, and we finished with a disappointing 14-7 record. The alumni, the press, other coaches, second-guessed me to death. About 80 percent of the letter-writers and phone-callers were uncomplimentary. I mentally catalogued their names and filed them away for future reference, and when we came back the next year and won the NCAA title there they were, the same 80 percent, slapping me on the back and telling me what a great coach I was. Talk about hypocrisy! 'Listen,' I told each and every one of them, 'I haven't changed. I'm not coaching any differently, I'm the same person—I'm doing exactly the same as last season—except now we've won the championship. Last year you called me a bum. Now you're calling me a hero. This isn't good, this is a poor perspective. Come on, fellas, grow up.' That was probably as gratifying a part of those championship years as any other thing."

Then there's the true story that will remind you of a score of B-movies from the 1930s and 40s. Unbeknown to the outside world, Bill Russell nearly flunked out of USF in his sophomore year. Intelligent, yes, but not very motivated. He simply didn't crack his books. So in the fall of his junior year, Woolpert called Bill in and read him the riot act. "Now look here, Bill," he said. "We want you eligible. It's important and imperative that you do a better job academically, because if you don't sharpen up you're not going to stick around here. From now on, we're keeping track of you in the classroom."

After the first week of school, Woolpert had USF's athletic moderator check up on Russell and he came back and told Phil: "Uh-oh, he isn't showing much aptitude."

Woolpert sent for Russell.

"Your marks are still down, Bill," he said. "From now on I'm putting you on a week-to-week trial. If you don't snap out of it—if you don't start hitting the books—you aren't going to play for me. And I'm not kidding! This is no idle threat!"

Russell was plainly upset, but he said he would try to do better.

Several weeks afterward, Woolpert talked to the moderator again. Bill's grades had not improved. That did it. Woolpert told the moderator, a priest, "I want to put Bill on probation. Basketball practice begins October 15th, but I don't want Bill out there until November 17th, after mid-term exams come out. I don't want him out for practice—I don't want him on the team—I don't even want to see him until he brings those grades up." The priest agreed to cooperate, with one reservation: First, he wanted Woolpert to clear this decision with the rector.

"So I went to the rector and leveled with him," Woolpert said. "When I told him I wanted to kick Bill off the squad, he looked at me wide-eyed. Finally, he said, 'You know, Phil, we've got the toughest schedule in the school's history this season. That includes Madison Square Garden. I agree with you totally that Bill has to get his grades up, but I'd prefer we put him on a kind of probationary-hold situation this semester, and then if he doesn't improve, next year lower the boom on him.' I couldn't believe what I was hearing. But he was the overall boss, what could I do? I went along with his decision reluctantly, and when I got home that night I phoned Bill's dad. Mr. Russell worked for the county—a great guy—just a beautiful human being. He was a regular big buster of a man, 6' 4", a massive man, but kindly, understanding. He asked me to come over and talk to him about his son. We sat in the living room and all the time I'm telling him about Bill's problem, his unwillingness to study hard, Mr. Russell sat quietly, staring at the floor, clenching and unclenching his fists. Finally, he looked up at me and said, 'Coach Woolpert, I love my son—I respect my son—but I expect him to do what he's supposed to do to get an education. I'll see that he does what he should. Leave it to me.' It was plain to see that he was very upset, very distraught.

"That was Friday night, and the following Monday our team captain told me that he was in the USF library, reading, when here came the Russells: Bill and his parents, Mr. and Mrs. Russell. Bill had his arms full of books, and they took a table off in a corner and sat there for two hours. Bill, his head buried in his books, never said a word, but it didn't take a mindreader to figure out his dad had laid down the law: hit the books or else. After that, Bill had no trouble staying eligible.

"Papa Russell had fierce pride. He once told me what it was like growing up in a white man's world. He said, 'You know, Coach Woolpert, I learned early, when I was working in Louisiana. I was doing odd-jobs for this elderly lady. I worked for her every day, and every day she'd put my lunch on the windowsill. I'd take it, but then I'd go out in the woods and instead of eating it, I'd dig a hole and bury it. This went on for two months, until one day she caught me burying it. She said, "Why, Charley, what on earth are you doing?" I explained to her that my pride wouldn't let me eat food that's been handed out the window. She said, "Well, I'm sorry, Charley. Had I known, I'd love for you to come in and eat at my table with me, but I just thought you preferred it the other way." That episode taught me we shouldn't take people for granted. It taught me we should speak up and clear the air when things bother us.' Mr. Russell was, and is, quite a man. He even went back to the NCAA championships with us—at USF's expense. What a PR man for the Dons. He charmed everybody."

After George Halas, Papa Bear of the Chicago Bears, retired from coaching a few years ago, he was asked in 1977 if he missed it. He said he never missed the Xs and Os of coaching but he did miss being down on the bench with the guys. Did Woolpert miss it?

Tanned, relaxed, in good health, it was easy to see that Woolpert was telling the truth when he said, "No, not a bit. Coaching has changed so much—and for the better, I think. If anybody were to offer me a coaching job today, I'd have to turn it down. I don't think I'm flexible enough to make the adjustment. The game has changed—the players have changed—conditions have changed. For example, take today's coach at USF. His approach to coaching is unique. He doesn't believe in curfews, he's against restrictions, regulations of any kind, so far as his players are concerned. His practices seem to be just fun and games. They don't worry about much of anything, except that everybody shows up and they have a lot of fun. Well, maybe, that's

not so far-fetched. After all, Dr. James Naismith always said he invented basketball for just one reason: *To have a lot of fun.* So to Bobby Gaillard's credit at USF, he treats his players as adults, and I like that, because too many modern coaches treat their athletes as infants, immature non-thinkers, and that's wrong. In any one-on-one human relationship you've got to recognize the other man's talents, emotions, the whole bit. Still, there is one thing about Bobby's coaching philosophy that bothers me: What is his team going to do when it must play a team from the old school? I mean, a team that is well-prepared, well-conditioned, well-disciplined? A team that is serious about winning? A team that takes its practices seriously? To me, practice is so important, so necessary in preparing for a game. It's great to have individual talents, individual skills, and individual freedom, but when the chips are down, you simply must have the cohesiveness of *team play*. And that doesn't come about by a lot of fooling around in the gym during the week. I felt that that was one of the keys to our success in the mid-1950s. We were a loose team, but well prepared. On game days, and before a game, the fellas would be laughing, whistling, singing, really enjoying themselves. They appeared so disorganized, so oblivious, I was embarrassed. I remember the day before we won our second NCAA championship we were having practice and many coaches were there to watch. As usual, my guys were nonchalant and looked so bad I turned them over to my assistant and ducked under the stands so the coaches wouldn't see me.

"At the Holiday Festival in 1956, we were having dinner at the same hotel as UCLA. The Bruins had a great ball club and were matched against us in the finals. It so happened that my wife and I were celebrating our wedding anniversary and my players surprised us with a gift. But before they let us open it, each member of the team had to stand and make a little speech in honor of the occasion. Meanwhile, the Bruins were sitting directly across the room from us, in silence, but very aware of us. John Wooden had a team rule about not talking at dinner. Well, our kids all knew the UCLA players, and they were singing and having all kinds of fun and trying to get UCLA involved. But the Bruins were having none of us. They wouldn't even look over at our table; just stared down at their plates and continued to eat. There was no conversation among them, just dead silence. We finished our meal on a hilarious high note and went on to the Garden in a great frame of mind. The result was we beat the hell out of UCLA later that evening to win the tournament. As my players described it: 'UCLA was beaten even before the players got out of the dining room.' The same thing happened to LaSalle the season before. I let my players go to the Garden early to watch the preliminary game—we were playing LaSalle in the finals, two hours later. I watched the prelim from up in the stands with my assistant coach. With five minutes left in the first game, I got up to join my players in the locker room and some woman grabbed my sleeve and said, 'Sir, aren't you the coach of the San Francisco team?' I said, 'Yes, ma'am.' And she said, 'You shouldn't be sitting up here, you should be back in your dressing room worrying about LaSalle and getting concerned.' The upshot was that as we were going to the locker room, suddenly here came the LaSalle team, climbing out of taxis, dressed in their uniforms, rushing to their dressing room, tense as a new bride. And my guys? As usual, loose as geese, they went out and played a great ballgame."

Woolpert always has been respected for his candor. On the subject of professional basketball, for instance, he will flat out tell you he doesn't like it. He hates the long season, the 24-second clock.

"The season should begin in October, quit in March," he said. "The pro schedule is ridiculous. Time and again Bill Russell has told me that there's no way most professionals can play at their peaks in January and February. Fatigue, boredom sets in; too much travel, too many games. I haven't changed my opinion of pro ball, and one reason is the 24-second clock. John Wooden favors it, he's told me, but I'm opposed to legislating how long you can keep the ball. As long as you make an honest attempt to play the game—as long as a team, through adroitness, through maneuvering, through the skills it has established can hold the ball, then that's tremendous, that's exciting. Another thing, it doesn't make much sense to say through legislation that you're allowed to play on only half the court, which, in effect, is

what the 10-second rule says. But everything considered, I prefer the college game. It is a much more skilled game. In my opinion, you can throw away all of the pro game except the last three or four minutes; until then it's just run and shoot, run and shoot, very little defense. Granted, I do like the pro game during the playoffs. That's when they really play basketball. But all that other stuff, forget it.

"If I was putting together a team today," Woolpert said, "I'd look for a willingness of the individual to subordinate himself to the other four players in order to coordinate as a unit. That's the one situation that most exemplifies basketball; what separates basketball from virtually any other sport is that it's a *team* game. When it's played as a team, then you really have tremendous skills and results involved. The nonpareil of all-around team play was Bill Russell, who had fantastic physical skills, but along with that had the greatest heart for the game of anyone I've ever seen, and the greatest willingness to subordinate himself.

"At forward, I think in terms of an Elgin Baylor—I haven't seen that much of Julius Irving—but a 6' 8" or 6' 9" or 6' 10" athlete who not only has the ability to score from outside, but the ability to drive, the ability to find the open man. As important as any other single factor is the ability to work without the ball; to make himself available in scoring situations, to create openings, to create leads for his guards and center and the other forward. Then, too, a tremendously important quality needed for any front line player is the ability to jump; not only that, but the ability to read a ball off the backboard. Reading the backboard is a skill which is not emphasized nearly enough. I have maintained for years that it is a technique that can be taught—it *should* be taught—because if you teach it to an individual, he's going to get to far more rebounds than people with even more technical and physical skills.

"So far as guards are concerned, I don't really care how big he is as long as he's mobile, or as long as he can use both hands equally well. Of paramount importance is his leadership ability, but the key to his play is the ability to see the court. That is, the ability to recognize crucial situations, the ability to recognize openings, the sense to smell out defensive weaknesses and exploit them, and certainly the ability to drive for the hoop. Bob Cousy is an excellent example. Bob had remarkable vision. Watching him play, most of us thought he had eyes in the back of his head; certainly in the side, because his was a skill you rarely see anymore: the ability to look straight ahead, and then, without even telegraphing with his eyes, to hit people in the perimeter, with split vision. Cousy was a master at exploiting both defensive and offensive skills and weaknesses; also a marvelous dribbler.

"The greatest physical specimen ever to play basketball was Wilt Chamberlain. He had the strength, the stamina, the size, the hands—he had everything but versatility to be a center. Personally, so far as physical skills go, I'd still pick Bill Walton or Kareem Abdul-Jabbar.

"In 1956, I took K. C. Jones and Bill Russell to Chicago to play in the All-Star Game. We'd just won the NCAA title, and when we got to our hotel rooms I received a phone call from Dick Harp, who'd succeeded Phog Allen at Kansas. I'd never met Dick before, but he called me and said, 'I'd like to talk to you. You've probably heard that I'm starting out next season with the big kid from Philadelphia—Wilt Chamberlain. Well, I know about the great job you did with Bill Russell and I'd like to talk to you.' I said okay, and we made a date to meet downstairs at the bar. We must have talked for two hours. Dick was on the spot. He said, 'Not only am I expected to win three NCAA championships in a row, I'm also expected to win every game.' I said, 'Dick, that's totally unrealistic, it's impossible. Why, there's no comparison between Chamberlain and Russell. When Bill first came to me, he was unknown, unheralded. He was unspoiled, nobody expected very much from him—they didn't expect much of *me*—so we started out together largely removed from pressure. But now you take Wilt—the big guy has been prostituted in high school, ruined, too many pressures. So I can't give you much advice as to how to handle him. But there's one thing I can do. I can ask Russell to have a talk with Wilt. I'm sure he'll be happy to do it.' Which was what Bill did. I don't know what they talked about, but I do know they've been friends ever since.

"I'll tell you how corrupt college recruiting got to be when Wilt came out of high school. This came from Bucky O'Connor, the Iowa coach. In 1956, we were playing the Hawkeyes

in the NCAA final and a day before the game Bucky and I shared a taxi together. I don't know where we were going, or why we were even riding in the same cab, but while traveling across town Wilt's name came up. Bucky said, 'Because of alumni pressure I felt I had to make at least a token effort to tempt Wilt to come to Iowa. So I called a contact at Overbrook High School in Philadelphia and said I'd like to come and talk to Wilt. The fellow said, sure, I could talk to Wilt, but the appointment would cost me $250. Wait a minute, I told him, what was he talking about? And he said that was the going rate for recruiters—$250.' When Bucky O'Connor told me that, I knew my coaching years were numbered. I knew it was just about time to get out."

I told Woolpert of an interview I had read, given by Al McGuire. The former Marquette coach was asked what changes he anticipated in basketball in the future, and McGuire said he thought the day was not far off when the students would pick the coach; further, the athletes will sue the coach if they think they are not getting enough playing time to help their professional chances. McGuire said he thought that the lane will be made wider and that anything that happens around the basket while a player is in the air will be legal. "I believe," McGuire said, "that after an offensive rebound the ball should be passed once before it can be shot again. And I think you're going to see a rule that will restrict a team's combined height on the court at any one time to maybe 32 feet." He said he also foresaw the day when the officials' whistle will be tied in with the clock so it will start and stop at the right instant. "I also think there should be a 24- or 30-second shot clock in the last five minutes of the game," McGuire said. "Something I'm not in favor of that will probably happen is the use of instant replay to review an official's call. But if the official is correct there should be a severe penalty—like foul shots or loss of ball—slapped on the protesting team."

Woolpert listened quietly, before commenting. Then:

"I've always been opposed to most rule changes; the more changes you make in the game, the more difficult it is to play, coach and watch it. Changes don't improve basketball all that much. For example, raising the basket is no answer; in some areas the little man would be given a break, but in others it will hurt him. Everything considered, I'd keep the game the way it is. Down the years, I opposed all the time changes: the 10-second rule [getting the ball across mid-court], the three-second violation, to name two. Once, I had a big argument with Henry Iba on the floor of a national coaches' convention. This was early in my career and the question was whether or not teams should be allowed to consult with their coaches during timeouts. I opposed the proposal, and the reason I opposed it was that it distracts from the players' ability to control the game. Iba said, 'Poppycock.' 'Leaders are born, not made,' he retorted. I told him, 'True, Hank, but if we adopt this measure we're not going to give the player with talent much chance. We'll be taking the play away from him.' In far too many instances today—in all sports—when there's a brief break in the action the opportunistic coach calls a player over to the sidelines for a consultation. This takes a great deal away from the player's versatility. There's simply too much over-coaching. If we, as coaches, have grounded our athletes properly and fundamentally throughout the past week—if we have exposed them to as many basketball situations as possible—then they'll react properly when certain situations crop up in the game. They will draw from experience, they will solve the problem.

"One reason I got out of coaching was that the pressure had become unrealistic. It's so exaggerated that the colleges are competing with the professionals for the entertainment dollar—and that's not what so-called *amateur* athletics are supposed to be about. What's happened to the fun-and-games aspect? Today, the schools depend far too much on athletics for income and to draw attention to themselves, and that's not right. I once wrote an article for a national magazine suggesting that the athletic department should be an integral part of the whole college curriculum—no more, no less—just the same as physics, biology, or English. If you make money, fine; if you lose some, too bad. But it's all funded by the general fund, and you don't isolate athletics as a special entity and say, 'Now, you must live or die on what you make or don't make.' All else lends itself to cheating, cutting corners, under-the-table payoffs—all the evils that threaten the very existence of college athletics. Something's got to give. I was amazed when the NCAA rejected the suggestion recently that a super conference be established. I liked the idea, because it would let the more ambitious schools get together and do their own thing. At least, that'd be more honest. With the super powers fighting for the bucks, the less affluent could then get down to a more realistic, honest approach to college athletics.

"Unfortunately, there's too much money entrenched in college sports—too much power. If changes for the better are to come, they'll have to be instigated by the general public through legislation. One of these days, people are going to wake up and ask themselves why college athletes aren't being educated. Hell, they're going to *demand* it. Too many recruits come into college unable to read or write—and they leave the same way.

"And that brings us to the bottom line. The alumni. The Old Guard gave me a pain in the pants. To be a successful coach, you're supposed to cater to them. The pressure groups, the booster clubs, the monied types galled me, always demanding to be heard, always trying to get their two cents in. It's one of the unpleasant phases of coaching. Rest assured, I was a very unwilling participant wherever the *kibitzers* were concerned, because, to put it quite baldly, most of them have never been sincerely interested in the welfare of the players. I wish they'd give college sports back to the kids."

THE EARLY YEARS

After the Blood, Sweat, and Cheers

When the blood, sweat and cheers of the first 87 years of college basketball have been strained through a comptometer and reduced to columns of figures in agate type, the thoughtful historian will be faced with a lot of disorderly scraps and threads snarled through the decades—pieces that begin nowhere and end nowhere. Such as:

This was a quarter of a century ago and Dr. Forrest (Phog) Allen sat and talked about basketball, there in the University of Kansas field house named for him. He was 81—six years older than the game itself—and he talked about Adolph Rupp, whom he had coached at Lawrence, and about Dr. James Naismith, who invented the sport and, ironically, was the only 'losing coach Kansas has ever had.

"And so I told Jim Naismith," Phog Allen said, "that I was going to be a coach, and he said, 'You don't *coach* this game, Forrest, you just play it.' And I said, 'Well, you can teach them to pass at angles and run in curves.' All through the land, I told him, no matter how small the town, a basketball gym became like a city hall, like a community meeting place. That's part of it, and the game. It's artistic, fast and clever. It has action and scoring. That's what people want. And then there's the emotion. There's so much that I don't think people can ever appreciate it in the right way. There's just *so* much emotion. Once, I asked Jim Naismith what *he* thought of it all. 'The appeal of basketball,' he told me, 'is that it is a game easy to play, but difficult to master.' And I said, 'You mean just like life?' 'Yes,' he replied, 'anybody can piddle at it, but to master it—yes, just like life, Forrest.' "

The late *Newsweek* sports columnist John Lardner, son of Ring but a bona fide original in his own right and at least as witty as his father, once classified basketball as a "back-and-forth goal game with a built-in stall or sputter," and as fascinating as a "leaky faucet."

To the uninitiated, Lardner's interpretation seemed justified. Basketball did appear to be a confused script for 10 athletes, punctuated by a bouncing, rolling, flying ball which sometimes ripped through the basket and sometimes didn't.

Then Bob Cousy, the old Holy Cross and Boston Celtics All-Everything, stepped forward and pointed out the special pull of the game.

"Basketball features planning to the nth degree," Cousy said. "Everything is calibrated in percentages. Take a simple play. Our two guards crisscross behind our pivot man, who has taken the ball up high near the top of the foul circle. The guy defending against our pivot man has dropped back to permit his teammates to follow the guards. If he continues to hang back the pivot can take a hook shot with no opposition. If he comes close to the pivot he risks having the pivot drive around him. It becomes a question of percentages—the relative costs of either alternative—and the game is full of such moments."

Some critics 25 years ago called basketball too sedate because it seemed to lack the awesome feature of bodily contact as known in, say, football or ice hockey. Such thinkers obviously never sat directly behind the basket at a college or pro game. Beneath the backboard the law of the survival of the fittest prevailed, with femurs, elbows and hips smacking against rib cages as

After inventing the game in 1891, Dr. James Naismith began coaching basketball at Kansas in 1898. A trained minister and doctor, he was more an advocate of spiritual and mental fitness than a teacher of basketball technique. In nine seasons at Kansas, his record was 54-60 (.474)—the only one of Kansas' five coaches with a losing career record.

players struggled for rebounds. The scramble for the ball called for so much strength that one acute student of the game remarked, "I'll trade 20 pounds for two inches of height anytime."

Time marches on.

On March 25, 1972, with 36 seconds left in a Big Ten game between Ohio State and Minnesota at Williams Arena in Minneapolis, Buckeye Center Luke Witte hit an easy jump shot to put his team comfortably ahead, 50-44. After scoring the basket, suddenly all hell broke loose. Ron Taylor, the Gopher forward, walked up to Witte and knocked him to the floor. When Witte started to get up, Taylor gave him a hand in an apparent gesture of help; Witte took it, rose half-way to his feet, when Taylor without warning slammed his knee into Witte's groin, flattening him again, this time unconscious. Ron Behagen, one of Taylor's teammates, then came over and began jumping up and down on Witte's neck and shoulders. Meanwhile, other Gophers ran madly around the court, looking for other Ohio State players to cut down.

When some semblance of order was finally restored, the game was called by officials and Ohio State was ruled the winner. Witte and teammate Mark Wagar were rushed by ambulance to a hospital in serious condition. Two days later, Big Ten Commissioner Wayne Duke suspended Taylor and Behagen for the rest of the season.

Ohio Governor John Gilligan labeled the Minnesota guerrilla tactics "the worst incident I've ever seen in sports." Few occurrences in the history of college athletics aroused so much national revulsion and attention. It remains one of basketball's darkest hours.

Northwestern Coach Tex Winter stated publicly he was against the rising tide of physical violence in college basketball. What concerned him, he said, was the no-harm, no-foul officiating. "What happens is that one team experiences national success doing one thing or another, and then everyone else mimics it," he said. "It happened with UCLA's full-court press, and now everybody is going to the strong physical players. I'm for college basketball remaining a game of finesse, not brute force. As it's played now, it's becoming like the pro game. Every time you try to make a move, you get knocked over. We don't need that. We've got a game like that already. It's called *football*."

Bill Russell has pointed out that basketball is as much a mental game as it is a physical contest. "It only takes a second to a second-and-a-half for a man to shoot," the former Celtics' star said. "I haven't checked, but I think there's only about 200 shots in a pro game. Thus only about 300 seconds are taken up shooting the basketball. That's about five minutes worth. So that leaves 43 minutes that the players have to be doing something else, something to set up or prevent shots. Games are won and lost mainly by what you do when you're not shooting."

In 1975, Dr. James Nicholas, founder of the Institute of Sports Medicine and Athletic Trauma at Lenox Hill Hospital in New York, made an in-depth study of the 30 most dangerous sports and concluded that basketball ranked No. 4, behind football, hockey, and boxing. He discovered that certain sports produce particular types of injuries. The most common basketball mishaps include kneecap dislocations, ruptured Achilles tendons, sprained ankles and scratched eyes.

As consultant to the New York Knicks, Rangers, Cosmos, and Jets, Dr. Nicholas said that few people realize that every year 17 to 20 million people require a physician for leisure-time injuries. Forty thousand people suffer crippled knees from sports annually. "Compare that figure with the 25 thousand annual polio victims of two decades ago," Dr. Nicholas said.

Combining the research of other physicians with his own, Dr. Nicholas produced a comparison chart that involved much more than difficulty and danger potential. He considered the physical, mental and environmental factors of each sport. He then rated them according to their demands on a player's total capacity. The subjective measurement scale ran from 0 (little or no involvement) to 3 (heavy involvement).

Basketball ranked fourth. Timing proved the most important factor in preventing injury, followed by practice, coordination and alertness. Intelligence ranked last. "We don't really know what intelligence is in sports," said Dr. Nicholas.

Dr. Nicholas' study was broken down into three parts: Neuromuscular (Physical) Factors, Mental and Psychometric Factors, and Environmental Factors. In detail, here was his scoresheet for basketball:

Neuromuscular (Physical) Factors
Strength, 2; endurance, 3; body type, 3; flexibility, 2; balance, 3; agility, 3; speed, 3; coordination, 3; timing, 3; reaction time, 3; rhythm, 2; steadiness, 2; accuracy, 3.

Mental and Psychometric Factors
Intelligence, 1; creativity, 1; alertness, 3; motivation, 3; discipline, 2.

Environmental Factors
Playing conditions, 1; equipment, 1; practice, 3.

While Dr. Nicholas is still trying to find out

Known as Lew Alcindor in his undergraduate days, Kareem Abdul-Jabbar was a UCLA All-American in the years 1967-68.

what intelligence has to do with sports, Dick Schaap, the author/TV sports commentator, thinks he's got it all figured out. In recent years, instead of going out and earning an "honest" living, he has ghosted books for Jerry Kramer and Joe Namath in football, Tom Seaver and Bill Freehan in baseball, Dave DeBusschere in basketball and Frank Beard in golf—six different athletes in four major sports. Now, with such intimate experience behind him, he has come forth with a theory, shaky as it is: as a group, football players are the most intelligent athletes.

"There are, of course, glaring exceptions, and not all of them are defensive linemen," Schaap conceded. "I remember one halfback who tackled English as if it were a foreign tongue. One quarterback built up a reputation for having a strong arm and a quick mind, but Namath said [the fellow] couldn't cross the street by himself. But most pro football players *did* serve four years on college campuses, and even though many of them emerged without degrees and unscarred by education, most of them emerged

with some knowledge, whether they wanted it or not—at least enough to play their complex game, the most cerebral of the major sports.

"The vast majority of professional basketball players went to college, too, but, apparently, their longer schedules forced them to miss more classes than the football players missed. Bill Bradley, who went to England on a Rhodes Scholarship and then came back and roomed with Dave DeBusschere and read the Congressional Record for relaxation, pulled up the average I.Q.; so did his roommate."

Few maneuvers have revolutionized basketball scoring so much as the acrobatic jump shot. Recently, fervent debate has centered around the question of its origin. Some claim it belongs to today's generation; others argue it dates back 30 or 40 years. Jimmy Ennis, who coached state championship teams at Everett (Washington) High School in the early 1940s, said the jump shot was sprouting wings even then, except no one knew what to call it.

"I had a guard nearly 40 years ago who'd drive to the top of the key, stop, jump, twist in mid-air, and let fly with both hands over his head," Ennis told me. "He was deadly with it. But at coaching clinics we didn't know what to call it. I'd tell the coaches: 'It's a jump, twist, and over-the-head-shoot-shot.' And that's just about what it was, too; nothing sophisticated about it at all."

Richard C. Montague, of Norfolk, Virginia, credits John Cooper, Missouri's 1932-33 star, with originating the jump shot. "Cooper's jumper was two-handed, both arms full length over his head," Montague said. "He started with his back to the basket at the free-throw line. After taking a pass, he would hold the ball perhaps 10 seconds or more, feinting, twisting and bending to work the guard behind him off balance. Then he would jump straight up, turn 180 degrees in mid-air and flip the ball overhead. From squarely in front of the basket it was a high percentage shot. Cooper was known to the Mizzou fans in those days as 'Jump Turn Johnny.'"

No one can knock John Wooden. As a college coach, he was a genius. Ten NCAA championships in 12 seasons at UCLA. But what was it like to play for him? Listen:

John Havlicek stands in Ohio State history as one of its most versatile athletes.

"We all wonder how he got the kindly grandfather image," spoke up one of his players several years ago. "To the outside world he was always smiling, and very modest, like a nice old man. But we saw him as he really was when he played the role of the coach. He could be tough, uncompromising, totally humorless. He wanted you to always say yes. If you didn't you had a 'bad attitude.' What bothered most of us was when coach threw in his 'going through life' philosophy, and told us this was how we were supposed to run our lives. We felt it was a little outdated. Once, when the season started, a half-dozen of the guys showed up wearing sideburns. Wooden gave a little speech. 'I don't have the right to tell you to cut off your sideburns,' he said, 'but I do have the right to say who makes the team.' The next day the sideburns were gone.

"A lot of coaches used to look at Wooden's record and say, 'Well, give me all that talent and I could win, too.' Maybe yes, maybe no. The truth is most coaches would have fouled up. Perhaps only Coach Wooden, with his special patience and his great strength of purpose, could have kept all those horses running and

working and winning together. Before a game, coach was very unemotional, very cool. He realized we'd won too much for an emotional pitch to reach us. Significantly, he hinted once that coaching would be a lot more fun without superstars."

"John Havlicek?" said Red Auerbach. "He'd have been a star at almost every sport. Basketball? He can throw a basketball harder and straighter than any man in the NBA. Swimming? Beautiful. Baseball? He'd have been a great shortstop. Football? John isn't the type to blow his own horn, but he once told me he threw a football 80 yards in the air. Before the Celtics got him from Ohio State in 1963, he had a tryout with the Cleveland Browns as a wide receiver. They eventually cut him, sure, but only because they had him at the wrong position. He was an all-state quarterback in high school. After the Browns let him go, other pro teams tried to get him. But I got rid of them all pretty fast. Why did I draft him? That was one of the best years for college talent I can remember. I had a choice of Terry Dischinger, Chet Walker or Havlicek. In college John had been overshadowed by Jerry Lucas. Everything at Ohio State revolved around Lucas in the pivot. John was not a great shooter or ball-handler because he didn't get the ball very much. But I thought he could play defense. And I thought he might be a swing player. I like a man coming off the bench to pick a team up. We had that kind of swing player in Frank Ramsey, but I knew Frank was on his way out. That's the main reason why I chose Havlicek. He came to my summer camp about a week after he was cut by the Browns. He worked out against other rookies. I watched him for about 35 seconds and I turned to Ben Carnevale, then the Navy coach, and I said, 'Holy smoke, Ben, this Havlicek is better than we thought.' "

Later, when Havlicek was told what Auerbach had said about his versatility, he laughed, embarrassed but pleased. After some prodding, he elaborated.

"A coach at Ohio State once told me: 'If you had played baseball here, it would have been a whole different show for you, a different life.' I'd never played tennis until I got to Columbus. It's a prestige sport, and where I came from, in the coal-mining country, there were no tennis courts. But I was tennis champion of my class. One day the Ohio State swimming coach told me I could have been a good swimmer. We never did any fencing in high school, but in college I was undefeated. Woody Hayes wanted me to come to Ohio State to play football. He used to introduce me to people as the best quarterback in the Big Ten—except that I didn't play."

For three years, Bill Bradley made Princeton one of the top college teams in America, rare for an Ivy League squad. An excellent student, model citizen and a Rhodes Scholar, never was he more brilliant on the court than in his farewell appearance, when he scored 58 points against Wichita State in the consolation game of the 1965 NCAA tournament at Portland, Oregon. That performance broke Oscar Robertson's record of 56 points in a tournament game and earned Bradley the MVP award.

Bradley said he played with detachment when he was at Princeton. He was particularly careful to control his emotions, he said, and let out only those feelings that made him more productive. He made it sound as if he were a machine, a robot. But later, after he started playing for the New York Knicks, he no longer led crusades for Princeton to show the world that a team of student athletes from the elite Ivy League could hold their own in stiff company.

"After surviving my pro initiation and winning a starting position on the team, I had stopped struggling," Bradley wrote in his autobiography Life on the Run. "I was in a safe, if competitive, status as a regular professional, and my play became more personalized. No longer did the severe discipline of the court prevent me from accepting the gentler half of my personality."

Before he retired from the game to jump feet-first into politics, Bradley allowed himself expression on the court. He said if he was angry or nervous, he let it show. "If I am in a great mood, I show it," he said at the time. "As I give expression to my feelings during play, I have a greater satisfaction and calmness afterwards. Playing creates a release for my emotional energy."

When a game was over, he said, the most important thing was the next game. He said it was vital that an athlete be able to recuperate from a defeat within 24 hours. "Such resiliency is not a bad character trait to take away from the sport," he pointed out. "But like so many of 'sport's lessons' it becomes over-simplified and even leads to insensitivity when applied to life."

Bradley, one of basketball's all-time intellectuals, once heard an old basketball man say that a certain coach had had a bad year—as if to say a bad season. It seems that the coach's wife had died and he had lost a large lawsuit. "There are some things for which there will not be another season," commented Bradley.

But "winning and losing is all around us. From the high school level on, athletes are prepared to win and they, in turn, convey to a larger public what it is to be a winner. Locker-room champagne, humility in victory, and irrefutable knowledge of a favorable, clear-cut resolution are what championships resemble from the outside. The winning team like the conquering army claims everything in its path and seems to say that only winning is important. Yet like getting into a college of your choice or winning an election or marrying a beautiful mate, victory is fraught with as much danger as glory."

The way Bradley sees it, victory, in sport as in life, has very narrow meaning and if exaggerated or abused can become destructive: a Frankenstein force.

"The taste of defeat has a richness or experience all its own," he said.

Twenty years ago Dr. Logan Wilson, then the president of the University of Texas, addressed a Texas Rotary Club meeting. He talked about college sports and the overemphasis on winning.

"The one thing worse than having a team that rarely wins is having one that season after season rarely loses," he said. "To me, the latter is *prima facie* evidence that an institution has compromised its academic standards. Although I have never heard of a coach or president being hanged in effigy when a school sweeps over all its opponents year after year, the advocates of de-emphasis might give thought to this possibility."

Actually, Dr. Wilson described himself as a realist rather than a reformer or cynic. He believed it was possible to maintain both a strong sports program and a strong academic program.

"Balanced perspective can combine these varied elements," he said.

What Bill Bradley said about the taste of defeat having a richness all its own was well illustrated by Bill Walton when he went back to Notre Dame with a UCLA team that hadn't lost a game in years. To the surprise of everybody but the Irish, Notre Dame zapped the Bruins. It was then that Bill Walton showed his values. He didn't slit his throat. He didn't react as though he'd just sat through a horror movie. He just walked off the court—*whistling the Notre Dame fight song.*

And on key, too.

Andrew D. Gilman, who once played soccer at the University of Pennsylvania, walked into a specialty sporting goods store in Manhattan recently and asked the manager for a pair of *sneakers.*

The manager paused, as if trying to recall a foreign expression or a word long deleted from the latest edition of *Webster's Dictionary.*

"You know," Mr. Gilman said, "those rubber-soled deep-treaded, canvas-topped, cotton-laced all-purpose shoes we used to wear for all sports except lawn tennis and bowling."

A light went on inside the manager's head.

"Oh, yes," he said, his eyes brightening, "I know what you're talking about. Some years ago, when we first opened, we carried something like that. But they were discontinued."

Mr. Gilman felt a sudden streak of remorse. It was almost as though he had just been told a dear friend died, or that he had been fired from his job. His worst fears were confirmed. The sneaker was dead.

For all those who grew up in the 1930s and 1940s, the sneaker represented gym class, the playground and, if you were good enough, varsity basketball. The playground variety were the worst. They were worn out, delapidated, holes-in-the-soles, splice-laced, low-cut and black—and smelled to high heavens. They were what my sixth-grade teacher, Mrs. Pakenham, referred to as "those things that give you falling arches and corns—they're bad for your health." What she really meant was that the stench from them was unhealthy for the whole class and the sight of them was greeted with pinched noses. She preferred we not wear them to class.

P. F. Flyers, Keds or Converse—we were never very particular about what brand we wore. No one gave too much consideration to color, weight, material, heel support or arch. You just put on your "sneaks" and went out and shot baskets in the gym or on the playground.

Remember how proud you were when you went down to the local store and bought your first ankle-high Keds, just like the ones they wore over at the high school or college? Even when foreign companies jumped into the market and they got more sophisticated, you still wore those old sneakers. It was cool to have a pair of Keds or Converse. They were status—they were what you put on your feet and wore to church, funerals, weddings, school, the county fair, picture shows, picnics, box socials, on your first date—*everywhere.* They were a Norman Rockwell canvas come to life.

Alas, the sneaker, the old all-purpose clodhopper, appears to have gone the way of *Collier's* and *Look* magazines, convertibles and the steam engine.

An era has ended.

Let's hear it now, all you old basketball players, for *sneakers*—for Keds—for Converse—for P. F. Flyers.

James Naismith: Basketball Evangelist

James Naismith, Divinity student, circa 1888. A purist, his philosophy was that too much stress was laid on the winning of basketball games, and not enough on the fine elements of true sportsmanship. Oldtime Kansas fans would have cringed had they heard modern followers try to recall the name of the person who started it all: "Wasn't he the dude who invented the ball?"

Mrs. Jack Naismith removed a small red leather Bible from the bookcase. "This," she said, "was given to my husband by his father, Dr. James Naismith, when he was in his teens." On the flyleaf was the date: May 7, 1917. She mentioned the name of basketball's sire as casually as if he were a clerk in the corner drug store.

Sixteen years after he died in 1939, the daughter-in-law still carried a vivid picture of Dr. Naismith in her mind. "He was exactly as he appeared, highly moral but in no sense stuffy," Grace Naismith remembered. "He had kindly blue eyes which crinkled at the corners, and wore a heavy, prickly mustache attached to a slightly square head on top of a stocky, straight body. An amateur boxer in his youth, he loved rock-'em-sock-'em body contact and had cauliflower ears that puffed out too much."

Within reach of the bookcase hung a portrait of bespectacled Dr. Naismith. It was the first formal photograph the inventor of basketball ever sat for, and it was a triumph—Sunday suit brushed and pressed and buttoned, a gold watch chain dangling from the vest pocket, unwrinkled dark tie on a triumphantly laundered shirt. He seemed to be getting mischievous amusement out of the business of posing. There was just the beginning of a smile on his lips; there was a twinkle in the round, direct eyes; a monument of character was there—kindly, forthright, wise and humorous.

"After all these years," he could have been thinking, "they bring me down here and set me in front of velvet drapes and tell me to watch the birdie. All those frustrating years developing the game of basketball, all those midnight hours burning the candle at both ends, all those miles going from town to town teaching the game and all those letters that had to be answered from foreign countries wanting to know more about my game. And now this. Well, it's a great life."

The years have rolled since they buried Dr. Naismith. His achievement as the originator of one of the most popular sports in the world rings more faintly each year in the memory of today's crowds. In the jet age of the computer and space ships, relatively few remember how panic stalked the tiny campus at the Young Men's Christian Association school in Springfield, Massachusetts, in 1891. The institution was a training school for athletic directors and YMCA secretaries. Its graduates went to posts all over the United States.

In the fall of '91, the physical education authorities of the country had arrived at the conclusion that perhaps the German, Swedish or French physical fitness systems had outlived their usefulness, did not give Americans the kind of P.E. work that would enable them to hold membership in the Y. Jim Naismith, then a young instructor, decided that what was really needed was a winter game that could be played indoors at night.

It was an irresistible challenge for the young man from Bennie's Corners in northern Ontario. He had dropped out of school at 14 to work on his uncle's farm driving teams, chopping trees and sawing logs. It was a drab life. He was going nowhere, and after five years he went back and finished high school. Then he enrolled at McGill University in Montreal to study for the ministry, but excelled in athletics. He graduated A.B. in 1887 with the highest honors given at McGill for all-around gym work. The university named him director of physical education and paid him enough salary to allow him to go on with his studies at the Presbyterian Theological College.

In those days, religion and athletics were looked upon as a strange combination. A football player named "Drunken" Donegan caught Naismith with a Bible under his arm one day and called him a sissy for studying psalms instead of going out on a spree with the rest of the boys. Jim promptly flattened him. The Donegan KO got Jim to thinking that perhaps he could preach better in the gym than from a pulpit. Well, why not? Sports could be used to help young men find themselves under controlled conditions. Then and there he abandoned dreams of a pastorate for a career in physical education and recreation.

Convinced that there was great potential for spiritual leadership in athletics, Jim Naismith enrolled at the Springfield YMCA school in the fall of '90. His department head was Dr. Luther Gulick, and the football coach was Amos Alonzo Stagg, himself a Divinity student when he attended Yale and made All-American at end.

Jim went out for football, and despite the fact he fleshed out at only 160 pounds, Stagg sent him in to play center. Jim wanted to know why he was playing center.

"Aren't I too light to be stuck in the middle of the line?" he asked.

"Jim," Old Double-A told him seriously, "I play you there because you can do the meanest things in the most gentlemanly way."

Typically, Jim Naismith preached a sermon at Springfield with two black eyes earned in a football game.

In class with Jim at the time were 18 male students, whose ages ranged from 26 to 30. They were the despair of the P.E. Department. They were training to become secretaries to YMCA executives and hated gym work; loved football and baseball and hated routine, boring P.E. exercises. But in order to graduate, they were required to take calisthenics an hour a day, and unless a game could be found as a substitute, formal drills would remain the order of the day.

Dr. Gulick picked Jim to design such a game after overhearing him claim that it was possible "to make up such a game and that mature young men do not necessarily crave physical fitness as much as some enjoyable form of recreation."

"All right, Jim," Dr. Gulick told him, "invent a game that will please your classmates. Make 'em happy. They're in your charge now."

Jim had just two weeks in which to produce a solution to a gnawing problem which two other instructors had found insoluble.

After trying to adapt football to indoor play and discovering that tackling made it far too rugged a proposition, Naismith visualized a game in which the ball would be *passed* instead of carried.

"I first tried to modify some of the existing

Outdoor basketball, complete with basket, was first played at Springfield, Mass., in 1892. The game was later moved indoors.

another stone. Recollection of the pastime suggested sending the ball toward the goal in a high curve. Jim conceived of placing a goal 10 feet above the floor at each end of an indoor playing area. But what to use for goals? Jim went to Bill Stebbins, superintendent of buildings at the school, and asked for two boxes, 18″ square.

Stebbins was curious.

"Boxes? What for?"

"I'm inventing a new game," Jim told him. "I need them to put on poles."

"Well," Stebbins wanted to know, "how do you play it?"

"The objective is to throw a large ball into the boxes," Jim said.

Stebbins disappeared and momentarily returned with two empty peach baskets. From them derived the name of the new game:

"Basket ball."

"To fully understand the fundamental principle of basketball," Dr. Naismith said in 1937, "you must appreciate the fact that football, for example, was rough because you had to allow the defense to tackle because the offense ran with the ball. Accordingly, if the offense didn't have an opportunity to run with the ball, there would be no necessity for tackling and we would thus eliminate roughness.

"The next step was to secure some kind of a goal through which the ball could be passed. In thinking of upright goals, the fact was brought out that the more force that was put on the ball, the more likelihood there was of having it pass through the goal. It then occurred that if the ball be thrown in a curve it would not be necessary nor advisable to put too much force on the ball.

"I decided that by making the goal horizontal the ball would have to be thrown in a curve, minimizing the severe driving of a ball. In order to avoid having the defense congregate around the goal, it was placed above their heads, so that once the ball left the shooter's hands, it was not likely to be interfered with.

"Then rules were made to eliminate roughness such as shouldering, pushing and kicking. The ball was to be handled with the hands only. It could not be drawn into the body and thus encourage roughness.

"The manner of putting the ball into play was then considered. Two individuals were se-

games so that they'd meet the requirements," Dr. Naismith explained shortly before his death in 1939, "but after experimenting with football, rugby, soccer, water polo, field hockey and lacrosse, my favorite, I failed to make any of them suitable for indoor play. I then left out the idea of any individual game and began to think of the fundamental principles of *all* games. I soon discovered that in all team games some kind of a ball was used."

One of Dr. Naismith's favorite boyhood games had been "duck on the rock," in which a stone was knocked off a boulder by throwing lected and took their stations in the middle of the floor. The ball was thrown up so as to land between them, giving as nearly equal chance as possible. The nearest approach to the ball needed was the soccer ball, which we chose. To get goals, we used a couple of old peach baskets, hanging one at each end of the gym. From this basketball developed."

It is significant that 12 of Dr. Naismith's original 13 rules were still part of basketball at the time of his death—nearly a half-century after he concocted his recipe. Here are the first rules as posted on the bulletin board in the gym at Springfield before the initial game was actually played:

"The ball may be thrown in any direction with one or both hands.

"The ball may be batted in any direction with one or both hands, but never with the fist.

"A player cannot run with the ball. You must throw it from the spot on which you catch it, and allowances will be made for a man who catches the ball when running if he tries to stop.

"You must hold the ball by the hands; the arms or body must not be used for holding it.

"There's to be no shouldering, holding, pushing, tripping, or striking your opponent in any way; the first infringement of this rule by any player shall count as a foul, the second shall disqualify him until the next goal is made, or, if there is evident intent to injure your opponent, for the rest of the game, no substitute will be allowed.

"A foul is striking at the ball with your fist, violation of Rules 3, 4 and such as described in Rule 5.

"If either side makes three consecutive fouls it shall count a goal for the opponents; consecutive means without the opponents in the meantime making a foul.

"A goal shall be made when the ball is thrown or batted from the *grounds* into the basket and stays there, providing the defenders do not touch or disturb the goal. If the ball rests on the edges and the opponent moves the basket, it shall count as a goal.

"When the ball goes out of bounds it shall be thrown into the field of play by the person first touching it. He has a right to hold it

Dr. James Naismith and Springfield College's Coach A. Hickox discuss the intricacies of basketball with the aid of a strategy board.

unmolested for five seconds. In case of a dispute the umpire shall throw it straight into the field. The thrower-in is allowed five seconds; if he holds it longer, it shall go to the opponent. If any side persists in delaying the game, the umpire shall call a foul on that side.

"The umpire shall be judge of the men and shall note the fouls and notify the referee when three consecutive fouls have been made. He shall have power to disqualify men according to Rule 5.

"The referee shall be judge of the ball and shall decide when the ball is in play, in bounds, to which side it belongs, and shall keep the time. He shall decide when a goal has been made, and keep account of the goals, with any other duties that are usually performed by a referee.

Basketball's original team posed in 1891 with founder James Naismith on the steps of the Springfield gym. Shown here, back row, left: John G. Thompson, Eugene S. Libby, Edwin P. Ruggles, William R. Chase, A. Duncan Patton; center row, Frank Maham, Dr. Naismith; front row, Finlay MacDonald, William H. Davis, Lyman W. Archibald. Amos Alonzo Stagg, later a famous football coach, was also a member of the team but was not on hand for this picture.

"The time shall be two 15-minute halves, with five minutes' rest between.

"The side making the most goals in that time shall be declared the winner. In case of a draw the game may, by agreement of the captains, be continued until another goal is made."

At first, the players in Naismith's class resented being guinea pigs and were plainly reluctant to cooperate with him. Jim Naismith was not one to give up easily, however. With bulldog tenacity and the fervor of an evangelist, he believed in his new recipe and carried the message to anyone who would listen. On the outdoor "court" he had measured off, with peach baskets erected on poles at each end, he was a man of action, moving here, hurrying there, shouting instructions, giving directions, talking a mile a minute, angry and impatient one moment, cajoling and praising the next. Slowly, the players began to relax. They were discovering that trying to maneuver a soccer ball into a peach basket was surprisingly good fun.

News of this game called "basket ball" quickly spread through Springfield like a fever. As many as 200 people flocked to the intrasquad contests.

Naismith's original conception had been not to limit the number of players. However, at Cornell, where P.E. teacher Ed Hitchcock Jr. introduced the game to his 100 students by letting them play all at once, 50 on a side, a mad mob scene resulted.

"What kind of game is it that makes idiots out of college students and causes them to act like jungle beasts gone berserk?" asked one disbeliever.

As an inventor of games Jim Naismith's reputation had suffered its first setback.

In 1895, he brought sanity into the game by limiting play to five men on a side. It has remained that way ever since.

The game started catching on across the country. Naismith took a team on tour to play exhibitions in Albany, Troy, Schenectady, Providence, and Newport. C. O. Beamis, physical education director, saw a game in Springfield and carried the word back to Geneva College. H. T. Kallenberg, a Springfield alum, wrote to Naismith for a copy of the rules and then taught the game at University of Iowa. The Brooklyn YMCA challenged several other New York branches, resulting in Greater New York's first basketball tournament. In 1893, Amos Alonzo Stagg introduced the sport at the University of Chicago. That same year W. O. Black graduated from Springfield and brought basketball to Stanford. A classmate, W. H. Anderson, launched it at Yale. And Vanderbilt was beating the Nashville YMCA, and Hamline was losing to the Minneapolis YMCA.

History is not clear on early intercollegiate play. The earliest known game to use five-man squads was Chicago vs. Iowa, January 16, 1896, though the Hawkeyes were actually a YMCA team comprised of Iowa students. A year later, on March 20, Yale trounced Pennsylvania, 32-10, in what is generally accepted as the first five-man intercollegiate game.

The Elis pioneered the five-man game and launched the first intersectional schedule with a western tour in 1900.

Cylindrical baskets of heavy woven wire made their appearance in 1892, followed a year later by the modern basket with an iron rim with cord basket. The soccer ball was replaced by a slightly larger ball in 1894, the ancestor of the modern basketball, although the present weight level was not reached until 1909. Backboards were introduced in 1895 to prevent interference from partisan fans, evidence that the homecourt advantage is as old as the sport itself. Crowds grew so rowdy and big that the

Dr. Naismith spent 40 years at University of Kansas. Here he and son James play their version of one-on-one. Jayhawk Theodore O'Leary, a 1932 Phi Beta Kappa graduate and Kansas basketball player for Phog Allen, testified: "To me, James A. Naismith was less the inventor of basketball than a mustachioed, middle-aged man who fooled around teaching fencing and wrestling and taught a boring hygiene class required of all UK freshmen."

playing areas were finally enclosed with chicken wire. The first cage was built by Fred Padderatz, a carpenter who managed the Trenton team. This prompted the Trenton *Daily True American* to editorialize: "The fellows play like monkeys and should be put in a cage." Bristol, Pennsylvania—where else?—was the first to use a genuine steel cage.

Dr. J. Fred (Doc) Bohler, renowned Director of Athletics at Washington State University for many years, learned basketball directly from Dr. James A. Naismith.

The late Dr. J. Fred Bohler, Director of Athletics at Washington State University for many years, once played in those screened-in courts.

"We frequently got stuck in the chicken-wire," Dr. Bohler recalled. "That's right. In a mad scramble for the ball, we'd go sailing head-long into the wire cage—and they'd have to get a crowbar to fetch us out. I tell you, old Doc Naismith didn't know what he started."

Historians point out that there were actually four types of basketball between 1892 and 1900. There was the *cage* game with constant action; there was a crashing, crushing football-like version, with no restrictions on dribbling; there was a passing game with dribbling limitations; and, finally, there was the "recreative" game in which the court was divided into sections, with each player required to stay within a section to avoid massing. This last version was a reaction to the notion that any number could play simply by splitting into two sides.

After five years at Springfield, Jim Naismith went to Denver and enrolled at the Gross Med-ical School. To meet expenses, he taught gym classes at the local YMCA. In 1898, he took a faculty position at the University of Kansas, where he remained for 40 years as head of the Physical Education Department. One of his star pupils was Forest C. "Phog" Allen, who, in time, grew into a legend almost as large as Naismith himself.

Phog recalled once that the first basketball court he ever played on was above an old livery stable.

"It had supporting posts every 10 feet down the floor, and was about 30 feet wide and 40 feet long," he said. "Then, there were the old armory courts, forerunners of college gyms, with their padded posts and their extreme dimensions of 30 feet by 127 feet. Amazing as it may seem, some of our first ranking college teams played on *concrete* floors. I remember playing on concrete in 1905 when we played the Buffalo Germans in Kansas City. There were no wooden floors in those days. Floors were built to endure the weight of horses and heavy artillery. Unfortunately, time stood still, as far as basketball was concerned. Forty years later, concrete floors were still in existence in some towns and still doing their parts to tie up agile young muscles and to cause shin splints and Charley horses and broken elbows. The best possible playing court was for years made of a 2-inch white maple tongue-and-groove flooring, one inch thick, laid upon a celotex intermediary and a subfloor of shiplap resting upon 2-by-12-inch supporting joists. The farther apart the joists were placed, the more spring the floor had."

Adolph Rupp, the man who won more games than any college basketball coach in history, admitted quite frankly that he knew very little about the game as a boy growing up on the Kansas plains. In fact, he never heard of Dr. James Naismith until he went to University of Kansas and enrolled in one of his physical education classes.

"I was born on a farm and we never got much news out there," reminisced the late Kentucky coach. "The only thing we knew was that we chopped wood and piled it up high so that we had enough to burn for heat. When the chores were done at night, we had our evening meals and our devotions. We went to bed at 8 o'clock at night, and got up in the morning in time to do our chores and get to school."

Recreational activity was hampered by primitive facilities and equipment.

"In those days the ball we had out on the farm was just a gunny sack stuffed with rags," Rupp remembered. "Mother sewed it up and somehow made it round. You couldn't dribble it. Then in grade school, we got a barrel and used that for a basket. The ball was a little bit better than the one we had on the farm, but not much. We had an old ball, and we'd have to blow it up every day and put a rubber band around it. We had to keep lacing it to keep it from falling apart."

Like Phog Allen and Adolph Rupp, the late Tug Wilson, captain of the 1920 University of Illinois basketball team before becoming commissioner of the Big Ten Conference, harbored memories of the game's Stone Age. He once recalled that there were only nine boys enrolled in his high school when he started playing basketball back before World War I.

"Basketball truly was still in its embryonic stage," Tug said. "We had no gym and played on an outdoor court. When it rained or snowed we had our games in the town opera house. This enabled us to pull off some pretty bizarre plays. One of our favorites was to disappear through one door under the stage and dart out the other, unguarded."

Two of basketball's first superstars were from the Big Ten, Wisconsin's Chris Steinmetz and Purdue's Elmer Oliphant. In an era when watching basketball was about as thrilling as watching putty harden (typical scores were 10-8, 15-12 and 17-9) the 6-foot Steinmetz tossed in 50 points against Beloit. Anxious to show off their scoring scourge, the Badgers signed up for nine straight games in the East. Oldtimers still talk about the sendoff that Madison gave its players. The home town sent up such a display of fireworks that the State Capitol Building caught fire and burned down.

Visiting teams were up against a stacked deck in those days. At Columbia University, for example, the Wisconsin players discovered that the baskets in the Lion gym were fastened on top of iron poles without backboards. Each time they shot, a Columbia player grabbed the pole and shook the ball off the hoop.

Chris Steinmetz was one of two Badgers who never missed a minute of action during that forage into the Mid-Atlantic states; the other

was sawed-off Bob Zuppke, later of football coaching fame at Illinois.

Before going on to All-America stardom at West Point, Hall of Famer Elmer Oliphant won 17 varsity letters at Purdue (1911-1913), including three in basketball. He is down in history as one of the greatest all-around athletes in college annals. On the wall of the trophy room at Purdue still hang four life-size pictures of him, togged out in his football, basketball, baseball and track uniforms. He also did some hitch-kick high diving.

During his career at Lafayette, Purdue never lost a football game to arch-rival Indiana. Against Illinois, despite a broken ankle, Ollie went back onto the field and kicked a field goal to win the game, 3-0. Knocked down in the closing seconds of a basketball game against Wisconsin, with Purdue trailing, 20-21, the 5' 7" Oliphant shot the winning basket—*while seated on the floor!*

With basketball still on legs as unsteady as a new-born colt's, game officials had about as much job security as a one-armed paperhanger with the flying hives.

"Incompetent officiating was a real threat to basketball's future," Phog Allen recalled. "The sport started out with one referee, then it was increased to two. Then they experimented with three and, finally, some authorities even advocated using four, one for each side and each end line. But as some coaches asked, voting down the proposal, 'Why increase the inefficiency?' "

The dean of all the early-day referees was Ernie Quigley. He had a no-nonsense personality and was hard on rules-violators. One night at Missouri he called a foul on a Nebraska man. Jumbo Stiehm, the Cornhuskers' vociferous coach, jumped off the bench like he'd been stabbed by a fork and started for the floor to protest, a brash violation. Out of the side of his eye, Quigley saw him coming.

"One free shot for every step it takes to get back to your seat!" he bawled. "Make 'em long or short."

With an abrupt about-face, Jumbo was back in place in two giant strides. Missouri got the two free throws.

Quigley was boss. Some of his calls made no sense whatsoever—but they stuck. He once banished a player from a game and when the irate

The 1904 Ohio State Buckeyes typified what the well-dressed college basketball team wore in those days. That's George Bellows, third from left, who later gained international renown as a painter.

coach questioned his action, Quigley looked him coldly in the face and replied, "Because I detected *malice* in his eyes."

Like most new organisms, basketball has been afflicted with growing pains down the years, partly because the rules were not standardized until 1934. There were times when as many as five sets of rules, not counting those for girls, were in effect and there were many variations to fit local conditions. To add further confusion, there was no uniformity of interpretation, so that basketball was a wrangling game, accompanied by charges that referees were biased and outright cheats.

For the first two years, the Springfield YMCA was the chief arbiter of the rules. Then the YMCA was joined by the AAU. The colleges weren't satisfied and in 1908 the National Collegiate Athletic Association assumed charge of the college rules. In 1915, the NCAA and AAU formed the Joint Basketball Rules Committee. There still remained numerous variations in the country, however, until standardization of the rules 19 years later.

Dr. Naismith invented basketball with a mere 13 rules. Many of them still remain: the officials still determine possession, violations, and fouls, including responsibility for physical contact that is other than incidental, and players may foul out of games; traveling is still a violation, so is goaltending; a team still has only five seconds to put a ball in play from out of bounds; and the winner is still the team with the most points.

Basketball is the only game devised in the United States with no roots in the sports of other nations. It first gained national impetus at the turn of the century when it was adopted by Eastern universities, with Yale and Pennsylvania among the pioneers. Other Eastern schools took up the game. In 1902, the Eastern Intercollegiate League was organized. Then the Western Conference swung into action, and soon the popularity of the sport rolled it along from the Atlantic Ocean to the Pacific, from the Gulf of Mexico to the Canadian border— and then throughout the world in 30 languages.

When Dr. Naismith concocted his recipe for

The knees have it. Kneeguards were an important part of protective equipment in 1914.

roundball, it was intended more as a ballet than a dock fight, but within a relatively short time it looked more and more like a rumble in sneakers and shorts. Games became so spirited that at one game the players actually tore out the side of the gymnasium. Stitches, then as now, were no longer found only in the basketball. They were found in the basketball players, too. A sharp elbow was as important to a guard as a good foul shot. For some, it was their only good foul shot of the night.

People flocked to witness the blood lust. Scores of the games could be kept in compound fractures as well as baskets.

The crowd got hotly in the act. At courtside you were in much more danger from a flying bottle than a right cross out on the floor. Violence begot violence. Violence attracted the vi-

olent. It posed a dilemma for school officials. Did a 25-cent ticket entitle a guy to bust up $500 worth of chairs, the eyeglasses of a bleacherite, the gym lights and anything else nearby?

Suddenly, basketball had become a world of explosions, where fans didn't shout, "Lovely shot, Slats!" but rather, "Get that other eye, Slim!" or "Punch him again, hit him again! Harder!" or the simple, "Kill 'im, Stretch!"

Now it was a world of knee-wrappings, tape, iodine, and "More plasma!" Blood was the real attraction of the crowd. Anybody's blood. The net result of all this was that it nearly did violence to the sport itself. A lot of schools backed up and started all over again.

"The game got completely out of hand," testified Dr. Walter Meanwell, who coached at

Those oldtime uniforms weren't much for the eye, but at Louisiana State University, in 1920, it was one-for-all and all-for-one spirit.

Wisconsin from 1911 to 1933 and is generally credited with doing more to launch modern basketball than anyone else. "It was so rough that many schools dropped basketball between the years 1905 and 1915. I decided to buck the trend and stress finesse. I'd done some experimenting with slum kids in Baltimore while attending med school in 1909, but because they were only kids nobody paid much attention to our record, even though we'd been very successful. So I put my ideas to work at Wisconsin."

Thus the "Wisconsin System" was born. Until then, most basketball offenses were static and unimaginative, with numerous long passes down court and across court; with waist-high dribbling and the forwards and center doing most of the shooting. Coach Meanwell put his

Badgers into five-man motion, using short passes and a revolutionary criss-cross and weave involving all his players, which never gave the defense time to get set. He also taught his players to pivot in motion, thus adding still another dimension to the short pass and the return pass to a man cutting. Finally, with so much fluidity going for him, it was inevitable that he pioneer the slickest offensive maneuver of all: the screen for the shooter.

The total effect of Dr. Meanwell's regimen was the first great dynasty of college basketball. In his first 10 years at Madison, the Badgers won seven Big Ten championships, with an overall record of 142 victories and 25 losses. His 1916 edition was heralded as "the greatest scoring machine college basketball has yet seen." It averaged 31.7 points per game, hardly a good 20

Dr. Walter Meanwell, originator of the fast break, did more to launch modern basketball than any other coach. In his first 10 seasons at Wisconsin, the Badgers won seven league titles and compiled a 142-25 record.

Arthur "Dutch" Lonborg was named basketball coach at Northwestern in 1927, and went on to one of the longest careers in Big Ten history.

minutes' production by today's standards. But, remember, that was in an era when the center jump after each basket was still in vogue. All-American center George Levis, and All-Conference Harold Olsen and Bill Chandler were the stars of the team. Against Iowa one night Levis popped in 11 field goals in less than 30 minutes.

So smooth was Meanwell's attack that it allowed Lyn Smith, a stationary guard, to slip through for four layups against Northwestern. That convinced a lot of coaches that the day of static, offensive zone play was a thing of the past.

Other early innovators who played leading roles in the game's steady advancement were Princeton's Dr. Joseph Raycraft, Pennsylvania's

Ralph Morgan, Ohio State's L.W. St. John, Yale's Bill Barber, and Stanford's John Bunn.

One of the more successful major coaches of the early era was Ward (Piggy) Lambert, who coached at Purdue for 30 years (1917-1946) and compiled a 371-152 record, including 11 Big Ten titles. Piggy—the nickname came from wearing a stocking cap with pigtails as a kid in Crawfordsville, Indiana—developed the uncanny ability to transform average material into stars. Among the nine authentic All-Americans he coached was 5' 10½" guard Johnny Wooden, a master dribbler and playmaker. Antiques still call him the greatest small man in the history of college basketball.

Obsessed with speed and the idea of moving the ball around, Lambert was an early advocate

Sports writers called All-American Johnny Wooden "the peerless Purdue guard" in 1930 as he led Coach Piggy Lambert's Boilermakers to their first undefeated season and Big Ten championship.

of fire engine basketball, the forerunner of the perpetual-motion game which was to become the pattern for basketball several years afterward.

Lambert looked for mental aggressiveness, good temperament, self-confidence, speed, and *then* size in his athletes. Size, so important today, rated *last* on the Lambert scale. There wasn't a man over 6′ on his 1934 Big Ten championship team!

"Mental attitude is the most important thing in basketball," Piggy insisted. "Never panic when you're behind in the stretch."

Though he stood only 5′ 6″, Piggy Lambert intimidated many a referee. Purdue officials assigned two student managers to sit alongside him at games and restrain him when he got the notion to punch a referee on the nose. "It was a scary feeling to be working a game, knowing that Piggy had never been wrong on a basket-

ball call in his life," commented one old-time whistle-tooter.

Starting in 1930, Purdue, under Lambert, rolled to six Big Ten titles in the next 10 years. The '30 gang was the Boilermakers' first undefeated team. That same season, the All-Big Ten selection was one of the most famous in league history. It included All-Americans Bud Foster (Wisconsin), Doug Mills (Illinois), Branch McCracken (Indiana), and two All-Americans from Purdue, "Stretch" Murphy and Johnny Wooden.

John Robert Wooden grew up on a farm eight miles from Martinsville, Indiana. At Martinsville High School he made the All-State team three years in a row. Six boys from the 1928 team went to six different colleges and were starters as sophomores. Kansas and most of the Big Ten schools invaded Martinsville to try to recruit Wooden, but Purdue got him

Wisconsin's "Old Red Gym" typified the tiny box-like floors of the 1920s, where the players often wound up in the fans' laps.

because of its engineering school and Lambert, an early advocate of the fast break. Wooden soon switched to a liberal arts major. He was not only named All-American three times, he led the Boilermakers to two conference championships and won the Big Ten medal for excellence in scholarship and athletics. A "floor guard" (as opposed to the "back guard" who rarely got to shoot) Wooden played at 5' 10½" and 183 pounds, and was so slashing and daring that sometimes Purdue officials stationed two men behind the basket to catch him after his wild drives. In a game against Indiana he was knocked to the floor near the free-throw line. Before he could get up, a rebound came to him and, still sitting down, he made the shot that won the game.

Dutch Fehring, a teammate of Wooden's who later joined the Stanford athletic faculty, recalled that Wooden had a way of stalling a game by incomparable dribbling. "He'd dribble from backcourt to forecourt, all around, and nobody could get that ball away," Fehring said. "He also had a way of taking off near the foul line and sailing up to the basket as smooth and

pretty as a bird. Or he would drive in for a layup with such determination that his momentum would carry him into the fifth row of the school band at the end of the court. He bounced off the floor so often that people called him the India Rubber Man."

Wooden was a fanatic on fitness. "They may beat me on ability," he once said at Purdue, "but they'll never beat me on condition."

Sportscaster Tom Harmon, who won the Heisman Trophy as a Michigan halfback, was a schoolboy in Gary, Indiana in the early 1930s, and used to go down to Lafayette to watch Purdue. "Wooden to the kids of my era was what Bill Russell, Wilt Chamberlain or Lew Alcindor was years later," he said. "He was king, the idol of any kid who had a basketball. In Indiana that was *every* kid."

Three members of the memorable 1929-1930 All-Big Ten team—Wooden (at UCLA), Mills (at Illinois), and McCracken (at Indiana)—all went on to become great college coaches. Another Midwest coach grouped with that trio was Dutch Lonborg. After a long search for a new basketball coach, Dutch was hired by

Northwestern in 1931. A star at Kansas, he got results in a hurry, giving the Wildcats their first undisputed championship his very first season. In 1933, they tied Ohio State for the title.

Other excellent college teams of the 1920s and early 1930s included Kansas, coached by Phog Allen, and California, which polished off four straight Pacific Coast Conference championships in 1924, '25, '26 and '27.

A new style of play was also launched in the 1930s. Rhode Island State College's Coach Frank Keaney devised a system featuring fast-breaking, long passes upcourt, and lots of shooting. Newspapers soon tagged RISC the "point-a-minute" team. Higher-scoring, free-wheeling basketball brought a new era to the game.

In spite of some increase in intersectional scheduling, most colleges still limited the majority of their games against teams from their own region. Consequently there were no national polls, no Top Ten, as the so-called experts of the day found it difficult to compare the merits of the outstanding teams from one section with those of another.

The Legend of Carr Creek

Like good bourbon, a good Kentucky legend is made out of corn from the hill country.

In the late winter of 1928 a handful of kids in an old Ford rattled down out of the little mountain village of Carr Creek, Kentucky, battled their way through the regional and state basketball championships, then went on to a 42-team national interscholastic tournament in Chicago, where they captured the hearts of a whole nation. The achievement remains one of the game's more intriguing stories. What they did rivaled even the Kentucky Derby that year in popular excitement.

Legend ran rampant as the rumor-mongers made up their own romantic fiction about the obscure little school of Knott County that suddenly found itself on the basketball map.

"The team was supposed to be made up of eight boys, all related, who comprised Carr Creek high school's entire male student body," reported writer Harold Peterson. "The team was said to have a homemade outdoor playing area of frozen ground on which its members practiced and played all games barefoot. One basket, rumor had it, was attached to a tree and the other to the side of the school. Richmond fans collected money to buy the sentimental favorites uniforms because they had heard that Carr Creek had appeared in the district tournaments wearing T shirts and overalls cut off at the knees. According to hearsay, only seven of the eight had uniforms."

Another rumor claimed the Creekers were without a coach, that they were tutored by a local doctor, a postman or a Yale engineering graduate.

When Carr Creek arrived at Lexington as one of the 16 state finalists, half the city turned out to greet the team. The boys lived up to advance fanfare. They were a colorful lot, impressed by all the hoopla and willing to play up to their reputation as waifs on the rise.

"We had to ride a log wagon to the railway station at Sassafras," said one player. "If we lose, we'll probably have to walk back."

It developed, when the truth be known, that Carr Creek did have a coach: Oscar A. Morgan, a graduate of Centre College, not Yale, and a grade school teacher. And the team did have an indoor place to play, though only 50 feet long, 30 feet wide, with only a 12-foot high ceiling. The team also played outdoors "whenever the weather was pretty." Said the team captain, "The fresh air is good for us. And as for wearing shoes, we don't feel handicapped with shoes on during the tournament."

With a budget of a mere $68.65, it was true that the Creekers had played in cut-down overalls, but it was not true that the eight players constituted the entire male student body. Actually, there were 18 boys in the school. Nor were all the players blood relations: there were only two sets of brothers and a cousin on the team.

"Center Ben Adams and Guard Gurney Adams were brothers," Peterson said. "Substitute Hermit Adams was their cousin, and substitute Herman Hale was the brother of Zelda Hale, the other regular guard. Forwards Gillis Madden and Shelby Stamper and substitute Carson Cornett, however, were not kinsmen of anyone on the team. All, with the exception of seniors Ben Adams and Zelda Hale, were sophomores."

Dressed in new blue-and-white game uniforms that had cost Richmond fans the then munificent sum of $55, the Creekers won their first game of the state B tournament, 31-11, before a full house. All five starters played every minute of the game.

After dropping behind Minerva, 8-4, at halftime, Carr Creek won its second game, 21-11. Then they destroyed the pretourney favorite, Lawrenceburg, 37-11, to win the B title.

As Class B champion, Carr Creek now challenged tough Ashland, a Class A finalist. At the end of the first quarter, C. C. led, 4-1. They still led, 6-4, well into the second period. Then Ashland's defense stiffened and the Creekers were held scoreless for the equivalent of two full quarters, while Ashland scored five straight points to take the lead, 9-6.

Late in the last quarter, Gillis Madden hit from outside to bring his team to within one point, 9-8. Now with but 20 seconds left, Shelby Stamper was fouled. Stamper's free throw sent the game into overtime.

Neither side could score through three consecutive overtimes. Ashland won the game, 13-11, and the state title in the fourth overtime, but Stamper, Madden, Ben Adams and Zelda Hale of Carr Creek won places on the all-tournament team. And no matter what the numbers were on the scoreboard, the Creekers had captivated the hearts of Kentucky. A fund-raising campaign was quickly organized to send Carr Creek to the national tournament in Chicago; fans raised not only enough for travel expenses but also enough to contribute toward a $5,000 fund for a new local gymnasium at Carr Creek.

"That should be enough to buy the materials," said Coach Oscar Morgan. "The boys and their parents can build it."

In the 42-team national interscholastic tournament at the University of Chicago, Carr Creek fought their way to the quarterfinals, where they finally lost to Vienna, Georgia. Again they were sentimental favorites, both with their fans back home and throughout the nation. The wealthy and famous of Chicago liked the mountain ballads the boys sang for them and saw to it that they had plenty of food and headlines.

When the Creekers got back to Kentucky, they were showered with invitations to banquets, baseball opening games, and vaudeville shows. They even turned up in the *Congressional Record* when Representative Fred Vinson lauded them in the halls of Congress.

Gurney Adams later returned to Carr Creek High School as a physical education instructor. He talked about the 1928 basketball team.

"It was the way everybody was so nice to us that stands out in my memory," he said. "Every place we went, people were for us. Even the team we beat would cheer for us in our next game. We just kinda went along with those big stories and didn't pay them no mind. We were just playing ball and having a good time."

Most of the original team settled in nearby communities of the mountains where they began the legend.

The rise of the basketball Creekers was like a dream, and for years afterward they were on the tongue of every man, woman and child of the bluegrass country who talked basketball.

Wonder Team of '29

Several years ago, Hank Luisetti was asked by his little grandson, "Grandpa, were you the greatest basketball player ever?"

"Some people say I was, Michael," the old Stanford star answered.

"Well, you're not as good as Rick Barry."

"Maybe not," said the originator of the one hand shot. "But what you don't know, Michael, what you can't know, is that the times are different. Very, very different."

A good deal of richly purple prose has been put forth in recent years on the subject of not only the greatest players, but also the greatest teams. Man for man, the authors declare after conscientious and coldly scientific consideration, this team or that could outfight a maddened bull elephant, outrun a virtuous blonde, outjump a kangaroo and outshoot a missile launcher.

There probably never can be an accurate measure of a team's lasting greatness, because styles change and there is no way of knowing how one era would actually do against another. But the debate goes on, as thoughtful researchers spell out, appraise, amplify and attempt to prove conclusively just how wonderful their favorites were. Still, whenever championship teams are mentioned, the St. John's "Wonder Five" is often ignored. Yet it is virtually impossible to think of the immortals without thinking of the Redmen of the late 1920s. It will never be possible to disassociate them and the game's greatest winning streaks.

In a four-year reign, St. John's won 86 games and lost only eight. In their last three years, they posted a fantastic 70-4 record. They were so good that they graduated intact from St.

John's to the pros and more than held their own against tough American Basketball League competition.

The coach of this all-conquering team was James (Buck) Freeman, an alert and eager drillmaster. Freeman was something of an explorer—inventive and adventuresome, tireless and dedicated. He was also a fundamentalist, and a stickler for infinite detail. At St. John's, he dictated even such decisions as how to slice the oranges which his players would suck on the bench—into halves, quarters, or eighths.

The philosophy that served Buck Freeman, since his beginning as an instructor in roundball, was enunciated before he was born by Mr. Kipling:

> When 'Omer smote 'is bloomin' lyre,
>   He'd 'eard men sing by land an' sea;
> An' what he thought 'e might require,
>   'E went an' took—the same as me!

Freeman's Homer was a composite, part Jim Naismith, part Phog Allen, part Howard Cann, part Piggy Lambert, part Walt Meanwell. Each had something Freeman required and he went and took it, with full permission of the copyright owner. Naturally, he tossed his own assets into the pot.

When Freeman went to St. John's, he discovered that the material lacked the depth and versatility of its top opponents. He decided he could compete on even terms only if he could utilize to the fullest what talent was available. After evolving a system of testing and grading the candidates, he picked the five best all-around athletes for his first team. He picked out a big center in 6′ 5″ Matty Begovich and surrounded him with a pair of flashy ball handlers, Mac Kinsbrunner and Allie Schuckman, an excellent passer, Max Posnak, and Rip Gerson, a hawk on defense.

The first five practiced as a unit, played as a unit, unconsciously fell into the habit of eating, dressing and even socializing as a unit, and to the coach's gratification a special esprit de corps came to characterize the group. Devoting much of their practice time to defensive work, they became harder to score against than any other team in the nation. In four seasons, only one team managed to score more than 40 points in a game against them. While the players were still freshmen—before they fully jelled as a unit—the semipro Crescent A.C. beat them, 43-35. The University of Scranton once scored 40 points against them, but St. John's still won, 41-40.

Freeman drilled his players hard. They worked on their assignments until they were almost perfect.

"We never beat ourselves," Freeman once said. "We stayed back until the other team made a mistake. None of my guys ever shot at the basket until he was sure he could score. All were accurate shooters. Our defense was no accident. My slogan was, 'Keep the ball away from them, the longer the better.' That's what I drilled into my players, and they responded with finesse. Kinsbrunner was an excellent dribbler and could often control the ball for 10 minutes or more. He got plenty of help from the others, who were also adept dribblers and joined in the freeze. Though Gerson was only 5′ 11″, his forte was ball-stealing and I always assigned him the job of guarding the other side's leading scorer. He was so aggressive, his hands were so supple, he frequently shut out the guy altogether. Gerson was the best defensive man of the era, no question about it. One factor that strengthened our team was that the kids liked each other. They worked together like a well-oiled machine. There was no jealousy, and no one tried to hog the limelight."

A smooth passing attack, each man acting as a cog in the machine, was developed even when the team was in its freshman year and had its poorest won-lost record (18-4). The next year they were 23-2—and the best still lay ahead.

By now, Gotham headline writers were calling the Redmen the "Wonder Five." Thousands flocked to the gyms wherever they appeared; almost always they were the overwhelming favorites. As juniors they won their first 10 games, before dropping a heartbreaker to Providence, 32-30, a stunning upset not only to their followers but also to Buck Freeman

"Let's not lose any more," Freeman told his players.

They didn't, ripping off their remaining 14 games to finish the season at 24-1.

As seniors, the Wonder Five continued to improve, both on offense and in freezing the ball. Ten opponents were held to less than 20 points, and only one team got as many as 30. They even held powerful City College of New York—a team that had blasted out 68 points in an earlier encounter—to an incredible nine points for the whole game, holding them pointless for all but two minutes.

St. John's opened the 1929 campaign like a missile off the launching pad. They won 13 in a row, giving them a combined record of 27 straight over two seasons. Then, after being upset by New York University for their only loss of the season, they ran out their college careers with a streak of eight to finish the year with a 21-1 record, and 42-2 over two years.

Begovich, Kinsbrunner, Schuckman, Posnak, and Gerson stayed together as a unit after graduation, first traveling as an independent team for two years, and then on to the pros for another five seasons, still billed as the "Wonder Five."

The old St. John's collegians had their share of glory in professional basketball until the original five broke up in 1938—11 years after it all started.

THE BEGINNINGS OF
MODERN BASKETBALL

Hank Luisetti: A Star Is Born

Once upon a time—and young people aren't going to believe this—the total score of a basketball game was often 25 points or less. In 1926, for instance, City College of New York beat Villanova, 11-9, and lost a tough one to Carnegie Tech, 13-12. CCNY also beat Dickinson, 15-7, and in a "high-scoring" game, defeated Temple, 15-14.

In a game against UCLA in 1932, Southern California held the ball for the last 15 minutes of the first half as the Bruin band fiddled and the fans burned. Finally, the band started playing a funeral dirge, the spectators showered the court with pennies and peanut shells, and Trojan star Jerry Nemer calmly read a newspaper. The second half was more conventional, however, and the Bruins went on to win, 19-17, which will give you an idea of the sort of shooting they did in those days. That same season Kansas clogged up a Missouri star's favorite shooting area, so the Tigers retreated to their backcourt and sulked. The two teams casually stood around at either end of the court. At last, four Missouri players sat down and four Kansas players did the same, leaving one Jayhawk to guard the basket. They'd probably still be sitting there, except Coach Phog Allen loved basketball too much to let the travesty continue, and in the second half he turned to his players and said, "Sic 'em!" Missouri won, 26-22.

Those two 1932 games, featuring the stall, were instrumental in getting a rule passed, beginning the next season, that the ball must be brought across the half-court line within 10 seconds.

Phil Woolpert, who always has hated the 10-second rule, remembers that back around that same time zone defenses and the fast break began to speed up and become a permanent part of the game. Heretofore, zones had been stationary, encouraged by tiny gyms, low roofs, the old-fashioned offense, and legislation against offensive stalling and screening and occupying the lane.

"The game suddenly became more sophisticated," Woolpert said. "Our major universities started building bigger gymnasiums, fieldhouses, to accomodate 10, 12, 15,000 spectators, and the coaches went right along with the times. Now there were fast breaks, much more scoring, and the good big man on offense and defense. Basketball became the best show in town.

"The skills that were important then are just as important today. And while techniques have improved—the offensive player in particular has become more adept—defensive skills have not changed all that much. As a matter of fact, defense today is not emphasized as much as it was 45 years ago.

"The big weapon was the two-handed set shot. To do it you simply shot the ball with both hands, either from an over-the-head position in front of your face or from below the waist with great wrist action. When I played for Loyola of Los Angeles, virtually all of us shot two-handed. Occasionally, one of the guys was off in a corner of the gym experimenting with different kinds of shots, but he was considered by his teammates as a renegade. 'Boy, that guy's a screwball,' they'd say.

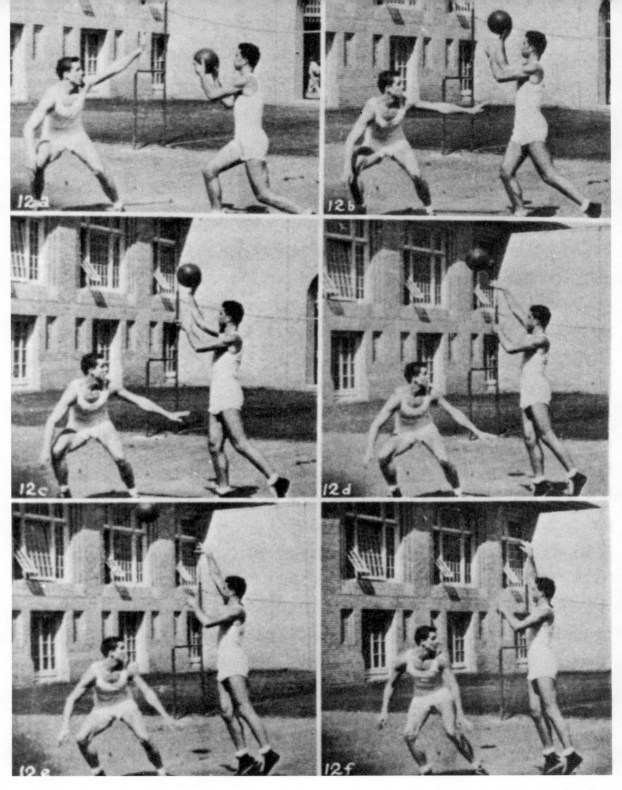

Stanford's Jack Dana and Ed Voss demonstrated for the camera here what the then newfangled one-hand push shot was all about.

"In those days, the center generally stood 6' 5" or 6' 6". He was considered a giant; today, of course, he'd be just another throwaway forward. Because there was no three-second rule, the jumping-jack centers of the early 1930s parked themselves under the hoop and waited for the ball. Some of them were excellent shooters, could pivot left or right and had great hands and tremendous jumping ability. They'd score pretty much at will if they got the ball.

The old underhand free-throw is demonstrated in three parts here. Fig. 15, finger position for passing and shooting; fig. 16, start of the underhand free throw; fig. 17, the followthrough.

That was pretty much the role of the center: to park himself near the basket, as close as the defense allowed, and make those points. There was a great deal of what we called 'scissoring' off the post man.

"The operating range for forwards in those days was generally what was called the '17,' or roughly 17 feet from the basket at the extension of the free-throw line. Their key weapon was the two-hander; the better the shooter the tougher it was to defense them. He did not drive for the hoop much. When he did drive, however, it was usually off scissors or off splits after hitting the center. A great deal of stress was placed on rebounding. I know that our coach—just about every coach at that time—used to harp about the so-called 'triangle.' That is, you had the two forwards breaking in from the angle and the center from the middle. That's all there was to it. It was considered great basketball technique.

"The guards, I think, were the most exciting players on the floor. They were the playmakers. They made things happen. Because there was no 10-second rule then, no pressing, they could take as much time as they wanted to bring the ball upcourt. The guards were the ballhandlers, the long set-shooters. I've seen guards who could pot 'em from 35 feet out with fantastic regularity. Let 'em get set, feet together and within range, and you were a dead duck. On defense, the guards always played out in front, while the forwards and center guarded the backcourt."

Johnny Jordan, the old Notre Dame coach, once said that Ed (Moose) Krause made the most spectacular shot he'd ever seen when the Irish played at Butler in 1933.

"Notre Dame trailed by two points, with

Ned Irish as he looked at 25 in 1934. The "boy promoter" was responsible for putting big-time college basketball into Madison Square Garden.

gym, he found all of us diligently shooting at the basket—stretched out on our backs."

Nearly 40 years since its inception, basketball was still an unprofitable sport both for the colleges, with their small, box-like facilities, and for the promoters who matched pro teams in armories and in dance halls. Joe Lapchick was a center on the Original Celtics and testified years afterward that they made very little money. "The man who managed the team got free bus rides," he said.

The first evidence of basketball's ultimate potential was provided by New York Mayor Jimmy Walker during the dark Depression winters. Walker, trying to raise funds for unemployment relief, organized a committee of sportswriters to promote basketball benefits in Madison Square Garden. On January 19, 1931, a college triple-header drew a full house; on February 22, 1933, a seven-game program that ran both afternoon and night attracted a total of 20,000. Bigtime basketball was here to stay.

Later, a number of people approached General John Reed Kilpatrick, the old Yale football star and president of Madison Square Garden, with schemes for promoting basketball regularly. Kilpatrick was more interested in ability than in security. He said he wanted someone with a concrete program. Up stepped Ned Irish, a University of Pennsylvania business graduate who had been working as a sportswriter for the *New York World-Telegram* at $60 a week. To supplement his salary, he moonlighted as publicity man for the New York football Giants.

At 25, Ned Irish was sharp-featured and thin-lipped. His voice was flat and colored by the accents of Brooklyn, where he once worked as a student sports correspondent at Erasmus Hall High School. His manner was brusque and humorless; except with old and trusted friends, he created the impression of a man preoccupied with people and things more important than the person or question he was facing at the moment.

When Irish approached Kilpatrick, he had both a plan of his own and backing, apparently from Tim Mara, owner of the football Giants. Irish proposed to run college basketball as a concession. As concessionaire, he guaranteed the Garden $4,000, which was then the average cost of renting the arena for one night. He

only seconds remaining," Jordan recalled. "All-America Krause, a junior then, was knocked to the floor during a scramble near the free-throw line at the Butler end of the court. Moose, flat on his back, somehow got his hands on the ball and shot. The shot was good, tying it up just before the game ended. Notre Dame went on to win, 42-41, in overtime. I happened to have been a sophomore on that Notre Dame team, and I remember all the details clearly, especially the aftermath. In the dressing room, the late Coach George Keogan complimented Moose on his great shot. He told the rest of us that Moose was the kind of player we ought to pattern ourselves after. So back at South Bend the next afternoon, when Keogan came into the

On December 29, 1934, NYU played Notre Dame as part of first regular college doubleheader at Madison Square Garden.

would handle scheduling, control tickets and direct the necessary publicity. The Garden was to share in profits above the guarantee on a percentage basis. Kilpatrick bought the package, and under terms of the agreement Garden basketball was established as Irish's dominion as long as he met the minimum of $4,000 a night.

On December 29, 1934, Irish matched NYU against Notre Dame, and this game, which began a rousing rivalry that ran for 23 years, attracted 16,188 fans. It brought the Garden something in excess of $4,000 and brought Irish roughly the equivalent of six months' pay at the *World-Telegram.* Suddenly, Ned Irish's future was as big as basketball's.

Irish could not quite believe what had happened. When his request for a leave from the *World-Telegram* was refused, he quit, but he clung to his job with the Giants as a hedge against the day when his promotions might end as abruptly as they had begun.

They did not end, because both fortune and opportunism were on his side. With strong teams from NYU, City College, Long Island University and St. John's serving as Garden home teams, plus the freshness of basketball's first blossoming, the 1930s were exciting times for the college game. Irish had bottled the excitement and, as concessionaire, he was accountable to no one for his methods. Any athletically ambitious college—which is to say, most major colleges in the U.S.—that wanted the attention of a showing at Madison Square Garden had to play for Irish on Irish's terms and on the date he assigned it. A few athletic directors griped over their cut ($500 on sellout nights in some cases), but Irish was Congress, court and executive of big-time basketball in America. "My terms or go back to your gyms," he reminded athletic directors.

For the next 15 years Irish's successes were continuous and unrelieved, and although he antagonized some college officials and newspapermen, the worst anyone could say about him was that he had the sneer of cold command.

The most historic night in the life of Ned Irish as a basketball promoter was December 30, 1936. That was the night that Hank Luisetti changed basketball.

There are those who say that Stanford's Hank Luisetti was the best college player ever. "I can't remember anybody who could do more things with a basketball," said Long Island's Coach Clair Bee.

There are those who say Luisetti was the best player ever. "I can't remember anybody who could do more things," Clair Bee, one of the best of the basketball coaches, once said. "He was an amazing shooter, a phenomenal dribbler and an awfully clever passer," said Nat Holman, another of the Original Celtics. "The thing I remember about him," added Joe Lapchick, "was his uncanny ability to control the ball while going at top speed."

"He was as far ahead of his time as Bob Cousy was ahead of the others later," said Jack Friel, who coached at Washington State for 30 years and saw plenty of Luisetti in the old Pacific Coast Conference. "In a poll of experts some years ago to determine the best basketball player of the first half-century, only George Mikan drew more votes than Hank. Historically, Luisetti is given credit for originating the running one-handed shot, but it wasn't new to us in the Pacific Northwest. Dave McMillan, who later coached in the Midwest, brought the shot out to University of Idaho, where he taught it to all his players; a moving, one-hand shot. So by the time we played Stanford and Luisetti in the P.C.C. playoffs, we were used to it; it wasn't new to us at all. But Hank was the one who popularized the one-hander. He went to New York and he wowed them with it. The coaches back there relied entirely on driving for the basket and on the old two-handed shot and they thought Luisetti was crazy. Some of them said that the one-hander wasn't basketball, but he converted them. Not only was Hank a spectacular shooter, but he was also a great rebounder, with good speed. You couldn't stop him on the break with one defender. He was always sensational. In our playoffs against him we held him to 18 points in two games, but we had to double up on him to do it."

"Luisetti was a myth, really," recalled Marv Harshman. "In those days, regional and national communications was largely the newspapers. Without television, we didn't get to see Luisetti. Nowadays, the kids get to see the stars perform on TV and can copy them. We're all great imitators, that's why basketball has advanced so fast. But there was no TV when Luisetti was at his college peak, so all we could do was try to envision how he shot that one-hander. Ironically, the first time I ever saw Luisetti in the flesh I played against him. I was a senior then at Pacific Lutheran University, he was one year out of Stanford and was barnstorming with the Phillips Oilers. They came through Tacoma and we played down in the old Exhibition Hall. We just stood around in awe—Hank Luisetti was, indeed, a legend in his time.

"It wasn't much of a contest. They beat us easily, but that was unimportant. What was important was that Luisetti took the time and trouble after the game to be clinical, to talk basketball with us. That's what I always liked about the athletes of the 1930s and 1940s— what I call the Romantic Era of Sports. They had class. Stars like Luisetti had the great ability to remain humble. In their playing—in their public relations—in their approach to their opponents—they harbored a great respect for everybody. I have always felt it was because they had a deep respect for the *game*. Unfortunately, we have lost a lot of that."

The game that made Luisetti—and set up Ned Irish as a basketball promoter—took place December 30, 1936, at Madison Square Garden on Eighth Avenue. At about 8 p.m. that evening, excitement lingered just inside the Garden's windowed doors. Inside the arena a crowd of 17,623, the biggest of the season, was noisily watching Georgetown upset NYU in the first game of a big holiday doubleheader. But that was merely a preliminary to the contest the crowd had really come to see: the match between Coach Clair Bee's Long Island University Blackbirds, with a streak of 43 wins in a row going for them, and the Stanford Indians, defending Pacific Coast Conference champions and 45-38 upset victors two days earlier over Temple, the second-best team in the East.

"Sure, they're good," said one skeptical New Yorker, "but we've seen wonder teams before. They come into the Garden and they fold. So what if Luisetti does average 22 points a game?" [An unbelievable figure in those days when there was a time-consuming center jump after every basket.] "We'll contain him."

Long Island was a slick ballhandling team. Its players could shoot from the outside to open up an opponent's defenses, and when they had succeeded in doing that, they could pass them dizzy under the basket. Furthermore, LIU was fiery and tenacious on defense.

Late comers continued to swirl into the

Garden in an unruly tide. A man caught and buffeted in the press at the door gasped as the breath was pressed out of him.

"If anybody takes this much punishment on the court, it will be the game of the century," he said.

In the locker room, Dr. Bill Northway, the Stanford team physician, was taping Luisetti's ankles. Outside, on the streets, the weather was windy and damp but warm for that time of year.

What the fans most wanted to see was Luisetti, who had been setting scoring records by shooting the ball, in defiance of accepted basketball orthodoxy, with *one hand*. After only a year of varsity competition, Luisetti was already a legend in the Far West. Hadn't he pumped in 32 points in 32 minutes against Washington? And what about the Southern Division championship game against Southern California, when, trailing by 15 points with 11 minutes to play, he suddenly broke loose, scoring 24 of his 30 points to win the title, 51-47?

In those days, the collegians rarely scored more than 45 points in a contest, and 20 points was considered unthinkable for one man. It was an era when the clock was rarely stopped, when free throws were awarded sparingly and when a center jump following every basket was required in most parts of the United States. A player who seemed able to score at will was extraordinary.

But the East had to be shown. Pacific Coast basketball was regarded by New Yorkers with contempt. The last time the University of California played at the Garden, for example, NYU trounced them, 41-26. This was the same Cal team that split four games with Stanford during the regular conference season.

Long Island University of Brooklyn was the class of the East, and the East was the class of the nation. They still played ball-control offense and man-to-man defense. They shot the ball in the traditional manner, with two hands, and they seldom shot at all until the ball had been worked in with six or seven passes or more.

Stanford? Well, the Indians were something of an enigma to Easterners. Stanford's attitude bordered on the frivolous. The players joked with New York reporters, and were observed rolling oranges into a cocked hat. Their unwavering fun spirit earned them the nickname

"Laughing Boys." And those who watched them shooting one-handed during practice were moved to laughter—or derision.

"I'll quit coaching if I have to teach one-handed shots to win," snapped Nat Holman, the CCNY coach and the ranking expert of Eastern basketball. "They will have to show me plenty to convince me that a shot predicated on a prayer is smart basketball. There's only one way to shoot, the way we do it in the East—with two hands."

John Bunn, the Stanford coach, had played for Phog Allen at Kansas and considered himself a traditionalist. He resented the intimations that he was some kind of radical. Athletics should be fun, he said, and one look at young Luisetti swishing one-handers from 20 feet away had convinced him there was room for innovation. So he gave his spirited players the freedom to develop their individual skills.

"On the attack," Bunn told the press, "we switch positions to meet changing situations. Luisetti might play the post, bring the ball downcourt or switch from the left to the right side at will. On defense we play a combination zone and man-to-man that I call a 'team defense.'"

To Bunn, switching positions was perfectly acceptable. To Eastern fans, however, it all smacked of anarchy.

It was hardly that, of course. For all of their liberated freelancing, the Stanford players were very disciplined and specialized. The left forward and fine all-around player was Howie Turner, the same size as Luisetti at 6' 2½". The guards were Dinty Moore, a tireless defensive specialist who stood 6' 1", and Jack Calderwood, a superb 6' 4" backboard man who answered to the nickname of "Spook" or "Frankenstein" because of his lumbering gait and foreboding mien. The tallest man on the starting five was 6' 4½" center Art Stoefen.

As Dr. Northway finished the taping, Luisetti playfully ruffled the physician's hair and pulled the necktie from beneath his vest for good luck. Then he and his teammates trotted into the packed arena. At first, the sight of so many people awed them. Art Stoefen remembered that the first thing he was conscious of was a giant neon sign. Then he looked up and saw what seemed to be thousands of fireflies. They were cigarettes glowing in the darkness. And

through the smoke, he finally saw people, people as far and as high as he could see.

Howie Turner recalled that he and his teammates were awfully nervous all of a sudden. None of them had ever been to New York before; most of them had not even been out of California. They needed something to loosen them up. Specifically, they needed what they always seemed to get: an incredible performance from Luisetti.

Long Island controlled the opening tap and scored first. On Stanford's first possession a pass to Turner in the right corner was slightly back of him and he started falling over the boundary as he lunged for it. Reaching the ball in time, he instinctively whipped it desperately in the direction of the hoop. He speedily regained his feet to assume his position on defense when he noticed that the referee was calling for a center jump at mid-court.

"Did that thing go in?" he asked Moore.

"It sure did," Moore replied.

"Wow!" cried Turner, and his teammates burst into laughter. Their tension broken, the Laughing Boys were finally in the relaxed frame of mind to play their freewheeling game.

Midway in the first half the teams were tied, 11-11, but already the handwriting was on the wall: LIU was flustered by the "team defense," the fast-break offense and Luisetti, who seemed to be all over the place at once, swiping the ball, rebounding, passing expertly and hitting his one-handers from every angle.

Luisetti remembers that his first field goal came after a fake and a pivot near the foul line. It was over the biggest Blackbird of them all, 6' 8" Center Art Hillhouse. "You lucky bastard," Hillhouse said to Hank. He didn't say a word when Hank's next shot dropped in.

Early in the game the crowd had been pulling hard for the home team, but when the Indians trotted off the court with a 22-14 lead at halftime, the fans, entranced by the black-haired Luisetti and his carefree teammates, gave them a standing ovation.

The second half was totally one-sided. Long Island was unable to score for a full seven minutes, and Luisetti was in complete control of the tempo. He shot only when it was obvious he should, preferring instead to wow the fans with his astonishing variety of passes. Still, he was the top scorer of the night with 15 points as the "Laughing Boys" from Palo Alto laughed their way to a 45-31 victory. Later that season he was named the outstanding athlete to perform in Madison Square Garden in 1936-37. The cheering New York fans, helpless Stanford captives, sensed they had just witnessed a basketball revolution.

There was no doubt about it, as the Metropolitan press acknowledged the following day. Wrote Stanley Frank in the New York *Post:* "Overnight, and with a suddenness as startling as Stanford's unorthodox tactics, it had become apparent today that New York's fundamental concept of basketball will have to be radically changed if Greater New York is to remain among the progressive centers of court culture in this country. Every one of the amiable clean-cut Coast kids fired away with leaping one-handed shots which were impossible to stop."

"It seemed Luisetti could do nothing wrong," added *The New York Times.* "Some of his shots would have been deemed foolhardy if attempted by anybody else, but with Luisetti shooting, these were accepted by the enchanted crowd."

The Stanford-Long Island University game was no mere intersectional upset. It was a pivotal game in the history of college basketball. It brought modern basketball to the world. Now players everywhere would begin shooting on the run and with one hand. The dull, deliberate style of play would give way to the fast break, the man-to-man would yield to the zone and combination defenses, and in 1937-38 the center jump after goals would be eliminated forever. Scoring suddenly grew, and a game that had served, in many areas, merely to fill the gap between baseball and football seasons abruptly began to enjoy tremendous popularity of its own.

There is no disputing that Hank Luisetti was the first *modern* basketball player. What amazed Eastern fans was not so much that he shot, rebounded, dribbled, passed and played defense better than anyone else, but that he did almost all these things in unorthodox ways. He dribbled and passed behind his back, and he appeared to shoot without glancing at the basket. When he drove, he soared like a hawk, looking left and right before he lofted the ball in mid-air toward the hoop.

"Hank could stay up so long he was like a ballet dancer," Turner said. "He could fake while driving at a time when people just drove, period. Forty years ago he was making moves that still are considered exceptional today."

"No doubt about it," said Howie Dallmar, a former coach and All-American at Stanford. "Hank simply revolutionized basketball. It would be unfair to compare anyone who played in his era with today's players. But no one now—I mean no one—is as far ahead of his contemporaries as Hank was of his. He was at least 20 years ahead of his time."

Angelo "Hank" Luisetti was born in San Francisco and played his freshman ball at Stanford in the 1934-35 season, averaging 20 points a game. In his first varsity appearance he tried nine shots from the floor against College of the Pacific and sank them all. Each year he was on the varsity he set new scoring records and as a senior he totaled 50 points in a game against Duquesne. His single-season record of 232 points survived for 12 years in the old Pacific Coast Conference before Stanford's George Yardley and Southern Cal's Bill Sharman broke it.

On March 5, 1938, Hank broke the national collegiate four-year scoring record against California in melodramatic fashion. With the historic point (No. 1,533) safely in the record book, he leaped for a loose ball and banged into Ed Dougery, the Cal forward. His head crashed against the floor, knocking him unconscious. He was helped from the floor as the partisan Cal crowd sat in silence. Had he smashed the scoring record and ended his career on the same night? No. Minutes later he reappeared. The first time he got his hands on the ball he scored. He finished the game with 22 points.

That was not the first time that season Luisetti had been resurrected. On January 23, he collided with USC's Gail Goodrich, father of the UCLA All-American of later years, and fell to the floor bleeding from a cut above the eye. He was quickly stitched up in the locker room, went back into the game and scored immediately from 30 feet out.

Angelo Enrico Luisetti was unique. Until he came along, basketball never had a hero—and it hasn't had one quite like him since. He was a reluctant hero, so modest that he had to be prodded into going for points. The first to insist that basketball was a team game, he was always trying to turn the spotlight over to his teammates.

Ward Lambert, the old Purdue coach and an ardent Luisetti watcher, said Hank was the answer to a coach's dream. "He could do the most fantastic things with a basketball," Lambert said, "but—and this is so important in basketball—he was also a superb *team* player. In a close contest at Palo Alto one night, Hank had been wowing the fans with his uncanny shooting. Suddenly he called a time out. 'Listen, guys,' he said, 'this isn't basketball. You're feeding me too much. Come on now, I'm not the only shooter on this team. Let's use our heads and play the game the way it's supposed to be played.' Another time, he narrowly missed six shots in a row—shots that drew groans from the crowd, they were so close. Finally, Hank went over to John Bunn and said, 'Take me out, Coach, I stink.' Bunn took him out, gave him a brief rest and then put him back into the game. Hank went on to score 10 important points to lead the Indians to victory."

Luisetti always seemed to come up with the clutch play. Once in an overtime period against UCLA he ripped a tie game wide open with six baskets; against California, he stole the ball five times and scored each time, forcing the Bears to abandon their game plan and switch to a new pattern. He once smothered Santa Clara with a 35-point barrage, and on another occasion he delighted a packed San Francisco crowd with a one-handed 50-foot basket. The night he led his team to a 92-27 blitzkrieg of Duquesne he needed a police escort to get back to the locker room. One of his teammates was Bebe Lee, who later coached at Colorado.

"One of the things they used to say about Hank was that he was a reluctant shooter," Lee said. "I guess so. He got as much kick out of passing off as he did from scoring."

Luisetti went into the Duquesne game averaging 22 points a game, but instead of shooting he began passing off. His teammates decided to teach him a lesson. They came busting down the floor on a quick break. Luisetti spun a pass to Art Stoefen, who dribbled once and threw the ball back to Hank underneath the basket. Hank again refused to take a shot and whipped the ball back to Stoefen. Stoefen tossed it right back. Luisetti scored. Then Howie Turner took a pass from Luisetti—and threw it right back to

Another star of the Luisetti era was Lou Boudreau, Illinois 1938, who had good hands and was a spectacular dribbler. He later took those hands to the Cleveland Indians and stardom as an All-Star shortstop and manager.

him. By then, Luisetti realized that all of his teammates were in on the plot.

"Aw, come on, guys," he pleaded. "Cut it out."

But it was too late. They had Hank on the hip. Every time the Indians got the ball, they fed Hank. Every time he passed to a teammate, the ball would come right back to him. By the end of the game, Hank Luisetti had set a record of 50 points.

"He broke the record with one of the most sensational shots I ever saw," said Bebe Lee. "Taking a bad pass in the corner and falling out of bounds, Hank heaved the ball like a baseball pitcher, with an overhand motion. The ball didn't even brush the rim, and Hank had his record."

Luisetti made the All-American team three times, was twice named College Player of the Year. His famous No. 7 jersey has been permanently retired at Stanford. After graduation he turned down lucrative professional offers, though he did play AAU ball for the Phillips Oilers, national champions. The coach was Chuck Hyatt, himself an All-American at Pitt. Hyatt had seen all the great stars of his era— Beckman, Holman, Dehnert, Banks and all the others who were gifted for basketball—but Luisetti was the apple of his eye.

"Hank was born for this game," Hyatt said. "He was born for it. I never saw him make a mistake. He was just one of those guys who come along once in a blue moon with just the right mixture of speed, reflexes, good hands, good eyes and, above all else, *class*. Boy, did he ever have class."

Luisetti's 1936-37 Stanford Indians were the first team from the West to sweep the East. Winners of 25 of 27 contests that season, they went on to claim the National Championship; along the way they won their second of three straight Pacific Coast Conference titles. The following season they traveled back to Madison Square Garden and beat Long Island and CCNY on successive nights, largely on the strength of Luisetti's hot hand. By then even Nat Holman was convinced: Hank Luisetti was no ghost, he was real.

In his last collegiate game, Luisetti scored 26 points in a virtuoso performance that defeated Oregon, 59-51, for Stanford's third straight Pacific Coast Conference title. Long before Hank left the game, the Stanford Pavilion crowd was on its feet giving him a standing ovation. Among the reporters covering the finale was Roy Cummings of the San Francisco *Call-Bulletin*.

"When future fans start talking about the basketball stars of their days," rhapsodized Cummings afterward, "those who witnessed Hank Luisetti and the Stanford teams of 1936-37-38 will shake their heads and say, 'My lad, you never saw Luisetti.'"

Recently, Luisetti reminisced about his first appearance in Madison Square Garden. "I guess," he said, "we didn't really know what we were starting that night. We actually had no idea that we would bring on a revolution. You know, I've thought about that many times over the years. I had no notion what that one game would mean to me. Getting all that publicity in New York changed my life, my whole life. It made me a national figure with stories about me in leading national magazines. Up until then, I had just been a local kid."

Now that he looks back at it all, he understands the significance. Modestly, he admits he wasn't too bad a ballplayer.

But Luisetti points to a trait most historians generally overlook. "Inside I guess I had the killer instinct," he said. "Inside I was serious as hell, even though on the outside I laughed a lot. I could play this modern game. Yes, I'd do well in any era. Maybe I wouldn't get as many tips, with some of these 7-footers around, because I wouldn't get in close—but I'd get my points."

Oregon Wins First NCAA— Then The War Years

By now, in 1937, people were yelling bloody murder that the rules committee had made a sissy's sport out of what had once been a grand old roughneck's game. Sam Barry, the USC coach, did not agree, and he said so.

"They've done nothing of the sort," he said. "What they have done is to take a dull, slow and unexciting game and turn it into a game of speed, skill and rhythm; a sport that is also an art; a game that is now filled with emotion."

Just as there was once the day of the flying wedge in football, Coach Barry said, so there was the day of the slam-bang, crash-through offense in basketball. It was speed and brawn in football; it was brawn and reach in basketball.

"In basketball, a coach took two fast men and called them forwards," Barry said. "He then took the biggest fellow in school and put him in at center for the tipoff. This fellow usually tipped the ball to a teammate, who threw the ball to the running guard, who held onto the ball until one of the fast forwards got free, and then he threw the ball in and the forward generally shot a basket. If the forward scored, the ball went back to center and another tipoff ensued. If one team had a tall center, or one who could outjump any opponent, that team usually got the tipoff and kept on running up the score.

"But today [1937], under certain rules which I have advocated and which have stirred up quite a controversy, that type of basketball has changed. The game today has speed, very little body blocking, cleverness and finesse. For several years I have fought for the elimination of the center-jump play, except at the beginning of each half, when it is still used to start play. I maintain that the elimination of the tipoff will make a more thrilling game. It will offer a fairer test of real skill. We have tried eliminating the tipoff on the Pacific Coast and have proved that it does speed up the game, that it produces more competition and gives the crowd a much better show. By stopwatches we have found that it adds four minutes of play to each game and the scores generally run from eight to 10 points higher. This is the way it works: At the beginning of each half, the tipoff is held as usual. Then, when one team scores, the side that has been scored upon is given possession of the ball under its own basket. This team, temporarily, is two points behind. Now it has a chance to make an offensive thrust. The players have a chance to show their skill at offense, working the ball down the floor—they must get the ball across the center line in 10 seconds, remember—and then a sudden drive for a score. The team does not have to trust to luck and a tall center to get possession of the ball to try for a basket. This tends to balance up a team. Every team must be as skillful on defense as offense. It opens up the game, with nearly every moment one of action. Somebody is threatening, trying to score, and that means action. Under my proposed rule, every team must have several plays for scoring, signals for defensive positions, and all five players on each team working as a unit on offense—not as five individuals."

Sam Barry got his way. The following season

the center jump was eliminated. The change revolutionized basketball, resulting in more playing time, higher scores, and patterned offenses and defenses.

Recently, one of Barry's adversaries, Washington State's Jack Friel, told me what it was like to coach in the era of the center jump. "There was always an element of strategy in getting ready for each team you faced," Friel said. "If you were going to be outjumped at center, you took a defensive position and did some gambling to cut 'em off and take your share of the tipoffs, which would be less than 50 percent if you were clearly outjumped. But about the only time it meant sure possession was when there was much difference in the size of the centers and the bigger boy could really tap the ball at a good range, either backward or forward. In one way, I actually liked the old center jump, because it gave the players time to catch their breath. The game wasn't quite so continuous then. You came back to the center jump after every score and there was that delay. I think the players, the coaches, the spectators, everybody, needed a little blow in a game as fast as basketball. But all considered, there isn't any question that today's game is much more exciting, vastly improved, without the center jump."

Always progressive, Friel has never been one to live in the past. Basketball today is so much better than the old game, he said.

"The jump shot has been the biggest change," he said. "Ironically, I didn't believe in the shot at first. I simply couldn't conceive of a kid jumping off the floor and shooting that accurately from the distance they do. I was soon converted, however, and the jump shot is the big weapon now. I think the present teams score more by accident, with their excellent jump shooters, than our old teams did by design. As a whole, the teams nowadays are better coached and better drilled defensively than they were in the old days. All we had on offense was the fast break, the two-handed shot, and, after Luisetti, the running one-hander. In the late 1930's and 1940's, it was pretty much post play—getting the ball deep to somebody, who'd hook or muscle himself in close for a shot. The hook shot became popular, mostly in the East; driving hooks, veering to the side of the basket and hooking right or left. The jump shot had

Oregon's Bob Anet got caught here between two Buckeyes, but the Ducks fought on to win the first NCAA basketball championship in 1939 with 46-33 victory over Ohio State at Evanston, Illinois. Oregon Coach Howard Hobson catered to home-state talent. Every player on his national championship team came from a radius of 200 miles.

Dr. Howard Hobson, coach of Oregon's 1939 NCAA champions, now in his mid-70s and living in Portland, says that two of his stars of that squad, All-American Slim Wintermute (above) and Laddy Gale, would have been standouts in any era.

not yet become vogue, and since you had to have something besides the set shot and the straight drive you learned the hook shot.

"Defense, in those days, was largely man-to-man, especially in the East. They wouldn't play zone back there because they figured it detracted from the game and soured the fans. The only way to play against the zone, intelligently, was to move the ball longer and faster than the zone could shift. The result was monotony. Now you've got the what-the-hell, shoot-from-anywhere jumper, a great crowd-pleaser, but where we had nothing but the set shot and drives, it took a lot of patience and poise and deliberation to crack open a zone defense. So the teams in the East, thinking about the turnstile count, turned their noses down on the zone and opted for the man-to-man. Once in a while I'd zone an opponent, but mostly I went man-to-man. Oregon? Howard Hobson zoned quite a bit—and won the first NCAA tournament with it in 1939."

In Eugene, Oregon, no one involved with the first NCAA playoffs felt any great compulsion to discuss anything as mundane as a national championship before the tournament began. Instead, they were relieved to have squeezed past California, 54-49 and 53-47, to win the Pacific Coast Conference playoffs and qualify for the 1939 NCAA Western semifinals at Treasure Island in San Francisco. There, the University of Oregon performed surgery on Texas, 56-41, and on Oklahoma, 55-37.

Traveling with the Ducks that season was L. H. Gregory, sports editor-columnist of the Portland *Oregonian* and an alumnus of UO. He once described his alma mater as "an athletically sick school," because it lost more than it won. Now he was one of its most vocal cheer leaders, coining such names as "Webfoots" and for the basketball team the "Tall Firs."

"Greg nicknamed them the 'Tall Firs' but they wouldn't be called 'tall' today," Jack Friel said. "Their center, Urgel "Slim" Wintermute, was 6' 8", and forwards Laddie Gale and John Dick both stood 6' 4". Their guards, Bobby Anet and Wally Johanson, were very quick and small. Their specialty was the fast break. They'd fast-break you to death; were hard to stop. Hobby once said: 'We use a fast break that's a bit unusual in that we use it all the time until the opportunity closes. It isn't an opportunity break. It's a break that we always attempt after we get the ball, with the two guards handling the ball on the way down, the two forwards down ahead and the center trailing for the rebound.' As an opposing coach, I can tell you that Anet and Johanson, usually Anet, would get the ball in the middle and take it downcourt so fast you hardly had time to set up; meanwhile, the other guard and the two forwards would run for the baseline via the outside lanes to complete the fast break. Defensively, Oregon zoned a lot. In fact, the Ducks zoned Ohio State in the NCAA finals. Hobby Hobson told me later, 'Those teams back there informally had a gentlemen's agreement among themselves not to use the zone. So when we sprung it on the Buckeyes, they had some trouble with it.' Hobby laughed about it. Out here on the West Coast we were used to it, and we got Hobby out of it, but he used it a lot and he used it in the national finals against Ohio State."

Jimmy Hull, All-American forward, was high scorer for Ohio State with 12 points in the 1939 NCAA tournament as the Buckeyes finished second to Oregon.

The setting was a small gym on the campus of Northwestern University in Evanston, Illinois. Blatantly, the Tall Firs reaffirmed what the experts had been contending all along: If Hobson went with the zone, it wouldn't be a contest. It wasn't. Oregon ho-hummed its way to an easy 46-33 victory. In doing so it earned itself a national reputation and the NCAA had itself a tournament.

Never before in the 87 years of its existence had Eugene seen the like of the milling mobs that gathered at the Southern Pacific depot and lined the parade route—"humanity deep"—to greet the returning champions. "When Hobson and his Webfoots wearily pushed their way off the train," wrote Dick Strite in the *Eugene Register*, "the pent-up frenzied shouts of 10,000 voices mingled with the clash of the University of Oregon band playing 'Mighty Oregon,' and booming fireworks—heralding the greatest athletic team in Oregon history."

Afterward, All-American Slim Wintermute was hugged by a Portland reporter, and he shrugged, " 'Twasn't anything at all." Then he paused, grinned and said, "Yes, it was."

With an estimated 18,000,000 basketball players in the world now, Forrest C. "Phog" Allen believed it was high time that everybody adopt a standardized nomenclature for the game. "The least you can do," he told a basket-

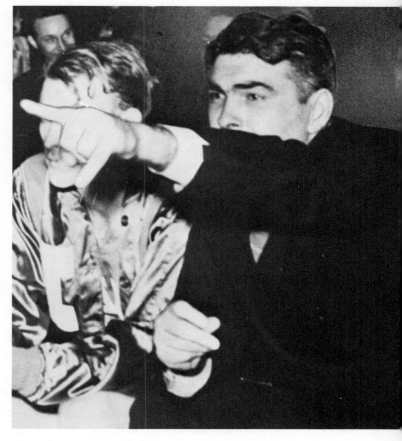

Away from a game, Indiana Coach Branch McCracken was a warm, pleasant man; during a game, however, he was something else again.

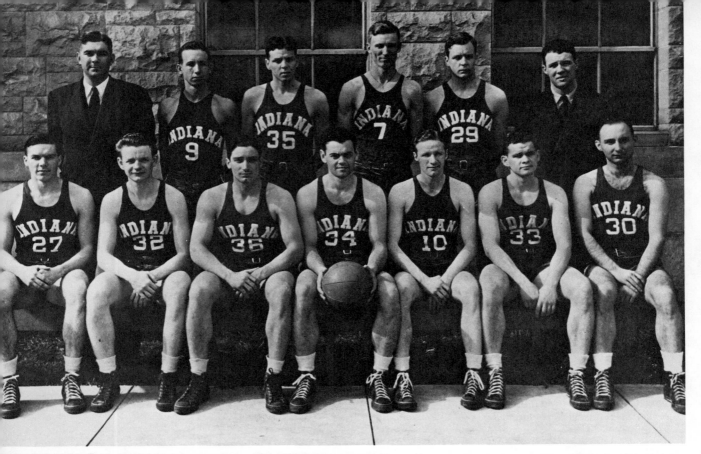

Indiana trounced Kansas, 60-42, to win the 1940 NCAA title. The champions: lst row, left: Jim Gridley, Herm Schaefer, Bob Dro, Captain Marv Huffman, Jay McCreary, Curley (Paul) Armstrong, Ralph Dorsey; second row, Coach Branch McCracken, Chet Francis, Bill Menke, Andy Zimmer, Bob Menke and Ralph Graham.

ball clinic, "is to learn how to speak the language correctly."

Dr. Allen said he had been giving it a lot of thought, and this was what he came up with:

Back court—not back half.

Backboards or bankboards—not backstops, boards, or banks.

Baskets—not buckets, rims, irons, rings, hoops, nets, or strings.

Blocking—not checking, picking off, smothering, or spiking. There is no legal block. Blocking and its synonyms are all fouls and should not be confused with screening.

Freeze—not stall, bulldogging, roping, backcourt game, or delayed offense.

Setups—not crips, follows, Sunday shots, guts, snow birds, lay-ups, dogs, suckers, bunnies, sleepers, or potshots.

Screening—not blocking or legal blocking. Screening is legal; blocking is not.

Shifting—not trading, switching, exchanging, sliding, or man-to-man.

Tip-off—not tap, jump ball, toss, center tap, or center jump.

Zone Defense—not mass, set, territorial, accordion, or elastic band.

When sifting through the rubble, it was clear that the West dominated the NCAA championship in its formative years. Six out of the first eight champions were from that part of the country—Oregon, Stanford, Wyoming, Utah, and Oklahoma A. & M. (twice). Indiana and Wisconsin won the other two times. For the East, it was the worst of times, though its time was just around the corner.

Jack Friel says he has a theory why the West's dominance became so complete.

"At the time," he said, "the East didn't have any big boys to speak of. They played a give-and-go, fast, good-looking, driving game of sound set-shooting, excellent ballhandling and all-around floor game, but they got to the point where they couldn't beat the Western teams because they lacked the big boys. Once they began importing recruits with size, however, the East-West matchups quickly evened out."

Two events marked the rapidly changing basketball scene during the 1939-40 season. On November 28, 1939, Dr. James Naismith died.

These are the Badgers of Wisconsin that defeated Washington State, 39-34, for the 1941 NCAA championship. First row, left: Bob Alwin, Bob Sullivan, Fred Rehm, John Kotz, Gene Englund, Charles Epperson, Ted Strain, Harlow Scott, Ed Scheiwe. Back row, left: Mgr. Morris Bradley, Trainer Walter Bakke, Ed Downs, Bob Roth, George Affeldt, Warren Schrage, Don Timmerman, Ted Deppe, John Lynch, Ed Jones, Coach Bud Foster, Asst. Coach Fred Wegner.

Western NCCA Champions Washington State battled their way into the finals of the 1941 national championship by beating Arkansas, 64-53, then cooled off against Wisconsin, 39-34, and had to settle for runnerup position. Back row, left: Coach Jack Friel, Dosskey, Butts, Harrington, Captain Ray Sundquist, Hunt, Mahan, and Dr. Wilbur H. S. Bohm. Front row, left: Gebert, Hooper, Gilberg, Lindeman, Zimmerman, Gentry, Akins, and Mgr. Wainscott. Dr. Bohm later went on as chief trainer of the Washington Redskins, New York Football Giants, Washington Senators, and Cincinnati Reds.

Precisely three months later, February 28, 1940, W2XMS, an experimental station and forerunner to New York's WNBC, televised the first college basketball game. The station featured the Pitt-Fordham and NYU-Georgetown doubleheader from Madison Square Garden.

In the Big Ten, Indiana finished second behind Piggy Lambert's Purdue Boilermakers, but the Hoosiers' "Laughing Boys" had beaten them twice during the regular season and were elected by committee for the Eastern Regional berth from District IV. It was Branch McCracken's second season as Indiana coach. Like Oregon's Tall Firs, he had a fast-breaking team built around Marvin Huffman, Herman Schaefer, Bob Dro, Curly Armstrong, Bill Menke, and Jay McCreary. It was a well-balanced squad, with any man a scoring threat. The Hoosiers ran away with the NCAA regionals, beat Kansas, 60-42, to win the national championship, and laughed all the way from Kansas City back to Bloomington.

The following year, basketball celebrated its 50th birthday. Wisconsin, which finished ninth in the Big Ten the year before, surprised everyone by winning its conference title from defending NCAA champion Indiana. The Badgers had a 14-game winning streak on the line against Washington State in the finals of the NCAA tournament.

The Cougar coach was Jack Friel.

"To get there," he recalled recently, "we beat Creighton, 48-39, and Arkansas, 64-53. My big man was 6' 8" center Paul Lindeman, with Dale Gentry, an All-American football end, at forward. They gave us plenty of muscle on the boards. On the other hand, Wisconsin was a very rugged, very solid basketball team; not overly tall, but strong. They played good, tight man-to-man defense, forcing us to go outside. Center Gene Englund, a regular jumping jack, was high for Wisconsin with 13 points, and sophomore Johnny Kotz, the MVP of the tournament, had 12. Kirk Gebert, our very clever floor general, topped both teams with 21 points. By modern standards, Wisconsin was not a big team. The players ranged from about 6' 2" to 6' 7". But they were durable, really tough on defense. As I remember, they didn't substitute much. They went all the way with eight players. I substituted a lot. In fact, I think I was one of the first to use the two-platoon

UCLA's Jackie Robinson, the first black to break major league baseball's color line, led the Pacific Coast Conference in scoring in 1940 with 148 points in 12 games.

Stanford's 1942 NCAA champions, left: Bill Cowden, Howie Dallmar, Ed Voss, Jim Pollard, Don Burness, and Coach Everett Dean, one of the leading tacticians of the day and author of books on basketball.

system. Basketball was developing into a racehorse game. I finally came to the conclusion that players really couldn't stay in there and pitch on defense; to play good defense, they needed some rest. So by 1941 I was substituting a lot, and after that I platooned all the time. In fact, we forced every team in the Northwest, and UCLA in the playoffs, to two-platoon with us. But platoons didn't seem to bother Wisconsin. In the championship game against us, they didn't play an especially fast game; it was more of a pattern game. Bud Foster, their coach and later president of the national coaches' association—very smart, very defensive-minded—had our number. We loved to run and he beat us by slowing the tempo of the game. Between the two teams there were only 73 points scored. Unfortunately for us, they had five more than we did (39-34)."

Recently, John Jarstad, who broadcast sports in the Pacific Northwest for 25 years, recalled having covered that contest as sports editor of *The Evergreen*, the Washington State student newspaper.

"That was the first time the NCAA ever held the championship tournament at Kansas City," Jarstad said. "To get there from Pullman, a bunch of us piled into a little two-door Olds and drove to K.C. We had a breakdown at Laramie, Wyoming, and one of our guys, a pretty good poker player, got into a poker game with some cowboys and won enough silver dollars to repair a burned out wheel bearing. We hopped from campus to campus along the way, staying at various fraternities to save money. The trip took three days of furious driving—the roads were all two-laners in those days. *The Evergreen* gave me $25 to cover my expenses, I remember; $25 for travel, hotel, food, tips. Let the IRS make something out of *that!*

"The tournament was played in a brand new auditorium, seating about 15,000, featuring all-blue leather seats. I remember those blue seats; really big-time in those days. Anyway, as gametime approached, I found myself sitting at the press table right next to the Mutual Broadcasting System's microphone. Mutual had decided to originate a national broadcast of the Wisconsin-WSC game and the local MBS station was asked to provide the origination. So

All-American Ken Sailors, 1943

Future national sportscaster, Curt Gowdy, a member of the 1941 Wyoming Cowboys.

they sent one of their local news broadcasters to do the game. I mean, he was there *alone*. He obviously knew very little about the two teams. Well, I got to shooting the breeze with him shortly before he went on the air and the upshot was he pressed me into helping him. At first, I concentrated on identifying the players for him, but then he turned the microphone over to me more and more and I wound up being what is commonly known today as a *color man*. A Howard Cosell, I wasn't; a Keith Jackson, he wasn't. But we made history, for that was the first coast-to-coast network broadcast of an NCAA championship basketball game. And that was how we went on the air. Afterwards, the guy slipped me $10 for helping him. There's nothing like starting at the top on a national broadcast."

The 1941-42 season had just begun when the Japanese attacked Pearl Harbor. For the following four years, college basketball was played on a reduced basis. Stanford won the first wartime NCAA title, despite the loss of all-American Jim Pollard, who was bedded down with influenza during the championship game. They won by beating Dartmouth, the Ivy League champion, 53-38. Howard Dallmar came off the bench to fill in for Pollard and outplayed Dartmouth's George Munroe, scoring 15 points to earn MVP honors.

The war caused important problems for college basketball. Whole teams were wiped out by the draft. Many schools dropped the sport for the duration. Some made freshmen eligible for varsity competition in order to keep their teams alive.

Out on the Western plains, Wyoming's All-American Kenny Sailors was the apple of everybody's eye. Exquisitely deft, Sailors was the practically perfect player, swift and sure on offense, overwhelming on defense. The Cowboys from Laramie battled their way into the NCAA finals with harried, come-from-behind wins over Oklahoma and Texas in the Western Regionals, then trounced Georgetown, 46-34, in the championship game. Sailors was named the tournament's MVP.

In those days, the merits of the NCAA tournament remained vaguely suspect. Its detrac-

In the final few minutes of the contest, Wyoming surged from behind to swamp Georgetown, 46-34, and win the 1943 NCAA championship at Madison Square Garden. Cowboys shown here, front row, left: Don Waite, Earl "Shadow" Ray, and Jim Reese. Back row, left: Jim Collins, Floyd Volker, Milo Komenich, Coach Ev Shelton, Lou Roney, Kenny Sailors, Jim Weir, and Dr. Philip O. Badger, president of the NCAA, presenting the championship trophy to Coach Shelton.

tors claimed that the National Invitation Tournament, the first big national post-season tournament (1938), attracted better teams. The issue was settled when Wyoming, the NCAA champion, and the winner of the NIT, St. John's, were matched to play in a Red Cross

Coach Clair Bee, one of college basketball's all-time super strategists, is shown here going over game plan with 1942 Long Island U. squad. Coach Bee's 82.7 winning percentage still ranks No. 1 among major coaches.

benefit at Madison Square Garden. Final score: Wyoming 52, St. John's 47. End of argument.

In 1943-44, some of college basketball's most exciting matchups were attributable to the war. Notre Dame vs. Great Lakes Naval Training Station, for instance. Forrest A. Anderson, later head coach at Bradley, played in that game.

"The most dramatic shot I've ever seen happened that night," Anderson told me. "The contest was played at Chicago Stadium and I was playing for Great Lakes. We were loaded, two of our stars being former Notre Dame players, George Sobek and Buster Hiller. We had a string of 20 straight wins going, and more than 18,000 jammed the Stadium to see if the Irish could upset us. George Keogan, Notre Dame's beloved coach for years, had died only two days before, and the Irish were out to win this one for George. Their spirit was tremendous. The pace was blistering all the way, and with only 10 seconds remaining we held a 54-52 edge. There

Considered by many the best all-around player since Hank Luisetti, 6'3" Bob Davies led Seton Hall to 43 straight victories in early 1940s.

The Illinois Whiz Kids took the country by storm in 1942. From left: Jack Smiley, Art Mathisen, Ken Menke, Gene Vance, and Andy Phillip.

was a scramble for the ball as it went out of bounds. Notre Dame was given the ball at mid-court. Two seconds to play. George Ratterman, the All-American football quarterback, passed to a little guy named Curran, who had been in our hair all evening. Curran grabbed the throw down by the end line, and Schumaker, our guard, was covering him so close that he almost had his hand in his face. Curran had no back-board to use as a guide, just the basket. Yet, with that huge paw in his face, he turned and threw the ball like a shortstop would throw to first base. The ball had no arch at all. It hit near the side of the rim, then dropped through the hoop. All this happened in two seconds. You couldn't hear yourself talk for a solid 10 min-utes. Finally, the game moved into an overtime, and we eventually won, 60-56. Ironically, George Sobek, a former Notre Dame man, scored the winning points for us."

The headliners in college basketball in 1943-44 were teenagers. Out of the tumult and the shouting rose such peach-fuzzed tykes as Utah's Arnie Ferrin, Kentucky's Bob Brannum, and Dick McGuire and Bill Kotsores of St. John's. But before the season ended, McGuire was

Though better remembered as a great football quarterback, Northwestern's Otto Graham was All-Big Ten in basketball in 1943.

Freshman Arnie Ferrin (22) was college basketball's fair-haired boy. In 1944 he led Utah to 42-40 victory over Dartmouth for NCAA title, and then beat NIT champion St. John's, 43-36, in Red Cross fund-raising game. Averaging only 18½ years of age, the Utes became known as the "Cinderella Kids."

They were so good that all but Menke made the All-Big Ten first team. Superstar Otto Graham of Northwestern beat him out—the very same Otto Graham of later Cleveland Browns fame.

Vadal Peterson, in his 17th season at Utah, had no choice but to go with youth. The military draft had stripped him of all else—experience, Skyline Conference competition (suspended for the duration), even the Utah fieldhouse (appropriated by the Army). Coach Peterson got permission to practice in a church gym and his schedule was mostly service teams. The Redskins played only three college teams. Wyoming, the defending NCAA champion, was not one of them. The Cowboys dropped basketball because of the war, leaving Utah with the District VII bid to the Western Regionals in Kansas City. Coach Peterson refused it, however, because he was not guaranteed expenses; instead he accepted an invitation to play in the NIT. The Madison Square Garden tournament included such powers as Kentucky, St. John's, Bowling Green, DePaul, and Oklahoma A. & M. Utah was knocked out of the NIT in the first round by Kentucky, 46-38.

Normally, that would have been curtains for the Redskins, but a strange thing happened to them on the way back to Salt Lake City. When Arkansas, with two stars injured in an auto accident, and Rice, co-champions of the Southwest Conference, withdrew from the Western Regionals, Utah was contacted again. This time Coach Peterson said yes, and sent his teenagers against so-so Missouri in the first round of the NCAA tournament at Kansas City. In a contest stressing defense more than offense, Utah won, 45-35.

Moving up a notch, Utah then blasted Iowa State, 40-31.

The Redskins matured with each game. Their offense had many sharp edges and they used a multiplicity of tricks to bedevil their opponents. The star of the team, of course, was a skinny freshman named Arnie Ferrin, 6' 3", an exquisitely deft playmaker who could shoot with either hand. Then there were Fred Sheffield, Wat Misaka, Herb Wilkinson, Dick Smuin, and Bob Lewis, averaging barely six feet tall. To win, Utah defensed unremittingly and worked hard for their points. Ferrin and

called to active duty, sent to Dartmouth in the military's college training program, and wound up playing for the Big Green in the NCAA tournament.

The team of the year was Utah, with its "Cinderella Kids" averaging 18½ years of age. They made people think of Illinois' "Whiz Kids" of the year before—Andy Phillip, Ken Menke, Gene Vance, Jack Smiley, and Art Mathisen—who, despite a 17-1 record, did not play in either the NCAA or NIT tournaments. Though the disciplined and aggressive Whiz Kids made hash out their abbreviated schedule, Coach Doug Mills was not able to keep them together long because of the military draft.

Sheffield were counted on to do most of the rebounding. Sheffield stood 6' 1" and was a winner of the NCAA high-jump championship.

Meanwhile, Dartmouth battled its way to the NCAA finals with a hard-fought victory over Ohio State, 60-53. Earl Brown, who had played at Notre Dame under George Keogan, was the Dartmouth coach and had a bewildering assortment of Navy and Marine reservists. Their success was attributable to Captain Audley Brindley, Bob Gale, John Monahan, Joe Vancisin, Harry Leggat, and Dick McGuire, a transfer from St. John's in the Navy's V-12 program. Brindley and McGuire were superb against the Buckeyes.

By this time, reporters referred to Utah as the "Blitz Kids," because of their aggressive tactics. On defense they swarmed all over opponents, forcing premature passes that often led to turnovers or harried, hurried shots.

The championship game was played at Madison Square Garden. Coach Peterson's strategy was to double-team Brindley and Gale with the ball, gambling that their teammates would be hesitant about shooting. Though they could never get a bigger lead than four points, the Redskins stuck to their game plan. Leading 36-32 with four minutes to play, they suddenly went into a freeze, forcing Dartmouth to press and foul. Twice Utah waived the free throw to assure possession of the ball. Then with the clock running down, McGuire stole the ball, but Ferrin got it back. Then Gale tipped in a rebound. Utah tried to freeze the ball once more—and again Dartmouth forced a turnover. With time virtually gone, McGuire got the ball, put his feet together, and sank a set shot just at the buzzer. Overtime.

Utah kept the game tied on the strength of Ferrin's four free throws. It appeared that another overtime would be needed when, with three seconds left on the clock, Herb Wilkinson whirled at the top of the key and hit a one-hander to make the final score, 42-40, Utah.

Utah was then matched with St. John's giant-killers in what had become known during the war as the Red Cross Classic: the NIT champion vs. the NCAA victor. Again the aggressive and disciplined play of Ferrin and his teammates won for Utah, this time 43-36. Hy Gotkin, Bill Kotsores, and Ray Wertis were held to 26 points, while Ferrin came off the

In 1945, Pfc. Gail Bishop, player-coach of the Fort Lewis, Washington Warriors, astonished Denver spectators by smashing the national AAU single-game tournament record with 62 points. After the war, he returned to Washington State, where he made All-Conference as a sophomore center in 1943, and earned All-America honors as a 6' 3" forward. Fast, versatile, a superlative two-handed and one-handed shot, an excellent rebounder, Bishop demonstrates here his jumping ability in a 1946 game against Oregon at Pullman.

floor with 17 and recognition as the best young player in America.

And so, for the second straight season, a team from the Rockies proved to New York that the NCAA champion was superior to the winner of the NIT.

But the quote of the year belonged to a renowned major college basketball coach (who shall remain nameless) when he was taken to task by an unhappy alumnus after being upset in the opening round of the 1944 NCAA tour-

George Mikan, 6' 9", the first of basketball's giants and superstars, dominated opponents for DePaul in 1945.

nament. In an attempt to alibi himself out of the corner, he blurted, "Hell, all my kids played like a bunch of amateurs."

It was, no doubt, time to do something about the goons; that is, the 6' 9" and 6' 11" and 7-footers who were dominating the hoops and the backboards. And so the intercollegiate legislators passed the goal-tending rule, making it illegal in 1944-45 to bat away a shot after the ball had begun its downward flight to the basket. The new rule, however, did not stop Oklahoma A. & M. from beating NYU, 49-45, to win the NCAA championship, with Cecil Hankin and 7' Bob Kurland leading the scorers. Coach Hank Iba, renowned for his methodical, slow-down offense, bottled up the Violets' fast break with a tight defense that stopped Sid Tannenbaum cold. The NYU star scored only four points. Kurland, with 22, was named the NCAA tournament's MVP.

Waiting in the wings for the Aggies was De-Paul. Champions of the NIT, the Demons had made a shambles of the record book. They had smashed 10 team records and George Mikan, their 6'10" superstar, an overwhelming scorer and boardtender, put his name in the history books with 10 individual records, including a high of 53 points against Rhode Island and a three-game total of 120.

No athlete dominated basketball as thoroughly as Mikan did during the war years. He represented an era. Even though he was so nearsighted he wore glasses a quarter of an inch thick, scorekeepers needed a computer to keep up with him.

Mikan began his college career inauspiciously. In 1942, the coach of a CYO team in Chicago arranged to get him a tryout at Notre Dame. George Keogan still coached the Irish and he told George, "Your height is a big asset and you have spunk, but you're hopelessly clumsy." Ray Meyer, who was Keogan's assistant, told George he should try another college. So George enrolled at DePaul.

When he arrived at DePaul he was surprised to find Ray Meyer. "What are you doing here?" George asked. And Meyer said, "I'm the new basketball coach."

The first thing Coach Meyer did was set up a rigorous training schedule for Mikan, with lots of rope-skipping, shadow-boxing, and running. In the gym, he personally practiced for long hours with Mikan, feeding him the ball from

Harry Boykoff of St. John's stood 6' 9" and weighed 290; in 1944, was a major reason why the goaltending rule became part of the game.

behind the free-throw circle, and, in alternating 15-minute periods, the future superstar polished his left- and right-handed hook shots and tap-ins.

Mikan had a tendency to pivot away from the basket instead of toward it. So that the ponderous center could learn to pivot correctly, Meyer placed folding chairs on both sides of him as he moved toward the basket. Mikan wound up with bruises all over his body after a week of workouts with his coach, but Meyer was eventually satisfied.

In a short time, Mikan developed a very good hook shot. His coordination improved. He gained confidence, grew taller, and learned to tolerate such spectator taunts as "goon" and "slats" and "monster." In 1945, he led all college scores with 23.9 points per game average; the following year he was No. 1 again with a 23.1 average.

Joe Lapchick once said Mikan was "the best feeder out of the pivot basketball ever had."

Mikan, himself, said his basic job as a center was to score and rebound. "But when my opponents ganged up on me, that meant some of my teammates were free," he said. "So I started concentrating on handing off or passing to players breaking around me," he said. "I also came to terms with myself. Once I got rid of my obsession that my height was a frightful bugaboo, I came to realize that for every shortcoming of an oversized body, there's a plus quality to compensate. For instance, I was able to scare off bullies without lifting a finger. Once when I was driving on a Minnesota highway, a car in front of me stopped short and I rammed into its rear bumper. The driver rushed at me, fists clenched. and shouted, 'Get out of that car!' I stepped out slowly and drew up to my full height. The driver's face went white and he backed off. 'All my fault' he said. 'Guess I shouldn't have stopped so short.' "

Mikan's major weakness was lack of speed. His teammates often took their time getting the ball into scoring position, because Mikan was late arriving at the keyhole. "Wait for Mikan" became a catch phrase among collegians all over the Midwest. But he was worth waiting for. Once he got there, it was almost a sure basket.

The big game of basketball's 1945 spring playoffs was the Red Cross benefit in New York

between NCAA champion Oklahoma A. & M. and NIT winner DePaul. At last, Kurland vs. Mikan. A press agent's dream. Get a few more matchups like that and some movie company was a cinch to do the life of Dr. Naismith, picturing him as a benefactor of the human race like Mme. Curie, Alexander Graham Bell, and Louis Pasteur. No other sports show in years was guaranteed to lift the hackles and stir the pulse quite so thoroughly as when Bob and George clashed on the court. Long, loose-limbed, almost gaunt, Kurland operated with a sort of scowling detachment, moving about the premises with glum deliberation. He'd lope gawkily around the court with his mouth open and pluck rebounds off the backboards like currants off a bush while waves of adversaries surged around him and bounced off in a sort of spray. When a fellow Aggie missed a shot he simply reached up and palmed the ball and pushed it down through the hoop. And Mikan? When he got his hands on that ball and started moving, he was a whole troop of cavalry, sabers drawn.

Mikan measured two inches less than Kurland's 7' from end to end and he looked and moved more like an institution than a man, with great grinding of gears. Willie Mays would have been hard pressed to throw a baseball over the top of Mikan. And he wasn't playing for Oklahoma A. & M.

The advance buildup in the Metropolitan dailies made great reading. But like pro football's Super Bowls, the game, itself, did not live up to all the hoopla. In what New York's biggest basketball brains promised would be the Game of the Century—in what was supposed to be the Battle of the Goons—a fevered match between the country's best two college teams—quickly deteriorated into a dreadfully dull show of conservative basketball. With only 14 minutes gone, the aggressive Mikan committed his allotment of fouls and was flung out of the game. His total points for the night added up to nine. That was the business for DePaul. With no Mikan to harass Kurland, the Aggies breezed to a 52-44 win—despite the fact that Kurland pumped in only 14 points himself.

The big winners were the promoters. Some 18,148 persons packed into the fastness of old Madison Square Garden. Among them was Michael Strauss Jacobs, the booking agent for fist fights. He was there to learn what mysterious magnet could draw that many taxpayers through rain and cold to watch college kids struggle over roundball. After the game, Jacobs stood leaning against the left shoulder of Ned Irish, the booking agent for basketball, who stood leaning against the wall as the horde filed out.

"Gad!" Mr. Jacobs was asked. "Can it be that you, too, have gone for this fad?"

Mr. Jacobs shook his head. He was not a basketball fan. No, he just loved to stand in the Garden and gaze upon a full house. To him, packed seats were more beautiful than a sunset or a fight manager made speechless by quinsy.

Both Mikan and Kurland were only mediocre on this night, but no matter. Mr. Jacobs confessed he hadn't seen their equal since the days when the most beautiful woman in the world was Peaches Browning.

Rupp, Cousy, and Ol' Bones
(1946-1948)

World War II was over. With the government paying their way on the G. I. Bill—tuition, books, and $65 a month—thousands of veterans marched back to school. The season of 1945-1946 promised to offer some of the best basketball in college history. The players were bigger, older, more mature, battle-wise. Forget the Knute Rockne fight talk routine. They were more sophisticated now.

Bob Kurland and George Mikan still reigned supreme.

For the second season in a row, Oklahoma A. & M. won the NCAA championship. As a matter of fact, the 1946 Aggies, 31-2, were the first to win *two* titles, consecutively or otherwise. Kurland piled up a record season high of 643 points, including 58 against St. Louis in the final home game of his collegiate career.

On the way to the national title that season, the Aggies had to beat Baylor, California, and North Carolina. Oklahoma barely got past the Tar Heels in the NCAA final. The score was 43-40 and Ben Carnevale, Carolina's coach, had to be thinking what the final score might have been had his star, colorful Bones McKinney, not fouled out of the game with 14 minutes yet to play.

At 6'6", Bones McKinney was so thin people were tempted to call him Slats. He looked as though he had never eaten a square meal in his life. He grew up in Durham, North Carolina, where he starred on a high school team that won 69 straight games. Originally, he enrolled at North Carolina State in 1940 on a basketball scholarship, before joining the army. After the

Coach Henry Iba congratulated his star center, 7-foot All-American Bob Kurland, after Oklahoma A&M won its second consecutive NCAA championship in 1946.

79

George Kaftan (12) and his Holy Cross teammates made history in 1947 as they became first New England team to capture the NCAA title.

war he transferred to North Carolina because he liked Coach Carnevale.

With his long, sad face, his funny construction and skinny nickname, Bones grew into a legend. He talked to himself as he legged it up and down the floor, gravely thanked the referee every time a foul was called on him, and intricately checked the scorer's table whenever he made a basket to be sure he got the credit.

McKinney went on to star in the pro leagues, he was an ordained Baptist minister, and head coach at Wake Forest. Once, as his team got set for the initial center jump, he turned to the crowd and said, "Pray ball."

For the first time since Dr. James Naismith outlined his game, a team from his part of the country (Massachusetts) won the NCAA championship. The 1947 honor went to Holy Cross, a school so poor it had no gymnasium of its own and had to play all its games on the road. Despite the handicap, the Crusaders, led by All-America George Kaftan, won 27 of 30 games, including the last 23 in a row and a 58-47 victory over Oklahoma in the NCAA finale. Kaftan was named MVP for his 18 points and unremitting play on the backboards. Center Gerry Tucker starred for the Sooners with 22 points.

While names like Kaftan, O'Connell, and Oftring dominated the Holy Cross boxscore in the title game, one substitute, a freshman, went practically unnoticed. He scored only two free throws. His name? Bob Cousy.

By now, college basketball coaches had gained the reputation as probably the sports world's worst "bleeders." People saw them as men who suffered pangs of anguish in every game. They made no attempt to keep their feelings to themselves. But a select few bled inwardly, often sitting with apparent calm until the tension became more than they could stand. Then they'd blow up.

The classic prototype of the inwardly bleeding coach was Joe Lapchick, whose St. John's Redmen, as usual, were one of the country's leading independents in 1946-47, and whose Harry Boykoff scored 54 points in a game against St. Francis that season. Joe took every defeat as a personal affront. He lost 15 pounds a season. When a campaign was over, he looked like a candidate for the graveyard, a 6' 5" toothpick of a man with new wrinkles on his face, new sadness in his eyes. During the season, he died a little each game, he'd get so worked up.

"You die because you have so little control over what happens," he said at the time. "This

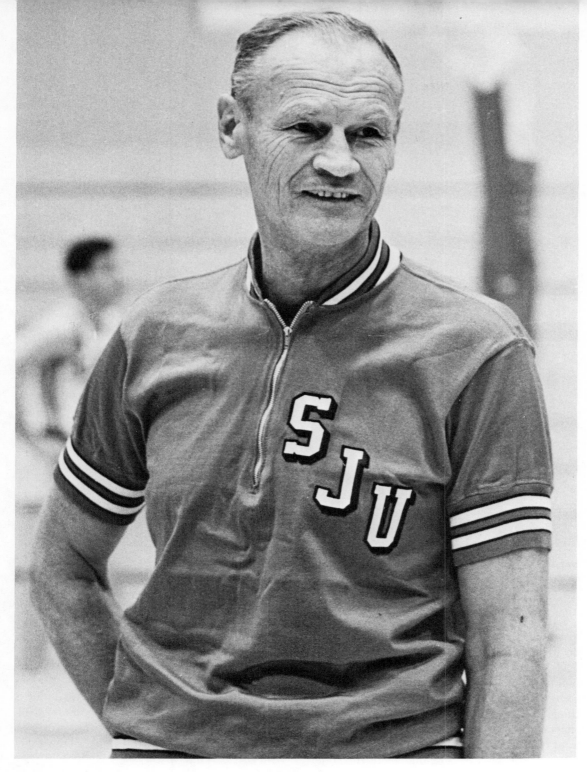

Joe Lapchick

is a humiliating business. There are no geniuses in coaching. The players make the coach. The coach who thinks his coaching is more important than his talent is an idiot. I know a young man who suddenly grew old trying to coach college basketball and who sat very quietly over breakfast one morning clenching his fists and saying softly: 'It's inhuman. I can bust my ass day and night. I can destroy my family life. I can get sick—and I did. And in the end, it all—and I mean it all—doesn't have a damned thing to do with how I've done my job. What it has to do with is whether some 19-year-old kid can make one lousy foul shot.' "

Led by charging, leaping All-American Ralph Beard (12), "Wah Wah" Jones (27) and Alex Groza (15), Kentucky smashed Illinois, 85-71, here on the way to winning its second NCAA crown in succession in 1949.

Later, years afterward, when Joe Lapchick reached the mandatory retirement age of 65 at St. John's, he said something which the genuine deep thinkers ought to mull over in their minds. It was over for him, he said, he was never going to coach again. "But I'll tell you something," Lapchick confided. "If I had the chance, there's only one route I'd like to go. I'd want to try it at a school where basketball is just a part of the total picture and where you could teach. I mean, where you could *really* teach. Who teaches today? Today it's a rat race. Today it's just one big recruiting contest. It proves nothing about either the coach or the kids. But if you went out and talked to the people who are really dedicated to the idea that a coach is a teacher, there's not one of them who wouldn't like to change the whole stupid system."

Now began the championship era of Adolph

Rupp. Four NCAA titles in the next 11 seasons. As a former pupil of Phog Allen at Kansas, The Baron of Lexington was an alert and eager student of the game, always exploring, always inventing. He was tireless and dedicated. He was the supreme drillmaster, a stickler for infinite detail, highly organized. Perhaps more than anything else, he was consistent. His won-loss record proved that. He won more games than any other coach in history.

In the decade after World War II, no college teams compared with the Wildcats. During 1945-1954, no one produced so many championship teams, All-Americans, or won so many games as the outspoken Rupp. In 1947-48, Kentucky's three-pronged attack of Alex Groza, Ralph Beard and "Wah Wah" Jones went 36-3, won the Southeastern Conference title for the fifth time in a row, then climaxed the season with a 58-42 rout of Baylor in the NCAA finals.

The 6' 7" Groza, brother of the Cleveland Browns' star placekicker Lou, was named MVP in the NCAA tournament.

Meanwhile, "Easy Ed" Macauley led the St. Louis Billikens to the NIT championship with 24 points on the way to a 65-52 win over NYU and All-America Dolph Schayes. The Violets' loss snapped a 19-game winning streak.

With the return of Groza, Beard, and Jones, the 1948-1949 Kentucky Wildcats established 22 NCAA team and individual records as they rolled over Villanova, Illinois, and Oklahoma A. & M. on the way to the national championship for the second season in a row. The NCAA finals were played in Seattle: Kentucky 46, Oklahoma A&M, 36. Groza was again named the tournament's MVP.

The top-seeded teams in the NIT were Kentucky, St. Louis, Western Kentucky, and Utah. All lost in the opening round. It was that kind of season. The NIT winner was San Francisco. All-America and MVP Don Lofgran, Joe McNamee, and Rene Herrerias put it all together to beat Loyola, 48-47, in a championship contest that left everybody exhausted.

The individual scoring leaders for the season were Villanova's Paul Arizin, who smashed the NCAA single game record with 85 points; William and Mary's Chet Giermak set a season record with 740; and St. Louis' Easy Ed Macauley gave future shooters something to think about as he topped the nation with a 52.4 field goal percentage.

As a freshman, Bob Cousy didn't see a lot of action. He rode the bench quite a bit in his sophomore season, too. Those were big years for Holy Cross. The Crusaders won the NCAA crown in 1947, made a great run for it in 1948 while finishing third, and Cousy had yet to be turned loose. But then the usually conservative Coach Doggie Julian, realizing Bob's potential, wound him up and let him go. Practically overnight, Cousy was a sensation—a genuine star and crowd-pleaser. No longer did he hold back. No more did he play as if one arm was in a sling. Suddenly it was Cousy whose dazzling passes wowed the fans. Suddenly it was Cousy whose behind-the-back dribbling provoked the cheers. Now it was Cousy who was the big star. Now it was Cousy who made the big basketball promotions pay off as never before. And it was

Easy Ed Macauley paced St. Louis University to 1948 NIT title as he scored 24 points and outplayed NYU's great Dolph Schayes. The Billikens defeated the Violets in the championship, 65-52.

Cousy that the kids of the playgrounds tried to imitate.

When most players tried to explain Cousy's greatness, they talked about his spectacular techniques, his peripheral vision and phenomenal reflexes. Not Bill Russell. Cousy and Russell were not in college at the same time, but they were teammates on the Boston Celtics, where Russell's preoccupation with the intricacies of the game brought fresh insights not only of his own play but that of Cousy as well.

"You want to know why Cousy was the greatest?" Russell asked. "Two reasons. First was his *imagination*. No matter what the situation was, he'd think of something new to try. He'd try anything. And he'd make it work for the second reason. His *confidence*. He just knew it was going to work. Some sportswriters said it must have been tough to play with Cousy—he did all these wild things, surprised you, fooled you and all that jazz. I'll tell you—he was the easiest to play with. You know why? When he passed you the ball, there was always something you could do with it, that's why. Some guys, they passed you the ball and there was nothing you could do with it except pass it back or eat it if you were hungry. But when Cousy gave it to you, there was a reason."

Another Cousy believer was Bobby Wanzer of the old Rochester Royals. Bobby once described for me what it was like to try to cope with Cousy's court magic. This was at Cousy's peak:

"When God handed out the physical qualifications for a basketball player, Cousy was over-endowed," Wanzer said. "He made him 6′ 1″ tall with a skinny body, but stubby, powerful legs that can run all night. He gave him extra large, sensitive hands and a great touch. He gave him a poker face that never tips off his emotions. Concentration is 90 per cent of basketball defense, with 10 per cent ability, but against a guy like Cousy it helps to have a prayer. There are some nights when he just can't be stopped. No matter how closely you guard him, he's still going to get those weird shots from all angles. He'll take shots no other player will attempt. And make them. That's where the praying comes in. I've seen him driving for a shot and while in the air shift the ball from his right to his left hand behind his back and flip it back-handed over his left shoulder

and into the basket—all in the same fluid motion.

"I start off a game by playing him very tight and hope I can worry him. Then if he misses a few early in the game, he might press. Playing him tight has its dangers because he's quick enough to break around and leave you looking silly if you relax the slightest. But it's better than standing off and giving him elbow room because then you invite disaster.

"He's the finest dribbler in basketball. There are two things that make him tough. A lot of guys are fancy dribblers when they're standing still. Couz is always moving, and he dribbles as well with his left hand as with his right, maybe better. A playground director named Morty Akin in Queens pushed Bob, a natural right-hander, into using his left hand. When Bob was only 12, Akin made him dribble by the hour with his left. Bob didn't have full control, but he got so he could move the ball back and forth from one hand to the other without breaking the cadence of his dribble. He wasn't dribbling behind his back or setting up any trick stuff yet, but he was laying the groundwork for it.

"In guarding Cousy I watch his body across the hips. Forget about legs and hands. He'll sucker you with fakes. But he can't make a break in any direction before moving his hips. Keep the hands high in front of him. That's an elementary principle of defense, but especially so in Couz's case because he's got so many shots. His best is a one-hand push, and lately he's been developing a jump shot to offset the taller guys guarding him. Primarily he's a right-hand shot, but he'll kill you with a southpaw hook if you overplay him to the right. You have to watch for screens. Against Cousy I scramble to stay with him and try to switch men as little as possible. The split-second switch of guards is enough for him to shake loose for a shot.

"Contrary to popular belief, Cousy hasn't got great speed. That's why quick men like Slater Martin and Ralph Beard can give him occasional tough nights. When they make a mistake, they still have the speed to recover and catch up with him. I don't have that kind of swiftness. I just try to hang on like a leech. And, of course, I pray."

Meanwhile, the coaching career of a former Navy officer was taking shape. During the war he had helped to get pilots in shape for combat

No. 14, Bob Cousy, ripped through NBA competition much the way he dominated college opponents at Holy Cross. Bill Russell called Cousy "the greatest."

flying. When he got out in 1946 there was no house to move into. He had been unable to keep the payments up and lost it. He immediately went back to South Bend Central in Indiana, where he had been coaching before the war, but some of his friends were not so fairly treated and he became disenchanted with the school system. When a job at Indiana State Teachers College in Terre Haute opened, he took it, bringing along a load of former Central High players just getting out of the service themselves. With 14 freshmen and one sophomore that first year, Indiana State had an 18-7 record. The same cast improved that to 29-7 the next year.

As long as he had taken the reluctant step from high school to college coaching, the former Navy officer figured he might as well go to a major university; both Minnesota and UCLA were after him. Minnesota offered more money, but the Gopher officials were delayed somewhere by a snowstorm on the day of decision and did not call when they said they would. The former Navy officer accepted the UCLA job and an hour later Minnesota got him on the phone—too late.

Which was how the Bruins came to get John Wooden as their head basketball coach.

The year 1949 introduced a new rule to college basketball. Now a coach could talk to his team during a timeout without penalty. Adolph Rupp obviously knew what to say to his Wildcats. The result was another NCAA championship for Kentucky. The only other major college to win two national basketball titles in a row was Oklahoma A. & M.

On their way to back-to-back championships,

the Wildcats smashed 22 NCAA team and individual records, and raced through 13 Southeastern Conference games without a loss. Then they rolled over Villanova, Illinois, and Oklahoma A. & M. to win the NCAA championship. Groza was high scorer of the tournament with a record three-game total of 82 points, and was named Most Valuable Player for the second straight year.

The *Associated Press* really started something in 1949. That was the season it started rating the teams in a national poll. Kentucky, 36-2, finished No. 1 in that first poll, and it has been a dogfight ever since.

MATURITY: THE FIFTIES

CCNY—Double Champs,
Then Chumps: 1950

The John Wooden system was based on upsetting the tempo and style of opponents. He did it by running, running and running some more. He mixed that up by hawking, by grabbing, by slapping and by hand-waving defense. His teams doted on harassing the man with the ball.

When he first arrived on the Coast, he told a UCLA banquet: "The fast break is my system and we'll win 50% of our games by outrunning the other team in the last five minutes."

It was no exaggeration. Most West Coast collegians played slowly and deliberately and several times against league opponents the Bruins actually had *five-on-zero* fast breaks.

Foes hated to play in the old UCLA gymnasium, a small place that steamed when packed with people, and was known, not without reason, as the B. O. Barn. Wooden insisted that if he was turning up the heat, as some coaches claimed, he was doing more damage to his running clubs. "I want a better place to play," he said, "but it doesn't displease me that the other teams dread to come in here."

Despite numerous division, league, and NCAA championships of later years, UCLA really was not a national power during Wooden's first 13 years there.

The season of 1949-1950 was dominated by City College of New York—the first team ever to win both the NCAA and NIT championships in the same year. More important, however, was the subsequent revelation that CCNY was among the teams involved in a shocking point-rigging scandal. Coached by Nat

Holman, one of the most respected names in basketball, CCNY opened a 17-5 season with only one veteran, 6' 4" Irwin Dambrot. They were not ranked among the AP's Top Ten, the All-America selectors ignored them. Then came tournament time. The Beavers upset Bradley, 69-61, to win the NIT, and then Bradley again, 71-68, to claim the NCAA championship. Leading scorer Ed Warner was named the NIT's Most Valuable Player, while Dambrot won the NCAA's version of the award.

Holman did a masterful job of coaching. He played five different men—Dambrot, Ed Roman, Ed Warner, Al Roth, and Norm Mager—at center, while Floyd Layne, one of the tallest on the squad, could move to corner or backcourt. In the NIT quarterfinals they faced the defending NCAA champions, Kentucky, 25-4 during the season. The Wildcats were smarting over an NCAA snub, their district's invitation going to North Carolina State. Coach-of-the-Year Rupp was fuming and intended to take his anger out on NIT opponents. He was proud of his team, which included 7' center Bill Spivey, 6' 6" forwards Shelby Linville and Jim Line, 5' 10" guard Bobby Watson, and 6' 2" Dale Barnstable. Kentucky was heavily favored. Final score: CCNY 89, Kentucky 50. It was Rupp's worst defeat. After the game, Rupp said, "City College will win it all." They did.

Details of college basketball's first big scandal still had not reached full flower when the 1950-

CCNY's 1950 NIT and NCAA tournament double champions. First row, bottom left: Mike Wittlin, Ed Roman, Joe Galiber, Coach Nat Holman, Irwin Dambrot, Norman Mager, and Seymour Levey. Second row, left: Floyd Layne, Arnold Smith, Ed Warner, Al Roth, Herb Cohen. Third row, left: Ronald Nadell, Arthur Glass, LeRoy Watkins, Ed Chenetz, Larry Meyer. Fourth row, left: Mgr. Al Ragusa, Asst. Coach Bobby Sand.

1951 season began. For the third time in four years, Kentucky again made a successful run for the roses. However, the Wildcats were fortunate to go all the way, since one of their two losses of the season was in the title game of the Southeastern Conference tournament against Vanderbilt, 61-57. But in a rule change that season, the NCAA berth went to the team with the best regular-season record and not the conference tournament champion, as in the past.

The NCAA members seemed to be ganging up on Kentucky. Now there were 16 teams in the tournament. But the expansion made little difference to the Wildcats. Like prairie fire, they swept through Louisville, 79-68, St. John's, 59-43, and Illinois, 76-74, to win the Eastern Regionals. That brought them into the NCAA finals at Minneapolis, where they blasted Kansas State, 68-58. Much of the credit went to MVP Bill Spivey, who scored 22 points, Frank Ramsey, and sophomore Cliff Hagan.

Individually, Duke's Dick Groat and Tem-

ple's Bill Mlkvy hogged the scoring limelight during the season. Groat totaled a record high of 831 points, while Mlkvy's 29.2 points a game established an all-time record in that department.

Groat was Duke's All-American Boy in both basketball and baseball. Writing for the NEA Syndicate at the time, I pointed out: "The Blue Devils think so highly of Dick Groat that they have published a brochure devoted entirely to his athletic career. Did you know that no less than 13 major league baseball scouts are dogging his heels? It's a new experience writing about a double All-America. Those who have followed his progress speak with such moving eloquence about Richard The Great that you wonder why he didn't play football, too. Certainly an athlete with his speed and natural ability would have made a fine ball carrier. 'Dick no doubt would have been a splendid football player,' admitted one Duke official, 'but we have decided to de-emphasize him by

The sparks behind CCNY's unprecedented double, left: Ed Roman, Coach Nat Holman, and Ed Warner.

Rated one of the top college playmakers in 1950, Bill Sharman went from Southern Cal to NBA stardom with Boston Celtics.

In 1951, Kentucky won its third NCAA championship in four seasons, as the national tournament expanded to 16 teams. One of the stars was sophomore sensation Cliff Hagan, shown here (6) scoring against St. John's on way to 59-43 win in Eastern Regionals.

limiting him to two sports.' Few players have commanded so much respect and attention as Groat. Other basketball stars pay him the unconscious tribute of halting whatever they are doing to study his movements. Hank Luisetti was the last to get that kind of adulation.

"Incredible as it may seem, they tell you that Groat is even a better baseball prospect. He led Duke to the Southern Conference title batting .386, and was virtually flawless at shortstop going to his right or left. Before he ever went to Duke, Groat's ballplaying was a legend around Swissvale High School in Pennsylvania and it became a standard of comparison. Dick does not talk much about baseball. 'But he had offers from 13 big league teams last Summer,' said Bill Strickland, Duke's assistant sports publicity director. 'One club offered him a contract and told him he could play shortstop the next day if he'd sign.' "

Now the basketball scandal of 1951 . . .
CCNY had just beaten Temple for an impor-

Dick Groat was a standout at both basketball and baseball.

tant victory and was traveling back to New York by train from Philadelphia. Spirits were high. Hadn't they played an almost perfect game? There was talk of winning another NCAA championship. "Allagaroo!" cried one of the cheerleaders with the team. Coach Nat Holman picks up the story:

"The kids were all in great spirits, having a good time celebrating their big win over Temple," Nat said. "They had played a whale of a game. As we neared New Brunswick (N.J.) a gentleman approached me, apologized and said, 'Nat, I have some bad news for you. I've got

orders to pick up some of your boys. But I don't want to make a scene.' He was from the office of the District Attorney of New York. I took my players aside one at a time and told them I wanted to speak to them when we got to Pennsylvania Station. When we arrived I told them individually, 'When they speak to you, tell them the truth. If your conscience is clear, you have nothing to fear.' "

The investigation was on. A heartbroken Clair Bee, coach of LIU, tried to pinpoint the reasons behind the scandal.

He said, "The players must have said to themselves, 'I'm bringing in all these fans and playing my heart out for them. Clair Bee is getting all the credit and Ned Irish and the college are getting all the gravy. Where do I come in?' The point system enabled fixers to approach players with propositions that seemed to take the curse off dishonesty. 'What's the difference, kid, if you win by eight points instead of 10?' they said. 'You're not letting down the school or the team. We're not asking you to lose the game. Just ease up a little. Everybody's making a good thing out of basketball. Don't be a sucker. There's $1,000 in it for you.' Boys who fell for that spiel were tragically wrong on two counts. There is no degree of honesty, of course. Shaving points was just as much a criminal offense, morally and legally, as throwing games. That, too, came inevitably when fixers forced players to go all the way by threatening them with exposure."

Judge Saul B. Streit, renowned for his austerity, presided at the players' trial. He had still stronger evidence to expose at the hearings. Two CCNY players, for example, were given athletic scholarships through forged entrance papers. City College officials later admitted that four other players had gotten in school the same way.

"Two players were in college and remaining eligible with IQs in the 80s," Judge Streit revealed. "One of the players, a so-called senior, was taking a class load consisting of nothing more than public speaking, oil painting, rhythm and dance, and a music seminar."

Basketball in a Fix: 1951

Dumb Dan Morgan, the last of the old-time prizefight managers, was a victim of The Disease. That is, he was a big bettor. He once estimated to me that he lost over a million dollars betting on sports. He bet on anything that turned up, if he could get anybody to bet on the other side. And if he couldn't, he'd change sides. Any way that suited the other guy suited him fine; any way just so he got a bet down. He was always ready and laying for a chance. There was nothing that Dan would not offer to place a wager on—and take any side you please. If there was a horse race, you would find him flush, or you would find him busted at the end of it. If there was a dog fight, he'd bet on it. If there was a cat fight, he'd bet on it. If there was a chicken fight, he'd bet on it. It never made any difference to him. He would bet on anything. I remember the time Hot Horse Andy's wife was sick, down with the gout, and it seemed for a while as if she wasn't going to get well, but one day Hot Horse Andy came around and Dumb Dan asked him how the missus was and Hot Horse Andy said she was much better; coming on so fast, as a matter of fact, that with the Lord's blessing she would pull through yet. "Well," Dumb Dan told him, "I'll give ya three-to-one she don't make it."

The first hint that college basketball was in trouble came to me while Dumb Dan and I sat at a table in one of those good steak houses not far from the old Madison Square Garden. It was one of those places where the glasses were thick and felt good in your hand and there was good lighting because the ice cubes in a drink on the rocks always gleamed when you raised the glass. With us was Dumb Dan's bookie, who reached into the inside pocket of his jacket and pulled out a packet of money which was held together by rubber bands at each end.

"New bills," he said. "My customers will feel great getting these."

The packet contained at least $15,000.

"What did they beat you on?" he was asked.

"Basketball," he said. "Ain't that something? I wish you could tell me what the hell I'm doing taking bets on basketball. But here I am. Those kids must be doing something. I don't know what the hell it is. But I figure something must be up."

"I always said," Dumb Dan said, "don't bet on anything that ain't got four legs." Morgan's specialty was horse flesh. "Listen," Dumb Dan continued, "I once had this bookie who used to tell what it was like to play basketball for this college team in New York. He didn't know anything. The day he got out of college he started to be an action guy. But when he was in school he didn't know anything—naive as hell. One night they played a game in the Garden and afterward the team was invited to a party at this club uptown. So they all went up. And they had a great time. Drinks, a big meal, plenty of dollies all around. The kids loved it. All for free, too. After that, my friend spent a lot of time there. Finally, after a long time, it dawns on him that the owners of the joint were betting on basketball and they were nailing his teammates and paying them to blow games."

"When was that?"

"He played for his school in the Garden in the year 1934, which is when I first heard of games being dumped. There were no point spreads in those days, either. If you took a contract it meant you went out and blew the game. The kids went all the way."

That was the first time I ever heard of college basketball games being fixed. And it took an old horse player to point out the facts of life to me: dishonesty in college sports is an old story.

A few weeks later, after a big upset, bookmakers all over let out a scream. The morning after the game, a guy called long distance from Minneapolis, saying, "I got murdered on that game. All the money came out of Philadelphia. You ought to investigate and write a story about it."

So they were betting big on college basketball, and there was lots of talk around town, and it all added up to only one thing—the collegians had to be heading for a mess. In wandering around to put the facts together you wound up listening to tales of unbelievable recruiting practices; of heavy betting going on all over; of the referee doing business in the Midwest; of some players receiving as much of $4,450 apiece for bagging games at Madison Square Garden during the season. Dishonesty in college basketball had become very widespread.

When the scandal finally broke, in February of 1951, it struck in many places, like a soap opera, and involved at least six colleges, four of them in New York City, and 33 players.

Twenty-one of the players pleaded guilty to "dumping"; 10 others, beyond the jurisdiction of New York District Attorney Frank Hogan, admitted their guilt. Some players and bribers were sentenced to prison, and the careers of several prominent coaches were ruined. This whole sordid affair killed big-time college basketball in New York for many years.

"Underlying the scandal," Hogan said in a formal report, "was the blatant commercialism which had permeated college basketball. What once had been a minor sport had been hippodromed into a big business."

Ned Irish, the chief hippodromer, refused to accept any responsibility, though the presence of gamblers at Garden games was as obvious in those days as major league baseball scouts are at an NCAA tournament. In 1944, I recall writing: "College basketball at the Garden has become big business, and college authorities and the big businessmen who are out to protect their own interests are busy these days laying plans to prevent big city gamblers from upsetting the

applecart. Last year, teams from all over the country played before crowds which averaged in the neighborhood of 16,000 a game. Now, fans are beginning to wonder what impact this sudden boom in basketball will have on the players. Not so very long ago Coach Phog Allen of the University of Kansas told a *Time* magazine reporter that big time basketball is becoming a 'dirty' business. Predicting an imminent 'scandal that will stink to high heaven,' he declared: 'Vadal Peterson, coach of the Utah team that won the NCAA title, knocked down a gambler who came to his room in the spring asking how much it would cost to have Utah lose to Dartmouth in the 1944 NCAA final. Professional gamblers already have caused two players to throw basketball games.' When Ned Irish heard the charge, he retorted, 'If Allen has any proof of dishonesty in basketball games at the Garden, he'd better come through with it.' Phog promptly telegraphed him the name of one player who had already admitted 'selling out' and had been expelled from college for the act. Soon after, Irish announced that in the future he will have 36 uniformed policemen, and almost as many plain-clothesmen and private detectives on duty with direct orders to stop all known gamblers from entering the Garden."

Despite the beefed up patrols, any sophisticated fan was still able to spot gamblers at a Garden college basketball game. It was business as usual. Some of the metropolitan reporters grew suspicious. It just didn't make sense. There, for example, was NYU leading Rochester by 15 points with only seven seconds of play remaining and 16,000 fans were on their feet excited as hell because a Rochester player had just been awarded two foul shots. He made the first one, missed the second, and the game ended with NYU ahead by 14 points, a seemingly comfortable margin. Yet the fans were limp over the "exciting" finish.

It just didn't make sense.

Oh, but it did. It not only made sense, but made dollars, thousands. The explanation was simple. Under the relatively new system of betting that had gripped basketball, NYU's 14-point victory actually had become a tight photo finish to those betting on the final score—which seemed just about everybody. The Violets had entered the game 13-15 favorites. That is to say, the bettor who took NYU had to win by more than 15 points in order to cash his bet. Rochester supporters, on the other hand, could afford to have their team lose, if the margin of defeat was kept under 13 points.

New York University's 14-point victory was what was known in the trade as a "middle finish," meaning that all those suckers who risked money on the outcome lost. So how come everybody lost and nobody won? Well, somebody *did* win. The bookie. The shrewd fellow with whom all bets were placed. He was the fellow who happily took 15 points from NYU bettors, who were forced to fork over their dough because their team won by only 14, and laid 13 points to Rochester backers, who also lost because their team was drubbed by 14.

In betting circles that 13-15 points quotation is known as a market or spread. It is the bookie's working margin, the edge that provides him with a profit percentage that ranges from 2½ per cent to 15 per cent, depending on the sport.

In the mid-1940s, the teams which produced the greatest gambling action in college basketball were the Big Ten, the Ivy League and those that competed in Madison Square Garden.

The prominence of the Garden in the basketball betting scene was causing grave concern in various collegiate circles. There was considerable popular credence being given to the suspicion that gamblers had already reached players in order to get them to put a game in "the middle."

"Oh, pooh-pooh," grunted one coach, "logic dictates that it is practically impossible for any player or group of players on one team to control the final score."

But he was wrong. Consider the facts: In 1945, reports of a fixed game between Brooklyn College and Akron forced authorities to cancel the contest. Later, five Brooklyn players admitted taking bribes to dump the game. A year later, a number of college stars playing in the Borscht Belt, a summer league, were caught dumping games and were fired. In 1949, a George Washington University athlete reported a bribe attempt.

The next time a report of a bribe popped up in the news was when Manhattan College star Junius Kellogg went to the Bronx District At-

torney. He was clean, but two of his teammates had accepted bribes. In came Frank Hogan, the Manhattan D.A., to take over the investigation. Before he was finished he had dug up more than 100 suspicious games dating back four seasons. The mess involved some 33 players from seven schools—CCNY, LIU, Manhattan, NYU, Kentucky, Bradley, and Toledo—who had conspired to fix scores of contests in more than 20 cities in 17 states.

The shocks rocked the country.

"If a man has any decent instincts at all," wrote Red Smith in the *New York Herald Tribune*, "He's got to feel regret—not sympathy, but a sort of pain, over the crooked basketball players who are going to jail. He's got to feel bad because they are young guys whose lives are ruined. But he's got to applaud the decision of Judge Saul S. Streit to put the crooks in a cage.

"There must be some deterrent to the spread of dishonesty in sports. Chances are it never occurred to the fakers that they could be put in jail for throwing in with sure-thing punks and dumping games for pay. Even the most stupid ones, who were dragged into college by the heels when they should have been working as longshoremen or grease monkeys, must have known that if the word ever got out, they would be put away as crumbs by the undergraduates and the neighbors and all decent associates.

"Yet it is unlikely they realized they could be caught and tossed into the pokey. It is time that realization was brought home to everybody. There has been far too much breast-beating about unfortunate, immature lads who were led astray by hoodlums. Everybody has been too ready to forget that the most doltish of students in ballroom dancing and finger-painting knew enough to count the money at payoff time. It is high time for the courts to teach what the colleges have neglected—that when you get caught stealing, there's a penalty for it. Maybe if that knowledge got around, it would make easy money look a little harder in young eyes."

Smith felt that the most shocking feature of the whole sordid scandal was the attitude expressed by mature men entrusted with the guidance of the athletes.

"It isn't any of the judge's business in the first place," said Matty Bell, athletic director of Southern Methodist, about Judge Streit's comments on recruiting and subsidization in the Southwest.

"The public doesn't understand," said Clair Bee, "that the players were not throwing games. They were throwing *points*. They were not selling out to the extent that the public believed, and somehow the players did not feel that what they did was wrong."

Admittedly, Red Smith said, the public's understanding of many aspects of the scandal was faulty. "Yet," he added, "one can't help believing it surpasses the understanding of some men who are supposed to set an example for boys."

Kentucky and CCNY were primary targets of the investigation. The probe revealed that the whole 1950 Cinderella team of City College was involved. Coach Nat Holman, once the brain and nerve center of the fabulous Original Celtics, for more than 30 years oracle of the sport he loved, recognized throughout the country as "Mr. Basketball," was heartbroken. He couldn't believe the evidence against his players; many skeptics couldn't believe he hadn't known. And he went on wondering why he hadn't known.

Only a week before, Holman had proudly accepted *Sport Magazine*'s Man-of-the-Year award for piloting underdog CCNY to an unprecedented sweep in the 1950 intercollegiate championships—the first team in history to win both the National Invitation Tournament and the NCAA title in the same year.

By January, ugly rumors about "shaving points"—keeping the point difference between winners and losers within a certain limit but not necessarily "throwing" the game—were approaching a climax. In defense of his sophomore-studded squad, Holman bristled, "I'll stake my reputation on the integrity of my boys."

Then the roof caved in. Three CCNY players were among the first to be accused by DA Hogan as "fixers," followed by four more teammates. Holman, who had always tried to teach decency, honesty and devotion to duty along with basketball, never completely recovered from the shock. He retired under pressure in 1954 and lived in relative obscurity thereafter.

Another coach who took the scandals so much to heart was LIU's Bee. The university had grown on its basketball reputation, and now, because of its involvement in the gambling mess, the sport was dropped for the next six years.

St. John's and Fordham were also under the metropolitan cloud of suspicion, but no hard evidence was brought against them by Frank Hogan. Meanwhile, Manhattan and NYU carried on with their basketball programs through the investigation.

While New York City teams suffered most of the early heat, down in the bluegrass country Adolph Rupp sounded the watchword of arrogant parochialism: "They couldn't touch our boys with a 10-foot pole." But when the smoke had cleared, the magnificent Kentucky team of the 1948 and 1949 championship years was shown to be the biggest offender. Some of the players, including two All-Americans, evidently had gone into business with the fixers soon after the 1948 Olympics. In retrospect, their superb 1949 record is all the more remarkable when you remember that the Wildcats won 32 of 34 games while controlling their point spreads and that their loss to Loyola in the National Invitational Tournament was a contest they fixed too well to win.

The investigation left the Kentucky basketball program in a shambles. Both the NCAA and the Southeastern Conference suspended the Wildcats for a year, and two players, by now all-stars in the NBA, were kicked out of pro basketball, causing the collapse of the franchise.

Bradley and Toledo? It was business as usual.

Later, some college coaches complained about the bad press that college sports received in 1951. They thought the newspapers played up scandals and ignored news that put athletics in a more favorable light. "The sporting press," one of them charged, "has let us down badly this year."

At least one successful basketball coach felt that the press had told it the way it really was. He was John "Honey" Russell, the Seton Hall University coach. Honey had put together some big clubs at Seton Hall and he had done it in the accepted manner. He had gone out and got the best ballplayers he could find. As one of the oldest names in sports—he came out of the gaslight years in professional basketball and was a lineman for the Chicago Bears before coming to the campus at South Orange, New Jersey—he was talking about coaching in colleges and he was making sense.

"The whole business is crazy," he said. "Scholarships, big national schedules, win the games or you lose a job—all of it is crazy. I feel very strong about that. If I had it all to do over again, I'd go some place where they didn't give scholarships and they played a simple schedule with schools right around the area. I'd go some place where all they wanted you to do was take a group of kids and teach them to play as well as possible and then if they lost or they won it wouldn't matter as long as they were getting something out of the sport.

"That's the only way they should have it. If it were up to me, I'd demolish the whole system of college athletics. And I'm a guy who has been around it all my life. I've had great college teams. I had one at Seton Hall with Bob Davies. You're not going to find any better than that. Then I had Bobby Wanzer and Frank Saul and Walter Dukes. So I'm not just some amateur making a speech. I've been through it. And I'm telling you, it isn't worth it.

"Thank the Lord that Seton Hall has decided to do something about it. The school is talking about pulling out of these big schedules and they're going to drop scholarships. But what makes me wonder is that nobody else is doing anything. I look around the whole country and it's the same. The recruiting is worse than ever. And they make up a schedule and all they do is try to make one long list of big games. Everything's got to be a big, tough game. Bring out the people, fill the joint. Plenty of noise and pressure. I haven't heard of one conference or one school outside of Seton Hall doing anything about what happened. They seem to think it's all going to blow over and things can go along the way they always did. Well, we know that won't happen. If they don't do something about it now, then they're going to have guys fixing games again in a couple of years. That's as sure as we're here. So why don't they do something about it?"

It was unfortunate that so many young men had to go to jail. It was even more unfortunate that when they went behind the wall they were not accompanied by their accomplices—the college presidents, the coaches, the registrars and the alumni. All compounded the felony.

"Regrettably," wrote Red Smith, "there is no law that can reach the educators who shut their eyes to everything except the financial ledgers of the athletic department, the authorities who enroll unqualified students with faked credentials, the professors who foul their academic nests by easing athletes through their courses, the diploma-mill operators who set up classes for cretins in Rope-Skipping IV and History of Tattooing VII, the alumni who insist on winning teams and back their demands with cash, the coaches who'd put a uniform on Lucky Luciano if he could work the pivot play. They're the bums who ought to go to jail with the fixers whom they encouraged. But they won't, and apparently they regret nothing except the fact that some crooks have been caught."

Several years after the basketball scandals I went into a pub in Brooklyn Heights and met an old geezer who had just returned from three years in prison, where the judge sent him for fixing college basketball games. He sat there with old clothes on and he was sick because he had a wife and three kids who had suffered terribly while he was in prison.

"I never want to hear about basketball again," he said.

"I don't blame you," a guy with him said.

"But somebody else will hear about it, don't worry," the guy said. "I got to wonder if they ever stopped doing business. I guess it will all come out again some day and some other poor bum will go to prison."

I saw him again late one night in 1960. St. John's had just played NYU in the Garden and it was, everybody wrote, the game that brought college basketball in New York back to what it was before the 1951 scandals broke.

"When do you think it will start?"

"Basketball?" he said. "I haven't even paid attention. But it'll start someday. Not yet, I guess. But someday."

Computerized Scoring: 1952-1954

It was a controversial osteopath, Dr. F. C. "Phog" Allen, who turned Kansas into a basketball power. In 39 seasons (1908-09 and 1920-56) he won 24 conference titles, two Helms Foundation national championships and the 1952 NCAA tournament. He was also founding president of the National Association of Basketball Coaches, the leader of the movement to make basketball an Olympic sport, and the second (770) winningest coach in college basketball history.

Each Fall, when a college abandoned its courses in blocking and tackling, it left a lot of athletes at loose ends. They had nothing to do except study, a most distasteful situation for young men with muscles.

Out in the Corn Belt, Dr. Phog Allen had come up with a solution in 1951-1952. He let some of the Kansas football players have a go at basketball. His protracted success as a coach at Kansas refuted the theory that blocking backs and defensive tackles didn't belong on a basketball court. The trend more recently had been to go along with the gangling tower of bones and ignore the larger tracts of meat. If you didn't answer to Bones or Slats or Stretch, forget it. But Coach Allen was old-fashioned. He liked lots of beef on his underlings.

While interviewing him that season, I reminded the good doctor that most basketball coaches frowned on using football players. "Kansas has done all right since I've been here—28 conference championships and a very good possibility we'll win the NCAA championship this season," he said. "Few, if any, of those titles were won without the help of at least one football player. What most people don't realize is that the two games are first cousins. Both are contact games. Any time you get two or more boys going in the same or opposite direction for a loose ball, you've got contact. Dribbling through a spread defense, for instance, is akin to a halfback running a broken field. There's an element of the forward pass in basketball passing. Football players are naturally tough and aggressive. They can stand shock without signs of distress. Nearly all of them have sturdy legs, and basketball is played as much with the legs as the arms. Football players aren't bothered by the pressure and banging of modern basketball. They thrive on contact. Many promising basketball players would be great if they didn't shy from body contact. Football players sometimes beat them out of varsity jobs by out-jarring them. A football player adds something extra to the basketball team—fire, hustle and aggressiveness. You're just handicapping yourself when you don't use them. You're subtracting something that you vitally need."

I pointed out to Dr. Allen that going from football right into basketball was a tight schedule. What about the academic life?

"Check and you'll discover that most athletes make their best grades in school when they're competing," he said. "They are sharp because of their competitive zeal. They budget their time better. They discipline themselves to do the job."

Kansas defeats St. John's, 80-63, to win the 1952 NCAA championship at Seattle on University of Washington court before a packed arena.

After finishing second to Indiana in 1940, Kansas went all the way to the NCAA title in 1952. Here are the Jayhawks who did it.

Mark Workman, 6' 9", carried West Virginia to the best regular-season record in 1951-52 Southern Conference race on way to All-America first team honors.

Dr. Allen made his point by winning the first NCAA championship in Kansas history. The Jayhawks outmuscled St. John's, 80-63, after the Redmen upset No. 1 Kentucky, 64-57, and No. 2 Illinois, 61-59, to earn a place in the finals. Ponderous 6' 9" Clyde Lovellette was Dr. Allen's chief weapon all season. His 33 points against St. John's won him the MVP award. Big Clyde ended his career with a national record of 1,888 points, smashing the old record of 1,886 set two days earlier by Dick Groat. Lovellette's 28.4-point-per-game average was another new record. Groat, with a 26-point average, led the nation in assists, while Louisiana State's Bob Pettit and Iowa's Chuck Darling both averaged 25.5 points.

Out in the Pacific Northwest, Johnny O'Brien became the first collegian to score more than 1,000 points (1,051) in one season, as Seattle University ran up a 29-8 record, including a sensational 84-81 win over the Harlem Globetrotters.

Freshman Tom Gola and Norm Grekin shared the MVP award as they led LaSalle to a 75-64 victory over Dayton to capture the NIT championship at Madison Square Garden.

For the third straight season, the AP and UPI All-America selections were the same: Chuck Darling, Iowa; Mark Workman, West Virginia; Clyde Lovellette, Kansas; Dick Groat, Duke; and Cliff Hagan, Kentucky.

After college, Lovellette turned down a $60,000 contract for three years from Milwaukee of the National Basketball Association for the security of Phillips Oil of Bartlesville, Oklahoma. Phillips, though prodded by an AAU investigating committee, refused to divulge the salary of the former Kansas center. Bob Hurt, a sports writer for a Topeka daily, who ghosted a national magazine article for Big Clyde explaining why he rejected the pros, admitted, "Lovelette knows no more about the oil business than I do."

A Minneapolis Laker official said, "Everybody knows Clyde is obligated to the Oilers because they paid his way through college, though it's one of those things you can't prove."

"Ridiculous," replied Bob Hurt. "Phillips worked too hard to get him."

Murray Olderman, who worked with me at NEA, flew from New York to Bartlesville to investigate the story. When he returned, he said, "While Lovelette was still in school at Kansas, a Phillips company plane carted Lovelette and his wife to and from their home in Terre Haute, Indiana, during vacations."

Winning was a great fetish with the Oilers. In the 16 years since they had sponsored a basketball team, they had won 709 games, lost only 84, including eight National AAU championships. A former rival AAU coach revealed: "It sells gas. Phillips men start practice in September, mixing work and play, and as the season progresses they gradually play all the time. No work until after the National AAU tournament in Denver. Their salaries continue and sometimes after the National bonuses are given if they win. Phillips tries to make everyone think they are pure but they aren't."

That was the story in 1953. It paid to be an amateur.

That old bugaboo, changing the rules, bobbed up again in 1952. No less an authority than Yale's Howard Hobson, formerly of Oregon and now chairman of the U.S. Olympic Basketball Committee, admitted to me that there was much room for rules improvement. To demonstrate, Yale and Springfield College experimented with what was advertised as "the basketball game of the future." The Elis won, 76-71, but the score was incidental. The game featured four rules changes which Hobson had been advocating since 1944:

The foul lane was widened from six to 12 feet.

Two free-throws were awarded for all defensive fouls.

It was compulsory that both free-throws be taken.

When a foul was committed by an offensive team, or when neither team had control of the ball, the offended team was awarded possession rather than a free-throw.

"In many ways, basketball is still in its infancy," Hobson said. "The game is still in the process of development and the rules have to change with it. The Yale-Springfield game reduced fouling more than 20 per cent. It was played in less time, the tempo was faster and more exciting. Widening the foul lane from six to 12 feet opened up the game and prevented wild scrambles under the basket. Yale, for example, had 21 drive-ins, Springfield 16. A defensive man thought twice before hacking an opponent to keep him from scoring. Our experimental game, however, is not conclusive evidence that my rule changes are the answer. Much is left to be done."

Springfield Coach John Bunn, who coached Hank Luisetti at Stanford and was past president of the National Association of Basketball Coaches, endorsed the Hobson Plan. "The advantages are far greater than any disadvantages," he said. It was encouraging to see someone trying to do something about giving the game back to the kids again.

Over the years, Hank Iba had become known as the foremost exponent of slow-motion basketball. So widespread was his reputation for deep-freeze tactics that even the Russians turned up using them in the 1952 Olympic Games in Helsinki.

But all that was changing. Basketball scores were rocketing upward. "The day is gone," Iba said, "when a team is likely to stop an opponent from averaging under 50 points a game." To support his case, he ran down a list of figures. In 1944, Oklahoma A. & M. held the opposition to 28.8 points a game. In 1952, the average rose to 45.4. And after the first 13 games of 1953, it was 50.8. Had the vaunted Aggies lost the touch? Or was it that the offense was catching up with the defense?

"It's a combination of the new rules and the emphasis on offense," Iba said. "Everyone has a stable of shooters today, kids who've been potting baskets since they were knee-high to a water bucket. It used to be that you had only one or two really good scorers on a team. Now everybody is a threat. You have to drop a net over all five men to stop them. Consequently, the scores grow larger. The defense just isn't what it used to be. Why, Navy's leading the nation with a phenomenal 92.3 points a game; they scored 126 points against Western Maryland. They're simply not teaching defense in high schools any more. The glamor hangs in scoring. So kids concentrate on shooting."

Ironically, Iba's 1952-1953 squad was the best

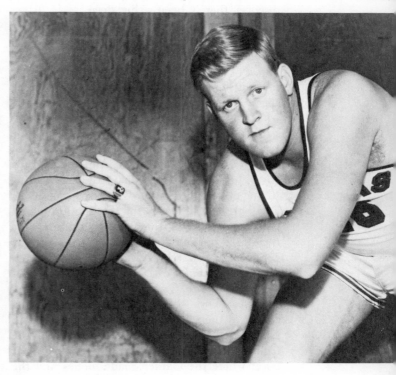

Clyde Lovellette, 6' 9", scored 33 points and won the MVP award at the 1952 NCAA tournament in Seattle.

bunch of shooters he had had in the 19 seasons he had been at Stillwater. They averaged 63.5 points a game. "On a good night," he said, "I believe my kids could match anybody in a game of run-and-shoot. But there's too much left to chance operating that way. Say your shots are missing. Then nothing can save you, except a tight defense. And, remember, the defense is much less likely to have a bad night than the offense."

As if the college booking agents didn't have enough problems, they were writhing on the horns of still another dilemma: an alarming slump in attendance. Less than 100 student tickets were sold at New York University for a game at Madison Square Garden. This, mind you, at a school with 56,000 enrollment. City College of New York, with a student body of 31,000, was averaging only 700 a game. Fordham, winner of 12 of its first 13 games in 1952-1953, was attracting only between 1,000 and 2,000 at home. "Folks just aren't coming out for basketball any more," said Fordham Graduate Manager Jack Coffey. "Check and you'll discover there's been a big decrease in attendance generally."

"What's the answer?" asked Jack Coffey, shaking his head sadly. "In a city of eight million, NYU, City College and Fordham aren't drawing flies. The rulesmakers haven't helped the situation any with their new shoot-till-you-win foul rule. Folks are tired of rat-race basketball. Yet Bevo Francis and his Rio Grande teammates drew 7,400 at the little town of Troy, Ohio, the other night. And the O'Brien twins, Johnny and Eddie, have the fans waiting in line every time Seattle University plays."

Whatever the reason for the diminishing interest in basketball, threatening to return it to the status of minor sport which it used to occupy, Ned Irish, who obviously was interested less in the morale of college students than of Madison Square Garden stockholders, warned the New York colleges either to get up the calibre of their teams or find some place else to play their games. In 10 doubleheaders of the regular 1952-1953 schedule six were below the point where the Garden made money and the colleges got a little take-home pay. "We need between 6,000 and 7,000 attendance for us to get off the hook and for the schools to get some money," Irish said.

The steadily declining post-scandal average dropped from 10,831 paid attendance in 1951-1952 to 7,947 in 1952-1953.

"College dates are there for next year if the colleges want them," Irish said. "But for how long they'll be there under the present conditions is another question. The directors expect me to do something without being told. If not they'll give me ideas."

Those who pointed an accusing finger at television were left with red faces when the case of Penn State was cited. The Nittany Lions' geographic isolation made them more or less immune from television and other metropolitan influences. But the gawkers refused to come out and gawk. Jim Coogan, the Penn State publicity man, confessed he couldn't figure it out. "It's downright unreal," he said. "Because we utilize a compulsory athletic fee to sustain a major sports program, for years we have barred the public on the grounds that the more than 10,000 students here should get first crack at the fewer than 6,000 seats. Last season it worked out well, averaging between 5,200 and 5,600. But this season, on a campus where neither television nor scandal is a factor, and where student leaders last fall violently protested setting aside 300 seats for the sports-starved faculty and public, only a handful are showing up."

When Syracuse traveled down to State College to play the Lions, only 3,279 rooters came out. Unbeaten Gettysburg, an extravagantly-touted bunch that season, attracted 2,612 when it came to town. "This," said Jim Coogan, "at a college where the students get in for nothing."

Never again, said Ron Bontemps, would he complain about basketball officiating in the United States. The lean, 176-pound former Beloit College star played in every game with the championship U.S. Olympic Games team at Helsinki in 1952.

"European officiating is the strangest I've ever encountered," he said. "I usually take the ball out of bounds and we were huddling on a time out. There wasn't any warning whistle when we decided to break up. I went to the sidelines, where an official was counting to five in Egyptian. Before I had a chance to take the ball, he said, 'Time's up,' and promptly threw it to the opposing team which was breaking for the basket. We couldn't complain. In Finland, a complaint got you a foul."

Bontemps said European-style basketball was wild and unpredictable. He said it was on a par with American high school basketball, although not even U.S. preps made so many cross-court passes. "Europeans waste so many opportunities to shoot," he said. "A player goes up to take a pot shot, but instead, at the height of his leap, passes off to a teammate who might be bottled up. I'd like to see Beloit College play the Russians, although they had fair height. One stood 6′ 6″, another 6′ 5″. We beat the Russians by 11 points in the championship game, but that isn't any conclusive evidence of the difference between the two teams. Olympic officiating doesn't permit aggressive defense. When the Reds chose to freeze the ball, we couldn't go after it. It meant a foul, and four

Olympic fouls and you're out. Europeans use a soft soccer ball that doesn't bounce well. They like to bank 'em off the backboard. I thought they'd crack the glass the way they banked shots, but the ball just plopped through like wet clay. Free throws were accomplished by just throwing the ball against the backboard as hard as possible. The playing surface of one court was so dirty that our hands were black before the game was finished. The balls wouldn't bounce true. Some of them were actually lopsided."

So went Olympic basketball in 1952.

At the outset, Indiana's 1952-1953 Hoosiers couldn't get unlimbered. Playing with all the agility of one who had just been disinterred, they lost two of their first three games. Then came the metamorphosis. They started playing

In 1953, Indiana won its second NCAA championship in 13 seasons with a heart-stopping 69-68 victory over Kansas. First row, left: Bob Leonard, Charley Kraak, Don Schlundt, Dick Farley, Burke Scott. Second row, left: Mgr. Ron Fifer, Dick White, Jim DeaKyne, Coach Branch McCracken, Paul Poff, Phil Byers, Asst. Coach Ernie Andres. Back row, left: Ron Taylor, Jim Schooley, Goethe Chambers, Jack Wright.

During the years 1952-1955, the big gun for Indiana was 6'10" All-American Don Schlundt, hooking in a basket here against Minnesota. Schlundt broke the Hoosiers' all-time career scoring record with 2,192 points.

as if all they read were Horatio Alger books. Through a home-and-home conference schedule of 18 games—the longest Big Ten season in history—they never lost again. The Hoosiers, putting it all together, attacked so fiercely that opponents thought they were playing the Russian army. They couldn't have won with machine guns.

The IU first five was composed of juniors Bob Leonard, Dick Farley and Charlie Kraak, and sophomores Don Schlundt and Burke Scott. "We were a young team that got progressively better as the year went on," Leonard said. "Coach Branch McCracken brought us up at the end of the season just right for the

NCAA tournament. He really wanted that NCAA championship. He always wanted to win, but the NCAA title was something special. He was a tremendous competitor. His street-fighter instinct wouldn't let him accept defeat. So he drove himself and he drove us. We were always in shape—and we had pride. Coach McCracken talked a lot about pride."

Indiana picked its way through an expanded 22-team NCAA field with all the skill of an acupuncturist. As the No. 1 team in the polls, the Hoosiers outscrambled DePaul, 82-80, in the semifinals of the Mideast Regional; and then devoured Notre Dame, 79-66, for the right to join Louisiana State, Kansas, and Wash-

In Indiana's first 25 games in NCAA tournament competition, the Hoosiers won 20. Here they defeat Louisiana State, 80-67, in 1953 semifinals at Kansas City. That's LSU All-American Bob Pettit up on the board.

Unanimous All-American, 6' 7" Bob Houbregs had the best hook shot in the history of basketball. He averaged 30 points per game in 1953 to lead the Washington Huskies to third-place finish in the NCAA tournament. He hits a 20-footer here in 74-62 victory over Santa Clara in Western Regional play-offs.

ington in the NCAA semifinals at Kansas City.

Out on the Coast, Washington had been touted all season as the greatest thing to happen to basketball there since cages around the courts were discontinued in 1929. The coach was Tippy Dye, who forsook Ohio State after winning the 1950 Big Ten title, and whose guesses and whose remedies had easily swept the Huskies past Seattle and Santa Clara in the Far West Regional.

UCLA's John Wooden was high on Washington's Bob Houbregs. He said the 6' 7" hotshot had a better hook shot than George Mikan.

"He hooks with either hand and pots 'em from all angles," Wooden said. "Against us, he dunked one in from about 20 feet away while standing near the baseline, back of the backboard plane."

Sports fame seldom outlasts the butterfly, but the legend of Bob Houbregs lives on. Recently, Marv Harshman talked about the former two-time Washington All-American. "There's one era of the game that reached its peak in the early 1950s and I don't know why it didn't continue," Harshman said. "It was epitomized by Houbregs, and I call it the Hook Shot Era. He was incredible. He could throw the running hook from the deep corner with amazing accuracy, better than 60 per cent. When he went into the pros he could still do it, but it wasn't a shot that the pros seemed to care for very much. All the same, I think Bob Houbregs was the greatest hook shooter in history. Coincidentally, that same season there was a little guy playing in the same city—at a little Catholic school, Seattle University—named Johnny O'Brien. He was also a fantastic hook shooter, maybe not so far out, but equally as deadly. He scored 43 points to lead the Chiefs to an 84-81 win over the Harlem Globetrotters. So there were two people—Houbregs and O'Brien—who literally captured the basketball world's imagination with their ability to execute and make this one shot."

The Huskies were imbued with the one-for-all and all-for-one spirit. This was evidenced by an incident that happened during a game against Northwestern earlier in the year. Houbregs and 6' 8" teammate Doug McClary leaped for a rebound, and while in flight batted the ball into the Washington basket. Houbregs was credited with the goal. Moments later, during a timeout, Houbregs sidled up to the referee. "Sir," he said, "it was McClary who tipped in the basket, not I. He should get the two points." The scorer reversed his decision.

When recruiting violations barred Kentucky from NCAA tournament competition, Louisiana State, led by sophomore Bob Pettit, won the Southeastern Conference championship, then trounced Lebanon Valley and Holy Cross for the East Regional title. Meanwhile, Kansas got into the Final Four by beating Oklahoma City and Oklahoma A.&M. in the Midwest Regional.

Seeing venerable Phog Allen among the final four reminded some reporters with long memories of the conversation he'd had with Dr. James Naismith, the founder of the game, back in 1908, when he decided to become a basketball coach. "But, Forrest," Dr. Naismith protested, "you can't coach the game of basketball. It's meant to be played, not coached."

Ignoring the advice, Phog Allen went on to disprove the dictum. In his first year on the bench he coached both Baker University and Kansas U., guiding the latter to a conference title. The next year, when Haskell Institute became the third team in his stable, Kansas again won a championship. But it wasn't until 1920 that Phog settled down in Lawrence for good and devoted his talents to making Kansas the spiritual headquarters of basketball.

The teaching technique of Phog Allen was as fierce and unconventional as the man himself. "You just do the playing," he told his boys. "I'll do the fighting and talking." In practice he lathered his players with phrases they heard in their sleep. "Guard as if your arms were cut off at the elbows . . . The knees are the only springs in the body—bend them! . . . Pass at angles, run in curves." When philosophizing on the game he used such terms as "pronation" and "supination" to describe hand and wrist action, and he liked to teach a "stratified transitional man-for-man defense with zone principles."

Allen's advice and opinions were trumpeted in the tones that brought him his nickname. During Phog's early coaching days at Kansas a student sportswriter heard him umpiring a baseball game and promptly dubbed him "Foghorn." Soon the label was bastardized to "Phog" by a reporter named Ward "Pinhead" Coble who decided he wanted "to doll it up."

Phog's record didn't need "dolling up." In 1953, he was the only college coach anywhere whose teams had won more than 700 games. This was the third time KU had reached the NCAA finals since the playoffs started in 1939.

It was not easy to find a satisfactory tribute for a man of Coach Allen's stature. But KU was prepared to try. A new 17,000-seat basketball gym was on the drawing board to be christened Allen Fieldhouse, defying a tradition that no KU building should be named for living men.

Louisiana State's All-American, Bob Petit.

It was a reasonable concession to a man whose athletes had already worn out two gymnasiums during his coaching career.

The saying around KU was that where Phog Allen was, controversy couldn't be far behind. So it had been in 1944 when Phog first warned that gamblers were toying with college basketball. "Allen's hogwash," was the retort of Nat Holman, whose CCNY players were caught deep in the mire of the subsequent scandal six years later. Press and rival coaches accused Allen of losing faith in basketball and American youth, but he stuck to his guns. He had the sad satisfaction of being proved correct.

In the semifinals, it was a case of Branch

Branch McCracken was not only a great college coach (451 wins, 277 losses, two NCAA championships, four Big Ten titles); as a player he made the college basketball Hall of Fame. During 1926-1930 at Indiana, he was the Hoosiers' high scorer for three seasons, was All-Conference for three years, Conference MVP in 1928, broke the Big Ten scoring record as a senior, and was unanimous All-American.

McCracken's Indiana Hoosiers doing just about whatever they wished against LSU. Despite the brilliant play of Bob Pettit, the Tigers were thoroughly confused by the IU defense and manpower and quickness. The final score was 80-67.

The second game stunned a lot of the handicappers. They had liked Washington. During the season the Huskies had paralyzed such powers as St. Louis, Ohio State, Northwestern, Minnesota, Utah, California, and UCLA, and they had looked good in the regionals. "Washington has everything, certainly the more gifted shooters," wrote one reporter. "The Huskies

will write finis to the Jayhawks' special dreams."

Those special dreams turned out to be a nightmare—for Washington. The same flaming emotion that had carried Kansas so stunningly to the semifinals completely buried the Huskies. The Pacific Coast champions must have thought they were under a *Kamikaze* attack. Kansas was like a bunch of piranhas. It wasn't so much a game as a presentation of the last rites: Kansas, 79-53.

Seething with revenge, Washington bounced back against LSU in the consolation game and shot the strings out of the net. Its second-half attack completely buried the Tigers, 88-69.

Indiana, anticipating its second NCAA title in 13 years, had a no-frills, no-nonsense approach to Phog Allen's Jayhawks in the championship game. To get that far, the team had consistently displayed one of the best-passing, quickest-thinking and smoothest-operating offenses in the U.S. of A. They did not disappoint their partisans. With 6' 3" Captain Bob Leonard and lanky pivotman Don Schlundt paving the way with instinct and intelligence, moving adroitly with or without the ball, following their shots and making important steals, the Hoosiers hung in there. The lead went back and forth. Finally, with 27 seconds to go and the score tied 68-68, Leonard was fouled. He made the free throw and that was how the game ended—69-68, Indiana.

After the game, Bob Leonard was asked how he felt.

"Great," he said. Did he want to elaborate? No, he said. There was nothing more to say. He had said it all.

Leaving the arena after the game, Branch McCracken plunged through a wall of Indiana rooters. A burst of shouting rose at the sight of him. "Hey, Branch!" "Hiya, Coach!" "Yay, Champ!"

An Indianapolis reporter listened and smiled appreciatively. "There's a sound," he said, "that will stay with him all his life."

Later, Al Lightner, who officiated the Indiana-Kansas game, told what it was like to referee a game for Coach McCracken.

"Away from the game, he was a pleasant, warm, game guy," Lightner said. "On the bench ... well—" Lightner grabbed his head in both hands, like a cantaloupe, and squeezed it. "Ohh," he said, "how that man could act. He'd jump, he'd stomp, he'd rage and rant when he didn't like your call. The technical foul was no stranger to him. Once, after hearing the play-by-play radio version of a game between Indiana and Ohio State, a local fan phoned McCracken the next day. He wanted to know why Indiana got pinned with a technical foul late in the game. McCracken explained to him that Indiana had too many men on the floor. Oh? And who was the sixth man? 'Me,' McCracken confessed.

"In the championship Kansas game, I nailed McCracken with two technical fouls for screaming at me. He went nuts and I blew the whistle. It could have cost him the NCAA title. Fortunately for him and his team, Kansas failed to cash in on either foul and Indiana won by one. The next morning, McCracken, who was quartered in the same hotel, bumped into me in the restaurant. 'Listen,' he said, 'I scalded you pretty good last night. Please excuse me. I'm only that way during games. I mean nothing personal. I hope you understand.' We shook hands and that was that. We went on to become pretty good friends—well, as good as a coach and an official can hope to be.

"What kind of coach was Branch Mc-Cracken? He was this kind of coach. He insisted that his players get their degrees. All he asked was that a boy have the proper mental attitude, do his best, and do what the coach told him. If he did, he could be sure he was going to get four years of college education, whether he helped the team or not. What kind of coach was Branch McCracken? When Indiana lost, he didn't check point totals, shooting figures, or the error columns. He looked at the personal fouls. If a player scored a lot but had no fouls, McCracken hit the roof. 'You're not doing your best!' he'd snap. An angry coach once accused McCracken of encouraging street-fighter tactics. McCracken denied any such thing, but said, 'But I don't discourage them, either.' What kind of coach was Branch McCracken? He attempted to legislate against basketball goons and got nowhere. So he went out and recruited them himself—and won with them. And he fought against the zone defense, but got nowhere. So he adopted the zone and won with that, too. What kind of coach was Branch Mc-Cracken? He was a *helluva* coach."

The leading scorer in the nation was Furman's Frank Selvy, who sizzled the baskets with a 29.5-point-per-game average. Johnny O'Brien

Furman's Frank Selvy smashed the major college single-game scoring record with a 100-point production against Newberry during 1953-54 season. On eight different occasions that year, he scored 50 or more points.

This foul by St. Joseph's Don Swanick set up the free-throw which enabled Seattle's Johnny O'Brien to break the national four-year scoring record of 2,599 points.

Seattle University's 5' 9" Johnny O'Brien became the first major college player to score more than 1,000 points in a season with this free-throw in 1952.

finished his career at Seattle with a 99-game total of 2,537 points on 838 field goals and 861 free throws—all NCAA records. Not bad for a kid from South Amboy, New Jersey, who stood only 5' 9" and got a basketball scholarship to Seattle University because its president, Father Lemieux, had been advised by mail that Johnny O was 6' 3".

Perhaps the best collegian in basketball was 6' 11" Walter Dukes, who led Seton Hall to a 58-46 win over St. John's to capture the NIT. As a newspaperman, I always wished he had gone to Duke. What fun the headline writers could have had with that one: *Duke's Dukes.*

Dukes was to Seton Hall of South Orange, New Jersey, what Clyde Lovellette was to Kansas. He was the biggest college name to appear at Madison Square Garden in 1953. Yet basketball was not first to him. He desired to be, of all things, a student first and a play and shotmaker after that.

I was covering college basketball around the Garden in those days and I asked Dukes, who came from Rochester, New York, what priority he gave the game. "It merely gives me an opportunity to get a college degree," he said. He was majoring in Economics, no cinch course. "I'm not interested in pro ball." He was much prouder of his B average than his scoring average, which was considerable. He said he aspired to be a lawyer, and was carrying courses that could be applied toward a law degree. "Taking time out to play college basketball is tough enough," he said. "Imagine the trouble I'd have traveling and playing four games a week as a pro. I don't believe I'd like to play basketball for a living, anyway. Just running up and down a hardwood floor throwing a ball through a hoop and not doing much else would dull my mind. I don't want to be a coach, either."

Center Dukes was bigger than George Mikan and far more mobile. He ran the 220 and 440 on the Seton Hall track team. He was a one-man gang. When a loose ball was being kicked around underneath the basket, he was a good choice to bend over, stick out his telephone-pole arms and wrap a hand around it. That didn't show in the score, but it killed the opponents.

Dukes was especially damaging on defense. One of his pet moves was to leap up when an opposing shooter began to wheel around for a pivot shot, slap the ball straight into the air, and then grab it and whip it downcourt.

He passed sharply, got the ball away quickly with the proper lead to it for the man heading for the basket. Coach Honey Russell said Dukes was the best he'd had around, and that included his tours with the professionals.

Wherever it is that old basketball coaches go when they die, Adolph Rupp wanted a reservation. This was in 1954, and there he sat, cursing his cruel fate. The year before, the NCAA had charged him with recruiting irregularities and barred Kentucky from Southeastern Conference competition. Then in 1953-1954, out of the doghouse once more, the Wildcats, 25-0, finished No. 1 in the AP poll but had no place to go when graduate stars Cliff Hagan, Frank Ramsey and Lou Tsiropoulos were declared ineligible for tournament competition.

"Well, James; well, Phog," Baron Rupp seemed to be saying to colleagues Naismith and Allen, "what new device must we overcome before they let us back in the NCAA championship competition?"

There were those who felt that the penalty imposed on Kentucky for recruiting violations was too harsh; that the infractions were based on unsupported allegations. Nonetheless, life went on and the Wildcats sat out the NCAA tournament for the second year in a row.

There was nothing compared to what Furman's Frank Selvy and Rio Grande's 6′ 9″ Bevo Francis did in 1954. Selvy, for example, scored 100 points in a game against Newberry, flaunted a season average of 41.7 points per game, hit 50 or more points in eight games, and finished with career record highs of 922 field goals, 2,538 points (1 more than Johnny O'Brien) and a 32.5 average a game.

On February 4th of that season, there was a story that came out of Jackson, Ohio, that set tongues to wagging. By the very nature of it, it

Opponents thought they were seeing double when they played Seattle U. in 1952. The fabulous O'Brien twins, Eddie, left, and Johnny, scored 62 points between them to lead the Chieftains to a stunning 102-101 upset of New York University at Madison Square Garden that winter. Eddie got 33, Johnny 29. A week later, Johnny set a new Boston Garden college record with 41 points, as SU topped Boston College, 99-86.

had to be true: a tall, big bag of bones named Bevo Francis had scored 113 points against little Hillsdale College of Michigan. The nation was skeptical, sure that the total was not legitimate. However, investigation proved that it was on the up-and-up. Bevo sank 38 field goals and 37 of 45 free throws for 113 points, breaking his own small-college record for most points scored in a single game. The contest was played on a 78′×47′ floor at Jackson High School; the normal college size was 90′×48′. Bevo made his points the hard way; very few came on tip-ins.

Gene Slaughter, the Jackson High coach, was there. He testified that Bevo controlled the boards magnificently and blocked shots the entire game. "He didn't lag behind and seemed to

LaSalle College's 1954 NCAA champions, front row, left: Frank Blatcher, Charles Greenberg, Bob Ames, Frank O'Hara, Charles Singley, Gary Holmes. Back row, left: F. O'Malley, Tom Gola, John Yodsnukis, Manuel Gomez, Bob Maples, and Mgr. John Moosbrugger.

be as determined to play a sound game as he was to score," Slaughter said. "Rio Grande played a man-to-man defense and used a full-court press the last quarter and a half. In the last four minutes, when it became obvious he might go over 100, Bevo's teammates deliberately fouled Hillside players, trading for possession. In the last quarter, Bevo took all but two of Rio Grande's shots from the field. In the last couple of minutes, when Bevo was near exhaustion and was a little late getting upcourt, his teammates waited to pass off to him. But when he got the ball, he just didn't miss. He scored 43 points in the first half and had 74 after three quarters. His defensive ability surprised me. I'd heard he just didn't play at all on defense. But he was a real smooth worker off those boards and he stuck right by the men he was assigned to guard. They got only seven points off him.

On the other hand, Hillsdale had three and four men guarding him. They just couldn't defense him. When he got the ball, jumped and turned, it went in. Hillsdale beat him to death, but they couldn't stop him. They'd keep fouling him—and he'd keep pouring 'em in. There was just no stopping him."

At the end of the season, Bevo Francis had an average of 48 points a game, and America had a new hero.

On the tournament front, the NCAA had been struggling for several years to wipe the NIT off the face of the map. There were signs it was succeeding. By threats, by restrictive rules, some colleges had been frightened away from the NIT. In a growing effort to corner the entire market, the NCAA expanded its tournament to 24 teams in 1954.

"The NCAA feels that it cannot have a gen-

Tom Gola shows the form that earned him the MVP award at 1954 NCAA tournament. The three-time LaSalle All-American scored 114 points in five games as Explorers won national championship.

uine championship as long as the NIT is around to take some of the top teams in the country," said a Madison Square Garden representative. "And there are those who feel that the NCAA is perfectly justified in some of the measures it has taken. The NIT has been particularly hurt this season by its failure to land LaSalle and Furman, although both apparently wanted to come."

LaSalle, of course, was its conference champion and understandably the NCAA insisted its various league winners compete in its own tournament. It had to go for the champions. The NIT went for color. Selvy and Gola would have added to the general luster of the 1954 NIT. The NCAA did not go for that sort of thing, but it kept the NIT from getting it.

Tom Gola, the NCAA's MVP, pumped in a total of 114 points as LaSalle outgunned Fordham, North Carolina State, Navy, Penn State, and, finally, Bradley to win the national championship. "He's a tough man to defend against," admitted the Bradley coach. "He seems to move in sections."

"Next time," advised a listener, "never mind his feet—watch the top section. That's the part that scores."

In the final AP poll, the nation's sports writers ignored the NCAA playoffs. They made Kentucky, the team that wasn't there, No. 1, and LaSalle No. 2. Down at Lexington, The Baron, wearing his brown suit and sipping his smooth bourbon, took the news in stride. "We deserved it," he said.

The Dons Do It: 1955-1956

The University of San Francisco, a small Jesuit school on a hilltop adjacent to the Panhandle of San Francisco's Golden Gate Park, was considered the dominant force, the best college team ever assembled, in the mid-1950s. Led by Bill Russell, K. C. Jones and Mike Farmer, the Dons won 104 games and lost only 10. From December 17, 1954 to, coincidentally, December 17, 1956, they won a record 60 consecutive games and two NCAA championships.

By today's standards their pace was slow and their shooting percentages poor, but as the first unbeaten champion in NCAA history they won as no team ever had before and as only six have since: North Carolina in 1957; UCLA in '64, '67, '72, '73; Indiana in 1976. The Dons' success was built around the rebounding, shot blocking and short-range scoring of Russell, the center, who was such a powerful inside force that after both championships the NCAA devised anti-Russell weapons. In 1955 it widened the free-throw lane to 12 feet and in 1956 it prohibited the guiding of errant shots into the basket.

Red Auerbach, who later coached him on the Boston Celtics, said that Russell had the biggest impact on the game of anyone in 10 years because he had instituted a new defensive weapon—the blocked shot.

"He has popularized the weapon to combat the aggressive, running-type game," Auerbach said. "He is by far the greatest center ever to play the game."

By Russell's own admission, he could block shots only five percent of the time. What made him so formidable, he said, was that opposing shooters didn't know which five percent it would be.

"Look, I could block shots," he said. "Okay. But if I'd tried to block all the shots my man took, I'd have been dead. The thing I had to do was make my man *think* I was going to block every shot he took. And how could I do that? Say I block a shot on you. The next time you're going to shoot, I *know* I can't block it, but I act exactly the same way as before, I make exactly the same moves. I'm confident. I'm not thinking any more but I got *you* thinking. You can't think and shoot—nobody can. You're thinking, will he block this one or won't he? I don't even have to try to block it. You'll miss.

"One time in college, K. C. Jones and I were chasing this guy who had the ball. We didn't have a chance to catch him, but we're chasing him. So K. C. yells over to me, 'I got him!' and I yell back, 'No, I got him!' And the next few steps I take, I hit the floor real hard so it sounds like I'm a lot closer than I really am. We *had* that guy. We had him thinking. Instead of going in for an easy layup, he tried to get off the shot and get out of our way at the same time. He missed.

"Here's something K. C. did to me one day. We're scrimmaging and he's on one team and I'm on the other. I'm bringing the ball up court and he's with me all the way. But I was sure I had him. I looked over at him and I could see he felt I had him, too. Then all of a sudden K. C. starts improvising. He starts jumping around and moving one way and another—things I never saw him do before. Now I'm worried. I'm thinking, what's he going to do next? You know what happened. I got all tangled up and fell down. That's right—one minute I'm sailing along, confident, and the next minute I'm sprawled all over the floor and K. C.'s taken the ball away from me and dribbles down for an easy layup.

"Basketball is a game of psychology. The psychology in defense, for example, is not blocking a shot or stealing a pass or getting the ball away. The psychology is to make the offensive team deviate from their normal habits. Basketball is a game of habits, and the player with the most consistent habits is the best. What I try to do on defense is to make the offensive man do not what *he* wants but what *I* want. If I'm back on defense and three guys are coming at me, I've got to do something to worry all three. First, I must make them slow up or stop. Then I must force them to make a bad pass and take a bad shot and, finally, I must try to block the shot. Say the guy in the middle has the ball and I want the guy on the left to take the shot. I give the guy with the ball enough motion to make him stop. Then I step toward the man on the right, inviting a pass to the man on the left; but, at the same time, I'm ready to move, if not on my way, to the guy on the left."

In Russell's opinion, shooting is of relatively little importance in a player's overall game. It is the other phases of basketball that make the difference. "If you're going to score 15 and let your man score 20 you're a deficit," he said. "If your value to the team is strictly as a shooter, you are of very little value. Offense is the first thing you learn as a kid in any sport: catch a pass, dribble, bat, shoot. You learn the offensive aspects of a game long before you learn there even are defensive aspects. These are the skills you come by naturally. Defense is hard work because it's unnatural. Defense is a science, not a helter-skelter thing you just luck into. Every move has six or seven years of work behind it. In basketball your body gets to do things it couldn't do in normal circumstances. You take abnormal steps, you have to run backward almost as fast as you can run forward. On defense you must never cross your legs while running, and that's the most natural thing to do when changing direction. Instead, you try to glide like a crab. You have to fight the natural tendencies and do things naturally that aren't natural. In rebounding, position is the key. No two objects can occupy the same place at the same time. Seventy-five per cent of the rebounds are taken below the height of the rim, so timing is impor-

tant, because almost everyone in college ball can reach the top of the rim. A really important part of rebounding is being able to jump up more than once. You have to keep trying for that ball. Sometimes you jump four or five times before you can get your hands on it. I used to practice jumping over and over again. When I was 6' 2", I could jump to the top of the rim 35 times, over and over."

When the 1954-1955 basketball season began, not even the hometown experts dreamed that USF would be playing in the NCAA finals at Kansas City in March. Much less did anybody consider the possibility that the Dons would run over All-American Tom Gola and defending NCAA champion LaSalle, 77-63, as they did when they wrapped up the national title.

In mid-December the Dons were still anonymous; nobody looked toward USF for All-America candidates, and Coach Phil Woolpert's record in four years at USF was a dismal 45-49. The team did not even have a home to play in; they rented the pavilion at nearby Kezar Stadium, borrowed the San Jose auditorium or used the Cow Palace when big-name schools like California and Stanford came to town.

Before the season started, Adolph Rupp, who at one time or another had been described as "brash," "ambitious," "arrogant," "ruthless" and "overbearing," wrote a letter outlining the 1954-1955 college basketball scene as he saw it. "Top teams nationally," he wrote, "will be LaSalle, Duquesne, Dayton, Iowa, Niagara and Alabama." Kentucky? Sorry, but three great stars had graduated from what Rupp called "the greatest team ever assembled in the United States." To replace one would be difficult, Rupp's letter explained. To replace all three was impossible. "This will be a season when Kentucky must rebuild," Rupp wrote.

Kentucky rebuilt so well that it was ranked No. 1 by January 3, 1955. The new Rupp, humble in November, was winning games like the old Rupp in December. Asked why his Wildcats continued to win, Rupp answered tartly: "Great coaching." The coach did not exaggerate. Over 25 seasons his teams had won more than 85 per cent of their games. When Kentucky beat Utah in December of 1954, the triumph was Rupp's 500th, a total with few precedents.

Coach Phil Woolpert's two-time, record-setting University of San Francisco national champions, 1956 edition. Top row, left: Tom Nelson, Gene Brown, Mike Farmer, Carl Boldt, Mike Preaseau. Middle row, left: Coach Phil Woolpert, Vince Boyle, John Koljian, Bill Russell, Bill Bush, K. C. Jones, Mgr. Bill Mulholland. Bottom row, left: Warren Baxter, Hal Payne, Jack King, Hal Perry, Steve Balchios.

There was no mention of USF in the Rupp letter, but after losing three games the Dons began to win ballgames and creep up in the AP poll. News dispatches from the Coast warned the country that "USF is going to be the team to beat." After the first of the year the Dons finally broke into the national ratings. On January 3, they were No. 5, behind Kentucky, North Carolina State, Duquesne and LaSalle.

On January 8, Georgia Tech, beaten five times in its first seven games, stunned Kentucky, 59-58, at Lexington on diminutive Joe Helms's backcourt steal and jump shot with 11 seconds to play. The Tech victory was its first win over the Wildcats since 1940, and ended Kentucky's string of 129 wins at home.

"We'll live on this one for a long time," cracked John "Whack" Hyder. The Tech coach hadn't forgotten the chiding his Engineers received from Rupp after losing to Kentucky for the umpteenth straight time in 1954. Rupp had said that the victory had been devoid of pleasure. "Beating Georgia," he complained, "is as ridiculous as kissing your sister."

For the second time in January, Georgia Tech was faced with playing Kentucky. This time the game was in Atlanta. By Kentucky standards the 2,000-seat basketball arena at Tech was a minor affair—the Kentucky gym seated 11,500. Before the game, blunt-speaking Rupp accosted Coach Hyder and demanded: "What's your aim in basketball here? What do you expect to accomplish with a place like this to play in?"

Whack Hyder thought for a moment and then clearly stated his aims: "First, I want my boys to adjust spiritually. Next, I want them to go to school and get an education. Next, I want them to give us their basketball time."

"You can't do that," Rupp said. "Boys aren't built that way any more."

That night Tech's boys were built that way. They wrecked mighty Kentucky, No. 1 team in the nation, 65-59, for an incredible repeat of the miracle of early January. Tech's iron men outfought the bigger Wildcats off the boards and led all the way. Little Joe Helms (24 points) and Bobby Kimmel starred for the Engineers. Exulted Coach Hyder: "It's the greatest thing since January 8th."

And Rupp? Old Adolph buried his face in his hands and said: "That shows you what'll happen when a team wants to win bad enough."

The defeat dropped Kentucky to No. 2 in the AP poll. And No. 1? Surprise—it was San Francisco. To stay. Like the earthquake, Nob Hill and the Golden Gate Bridge, the Dons were speedily becoming a Bay Area institution.

The 1955 NCAA championship matched USF against LaSalle, the defending champions. The Dons got there by beating West Texas State, 89-66; Utah, 78-59; Oregon State, led by 7' 3" Wade Halbrook, 57-56; and Colorado, 62-50. Meanwhile, LaSalle, No. 3 in the final AP ratings, polished off West Virginia, 95-61; Princeton, 73-46; Canisius, 99-64; and Iowa, 76-73.

Shortly before the finals at Kansas City, Coach Ken Loeffler of LaSalle reviewed his strategy. "I think we just can't let that big guy [Russell] get the ball," he said. "Once he gets his hands on it, he shoots. We can stop him only by keeping the ball away from him."

Russell was asked how he felt about playing against three-time AP All-American Tom Gola. "I'm not worrying about Gola, I'm just trying to help my team win," he said. After a moment's reflection, however, he added, "But, man, that Gola would really give the coach an ulcer."

Phil Woolpert pulled his big surprise that night when the teams took the floor. K. C. Jones, 6' 1" tall, was assigned to guard the 6' 7" Gola. Jones got the job after he had startled the big crowd and the Dons' bench in the semifinals against Colorado with his acrobatic leaps around the basket. "I figured that K. C. might be able to handle Gola," Woolpert said. "With Jones on Gola, Russell could stick around the basket on defense and handle rebounds. Fortunately, the strategy worked perfectly. Gola scored only 16 points—a bad night for him. K. C., with his amazing shooting from outside, hit for 24 points to lead all scorers."

Superb as K. C.'s performance was, Russell still remained the brightest star in the San Francisco galaxy. He clogged the middle to keep LaSalle from driving, snared 25 rebounds and batted away several shots by the Explorers. But it was on offense that Russell broke the game open and won the hearts of the crowd. Operating from the post position right by the basket, he pocketed 18 points during the first half. LaSalle simply could not keep Russell's hands off the ball. His tap-ins were particularly deadly. Timing his leaps perfectly, he'd soar into the air just as a shot by a teammate floated in toward the basket and tip the ball into the basket while LaSalle defenders impotently stretched and strained beneath. USF's first national championship was never in doubt.

The supreme tribute to Russell came from the venerable Coach Phog Allen of Kansas. Allen, who was known to reach for the rule book whenever his Jayhawks were in trouble, watched Russell against LaSalle and shuddered. "I'm for the 20-foot basket," he said.

Bill Russell became an All-American that night, and Phil Woolpert the Coach of the Year.

And the San Francisco Dons were no longer orphans begging for a place to play. Appreciative San Franciscans had already raised $350,-000 toward a $700,000 gym the Dons could call their own. The future was bright for both USF and Coach Woolpert. Only one member of his championship starting five was graduating, and Bill Russell—a junior—would be among those present in 1955-1956.

From the moment Bill Russell began to lead San Francisco into national prominence, people wrote and talked about him and his phenomenal feats. From the Bay Area the word filtered east of the Mississippi that here was a "discovery" almost as big as the gold strike of '49. He was truly one of the real giants of the game. By March of '55, when the Dons beat LaSalle for the NCAA title, he was accepted nearly everywhere as the best college basketball player in America.

There remained, however, a hard core of non-believers: the Madison Square Garden skeptics who, through the years, had watched stars like Luisetti and Mikan and Cousy and Macauley and Gola perform their magic and were seldom convinced by mere words alone. They were determined to see Russell and judge for themselves.

So in the winter of '55, as Coach Woolpert brought the nation's No. 1 team—and No. 1 player—into New York for the annual Holiday Festival Tournament, 18,500 packed the arena to see for themselves. At first they greeted Russell with a stubborn silence. Then, when he failed to shoot like a Carl Braun or dribble like a Bob Cousy or feed like a Dick McGuire, their silence changed to hoots and jeers for him. On offense he ambled lazily to a spot near the free-throw lane, almost reluctantly took passes from his teammates and quickly shoveled the ball away to someone else. And finally, when the man guarding him strayed away momentarily, Russell began to shoot from a distance of a dozen feet—and missed badly, not once, not twice, but three straight times, easy little shots. What then, asked the crowd, *could* he do?

Finally, Russell settled down and went to work. He convinced them there were skills to the game other than dribbling or passing—or even shooting. As the tournament progressed and USF moved steadily ahead into the finals, the looks of doubt and the hoots of derision changed into looks of incredulity and awe. For the things which Russell could do he did better than anyone in college basketball. All the words they had read had not really prepared the big

crowd for Bill Russell. They had come to see; what they saw was a 6' 10" college senior who could drop off his man on one side of the court, take two giant strides and soar above the basket to block a shot by an unguarded forward flashing in from the opposite side of the floor. They saw a man who had such amazing spring that he high jumped over 6' 7" without working up a sweat and had the speed to run the quarter-mile in 49.6 seconds. They saw a man with tremendously long arms, long even for a man of such height, and with hands which curled around a basketball like a small boy's grasped a large orange. They saw a man with the reactions of a lightweight fighter—quickness and timing that covered the floor like a shadow at dusk—and great competitive spirit beneath an almost phlegmatic exterior; a spirit, by the way, he credited to his high school coach, George Powles, who taught him how important heart and attitude is.

Finally, the Garden crowd saw a player who came down with 62 rebounds against magnificent athletes like 6' 7" Tom Heinsohn of Holy Cross and 6' 5" Willie Naulls of UCLA; a player who went up, time and again, to pluck a wild shot by a teammate from the backboard and cram it down through the basket while both opponents and teammates watched helplessly from below; a player who was deadly on soft little hook shots right under the basket; who made it the height of absurdity for an opponent to try to pass through the middle area he was guarding; who batted so many seemingly sure shots away from the basket it was discouraging to anyone with his hand on the ball and a goal-shooting gleam in his eye.

Without Russell, San Francisco's 33-game victory streak would never have survived the first round of the Garden tournament. His 22 rebounds, 26 points and a basketful of blocked shots brought the Dons from behind and saved the night against LaSalle. To his credit, USF won, 79-62. Against Holy Cross in the semifinals Russell outmuscled tough Tommy Heinsohn in a man-to-man duel they still talk about around New York. In Holy Cross' opener against Syracuse, Heinsohn had scored 36 points; Russell stopped him with 12, scored 24 himself, had 22 rebounds and batted away half a dozen more. San Francisco won, 67-51.

The finals of the Holiday Festival Tournament became an all-California brawl: San Francisco vs. UCLA. On that night Russell's teammates virtually gave him a night off in appreciation of his earlier efforts. K. C. Jones and the rest of the Dons ran rings around the Bruins, outshooting them, outrebounding them and forcing them into errors with a defense so tight it was frustrating. The final score was 70-53. Under no pressure to come through with another big production, Russell took things relatively easy. Nonetheless, he seized 18 rebounds, scored 17 points and won unanimous vote as the tournament's MVP. Once and for all, Bill Russell left no doubt in the minds of Easterners that he was the most formidable basketball collegian in the world.

As the 1955-1956 season progressed, the chief riddle that confronted college basketball after nearly two seasons was when—and how—was anyone going to stop San Francisco? By mid-March, 1956, over a stretch of 51 games, 25 of them that season, the defending NCAA champions had gone undefeated. Bill Russell was almost unanimously accepted as a super star. K. C. Jones had bewildered opponents with leechlike guarding and sparkling leadership and earned an All-America status in his own right. The Dons had height and speed, great depth, great coaching, and a reputation as the finest defensive team in the country.

"Better than the Kentucky team of Groza, Beard and Jones," Duquesne's Dudey Moore once called them.

"I believe San Francisco could enter the pro league and hold its own with all but the very top teams," said Chuck Taylor, basketball's touring ambassador.

"You can't stop Russell," said UCLA's Johnny Wooden. "The best you can hope to do is contain him. And you can't even contain him on defense—he contains you."

Going into the NCAA tournament, the immediate concern of Coach Phil Woolpert was the absence of K. C. Jones. After serving as captain of the Dons through the season, he was lost for the playoffs because of the NCAA four-year rule. There was a good replacement named Gene Brown—classified by Dudey Moore as "the best substitute in the country, a star on any other team"—and what sophomore Brown would cost USF in defensive ability he could

Former college All-Americans Tom Heinsohn, with ball, and Bob Pettit (9) went head-to-head in NBA competition in 1957. Heinsohn and Togo Palazzi led Holy Cross to NIT title in 1954.

almost make up in crack shooting. But K. C. Jones was still K. C. Jones, and he would be sorely missed.

"UCLA," said Washington Coach Tippy Dye flatly, "can whip San Francisco without Jones on the floor."

"We have improved a great deal," admitted Johnny Wooden, "and perhaps the loss of K. C. Jones will hurt them. However, they've still got Russell and he's the ballclub."

Bill Russell (back to camera) scored 25 points as he led University of San Francisco to an 83-71 victory over Iowa here in the 1956 NCAA final at Evanston, Illinois.

score more points against the Dons than any other team all season. But there was another side to the story: San Francisco, usually content to play control basketball, proved it could run, too, and wound up with a high of its own for the season—and a date in the semifinals with Southern Methodist University.

As the four semifinalists—Iowa, Temple, SMU, and USF—got ready for Evanston, Illinois, most of the professional forecasters saw San Francisco over SMU ("too much Russell") and Iowa over Temple ("too much height," said Kentucky, which had lost to both teams). In the finals, few were willing to bet that even Iowa, a truly fine team, could stop the defending champions, or even make them break out in perspiration.

In the semifinals, San Francisco met a good SMU team, one of the best in Southwest Conference history. The Mustangs had won 25 games against only two defeats with a mixture of accurate shooting, adequate height and superb balance. But the Dons almost made a farce of the contest. With the radarlike outside shooting of Harold Perry and Gene Brown and with 6' 7" sophomore Mike Farmer left practically unguarded while SMU fell back to double-team Russell, USF soared off to a 40-19 lead. This left Russell with little to do except gather in most of the rebounds, bat away some SMU shots, intercept a few passes and generally tidy up around the baskets at both ends of the floor.

The final score was 86-68. Russell didn't think he played a very good game. "Farmer and Perry and the others played well, but I didn't," he said. "Still, we won and that's what we came here for."

Coach Doc Hayes of SMU, after watching Iowa fight off a stubborn Temple, 83-76, in the other semifinal, said, "San Francisco can beat Iowa. San Francisco can beat any basketball team I know of. San Francisco," he added thoughtfully, "can beat the Russians."

The following night, with 11,000 observers watching in amazement at Northwestern University's McGaw fieldhouse, Iowa bolted off to a 15-4 lead in the first few minutes of the first half. The score left everybody feeling strangely like the occupants of a car crossing Death Valley; the mirage was there and they could see it

But even without Jones, USF resembled nothing so much as the best college basketball team ever invented as the opening rounds of the NCAA playoffs were played. The Dons stretched their victory streak to 53 games by disposing first of UCLA, 72-61, and then Utah, 92-77. Russell played like a demon and Gene Brown scored 41 points in the two games. Russell scored 21 against UCLA, 27 against Utah, picked off 45 rebounds and blocked over two dozen shots with his uncanny defensive moves around the basket. UCLA's highly touted Willie Naulls and Morris Taft each scored 16 points, below their season average, and that was that.

Utah, after outrunning Seattle University, 81-72, in the other second-round game, tried the same tactic against USF and did manage to but they knew that as the journey progressed it would begin to shimmer, dim and finally fade away. And they were right.

In a few minutes the Dons settled down to their night's work and the mirage disappeared like spent fog. All that remained was the nightmare of Bill Russell scoring 26 points, coming down with 27 rebounds and knocking away a dozen Iowa shots. He so befuddled Bill Logan that the 6' 7" Hawkeye center who had scored 36 points against Temple abandoned all attempts at scoring from underneath the basket and finished the game with only 12 points. The final score was 83-71, and for the second year in a row the Dons graciously accepted the big silver trophy for another NCAA basketball championship.

The only thing that prevented Russell from winning the writers' award as MVP in the tournament was the most astounding shooting exhibition in NCAA playoff history, a 48-point spree by Temple's phenomenal 5' 11" guard, Hal Lear, which helped the Owls to win third place over SMU, 90-81.

Coach Phil Woolpert, who had remained noncommittal for two years while others persisted in ranking his Dons as possibly the greatest college basketball team in history, finally had to admit they probably were. "This team is the finest I've ever seen," he said. "I can say that in all honesty now. It has done everything asked of it. The difference, without a doubt, was Russell."

While legions saluted Bill Russell, the biggest tribute paid him was perhaps from the rules committee of the National Basketball Coaches Association, meeting at the Edgewater Beach Hotel on Chicago's Lake Shore Drive. On the agenda in its executive session was a proposal to prevent any future Bill Russells from vaulting into the air and slapping the ball *down* into the basket. It was a problem which no one worried much about before Bill Russell. It was the coaches' way of bidding goodby to an era—and taking steps to prevent it from ever happening again.

Six-foot Guy Rodgers (shooting) proved there was still a place in basketball for the smaller man as he led Temple to a 27-4 record and third place in the 1956 NCAA tournament.

Tar Heels Overcome The Stilt: 1957

He was, without doubt, the most publicized rookie in college history. Before Wilt Chamberlain had even tried on a Kansas uniform, most basketball authorities had already conceded the next three NCAA championships to the Jayhawks.

"He'll be even more dominant than Bill Russell," spoke up one coach. "Hell, he shouldn't even bother to suit up. He should report directly to the Hall of Fame."

Such was the build-up that greeted 7-foot Wilton Chamberlain at Lawrence, Kansas, in 1955-1956, his freshman season. Hundreds of schools had attempted to recruit Wilt the Stilt, but Dr. Phog Allen won. Ironically, Coach Allen would never get to use the sensational center from Philadelphia. He reached KU's compulsory retirement age of 70, and despite an effort to pass a special resolution permitting him to remain on the university payroll for three more years, Coach Allen was obliged to turn over the coaching assigment in 1956 to his long-time assistant, Dick Harp.

Chamberlain's basketball credentials were awesome. At Overbrook High School in Philadelphia, he had averaged 37 points a game for three seasons—45 points a game as a senior, although he frequently played only half the time because of the lopsided leads he ran up.

In November, 1955, Kansas put Chamberlain on public display for the first time as a member of the frosh five in its annual preseason game with the varsity. This normally meaningless game attracted a crowd of 14,000, including most of the coaches from the other Big Seven Conference schools. Among them was Jerry Bush, the Nebraska coach. Bush confessed he was there to memorize every move Chamberlain made.

That night, a plainly nervous Chamberlain scored 42 points against double- and triple-teaming defenses. It didn't take Bush long to decide that this was only a sample of what was going to happen when Chamberlain became a varsity player in 1956-1957. In fact, a single characteristic maneuver was enough to shape the Cornhusker's opinion. Chamberlain drove to the top of the keyhole and went up for what appeared to be a one-handed jump shot. But he didn't come down. He kept soaring, floating, did a full twist so that his back was to the basket, shoved his arm behind him, rotated it in helicopter style and dunked the ball in the net. He landed in the fifteenth row of the seats behind the basket.

From behind the scorer's table, Bush was heard to mumble, "I feel sick."

In the whole disorderly history of college recruiting, the case of Wilt Chamberlain was one of the most contentious. Alumni from other colleges still grouse over their failure to land him. Newspapers, especially in the East, openly questioned the manner in which he was wooed. Remember Phil Woolpert's comment: "The going rate to talk to him on the phone was $250." Throughout his high school career, Chamberlain was constantly badgered by college alumni, some of whom seemed willing to violate the Lindberg Kidnapping Law to bring the 19-year-old youth to Alma Mater. Usually, a high school athlete is courted largely when a senior. With Chamberlain, the rush was on when he was still a sophomore.

"Nobody gave me time to think," he has

Wilt Chamberlain, the No. 1 draw in college basketball in 1957, averaged nearly 30 points a game and carried Kansas to second place in NCAA championship. Only a sophomore, the 7-foot sensation nearly swallows the works—hoop, net, and ball—against Colorado.

since said. "Every day when I'd come home from school, somebody would be in my living room, there would be four or five letters on the bureau and my mother would tell me at least two people called long distance and would call back later. When I flew out to Dayton to see the campus, they had me eat my meals in a hotel room. When I figured out why, I crossed them off my list. I also crossed off a lot of other schools because they never had gone in for black athletes. A couple of schools in Florida made a mistake and wrote me. South Carolina, too. They didn't know I was black. I let 'em find out for themselves. I didn't like some of those recruiters. They tried to take advantage of my age by flattering me with all kinds of talk. Then they'd start in building up their own importance in business, telling me how big they were. Like they owned the school as a sideline. Seems they all had the same phrases: 'Make it worth your while,' or 'We can afford'—you know, leading up to some offer if I promised to come to the school."

Wilt visited so many campuses that he was hazy on numbers and places, but a sample list included the University of Washington, Oregon, Dayton, Denver, Cincinnati, Illinois, Indiana, Michigan, Michigan State, Iowa and Northwestern—along with Kansas, of course. The Jayhawks started thinking of Chamberlain in 1952, when Don Pierce, the Sports Information Director, spotted a photo of Wilt in an out-of-town newspaper and ripped it out. He circled it in red pencil, marked it "Doc"—an Allen nickname—and passed it along. Allen promptly tacked the picture on his office door so he wouldn't forget it.

"I didn't think it was any good rushing him too soon," Allen said. "He was only a sophomore in high school. But in February of 1955 I thought it was time to move. I made my contacts with the alumni, and then went to Philadelphia with Lloyd Kerford. We didn't announce ourselves. We went to a game he played against Germantown High, and attended a YMCA banquet afterward. I talked to Wilt's mother more than I did to the boy himself. I wanted to convince her that Kansas was a sane place for a boy to get an education and play basketball."

It was after his second tour of KU, in May,

that Chamberlain sent word to Kansas authorities that he'd enroll. Because the competition for Wilt had turned into a national sportspage story, Chamberlain knew it would be a long while before he heard the last of it. "They'll say things, no matter where I go," he snapped. "I can hear 'em now: 'You must have got a mint.' "

Phog Allen was ready for the skeptics.

"There wasn't one cent involved in bringing Chamberlain to Kansas," he said. Later, he answered one persistent reporter by saying, "I don't know how much he got. I never asked him."

The new head coach, Dick Harp, 39, understandably felt that he was on the spot with Chamberlain. "Here it is my first year as varsity coach," he said on the eve of the 1956-1957 opener, "and everybody expects me to go through three years unbeaten. But it's a nice spot. I like it. Who wouldn't?"

In previewing the season, few experts noticed anything beyond Wilt Chamberlain. "By the middle of the season," one veteran coach summed up bleakly, "Chamberlain and Kansas will be off by themselves."

After the midyear break in early February, Wilt and his Jayhawks (13-1) were not doing badly. But they had company. For example: North Carolina (16-0), which launched the second half of the season by breezing past Western Carolina, 77-59; Kentucky (16-3), which trounced Florida, 88-61; and UCLA (15-1), which defeated Oregon State, 64-53.

The lone loss on the Kansas schedule came on January 14 at Ames, Iowa. Two nights before the game was to be played on their home court, Iowa State's Assistant Coach Bob Lamson had a dream. The next day he took it to Head Coach Bill Strannigan, who rehearsed it with the team for 30 minutes and decided to buy it. The next night it worked like a dream.

For a year, even before he graduated from the frosh squad to the varsity, rival coaches had been trying to devise ways and means of stopping Chamberlain. In his dream, Lamson saw State's big center, Don Medsker, playing in front of the Kansas cyclone, Chamberlain, where he'd grab at passes aimed for Wilt, and the forwards (Crawford and Vogt, who played the backcourt in the zone defense) applying a pinch on the big fellow. The one on the far side from the ball would move in behind Wilt and block off the boards. The guards, Thompson and Frahm, and the loose forward were free to go after the outside shooters. This, of course, was permitting Kansas some leeway on shots from the corners, but since there was no backboard to serve as a target and as a deflecting bank, many of those shots were going wild.

And that's just about the way the game played out. Chamberlain did not score a field goal in the first half. All told, he got only five baskets and seven free throws.

Coach Strannigan, a realist, was well aware than an ordinary offense, coupled with his assistant coach's dream defense, would not do. If his players took their normal number of shots and made a fair percentage of them, Iowa State would lose the ball almost every time they missed because Chamberlain was such a sure rebounder. So Iowa State played the percentages when they yielded space for corner shots, but not when *they* had the ball. They shot only 38 times. They made 13. In between, they kept the ball in circulation, whipping it around constantly until they shook a man loose enough for a clear try at the basket.

The game ended in an explosion of excitement when Don Medsker sank a 15-foot jump shot just ahead of the final buzzer. That made it 39-37, Iowa State.

After the bedlam had quieted, Bob Lamson revealed himself as something of a perfectionist among dreamers. In his dream two nights before, he said with slight disappointment, it was Gary Thompson, the team's top scorer, who sank the winning basket in the last second. Disappointed on more substantial grounds, Kansas Coach Dick Harp said grimly, "We play State again, February 2. Put that down. February 2."

Sweet revenge. On the second day of February, Kansas reversed the decision, 75-64. But the endless patterns of defense that coaches plotted to hold Chamberlain continued to have a noticeable effect. He scored only four points in the first half against Iowa State and was held to a disappointing (for him) 19 in all.

So far, Chamberlain's point average was 29.79 a game, below expectations, although it led the country. He was under challenge from Chet Forte (29.64) of Columbia, a hard-driving guard. Still, it is easy enough to see how Forte was overlooked amid the ecstatic forecasts that the 7-foot Wilt the Stilt inspired. Forte was the smallest man on a small Columbia squad. He stood a mere 5' 9".

As the 1956-1957 college basketball season passed the halfway point, the only major unbeaten team left, North Carolina, moved ahead of Kansas as the No. 1 ranked squad in the nation. Led by Brooklynites Pete Brennan, Joe Quigg and a whiz-bang with the fine old southern name of Lenny Rosenbluth, nine of the 12 varsity Tarheels were from metropolitan New York. The fact that Head Coach Frank McGuire was recently from St. John's University and a native New Yorker was purely incidental. Or so McGuire said.

Coach McGuire, whose tact and friendly personality made him a favorite with Broadway regulars, saw nothing surprising in the Yankee infiltration at North Carolina. "I use five or six scholarships each year," he said. "I make sure the kids receiving them are topnotchers. If they come from New York—well, they come from New York."

Another time, McGuire's explanation was more facetious. "New York is my personal territory," he claimed. "Duke can scout in Philadelphia and North Carolina State can have the whole country. But if anybody wants to move into New York, they need a passport from me. I do my own scouting. All the people in New York are my friends. No one gets paid for helping, but everybody looks out for me. The whole police department looks for players for me. So do the high school coaches, so do the Brothers at the Catholic schools. Even the waterfront looks out for me. No one gets paid. Why shouldn't I get the New York players? After all, that's my home territory."

North Carolina and Kansas were definitely on a collision course. Those who had seen the Tarheels believed their chances were excellent if it came down to a shootout—in spite of the Big Fellow. The word filtering out of Lawrence was that Dick Harp was having difficulties. Foremost was the Jayhawks' tendency to play at considerably less than full effort all season, trusting to Chamberlain to pull them through somehow. Harp also had a problem with Wilt himself, at best a fitful and moody young man, who was starting to show that he was not equipped to cope with the flood of attention that followed him to Kansas. The stares, the cameras, the reporters' questions and the rumors that followed him wherever he went were taking their toll. He withdrew within himself to the point where even during practice sessions in an empty stadium, he appeared to be miles from the scene in spirit. During a game, before the capacity crowds he always drew, he seemed to do his best to avoid any move that would cause any special notice. On offense, he took his position in the post and remained rooted for most of the action, coming to life just long enough to block a few shots and dunk a few buckets to save the game for Kansas.

Before the first Iowa State game, Coach Harp tried for hours to talk Chamberlain into a relaxed frame of mind. He also tried to impress the rest of his Jayhawks that out on the court they were not just four anonymities surrounding a star. By game time he had nearly talked himself out.

Whatever his problems, Chamberlain continued being the No. 1 draw in basketball. By checking the number of automobiles which passed through the eastern and western turnpike exits at Lawrence on Saturdays when Wilt was playing in a home game and on Saturdays when he wasn't, the Kansas Turnpike Authority concluded that the Big Fellow pulled 1,665 extra cars over the road at an average rate of 97¢ per car, or $1,615.05 every time he trotted out on the court. Since the turnpike was 236 miles long, he was worth $6.84 per mile per Saturday, and $16,150.50 a year. Someone took the trouble to figure that if KU continued playing 10 games per season at Lawrence, Wilt would have produced $48,451.50 in extra revenue for the turnpike before he graduated.

Joe Gilmartin, Sports Editor of the Wichita *Beacon*, proposed renaming the stretch of four-lane road between Kansas City and Wellington the Wilton Chamberlain Memorial Highway.

On the night of February 11, Nebraska and Missouri were playing a close, ball-control game at Lincoln. At the start of the second half, Missouri grabbed the tipoff and all five Cornhuskers hustled downcourt and conscientiously set up their zone defense. The Tigers thereupon scored possibly the easiest two points in all basketball history—for Nebraska had surrounded the *wrong* basket.

That may have been the only truly startling development of the whole 1956-1957 season. In just about every section of the country, form held true. Even Iowa State's last-second defeat of Kansas could have been—indeed, *was*—predicted. It was to Dick Harp's credit, however, that his team recovered quickly and won its conference title easily. That went also for undefeated North Carolina and San Francisco and West Virginia and SMU and St. Louis—among others—all of whom held firm under the season-long pressure of being their league's title favorite. Kentucky, too, despite Coach Rupp's early estimate that this was his "weakest team in years," was no exception. No one, including the members of his squad, believed Rupp. The closest approach to a conference upset was Michigan State's showing in the Big Ten—10 straight victories and an NCAA bid after three straight losses.

"If form continues to hold," declared a handicapper, "this year's NCAA semifinals will find California, Kansas, Kentucky and North Carolina playing for the national championship in Kansas City. No team in the eastern draw seems capable of stopping Carolina and the same is true of California in the Far West. In the Southwest the key game is Kansas vs. SMU in Dallas. Here will be staged the keenly anticipated duel between All-Americas Jim Krebs and Chamberlain. In the Midwestern draw, Kentucky will have its hands full with Morehead State, but tournament victory has long been a habit with Kentucky and a loss would be a definite upset."

But California and Kentucky fell along the wayside. Taking their places in the Last Four were San Francisco, winner over the Bears, 50-46, in the Far West Regional; and Michigan State, which stopped the Wildcats, 80-68, to win the Mideast Regional. Kansas won the Midwest Regional in Dallas entirely on Chamberlain's ability to intimidate his opponents. The tournament was won in the first game against a Southern Methodist team armed with everything it needed, including three years of tournament experience which should have made it immune to pressure jitters. But, conscious always of the Big Fellow and shooting with only half an eye on the basket, SMU was blown away, 73-65. Then in the Midwest championship game, Oklahoma City did even worse, 81-61. Chamberlain scored 66 points in the two games. Meanwhile, North Carolina earned its ticket to the NCAA semifinals by defeating Yale, 90-74; Canisius, 87-75; and Syracuse, 67-58, in the East Regional.

A scouting report on the Last Four saw things this way:

Rebounding: "Kansas must be given the edge only because of Chamberlain, the nation's percentage leader. Aside from Wilt, Kansas is in last place in height, with Carolina and San Francisco in a tie for first and Michigan State third."

Shooting: "In cold statistics for the regular season, Carolina (43.3) led Kansas by 4 percentage points, Michigan State by 4½ and San Francisco by close to nine in accuracy from the floor. In free throws, they led USF by 1½, Kansas by seven and State by seven. Such figures, however, are unreliable guides to a single-game performance under championship tournament pressure."

Defense: "Coach Phil Woolpert's ability to teach aggressive defense tactics—man-to-man—demands that San Francisco be accorded top ranking here, since they have limited the opposition to 55 points per game this year. Kansas, also, has held its rivals to a low average (58 pts.) and must be placed on the same level with the Dons. Their defensive success begins and ends, of course, with Chamberlain. Neither Michigan State nor Carolina is in the same class as Kansas and USF in this area."

Summing Up: "Any reasonable estimate must reach the following two conclusions: 1) Kansas and Carolina will meet in the finals. 2) The outcome will hinge on whether the Tarheels can maintain their poise or whether Chamberlain will continue his psychological and physical mastery over five rival players. Oddly enough, the tournament, to date, has shown Chamberlain to have some glaring faults—he cannot defend adequately against a hook shot and he has an effective range of only about eight feet from the basket on offense. He may, once in a while, hit some whirling jump shots from farther out than that, but he does

not do it consistently, and no team that plays Kansas ever worries about Wilt when he is that far away from the target. He is also an abominably poor foul shooter. He has tried everything—overhand, underhand, left side, right side, outside. Maybe he'd better go to a shrink. He is convinced he just can't shoot the damn things. When the rest of the team shoots fouls in practice, Wilt just turns the other way. He says there is no point in watching, since he can't shoot them at all."

Chamberlain opened his two-night stand in Kansas City before as wise and hard-eyed an audience as could possibly be present—coaches and athletic directors from every state and conference in the country. Despite his featured billing, he quickly acquired two rivals for the applause of these experts. The first game on the program—between North Carolina and Michigan State—was merely a *triple-overtime* heartstopper that was won by the Tarheels, 74-70. The second performance to compete with the Big Fellow's starring role was provided by his own fellow Jayhawks, who, in their following game with San Francisco, played classic basketball in every department—outdefensing the No. 1 Dons, and fast-breaking them to death and outshooting them with an accuracy percentage of 59.6. In the destruction of the Dons (80-56), however, Chamberlain was the chief bulldozer. He blocked, he dunked, he ran, he rebounded flawlessly. Pro scouts sat in the stands and drooled.

After the game and all the next day, coaches speculated on the playoff between the two winners. "Kansas in a rout," one coach predicted. "Kansas, but it'll be close," speculated another. Opinions were heavily one-sided in favor of the Western Champions.

Little Tommy Kearns, 5' 11", North Carolina's bandit of a guard who loved to steal the ball and drive for the basket, spoke up briskly but without heat. "We're a chilly club," he said. "We play chilly all the time. I mean, we just keep cool. Chamberlain is not going to give us the jitters like he did to San Francisco and some of those other teams."

The first 10 minutes of the championship contest seemed to prove Kearns's point. N.C.'s shooting percentage was perfect—100 percent,

Star of North Carolina's national champions in 1957 was Lennie Rosenbluth, shown here being fouled by John Green of Michigan State in the NCAA semifinals.

in fact. It did not miss the basket once in those first 10 minutes.

On offense, Carolina started in low gear, gradually speeding up the tempo until a sudden spurt or quick pass freed a man clearly for a shot. If that man sensed he was not totally free, he didn't take the shot but instead put the ball back into circulation. There were misses, true, but by halftime they had outshot Kansas, 64.7 percent to 27.3 percent. All-American Forward Len Rosenbluth was high scorer with 14 points and had missed only two attempts. Kearns was two for two, but his ball control was superb. Carolina led at halftime, 29-22.

The second half was almost a carbon copy of the first 20 minutes, except that Kansas improved its shooting percentage a few points, while N.C.'s slackened off several digits, and Rosenbluth, a whale of a clutch shooter, fouled out of the game. At the end of regulation play the score was tied at 46, the first tie in the history of the NCAA finals. What a predicament for North Carolina—a team which played through a fatiguing triple overtime only 24 hours earlier and faced once more with the same prospect. But now the Tar Heels were without the services of their most accurate shooter.

Only two points were made by each team in the first five-minute period, and none at all in the second overtime. In the third the score was tied twice until, with six seconds left on the clock and Kansas leading, 53-52, Joe Quigg was fouled. Displaying the sort of cool that Tommy Kearns spoke about the day before, Quigg made both free throws to win the game, 54-53. Through 55 marvelous minutes of electric basketball, North Carolina gave Wilt the Stilt the proper respect, but if there were any jitters the Tar Heels didn't show them.

They maintained their poise, stuck to their game plan and won an upset NCAA championship that few people, experts and laymen alike, thought they could do. It had been no easy road. To get to the end the boys from Chapel Hill had had to win 32 straight games.

North Carolina thus matched the feat of the San Francisco Dons, who won the national title in 1956 with an undefeated record. Although hurt by the loss of Bill Russell, USF ran its winning streak to 60 games at the start of the season for an all-time college record. After that

Joe Fleishman   Bob Lennox   Young Rosenbluth   Joe Quigg   Pete Brennan   Buck Freeman   John Lacey

Frank McGuire

To win the 1957 national championship, Coach Frank McGuire and his North Carolina Tar Heels rolled over 32 straight opponents.

One of the sensations of the 1957 college season was West Virginia's ambidextrous "Hot Rod" Hundley. Here he scores with his left hand against Miami in the Orange Bowl tournament.

little was heard of the Dons nationally until they suddenly bobbed up and knocked off California and Michigan State to finish third in the NCAA tournament. Ironically, it was the Olympic team of Russell and K. C. Jones that gave the Dons their first (unofficial) loss that season. Illinois later officially ended the 60-game streak.

San Francisco held the record for extended excellence until UCLA came along with its 88 wins in a row during the Bill Walton era. But the former Don players give away nothing to the more modern teams. "I just can't conceive a club with Bill Russell losing," says Stan Buchanan, a forward on the '55 team.

Added Bill Russell, "We beat everybody."

All told, seven members of the 1955-1956 USF basketball team went on to become lawyers. And Jim Cunningham, a guard on the squad, was elected to Congress.

There's one final footnote to the 1956-1957 season: In Evansville, Indiana, Mississippi State was scheduled to meet Evansville College in the final game of Evansville's invitational tournament. As tipoff time approached, Don Ping, Evansville's athletic director, read a prepared statement to the assembled spectators. It explained that Mississippi State's representatives had been called home suddenly by their school administration. It seemed Mississippi State would not play because there were blacks playing in the tournament.

The players kept getting taller—and rougher—as the game swept along in the late 1950s. Examples, left: Boston U.'s Bob Cumings got an assist on the back of a Wyoming defender to score; in center photo, Minnesota's Dave Tucker (34) took ball away from Frank Howard (11) of Ohio State; Jim Palmer, photo on right, one-handed rebound halfback-style for Dayton. Bottom photo: Phil Dye of Southern California made a basket against Oregon just before landing on his head.

The Baron Gets His No. 4: 1958

Ever since 1952-1953, when Kentucky was obliged to cancel its schedule because of alleged violations of the NCAA code, Adolph Rupp, jowly and bulky and 56 now, had had only one thought, one bitter, consuming ambition.

"I will not retire until Kentucky wins another NCAA championship," he said, over and over.

At the start of the 1957-1958 season, The Baron, an open-eyed realist, could hardly have hoped for much more than his 18th Southeastern Conference title, if that.

"I got a collection of *fiddlers* when I need *violinists*," he said. "Oh, they're pretty good fiddlers; be right entertaining at a barn dance. Unfortunately, we're not scheduled to play at any barn dances. To play in Carnegie Hall, you need concert violinists—and I ain't got any of those. My fiddlers? They fool around and fool around with maybe two or three minutes to go. Then they look over at the bench and see that I'm not too happy—and then they get busy and win by one or two points. In the meanwhile, see, they drive me crazy. They aren't the greatest players in the world. All they do is win."

Recently, two college athletes tried to recall the name of the man who went from Kansas to Kentucky to the Naismith Hall of Fame. "Adolph Rump," said one. "Rudolph Hupp," said the other. For the record, it was Adolph Rupp, who warmed the bench on Coach Phog Allen's national championship Kansas team of 1923, then went on to coach at Kentucky for 41 seasons and win 874 contests, No. 1 on the all-time charts. When he lost the distinction as the winningest college coach to his old player, Dr. Allen stayed in character by saying, "Bless his bones. If Rupp can count that high (771 in 1967), he can have the record." Rupp then went on to win another 103 games for the all-time high.

Rupp dubbed them the "Fiddlin' Five" and in many ways they were his favorite team.

"I'd have to say the 1957-1958 season satisfied me more than any other," Rupp admitted before he died in 1977. "Probably because the players didn't have a great deal of talent. But they won."

The fiddlers were the holdovers of what Rupp had termed possibly his worst team in years. But the clue—for all who had eyes to see—was in that word holdovers. He had a starting five of four seniors and one junior. All had had three years of the not-so-subtle Rupp discipline that molds basketball players. It was an ancient system of "Yes, sir" and "No, sir"—of orders given and orders carried out—of regimentation or else. Sample:

In one game, Kentucky played a dismal, scrambling first half. During the 15-minute rest period in the dressing room Rupp unceremoniously placed towels in front of five chairs and ordered his starters to sit. Then he pulled the plug.

"Beck!" he screamed at Ed Beck. "You are a sorry, no-good, goddamn shrinking violet! I brought you up here from Georgia when you were nothing but a worthless, clumsy ox. I have given my blood and sweat trying to make something respectable out of you. I have failed. There's nothing I can do about that now."

Pause, utter silence. Then the sage of the blue grass shifted into high gear.

"But what really scorches me is that I have fed you for four years. You have eaten off Kentucky's table for four years and we have wasted every morsel. And now, right here in this dressing room, while you are losing an important game, I want you to vomit up every bite of food you have eaten at the University of Kentucky."

Rupp let that sink in, then turned to the other four starters: "And that goes for the rest of you bastards, too!"

The Wildcats ultimately won the ballgame.

Kentucky played its games by strict patterns laid down by Rupp; with hardly a single freelance move, they ran their patterns, getting better and better at them as the season wore on, and won the Southeastern title against competition which was far superior to that of many previous seasons.

The NCAA tournament's early rounds pro-

duced a number of extremely hard-fought contests and spectacular upsets (Manhattan 89, West Virginia 84; Notre Dame 94, Indiana 87; Kansas State 83, Cincinnati 80; Seattle 69, San Francisco 67) which had to be taken into account in any evaluation of the semifinalists—Temple, Kentucky, Seattle, and Kansas State. The handicappers had the Final Four analyzed this way:

Rebounding: Seattle had the best record, but compiled it against the weakest schedule. K-State had an edge in front-line height. Kentucky was above average and well balanced at both ends of the court. Temple's relentless pursuit of the ball brought fine results on the offensive board; only fair on the defensive board.

Shooting Accuracy: Again, Seattle was first with a percentage of just over 45, led by Jerry Frizzell and Elgin Baylor; the other three teams were fairly even around 40 percent. K-State's height advantage was sure to help in the final rounds. Kentucky's excellent screening and Temple's great speed upcourt were balancing factors.

Defense: Temple and Seattle had the greatest margin (16 points) over opponents in regular season games—Temple with tough, tenacious zone exclusively. Kentucky and Seattle were strictly man-for-man; K-State switched. All four were fast-breaking teams, and Temple's speed was a big asset in getting back to set up a zone.

Kentucky and Temple were paired to meet in one of the two semifinal contests at Louisville. Temple was out to avenge an early-season, triple-overtime, two-point loss to Kentucky on Kentucky's home court. A lot of the professional handicappers liked Temple's chances. The key player in Coach Harry Litwack's effective zone defense and director and ballhandler on the fast break was the brilliant and graceful All-American, Guy Rodgers. There was no better strategist or feeder in the country than Rodgers—and few in the pro ranks.

On the other hand, the glue in the Kentucky works was Center Ed Beck, intelligent, strong defensively but lacking in the natural aggressiveness necessary for generalship. But if the Wildcats, with their highly disciplined, strictly patterned offense (usually accurately designed by Rupp to take maximum advantage of an opponent's weak spots), got off to a fast start, simple momentum rather than floor direction would keep them going. The Wildcats screened cleverly for John Cox and Adrian Smith, and Beck handed off beautifully to Vernon Hatton and John Crigler from his high post.

Kansas State's none-too-mobile offense was run by Guards Roy DeWitz and Don Matuszak. But the bellwether of the team was neither of these, nor was it the high-scoring Bob Boozer. It was Center Jack Parr, a likable but moody young man who lifted or depressed the emotional pitch of his team by his play in the early minutes of a game. Against Kansas' Wilt Chamberlain earlier in the season, his blocks and rebounds on defense were devastating. "If he can have a night like that against Seattle, he just may elate and spark the rest of the team to heights of some brilliant basketball," said K-State Coach Tex Winter, who had handled Parr with the affection and concern of a father all year. "He must be ready for his best effort or suffer the indignity of watching the championship game from a seat in the grandstand." With Boozer and Wally Frank, Parr helped make up a front line that stood 6' 8", 6' 9", and 6' 8".

Seattle, too, had its bellwether in the sharp-shooting Elgin Baylor. At 6' 5" and 225 pounds, he was such a powerful, punishing player that his teammates were positive he could win the heavyweight championship of the world had he wanted to train for it. Around the West he was known as a four Band-Aid player. The man assigned to him usually stocked up with liniment and aspirin and approached his task with all the zest of a man assigned to defuse a live bomb with a hairpin.

Almost every good team has what is known as a "policeman" or "hatchetman," whose duty it is to intimidate the other team, to show them who's boss when they want to play rough. With Kansas it was Wilt Chamberlain; with Seattle, it was Baylor, a pile of muscles with the disposition of a starving bear. When anyone tried to eviscerate him, Baylor simply retaliated with a few elbows, and the antagonist put away his cleaver and kept his distance.

When Baylor had the ball the opposition usually scattered like crapshooters at the sight of a cop, leaving the deadly business of stopping him to the luckless fellow who was hired to do it. To the unschooled fan, what Baylor did was not spectacular. He rarely swished in 30-foot outside shots. He didn't have to. He bulled his

way to the basket and, because he had such incredible sleight-of-hand under it, he dumped in what the players called "garbage"—40 to 70 points per game. It was done so unobtrusively the fan in the upper balcony was frequently surprised at the end of the game when Baylor had outscored any other two men on the floor.

As basketball players go, Elgin Baylor was not big. On road trips, he didn't have to sleep side-saddle in hotel beds or stoop over to shave in the mirror. But he was big for the things he did.

His coach at Seattle Univesity was half-Irish, half-Italian John Castellani, a peppery, fast-talking, sharp-dressing 32-year-old. He was in his second season at Seattle. When the Chieftains lost four of their first eight games, Castellani was twice hung in effigy in downtown Seattle. To his credit, he kept his electric intensity, gained a measure of control over it and, more important, finally gained control over his play-

Elgin Baylor filled out considerably from the time he starred at Seattle University (left) to the time he became All-Pro with the Los Angeles Lakers at 6′ 5″ and 225 pounds. At his peak, he was such a powerful, punishing player that fellow Lakers were positive he could have won the heavyweight championship of the world had he wanted to train for it.

ers. He drove them relentlessly through the rest of the season, and they suffered only one more defeat. His leadership won Seattle entry into the NCAA championship tournament and three stunning preliminary victories over Wyoming, San Francisco and California. It also won the Chieftains vast popular support around the country.

The problem of what to do about the offensive versatility and the apparently unstoppable rebounding of Baylor was a problem that hadn't been solved by very many coaches. Portland Coach Al Negratti told Castellani after Baylor had scored 60 points against his team: "John, we almost had you. If we could have held Baylor to 54 points, we'd have won."

"Finesse usually happens in small people, about 5' 9"," said Marv Harshman. "But Baylor was so quick of mind and hand he got his shots no matter how good the defense was. You had to be fast to rebound a Baylor miss—if you ever got one. He came up with the second and third try on the same ball. I coached against Baylor. At the time, I was at tiny Pacific Lutheran University. It was one of the best teams I ever had; 31-1 and runnerup to Tennessee State in the NAIA. Well, we played Baylor's team in Seattle and he destroyed us, by himself. We couldn't control him. He scored something like 50 points. Our biggest problem was fouling out; that is, the people assigned to guard him left the game early. Elgin had it all—rebounding, shooting, drive, heart—and the finest sense of *timing* of any ballplayer in the history of basketball."

Despite the sharpshooting Baylor, Seattle was strictly a freelancing team which could be ignited by any of three or four good outside shots—Baylor, Don Ogorek, Frizzell and Charlie Brown. They would have to rely on outside shooting when they met K-State in the semifinals, because their famed fastbreak was expected to be stalled as often as not by State's height and tenacity under the boards. Since they were good at it, they were counted on to push State to the limit; nonetheless the handicappers picked K-State over Seattle. What the oddsmakers failed to take into consideration, however, was Seattle's finely-fashioned victory over San Francisco, adjudged by many the best team in the nation, in the Far West Regional. It gave the Chieftains a momentum of morale

which brought them to Louisville in high spirits and convinced they were the team to beat. It was a significant advantage.

It was a tossup whether K-State's hard-fought, 83-80 overtime victory over Cincinnati in the Midwest semifinals sharpened them for Louisville or, coming as it did after a typically rugged Big Eight schedule, exhausted them further.

What about Temple? It had to scramble to edge well-drilled Maryland in the East Regional semifinals, 71-67, but was never in trouble against Dartmouth (69-50) in the championship game and now rode a 25-game winning streak. In addition, Temple looked forward to the rematch with Kentucky—Rodgers was especially determined to close out his All-American career in victory. Temple's vastly underrated Jay Norman had a reputation of handling just about anyone around the backboards.

In its semifinal against Temple on Friday night, Kentucky came perilously close to defeat. The Wildcats had to battle for their lives to stave off the Philadelphians. They passed and ran and ran and passed until they found the tiniest chinks in one of the toughest defenses in the nation; that kept them even in a see-saw game until they made good on a last-minute Temple error and won, 61-60. Rupp was within one step of his goal now, but no one knew better what a big step it was.

Rupp could have had few real worries about his own attack against only a so-so overall Seattle defense. The Chieftains earned their way into the NCAA final via a superlative 73-51 victory over Kansas State, a team which appeared exhausted in body and spirit after a grueling season. Then to accentuate the negative, State lost to Temple in the consolation game, 67-57. For a team that was favored by some experts to go all the way, the 1958 NCAA experience left K-State shattered.

Rupp did not mess around trying to come up with an answer to what to do about Elgin Baylor. It was obvious 12 hours before the contest that he had decided there was *nothing* he could do about the Seattle star; he just didn't have the height or the skill. There was only one course open: get rid of Baylor. Which was what he did.

He did it through John Crigler, easily the

most underrated player in the 1958 NCAA tournament. Dedicated to winning basketball games, as he made it clear so often, Rupp set up fast-moving patterns that forced Seattle into a constant switching of defensive assignments until Baylor was left guarding Crigler and Crigler was left with the ball. Baylor must have thought he was watching a horror movie; Crigler had the maneuverability of a dragonfly. The crux of Baylor's problem was that at the instant he was forced to switch to Crigler, John took advantage of a confusing series of legal blocks and was already a half-step ahead of Elgin and pounding through an open path to the basket. Baylor really had very little alternative; either concede two points each time or try to stop Crigler without fouling him. Baylor chose to risk the fouls—and lost. Before the contest was 10 minutes old he had been charged with three. Inevitably, there were a full 30 minutes to play when the issue was decided. Kentucky did not relax the pressure. It continued to feed the ball to Baylor's man, and Baylor was obliged to give him plenty of room for drives or shots or stick to him like plaster of paris and run the risk of fouling out.

In the second half, Coach Castellani altered his strategy by changing to a zone defense. Trying to stave off the loss of Baylor for as long as possible, he positioned four men out front and kept Elgin under the basket where, at least, he was of service off the backboard. The problem with that thinking was that the four men out front ran themselves bowlegged attempting to cover five Wildcats. The result was sharpshooting Johnny Cox or the superb jump-shooting Vernon Hatton always seemed to be clear in a corner or near the top of the key, where they turned out the lights on any quixotic idea Seattle had about winning the national championship.

Yet, handicapped as he was by fouls and by a nasty rib injury, Baylor still scored 25 points in flashes of stunning offensive play, and passed off daringly and well to his teammates. But it was not enough. The SU hopes went aglimmer as Kentucky won, 84-72.

The Baron had his fourth NCAA championship.

There is a postscript to the 1957-1958 season. At the end of the Spring semester, Wilt Chamberlain, a junior, left Kansas almost as mysteriously as he had entered. There were the grim, inevitable rumors (vehemently denied on both sides) that he could not get along with Coach Dick Harp. There were other stories that Chamberlain, highly sensitive, didn't find the natives of Kansas as anti-Jim Crow as he had anticipated. But all Chamberlain would say was that he could not afford to stay. The Harlem Globetrotters were dangling a $65,000 offer in front of him. Owner Abe Saperstein was prepared to pay for his services. Bill Russell had received a similar proposition in 1956 but turned it down.

"Saperstein came to see me and my coach, Phil Woolpert," Russell explained later. "At first, I was really interested. But all Abe said to me was hello and goodby. All the time he was there he talked to Coach Woolpert. He told Woolpert what he could do for me and how much money I'd make and all that jazz. He never said a word to me. He treated me like some kind of idiot who couldn't understand what the conversation was all about. I made up my mind right then that I'd never play for him."

In the end, Chamberlain had no such qualms about Saperstein. He gladly signed on the dotted line and at the end of the year was $65,000 richer.

As the various All-America selections for 1958 were announced, it was increasingly evident that the five best college players in the country were all black: Guy Rodgers of Temple, Oscar Robertson of Cincinnati, Wilt Chamberlain of Kansas, Elgin Baylor of Seattle, and Bob Boozer of Kansas State. And a second All-America five, all black, could just as easily have been John Green of Michigan State, Tom Hawkins of Notre Dame, Gene Brown of San Francisco, Jay Norman of Temple, and Wayne Embry of Miami (Ohio).

It was George Gregory's conviction that one of the big reasons for this phenomenon was the fact that the average black family was eating better. George is down in history as the first black All-American basketball player. In 1931, he captained the Columbia University team.

"The day I was elected captain, I went home and celebrated by eating a mustard sandwich for dinner," he said. "That's all we could afford.

Wilt Chamberlain stretches his 7-foot frame against Oklahoma's 6' 5½" Bill Ashcraft in 1958, The Stilt's last season at Kansas.

I learned to play basketball on cold, dark basement courts where you had to dribble around a furnace to take a shot. But times change, and by 1958 the average black athlete was no longer living on mustard sandwiches."

There were, of course, other reasons why blacks were achieving first-rank status in campus basketball across the U.S. Gregory, who rose to Commissioner of Civil Service in New York City, had a theory.

"At first," he said, "competition for athletes was limited to football men, but as colleges began to appreciate the prestige that came with winning basketball, the bidding for good shooters became as fierce as the scramble for good quarterbacks and 250-pound tackles. This increased opportunity for a free college education always had been an incentive for all athletes—white and black—but for the black it came at almost the same time when he was being welcomed in ever-larger numbers anyway by the bigger schools. By 1958, the average state college was making 20 full basketball scholarships available. And at those schools where there were no racial bars the black athlete was getting his share of the scholarships.

"There remains, of course, the fact that basketball is a team game—a symbol to the black, when he plays it, of his approach to full American citizenship. Blacks enjoy a deep psychological thrill from playing in a mixed group. He has a sense of belonging, of being wanted and needed and of making a contribution."

Black athletes surely made their contribution to basketball in 1958. A change in the free throw bonus rule, awarding the extra shot only after six team fouls in each half, generally lowered scoring averages. The only players to average more than 30 points a game were Oscar Robertson, Elgin Baylor, and Wilt Chamberlain—all black. The 6' 4" Robertson's 35.1 points a game made him the first sophomore in history to win a national scoring title. For Oscar, it was a triumph of finesse over sheer height—he scored through the mastery of every shot in the game, not just by basket-stuffing.

Skin color is a crude guide to black and white styles of play, but there is a difference. When you talk about "black" basketball, you're talking about speed, mobility, quickness, acceleration, "the moves, *rhythm.*" Rhythm is what black players talk about a lot; feeling the flow of the game, finding the tempo of the dribble, the step, the shot. It is an instinctive quality.

If there is a single trait that characterizes "black" basketball it is leaping agility. Bob Cousy once said that "when coaches get together, one is sure to say, 'I've got the one black kid in the country who *can't* jump.' When coaches see a white boy who can jump or who moves with extraordinary quickness, they say, 'He should have been born black, he's that good.'"

There is another kind of basketball in America, too. It is "white" basketball. It is a mechanical, precise development of skills, without frills, without flow. But it is effective. It is jagged, sweaty, stumbling, intense. "A *black* player overcomes an obstacle with finesse and body control," Cousy said. "A *white* player reacts by outrunning or outpowering the obstacle."

"White" basketball, then, is the basketball of patience and method; with execution, with constant running, with the same play run again and again. "Black" basketball is the basketball of electric self-expression.

Perhaps the most classically "white" position is that of the quick forward, one without great moves to the basket, without highly developed shots, without the height and mobility for rebounding effectiveness. What does he do? He runs. He runs from opening jump to the last horn. He runs up and down the court, from baseline to baseline, back and forth under the basket, looking for the opening, for the pass, for the chance to take a quick step and the high-percentage shot.

In dramatic contrast, the "black" style is of the stuff that makes legends—leaping from the foul line and slam-dunking the ball on the way down; going up for the layup, pulling the ball to the body and throwing it under and up the other side of the rim, defying gravity and probability with moves and jumps.

Bob Ryan, basketball writer for *The Boston Globe* and *The Sporting News*, several years ago picked a classic all-star roster of blacks and whites, breaking it down according to style of play:

BLACK "BLACK"	WHITE "WHITE"
Julius Erving	John Havlicek
Connie Hawkins	Mike Riordan
Bob McAdoo	Sven Nater
Nate Archibald	Jerry Sloan
Earl Monroe	Dave Twardzik

BLACK "WHITE"	WHITE "BLACK"
Paul Silas	Rick Barry
Bill Bridges	Billy Cunningham
Nate Thurmond	Dave Cowens
Norm Van Lier	Pete Maravich
Jim McMillian	Paul Westphal

As something of a postscript to the White "Black" lineup, "Pistol" Pete Maravich was one of the few white players ever offered an authentic bid by the Harlem Globetrotters.

Until 1970, it was customary, whenever writing about Kentucky basketball, to refer to Coach Adolph Rupp's Wildcats as "well-drilled, usually undefeated, lily-white." Then, whoops, one was obliged to look again at the start of the new decade, as Rupp changed the phrase to read: "Well-drilled, undefeated and *integrated.*" The Baron went out and recruited a black—Tom Payne, not only the first black player in the 68-year history of Kentucky basketball but the tallest player as well (7' 2½"). Rupp, 69 years old and nearing retirement, finally made the black man's acceptance official.

Blacks have become so highly accepted, as a matter of fact, that it is not unusual today to see seven, eight, even nine of them on the floor at the same time in a college or pro game, while whites line the bench waiting for some token action. All of which prompts my friend, Elmer Alskog, to jest: "I'm going to start a league for white castoffs—for whites who can't make the black teams."

Newell Makes Point With Defense: 1959

"Basketball," said Pete Newell, head basketball coach at the University of California, in 1959, "is a game of mistakes. The team making the fewer mistakes generally wins."

During Newell's reign at Berkeley, the Golden Bears rarely made more mistakes than an opponent. In fact, the 1958-1959 Blue and Gold on the average made only six ball-control errors a game compared with their opponent's 15, and since Coach Newell figured control of the ball was worth about 1.5 points, that gave California a 14-point head start before the teams even took to the court.

As a result of such attention to detail, the 44-year-old Newell, an intense perfectionist (his 6' 1½" frame usually shrank from a trim 180 pounds to a nerve-wracked 165 each season) was able to accomplish much with players of ordinary ability.

Newell's first major coaching position was at the University of San Francisco, where he surprised almost everyone by winning the National Invitation Tournament in 1949. After four seasons at USF (1947-1950) he went to Michigan State (1951-1954), where he took a team that had won only four and lost 18 and, within a year, had it holding its own in the tough Big Ten.

His greatest accomplishment, however, was at Berkeley. He coached there during the years 1955-1960, during which he won 118 games, lost 44; won four Pacific Coast Conference titles and finished first (1959) and second (1960) in the National Collegiate Athletic Association championship tournament.

To many Californians the NCAA victory in 1959 ranks even yet as the Bears' greatest ath-letic achievement. Indeed, it was a truly remarkable team victory. Not one player on the team had been All-State or its equivalent in high school, and only one, Captain Al Buch, had ever received any sort of outside attention for his play in college. He made the West Coast NCAA squad, but, at that, he was tied in the voting for last place on the *second* team.

Newell was a modern guy with old-fashioned ideas about how to win championships. Hard work was his credo. To begin with, he demanded that his athletes be in top physical condition. For the first two weeks of preseason practice they did nothing but exercise in the gym and ran on the punishing hills behind Berkeley. "Sometimes we have to wear an opponent down," he told his players. "You have to be conditioned to play the last five minutes of a game, not just the first five."

In the gym Newell had ideas about everything, ranging from the position of the feet to the use of vision. "Practice habits are game habits," he cautioned his team. "If your individual habits are sound, then our team habits will be sound. You should be constantly trying to minimize your mistakes."

In practice, Newell required each player to shuffle with his knees flexed, one hand up, the other down, for 20 minutes at a time. "This is the correct defensive posture," he intoned. "Any other way is wrong. You shuffle because that allows you to slide with the man you're guarding. If you cross your feet instead of shuffling, you might lose your balance. Knees are flexed because you have to bend your knees before you react. So be in that position. Why wait to get to it?"

Newell also expected his players to learn to dribble and pass with either hand; also had to be ambidextrous with their feet. "We do not," said Newell in 1959, "subscribe to the theory that because a boy is naturally right-footed, he should always have his right foot forward. When he is playing the ball, his inside foot (the foot closest to an imaginary line drawn between the baskets) should be extended. This permits him to better defend vulnerable areas where he cannot depend on defensive assistance from teammates. These vulnerable areas are the sidelines and the backline."

In addition, the inside hand was supposed to be raised. "The hand should be in the shooter's face to disconcert him," Newell explained. "The other arm should be extended almost parallel to the floor to deflect passes. We condition arm muscles so the arms can be held up over protracted lengths of time. In boxing, it's fatal to drop your hands. The same is true in basketball."

Newell ran his practice games at fast and slow speeds. The Bears practiced like that so they could accelerate or decelerate in a game. They used tempo as a weapon. The theory was to confuse the other side. "We want to make the other team play the game we think we can play better than they can," Newell said, "and this we can do by making them play at a speed they're not used to. When we play a ball-control team, we try to force them into a faster tempo of play. When we play a fast-breaking team, we try to slow down the tempo with ball control. The fast break itself we stop by pressure on the rebounder. If he has pressure on him, he can't throw. We also choke the outlet pass to the guard out to get the pass. And we don't retreat. A man-to-man aggressiveness is very important. We don't concede."

California was at its best defensively.

"There are certain nights when you are off offensively," Newell said. "You'll have nights when you are off defensively, too, but your offensive performances vary more. Also, the good defensive team seems to come up with an above-par performance defensively when its shooting is off. The players seem to realize that through increased defensive play they can offset a poor shooting performance and still win the game. Man-to-man responsibilities are the dominant aspects of our basic defense. Along with this, we incorporate the press defense in various forms. We're usually in one form of a press throughout the game because it is important always to have pressure on the ball. Through our pressure, we are trying to increase an opponent's mistakes."

Newell also had theories for holding down errors on the offense. "We want to get the shot opportunity in a good-percentage shooting zone," he said. "We're not concerned with driving all the way to the basket for the layup or cripple shot. We're content with a 10-footer. The more you drive into the basket, the more you risk losing the ball. We rely on execution. If we feel we can get the execution, we can get the shot, regardless of the defense."

Newell said there was a reason why he never took a game lightly. There was a good reason, he said, for his do-or-die intensity before, during, and after ballgames.

"The team feels the way I do about a game, and if I ever stopped taking a game seriously the team would do the same," he said. "So, I prepare myself mentally that each game we play is a real tough game. And each season we play is a real tough season. You can't allow yourself to relax. Every 15 minutes before a game, I wonder why I ever went into coaching. One day I'll have to get out. I don't want to be coaching when I'm 60. I simply couldn't go through 16 more years of the tension that goes with each season."

At the height of the 1959 season, with Cal and Washington in a dogfight for No. 1 position in the P. C. C., Newell was as fidgety as a cat on a hot tin roof. He looked for bobby pins on the street to bring luck, and he'd lost 15 pounds. His stomach was too turbulent to keep much food, and on the day of a game he kept going on 20 cups of coffee and maybe two packs of cigarettes. During a game he allowed himself the luxury of chewing on wet towels set aside by the team manager. Once in a while, he inadvertently took some salt into his system by biting into a towel that a player had used to mop his brow. *What price glory!*

"Geography determines championships," was the succinct summing-up by LaSalle's wise old warrior, Coach Dudey Moore, of the long-held view in basketball circles that a team playing on its home court had an incalculable advantage. Well, that wasn't true of the NCAA early rounds in 1959—because no team had a home-court edge. Starting with the quarterfinals, all games were played on neutral courts. So picking a probable winner was a risky business. The plain fact was, no team stood out.

Kansas State, with the best record (23-1) at the end of the regular season and a tall, veteran crew, should have rated top preference, except for one key psychological factor that was an important consideration in the upcoming NCAA tournament. Most of the K-Staters had made the trip to Louisville in 1958, and disappointed everyone with two games in which they played the poorest basketball they displayed all season. Coach Tex Winter tried all year to remove this nightmare from the memories of his players. But when the chips were down, in the Midwest Regional championship game, they lost to Cincinnati, 85-75.

K-State had plenty of company. The year's NCAA championship competition became known as the Tournament of Upsets. Never before had so many favored teams been so outrageously trimmed by underdogs. Navy's 76-63 slaughter of North Carolina (20-4) in the very first round started the string of surprises, but it remained for the team that entered the tournament with one of the worst records (16-10), Louisville, to wreck all predictions and national ratings. Even the Cardinals' record was misleading, because, in the matter of success in road games—always the test of a team's poise and ability—they appeared sadly inept. They had lost nine of 11 games away from home.

If ever there was a dark horse, it was Louisville. Despite its mediocre record, the Cardinals proceeded to take apart Eastern Kentucky, 77-63, at Lexington, and then advanced to the Mideast Regionals at Evanston, Illinois, where it continued the rampage over the defending champion, Kentucky, 76-61, and Michigan State, 88-81. Pesky Louisville did some early wobbling against Kentucky—after 10 minutes, the Cards were 15 points behind—and then Michigan State (a 74-69 winner over touted Marquette) until Coach Peck Hickman found the right defense; then outside sharpshooters Don Goldstein and John Turner did the rest, hitting on better than 50 percent of their long-range shots.

Could the Cardinals continue this inspired tear in the final round? The answer was yes, if the amazingly accurate shooting held up; that could demoralize any opponent. The answer was no, if the many sophomores on the team threw the ball away too often.

West Virginia would be Louisville's opponent in the semifinals. Since the NCAA championship playoffs were being staged in Louisville, the home-floor advantage theory would be given a thorough test. West Virginia gained its place in the semifinals on the strength of two outstanding performances by Jerry West in the regionals at Charlotte, North Carolina. Against St. Joseph's he had 36 points and 15 rebounds; against Boston U. he had 33 and 17. And he was his team's best defensive player.

Jerry West was brought up in the family of a coal-mine electrician in the tiny town of Chelyan, West Virginia (pop. 500). From the beginning he displayed the intensity and purposefulness that were to carry him to the heights. As a small boy his mother had to threaten to punish him for sloshing around for hours in the rain on his makeshift backyard basketball court. Years later, at West Virginia, his diet during the season was reduced to bananas and steak. Before a game he often retched into a towel; afterward he would bolt down sleeping pills like an addict, then lie awake all night. He lunged and tumbled after every loose ball, and people used to say that Coach Fred Schaus's assistant, George King, was under strict orders to dive under West any time it looked as if he might fall.

One of Jerry's big problems was depression. He would miss two or three shots and then he would begin to press. He would get down on himself—never on anybody else on the team, or even the officials—but his depressions would last as long as a week or 10 days.

"Once I was really concerned," Schaus recalled. "He'd been moping around for I don't know how long and we had a game with Holy Cross coming up that was going to be on national television. Two days before the game I had George King take him to lunch, but George couldn't find out a thing. When the game started we controlled the tip and quickly got the ball downcourt to Jerry for an easy layup. He missed it. I almost died. Right there on the bench I almost died. I thought we were finished for sure. But then, almost before you knew it, he straightened himself out. I don't remember how many points he scored, but it was plenty and we won. I've since quit worrying about his moods. His high school coach once told me—and it's true—Jerry never had two bad games in a row."

Invariably, when it came time to assay West's rank among the modern All-Americans, the question of his size was discussed. His 6′ 3″, 185 pounds, about average for a backcourt player, was deceiving. What wasn't often taken into consideration was his exceptional wingspread—81 inches from fingertip to fingertip when standing like a crucifix against a wall. Actually, Jerry had the reach of a player 6′ 9″ or 6′ 10″.

In college, West was more or less a one-handed shooter; opposing guards played him a full step to his right. He spent long, lonely hours on the court working out that weakness. He had the quickest shot in the game—it took no more than half a pick to get him free. He moved exceptionally well without the ball. Because of his speed he made everything look rather routine.

After scouting West for the Boston Celtics, Red Auerbach said, "You never really stop him. You try any number of ways—play him close, loose, keep him away from the ball, and even then he'll get his 25 or 30 points. He creates many problems for a defense, and he is very exciting because of the range of his long shot."

There was one intangible that nobody talked much about because it was hard to judge accurately, or even to judge at all. West seemed to have a settling influence on the Mountaineers. He was not a complainer. He did not bait officials. In his seasons at Morgantown, he had not drawn a technical foul.

"But if I were a coach, I'd take Cincinnati's Oscar Robertson," Jerry said honestly. "He's a better passer and a better dribbler. He has bigger hands and his ball handling is superior. He has quicker reactions. He's unbelievable."

In the Midwest Regional final at Lawrence, Kansas, No. 1-ranked K-State, after shooting down DePaul, 102-70, figured it knew how to stop Robertson, who led Cincinnati to a 77-73 victory over Texas Christian. But Oscar had other ideas. Finding himself double-teamed, he turned feeder, passed off for 13 baskets and the Bearcats won by 10 points.

Normally diffident and noncommittal, Robertson was completely unresponsive to re-

"Jerry West never had two bad games in a row," said West Virginia Coach Fred Schaus, shown here.

porters' questions after the game. His only post-game comment was typical: "Well, we won; they lost." Actually, Oscar was naturally a warm and friendly young man and delivered such replies with an engaging smile. He just didn't have anything to say, he said. The game was over and he was already looking ahead to the next contest.

Long before "Roots" made it a national passion, Oscar followed his Indianapolis family's origins in Tennessee all the way back to Africa. He discovered that his forebears had been slaves and that his great-grandfather, before his death at the age of 116, was considered the oldest living American. When he chose to talk about himself, Robertson could be candid. He told a reporter that he'd once been a tough little slum kid who had to be tossed off his high

California's Darrall Imhoff, 1959.

school junior varsity team before he learned to behave.

Oscar grew up to 6' 5" and 195 pounds. That was not an unusual pairing of physical factors, but in him they were so superbly blended and proportioned (and were driven by such a fission-fast nervous system) that he achieved the graceful, swift appearance of a large, lithe cat. In the flat, he appeared to flow like oil over the floor, hunched protectively over the ball as he dribbled; airborne, he hung, magically, for long moments while he decided whether to shoot or pass; in one spot, he was yet in motion, feinting with hands, faking with head, weaving on a pivot. Those skills earned him the national scoring title in 1958 (35.1 points per game) and a total of 984, including 56 points in one game

against Seton Hall at Madison Square Garden—all records. Least noticed but probably most important of all was the fact that he led the Bearcats not only in scoring but in rebounding and assists as well, a combination which reflected his incalculable value as a team player.

But Cincinnati Coach George Smith had a problem. Oscar was a junior and had made it abudantly clear he had learned just about everything he could as a college player. There were rumblings that he was losing interest in his studies. "Statistics, theories of economics," he was heard to complain, with a wave at the books on his desk. "I can't work at that stuff. It *bores* me." He was, it was noted, an excellent student in high school, a fair student in his sophomore year at Cincinnati, and a poor student as a junior in 1959. It took no mind reader to guess that the NCAA championship tournament could very well be Robertson's last games as a collegian.

In the western half of the NCAA draw at Louisville, the irresistible force of the Bearcats were scheduled to meet the immovable object of California's hard-nose defense. To get there, Cal, whose towel-chewing mentor had always gained more satisfaction out of harassing opponents into errors than in smothering them to death with baskets, beat both Utah and St. Mary's. The Bears' constant pressure held both Utah (71-53) and St. Mary's (66-46) to their lowest scores of the season. California finished the regular season as the nation's best defensive team, though in low-scoring, ball-control territory. Darrall Imhoff was the leading rebounder, while his teammates were generally poor on the boards. But Buch and Fitzpatrick formed a strong, good-shooting backcourt combination, and if they got hot, they were devastating. Yet if California fans wanted the truth, the handicappers weren't giving the Bears much chance to go all the way, despite that vaunted defense.

"A good defense is the best offense."

Many a coach had mouthed that saw, but never was it truer than when California played Cincinnati. Pete Newell's well-disciplined Bears, hounding, clinging and never more than a breath's length from their opponents, snared the Bearcats in their switches. Meanwhile, Cal attacked deliberately and cautiously from its slow-down offense. With the score tied and about three and a half minutes to go, the Bears tried desperately to contain Robertson. Suddenly Oscar drove to the baseline, close in to the basket. He went up for his jump shot, and Darrall Imhoff, Cal's baby-faced 6′ 10″ stringbean center, blocked it. On the subsequent critical play, the Bears took plenty of time setting up. Imhoff worked himself clear in a low post position, took the pass and threw in a left-handed hook to put his team ahead, 56-54. There were two minutes to go. Seconds later, Robertson went in for almost the identical shot as before, and Imhoff blocked that one, too. California was ahead to stay and finally won, 64-58. Imhoff was the leading scorer with 22 and his team's top rebounder.

The fact that California's defense held Cincinnati to 58 points (26 under its average) and Robertson to 19 (13½ under his average) did not, actually, tell the whole story. What was significant was that the defense allowed the Bearcats to get off only 56 shots, far below its normal average—not at all the kind of game it liked to play. For their part, the Bears, despite their deliberate offense, took 73 shots in the face of Cincinnati's less-efficient defense. That was the reason they were playing West Virginia for the championship and Cincinnati had to settle for Louisville in the consolation game.

In the other half of the semifinal draw, the free-wheeling Mountaineers caught plucky Louisville with its emotional tanks drained dry and ran the hometown Cardinals into the boards, 94-79. Jerry West, with 38 points, was the major problem. Peck Hickman, the Cardinals' puckish coach, facetiously gave his formula before the game for defending against West: "My boys pick somebody they think they can lick and then tie into him. The poor guy who gets to pick fifth gets stuck with Jerry."

Cal's game with West Virginia was different from its semifinal encounter in one important respect. The Mountaineers nearly matched the Bears with an excellent defensive exhibition of their own, especially a zone press that actually threw the Bears off stride for lengthy periods. This press put two men on the Californian with the ball, but involved a lot of running around by the defenders as the Bears zipped the ball from one side of the floor to the other. Naturally, there was great risk in such a defensive tactic, because it left a Bear free at all times.

For California, the trick was to find the open man; West Virginia had to get to him before he could shoot.

While California's man-to-man defenders managed to slow down the quick Mountaineers to a relative walk, they couldn't stop West, who fed off magnificently and led all scorers with 28 points. Midway in the first half, West Virginia took a 10-point lead. It appeared that the Mountaineers could play the Pacific Coast Conference champion's slow game as well as its own fast one, and win at that, too. But Pete Newell's disciplined charges didn't panic. They stuck to their deliberate offense patterns, moving to options when the set plays were zapped by West Virginia. This tenacity first brought the Bears even and, finally, to the lead. At halftime, the score was 39-33 in favor of Cal.

West Virginia came out for the second half all fired up—perhaps too fired up. High as moonshiners on a Saturday night, the Mountaineers committed a number of foolish turnovers, and California took advantage of every one to go ahead by as much as 13 points. West Virginia went into the zone press, got control of itself, and fought back to within four points several times. But California simply refused to give up.

The score was 69-64 with two minutes left. Here Darrall Imhoff started rising to the occasion. Suddenly, he was a one-man-gang gone wild. Moving with the ponderous gait of a dowager coming down a church aisle, he blocked shots, deflected passes, cleared himself for passes when a teammate with the ball was dangerously close to being tied up by the West Virginia press. He was one vital cog in a well-drilled, disciplined machine.

With 52 seconds to go, Cal's lead was shaved to one point. West Virginia was pressing splendidly, had stolen the ball repeatedly in the previous few minutes, and now it was anybody's game. Then Imhof got the ball near the base line, a good 20 feet from the basket, and tried another hook. It was a poor shot; it rolled around the rim and fell off. But Imhoff somehow recovered, clutched the rebound of his own shot and, while off balance, banked the ball perfectly off the board and through the net. That put the Bears ahead, 71-68, with only 15 seconds left. Being careful not to foul, California conceded a shot and a final basket to West Virginia, and won, 71-70.

Jerry West

Pete Newell had made his point: A good defense wins ball games.

In the consolation game, a more relaxed Cincinnati came back to put down Louisville, 98-85, for third place. Oscar Robertson scored 39 points to lead the nation's major college scorers with a 32.6 average and set an all-time two-season record of 1,962 points. He was so satisfied with himself that he decided then and there to come back the next season and play out his senior year.

WHO OWNS BASKETBALL?
THE SIXTIES

Year of the Buckeyes: 1960

By 1960, college basketball's bursting vitality was in evidence from coast to coast. The evidence: in the past five years, national attendance had increased from 10 million to 15 million; there was a flock of shiny, new arenas; and the number of coaching and player clinics had tripled. But the surest proof of all of how far the game had come was the fact that it was now a major sport at more schools than any other activity. The competition among 1,000-odd college basketball teams for good high school prospects was even matching the mad scramble for football players.

In the test to determine the best college team, California and Ohio State met in San Francisco's Cow Palace in the final round of the 1960 NCAA championships, March 19. Billed as one of the classic patterns in sport, the game reminded oldtimers of the Tunney vs. Dempsey heavyweight fight: boxer versus slugger, great defense opposing great offense.

California led the nation in containing rival scoring; Ohio State led in points per game. The scouting report on the Bears revealed: "Overwhelming board control by Darrall Imhoff and Bill McClintock plus traditionally tight Coach Pete Newell defense limits rival to a minimum of shots. Deliberate offense works so well because scoring power is spread through squad." On the other hand, the Buckeyes were big, fast, deep and deadly accurate shots, hitting close to 50 percent on field goals, the nation's top scorers. "Powerful on the boards," reported one scout, "leading to fast breaks that stun rivals. Has 20-point-average margin over all opponents this year."

Logically enough, the California and Ohio State playing styles were completely different.

The Bears used their rebounding power to upset their rivals by forcing them to play at California's deliberate tempo. Ohio State used its excellent control of the backboards to fast-break endlessly, destroying the opposition's defense by simply running away from it. Both teams had individual stars—Imhoff at Cal, Jerry Lucas at Ohio State—but their court styles placed great reliance on team play. Skill and confidence ran deep in both squads.

California, 24-1 during the regular season, was a veteran crew, coached again by the wily Newell. Ohio State, 21-3, was largely a sophomore team, coached by young Fred Taylor, in his second season in major college basketball. From every angle, and whoever won, it was bound to be an exciting final contest. The vast majority of expert opinion favored California, first because the Bears had a great stake in the outcome as defending champion and, second, because Coach Newell had a genius for instilling self-discipline in his athletes—and this was an especially valuable asset in the pressure of tournament basketball.

"And yet," hedged one reporter, "California might indeed be the better of the two teams and still lose this one game."

The plausibility of such an upset jammed the Cow Palace.

To earn the right to play Ohio State, Cal was forced to beat Cincinnati in a down-to-the-wire semifinal thriller the night before. Led by superstar Oscar Roberston, Cincinnati (25-1) arrived in San Francisco determined to reverse its defeat at the hands of this same California team in 1959 at the very same stage of the NCAA tournament—the semifinal round. Cincy brought its school band and hundreds of home-

Ohio State's Jerry Lucas, 6' 8", 230 lb. center, seemed to have springs in his legs. During his rein at Columbus, the Buckeyes won three Big Ten titles, one NCAA crown, and twice were runnersup in the national tournament while winning 78 of 84 games.

town followers, and Big O and his teammates tore into the Bears with gusto. They had a basket within five seconds, another shortly thereafter, and with nine and a half minutes gone, they had a nine-point lead, 20-11.

There was nothing wrong with California's defense; it was working well. The Bears stole the ball repeatedly and then missed the easy layups. They made all their points on difficult shots after careful execution of set plays. They managed to contain Robertson—he didn't score his first field goal until two minutes before the end of the half—but his sharp passing accounted for most of Cincinnati's points.

Just before intermission, the California defense began to pay off; then they caught and passed Cincinnati and left the floor ahead, 34-

30. It was hardly a lead large enough to calm the nerves. Cal still had a rude jolt coming.

After play resumed, Cincinnati refused to crack despite Cal's continued defensive pressure. With a minute and a half to go, Cal led by only three points. Here Cincinnati made a series of costly errors that led to two quick baskets by Earl Schultz, the Cal guard, and that was the ballgame. Cal won, 77-69, plainly a victory for defensive basketball. The ability to force Cincinnati into mistakes in ballhandling had saved the day.

In the other 1960 semifinal contest, Ohio State had an easy time beating New York University, 76-54. The Buckeyes impressed few witnesses that night, because NYU was terribly tense throughout the game and definitely out of its class. The next morning, most of the experts were certain that California would have little trouble in beating Ohio State.

In the Cow Palace that Saturday night, however, Ohio State surprised just about everybody, including the oddsmakers who had made California the favorite by five points. Few had considered the hard facts. Only three teams had beaten Ohio State in 1960—all on the road—and each victor was obliged to score a minimum of 96 points and, on two occasions, make better than 53 percent of its shots. The Bucks were a tall, rugged bunch of native Ohioans who had been playing basketball since elementary school days. They were patient, poised veterans, though several of the best were still only sophomores, and they were intelligently coached by youthful Fred Taylor.

At this stage of his development, Jerry Lucas was an agile, nerveless kid of 19 who played 40 minutes of every game without changing his deadpan expression. He seldom made a mistake. When his team took off on a fast-break downcourt, as it did at every opportunity, Lucas trailed the leader and always managed to be hovering around the rim of the basket to stuff in the shot if it missed. On a team that boasted a flock of fine shooters, he was uncommonly accurate, with a delicately soft shooting touch.

Jerry Lucas was an exceptional young man. He was about as good as they came, both at basketball and in the classroom. In a vintage year for new basketball talent, a lot of people felt he was the best of the crop, highly skilled at every facet of the game though he was only a sophomore. He ranked among the top five in scoring, rebounding and field-goal shooting, and he was the principal reason why Ohio State was a leader in all three departments. At the same time, he averaged a shade under straight A in OSU's College of Commerce, which was something of a comedown for him after being an A student for four years in high school. In his freshman year at Columbus he carried 49 credit hours, far more than normal, and earned 42 hours of A's.

"I was always interested in my classwork," Lucas said. "Before I started first grade I already knew third-grade arithmetic, because my parents had taught me, and from then on I wanted to get good grades."

His attitude toward studies was the reason Lucas chose Ohio State over the more than 150 other colleges that were after him while he was still at Middletown, Ohio High School. He said that Ohio State was the only school that talked to him first about his education. "All the others talked only about basketball," he said. "They didn't understand that I didn't want an athletic scholarship anyway. I wanted an academic scholarship, and that's what I got." So no matter what happened—even if he hadn't made the team—he still got his education. That was the way he wanted it.

From the fifth grade on—in more than 125 games in elementary school, junior high and high school—Jerry participated exactly once in a losing effort, and that was a one-point loss in the last game of his high school career.

In his career under the teachings of an excellent high school coach, Paul Walker, at Middletown, Jerry scored 2,460 points, breaking the national record of 2,252 set by Wilt Chamberlain at Philadelphia's Overbrook High.

Lucas went to Ohio State with so much basketball experience behind him that he didn't suffer at all from the Big Ten ruling which forbade inter-school competition by freshmen. He led the Buckeye frosh team to a number of victories over the varsity in practice games, and scored 92 points in the last two of the season. Fred Taylor, the varsity coach, could hardly wait to build an attack around Jerry, and so he didn't. "We planned our varsity offense around Jerry even though he was still a freshman," Taylor admitted later. "We put in the whole kit and kaboodle. The boys learned the offense just

Two reasons why Ohio State won most of its games in the early 1960s were Larry Siegfried, left, and Mel Nowell.

the way we were going to play it with Lucas in 1960."

Lucas was chosen on one All-American team before he had even played his first varsity game. In a tough December schedule that started out with four games in seven nights and included five road games against first-rank teams, Jerry sank shots at a .612 average. He made 50 of 63 free throws, including 25 in a row. He had 158 rebounds for an average of 17.5, and scored 252 points for a 28-point average. Against Kentucky he awed the basketball-wise Lexington crowd with his remarkable selection of shots, most of which were not guardable. He hooked accurately with both hands, took a full-spin one-handed jumper and drove well. A sequence of shots in the Kentucky game included a tip-in on a follow-up, a spin from the circle, another spin, a hook from the side, and a driving layup. In the pivot he handed off with precision to cutting guards Larry Siegfried or Mel Nowell, often merely opening his hands and dropping the ball into perfect position for them as they scooted by and under him. Against a zone defense which double-teamed him, his feints repeatedly drew defenders away from the ball, leaving one of his forwards (Joe Roberts, John Havlicek or Dick Furry) free for a shot. And if the shooter missed, Lucas was usually there for the tip.

If there was a soft spot in Jerry's game it was on defense, though he had far outclassed every pivotman he had faced all year with the exception of Utah's fine 6'9" sophomore, Billy McGill, who had hit for 31 points against him earlier in the season. Now it was going to be Lucas' task, in the championship game against California, to guard All-American Darrall Imhoff, who had scored 25 points against Cincinnati in the semifinal round.

Lucas showed right at the start that he was equal to it.

California began poorly, as it had done against Cincinnati. The Bears conceded two quick baskets and was soon behind, 18-8. Lucas gave Imhoff room only when he was far away from the basket; in close, he was always between Imhoff and the ball. Actually, every one of the Ohio State players was beating Cal at Cal's own game—defense—at the same time the Buckeyes were on the way to a fantastic shooting percentage. In the first half, Ohio State took 19 shots and scored on 16. Lucas hit five out of six; Joe Roberts, Mel Nowell and Larry Siegfried sank all nine of their attempts. The team percentage was an amazing .842. California's was .296. The halftime score was Ohio State 37, Cal 19.

Still, very few in the noisy capacity audience of California partisans were ready to throw in the towel. Cal had a reputation for coming out for a second half far behind, and its persistence in forcing rival errors had brought victory.

Pete Newell sent the Bears back into play with a crushing press defense, and within five minutes had narrowed the gap to 42-29. Perhaps their come-from-behind breakthrough was at hand after all. But the press proved to be Cal's undoing. Converging on the Ohio State man with the ball, Cal was forced to uncover a free man somewhere, and after a brief period of adjustment the boys from Columbus began to find him. Several furiously fast scoring breaks with more than five minutes still to be played sent the Bears back to Berkeley as losers. When

the smoke had cleared, the Buckeyes' shooting percentage was still an incredible .767.

There was no longer any doubt about which was No. 1, and Fred Taylor started sending in his substitutes freely. The reserves had little difficulty holding Ohio State's 20-point spread, and the Big Ten champions won, 75-55.

Not only did Ohio State demonstrate it had a firepower, it also proved it knew how to handle itself when the other team had the ball. Unwilling to concede a good shot, State choked off the Cal attack to such a degree that it finished the night with a .339 shooting percentage.

Afterwards, Newell, who was retiring from coaching to be Cal's athletic director, refused to offer any excuses for his team's poor showing. One sympathetic San Francisco reporter suggested that maybe the tough Cincinnati game had taken something out of the Cal players. No, said Newell, Ohio State had also played the night before. Well, then, the reporter said, wasn't so-and-so's leg bothering him, and wasn't so-and-so fighting a cold? No, no, no, said Newell. California was beaten by a fine team. "You have to give Coach Taylor the credit."

It was a typical news conference performance by the honest, gracious Pete Newell. Across the Cow Palace in Ohio State's dressing room Fred Taylor was equally gracious in victory. He told the press how the summer before he had gone to Newell for some coaching tips. He pointed out that his 1959 Buckeyes had the worst defensive record in Ohio State's history. He had to do something, he said, and he knew that Newell was the best in the business at teaching defense. So he asked Pete to help him and Pete did. "He showed me everything," Taylor said. "He confirmed some of my ideas, and he gave me the courage to try things I was afraid were too radical. Last season, our boys couldn't have caught Marilyn Monroe in a phone booth. Now look at them."

Fred Taylor confessed that he borrowed many of Pete Newell's ideas. And on the evening of March 19, 1960, they paid off for Ohio State . . . against Pete Newell.

Cincinnati's Oscar Robertson, possessor of more baskets (1,052) and more points (2,973) than any other major college player in history, led the nation in scoring for the third straight year. The Big O piled up 1,011 points in 30 games for a 33.7 average.

This was the collegiate Oscar Robertson of 1960, Cincinnati's three-time national scoring leader.

Other 1960 statistical champions included Jerry Lucas, field goal shooting, 283 for 443 and 63.8 percent; Xavier's Billy Kirvin, foul shooting, 78 for 89 and 87.6 percent; College of Pacific's Leroy Wright (for the second time), rebounding, 380 in 17 games for 22.3 average; team offense—Ohio State, 2,532 points in 28 games for 90.4 average; team defense—California, 1,486 points in 30 games for 49.5 average.

High and Mighty Cincinnati: 1961

After 14 weeks of competition, closing with an ugly scandal that threatened to wreck college basketball for the second time in 10 years, the 1961 season ended with Cincinnati's streaking Bearcats successfully disposing of the notion that they were nothing without the Big O, who had graduated.

When 504 basketball coaches arrived in Kansas City in late March for their annual convention and the game's national championship, they were treated to the most memorable basketball doubleheader ever played in a national tournament.

The teams involved were Cincinnati, Utah, St. Joseph's and "unbeatable" Ohio State.

The program began at 7 p.m., and by the time it ended nearly five hours later the 10,700 limp patrons in the K.C. concrete Municipal Auditorium not only had seen a consolation round first game that went to four overtimes, but had witnessed a nervy bunch of underdog Bearcats outfight, outplay and eventually outscore Ohio State, the heretofore nonpareil of college teams.

The Buckeyes arrived in Kansas City with a string of 31 consecutive victories over the past two years, and as the defending national champions, their greatest strength was their unemotional-as-a-machine composure. They always played as if the thought of losing had never occurred to them. Even when they trailed patched-up Iowa, 59-52, with only 3:36 to go, they didn't lose their poise. For more than 36 minutes the Hawkeyes, minus four starters through academic deficiencies, had out-rebounded, out-shot and out-hustled the unbeaten Bucks while 13,500 feet-stamping Iowa fans howled for the kill at Iowa City. Don Nel-

son, Iowa's sharpshooting forward who scored 27 points, had been more than a match for OSU's Jerry Lucas, who scored 25. Then, with time running out, obstinate Ohio State turned to their half-court press, pulled off four quick steals for 10 straight points, the last four by Larry Siegfried and sub Gary Gearhart, and subdued the Hawkeyes, 62-61. Fred Taylor, the Ohio State coach, was obviously shaken by the close call. "They just grabbed us off our feet," was all he could say.

In Jerry Lucas the team had one of the very best basketball players of the era. When opponents attempted to double- or triple-team him, captain Larry Siegfried and Mel Nowell would shoot from outside,—where they averaged nearly 50 percent of their field-goal attempts. Lucas, himself, was one of the highest scorers in the country. He could have been at the top if he elected to shoot more baskets, but he preferred to share honors with his teammates. He threw the ball to them more often than at the hoop.

On defense Ohio State had John Havlicek, a onetime high school quarterback who was as smooth as Johnny Unitas and as tough as Bobby Layne. He always guarded the opposition's toughest man and usually stopped him cold. Havlicek was an athlete in the Walt Whitman sense. He was in many ways the heart and soul of the Ohioans. John was as dependable as Arizona sunrise. "I used to pray in a tight game they'd give him the ball," Fred Taylor often said. Havlicek seldom had moods. He seldom threw a shoe or pounded a locker. He was "Mr. Clutch" and "Ole Reliable" and "Mr. Endurance" all rolled up into one. While Lucas, Siegfried and Nowell drew most of the newspaper attention, it was the indefatigable Havlicek that drove the Buckeyes to the astonishing record of 78 victories in 84 games during his varsity career.

Larry Siegfried was the only exception to Ohio State's peaceful aplomb. Coach Taylor called him a "role player." Larry often would wave his arms, telling the team what the defense was and moving men around like pieces on a chess board. This despite the fact that his alert teammates had already recognized the defense, but Siegfried was showing the house he was captain. When Lucas began putting inner soles in his shoes so did Siegfried. Lucas wore his sweat pants when introduced before a game. So did Siegfried. When forward Rickie Hoyt was hampered by an arthritic condition and started wearing a corset, Siegfried asked the trainer for a special hip pad. But if Siegfried was something of an actor, he was also a magnificent all-around basketball player.

Credit for Ohio State's workmanlike attitude went, of course, to Coach Taylor. Despite his youth (34), he had just been named Coach of the Year for the second straight year. A season of having every opponent point for his team had left him tired and tense. But it hadn't marred the color of his speech. "A real barn-burner," he said when his team beat Louisville by a single point, 56-55, in the NCAA regional tournament at Louisville.

With a trip to the final rounds of the national championship in Kansas City at stake, Man o' War could have raced eight furlongs down Walnut Street with Lady Godiva up and gone unnoticed in Louisville. Tickets selling for as much as $30 each had been impossible to get for two weeks, largely because three Kentucky schools, Louisville, Morehead State and Kentucky, were bunched in the regional with Ohio State. Meanwhile, thousands of fans had come into town from Columbus, with their own bands, their own bottles and their own certainty Ohio State could defeat any team from Kentucky.

On opening night, Friday, Louisville caught the defending champions cold. They crowded three men around Lucas. The Buckeyes were so shaky they could only hit one outside shot in the first 20 minutes, and Louisville had a 5-point lead with three minutes to play. That should have been enough. But a jump shot, a stolen pass, and a three-point play by Ohio

State tied the score. Then, with less than a minute to play, handsome John Turner, with 24 points to his and Louisville's credit, bounced the ball off his toe. Ohio State came up with it, and when an emergency scoring play failed, Havlicek—Mr. Clutch—improvised a 20-footer with six seconds left. Refusing to quit, John Turner had two foul shots with one second to go, and saw the tying point roll off the rim as Ohio State won.

Held to nine points, his lowest total since grammar school, Lucas had also made nine errors. "I was guarded so tightly I felt like I was in jail," he said.

Lucas had his freedom the following night, however, as he made 14 of 18 field-goal tries, scored 33 points and captured a rousing 30 rebounds to lead his team to an 87-74 win over Kentucky. Adolph Rupp, the master strategist, had his team play its classic man-to-man defense, but two men fouled out trying to cope with Lucas.

"That team," said Rupp, "is truly great. They're going all the way."

Coach Taylor, still concerned over the way his team played against Louisville, took the Buckeyes back to Columbus for three days of furious and exhausting practice. "Now they're head-hunting again," he reported afterward.

When the season began, Missouri Valley fans just about conceded the title to powerful Bradley. But as the year wore on, it became more and more apparent that defending champion Cincinnati, even without Oscar Robertson, was the team to beat. Oscar had been succeeded by Tom Thacker, a brilliant 6' 2" sophomore who moved swiftly, shot skillfully, defended well and was equally at home in front court or backcourt. Late in the season, Thacker scored 22 points, including the winning basket with eight seconds to go, and Cincinnati upset first-place Bradley, 73-72.

In the NCAA regionals at Lawrence, both Cincinnati and Kansas State had no trouble beating Texas Tech and Houston respectively on the first night, and their game against each other appeared to revolve around Cincinnati's 6' 9" Center Paul Hogue, who resembled a large oak tree that had been granted the power to move—fast.

But Hogue fouled too much. Ed Jucker, the Cincinnati coach, figured he was beaten if he had to bench Hogue, and Kansas State Coach

Cincinnati's 6' 9" Center Paul Hogue resembled a large oak tree that had been granted the power to jump to the moon and move—fast. He was the NCAA tournament's MVP in 1961.

Tex Winter thought he would have a good chance if his team stopped Hogue. Both were wrong. Trailing, Cincinnati was forced to bench Hogue when he got his fourth foul as the second half started. In came a sub, but Cincinnati continued to control the boards, finally caught Kansas State with 10 minutes left and went on to win, 69-64. It was Cincinnati's 20th straight win, thanks as usual to its tenacious defense.

Defense had nothing to do with determining the winner at the Portland, Oregon regionals. Utah, given a big lift by 6' 9" center Billy McGill, did what it had been doing all season—exhausting an opponent with its fast-break attack and then romping to an easy victory. The Utes did it against Loyola of Los Angeles, 91-75, and against surprising Arizona State, 88-80. The latter had pulled the Western tournament's biggest upset by soundly thrashing Southern California, 86-71.

The four teams going to Kansas City to fight it out for the NCAA championship had an intriguing combination of traits and talents. Ohio State and Utah had superb offenses with fast, accurate attacks and ranked second and third nationally, with shooting percentages of .495 and .494. Cincinnati and St. Joseph's had more deliberate—and less effective—offenses, but Cincinnati had its defense and St. Joseph's had that tournament intangible: the role of underdog with nothing to lose.

Louisville proved that Ohio State could be cut down, but St. Joseph's, which played the Buckeyes in the semi-final, was not the squad to do it. In Jack Egan the team had a very good jump shot, but the guards were too short at 5' 8" and 6' to handle 6' 4" Larry Siegfried and 6' 2" Mel Nowell, nor did St. Joseph's have the height in the front court to try Louisville's gamble of putting three men around Lucas.

In the small dark hours of the night before playing Ohio State, Jack Ramsay, the balding, insomniac St. Joseph's coach, had a nightmare. He pictured himself standing on the bench shouting for time out, but nobody would stop the game. That's about the way it turned out the next night, too. His team played poorly, and Ohio State won, 95-69.

A clue to what was in the offing in the finals came in the second game of the semifinals when Utah was harassed to death by the magnificent Cincinnati defense. This Cincinnati defense was the most baffling and surprising basketball development of 1961. For the previous two seasons Cincinnati had been expected to win an NCAA crown with its one-man team, the Big O, only to come up short in the semis each time. Now, in 1961, Ed Jucker, in his first year as head coach after seven years as an assistant, made an important change. He got rid of the traditional run-and-shoot style of Cincinnati basketball and replaced it with a controlled offense and a tight defense. Instead of using one man he used all that the rules allowed—five. The switch took time and patience. Cincinnati lost three of its first eight contests, one by 17 points to St. Louis. The one-sided defeat alarmed Coach Jucker so much that he called his players together.

"You guys can still win the conference championship if you get tough," he told them. After a loss to Bradley, they got tough, indeed, and won 20 in a row.

Bob Wiesenhahn, 220 pounds of raw muscle who averaged 10 rebounds a game, was the toughest Bearcat of them all. He got help from the even more noticeable Paul Hogue. With this pair on the floor at the same time, the Bearcats were outrebounded only once that season. In addition, Cincinnati had Carl Bouldin and Tony Yates, whom one rival coach called "the finest pair of guards I've ever seen on the same team."

Coach Jucker was obviously sky-high when his stingy defense made a shambles of Utah's vaunted fast break and won easily, 82-67.

"Just one more," roared the Bearcats in their dressing room after the game.

By contrast, Ohio State's quarters after the St. Joseph's game were quiet and businesslike. They discussed plays and strategy for the championship showdown and then soberly walked back to their hotel.

On the following afternoon, Fred Taylor gave the team its scouting report on Cincinnati. In his instructions he pointed out that much of Cincinnati's success was credited to rebounding, especially by Hogue and Wiesenhahn, who bombed the offensive boards and were not unwilling to push and shove to get up over opponents.

"Hogue is a bit reckless with his ability as a duke man," Taylor wrote in his report. "Make him foul."

All season, Cincinnati had lived like a man on the edge of a cliff because of Hogue's fouling. He got in two scuffles in the Utah game. Now he was going to face Ohio State—just the driving offense to force Hogue to foul.

By game time, Ohio State, with no mean defense of its own, was a solid favorite. It looked like wise old Adolph Rupp was right: OSU all the way.

St. Joseph's required two and a half hours and four overtimes to beat Utah, 127-120, in the consolation game. The fans had barely settled back in their seats from that breathtaking contest when the championship game began. In a very few minutes Cincinnati let everybody know that this was going to be a game to remember, too.

Jerry Lucas, playing a whale of a game for Ohio State, was forced to station himself 15 feet from the basket to be effective. He kept OSU in the game by hitting one-handers from there, but the Bearcats kept the rest of the Buckeye offense bottled up and looking strained and slow. Cincinnati maintained reasonable control of the backboards, took only the best shots and forced the game into a pattern they liked—a grudging defensive battle. Ohio State had been accustomed to testing an opponent's weaknesses and traits early in a game, but now their plays were failing as Cincinnati made use of a special strategy of switching defensive assignments.

Despite their frustration, the Buckeyes led at halftime, 39-38. It was, in the phraseology of Fred Taylor, "a real barn-burner."

In the second half, both the Bearcats and Buckeyes showed their poise under pressure. With 11 minutes to go, Cincinnati forged to the front by six points on five jump shots by Carl Bouldin, whom Taylor noted in his scouting report as the team's "best outside shooter."

Ohio State stormed back to go ahead by five, only to lose the lead again before the regulation game ended 61-61. In the overtime, Cincinnati quickly went ahead and didn't give OSU an opportunity to get even. The final numbers were 70-65, and Cincinnati was the new NCAA champion in a truly amazing upset.

"It was a beautiful basketball game, played by both teams with the pure poise and aggressiveness that the sport demands at its finest," remarked *Sports Illustrated*'s Ray Cave afterward. "A champion had been beaten, but by no fluke."

There was no second-guessing or sour grapes,

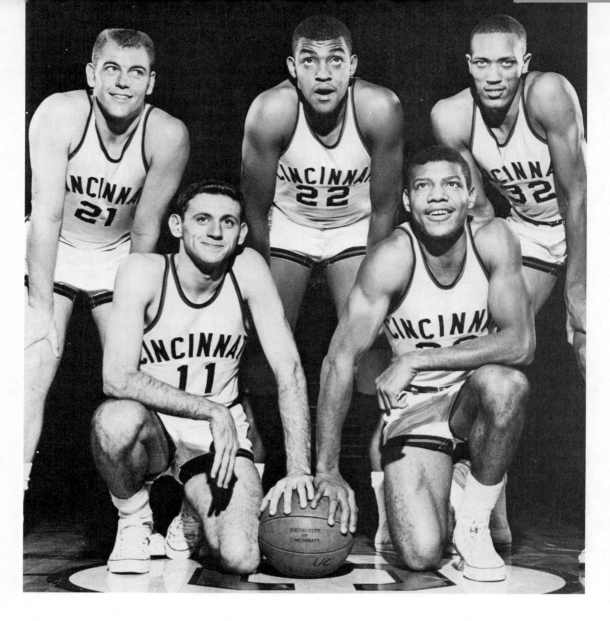

Cincinnati's 1961 national championship starting five (top left, clockwise): Ron Bonham, Paul Hogue, George Wilson, Tony Yates and Larry Shingleton.

because there was simply nothing to second guess. Cincinnati had come into the game with its new style of basketball and made it work to perfection. It had run its offense carefully, making adjustments quickly when OSU changed its defenses. When Bouldin made his five straight crucial baskets from outside, for example, Siegfried was forced to stop helping guard Hogue and to concentrate on his own man, Bouldin. This left Hogue more open and Bouldin began at once to pass the ball to him.

After being charged with four charging fouls early in the contest, the Bearcats didn't make another after they saw how closely the referees were calling that particular violation. They made only two other errors that cost them possession of the ball before they could shoot, compared to 11 for Ohio State.

While Lucas managed to get 27 points, the Cincinnati defense forced the normally fast Buckeye offense to become overly cautious, averaging only a shot a minute through the second half and the overtime.

The trophies were awarded immediately after the game, and battler Larry Siegfried, unaccustomed to second place, mirrored his personality with his reaction. He threw a towel over his head to hide himself from the crowd, and cried.

Bribery, Fraud, and Prison Bars: 1961

The ink on the court orders committing college basketball talent to prison was hardly dry when Dr. Phog Allen again raised the storm warnings on gambling. All during the latter part of the 1950's, even after retirement, he kept hammering away on the subject, telling of an attempt by a "big cigar" to fix the referee of certain games in the Midwest. (The referee denied it.) Nevertheless, Phog thundered on.

"The same guys that used to be in this ugly business are back in it," Allen said. "They're just a little more coy and careful now. And there are teams right now that are in business for themselves, and nobody else."

Before he bowed out, Dr. Allen said he wanted to see his college brethren appoint an athletic czar to police such evils as gambling. "Unless we have better enforcement," he warned, "some more fine American kids are going to be dragged into the slime." Not that the good doctor believed in coddling athletes; after all, when he was coaching he sometimes got his teams in the right mood for a game by showing them movies of a mongoose and a cobra fighting to the death.

For the second time in 10 years, bribery and fraud once more shook college basketball. True to Dr. Allen's warnings, news of the latest wave of fixes broke into headlines in late March, 1961. Actually, Scandals II was six months in the making.

It all began to unfold when New York City detectives were sent down to the University of North Carolina to bring back several athletes for questioning. Within days it developed that three students at the University of Connecticut had also been questioned. According to the po-lice report, they were members of the basketball and football teams.

The office of New York District Attorney Frank Hogan had been investigating college basketball for two years, but work on this specific case began on September 24, 1961. That was the day a New York gambler named Aaron Wagman was arrested in Florida after trying to bribe a University of Florida player to fix a football game. Wagman was released on $20,000 bail but was put under surveillance. He led the detectives all over the country until the scope of his operation became clear.

Wagman rarely dealt directly with the athletes he bribed. He had "contact men," nearly always fellow students of the athletes, on a dozen campuses. Such a student would call Wagman in New York when he and the player were ready to fix a game. Wagman, who had little working capital, would then go to a big-time gambler and borrow enough money to pay the bribes involved and to make his own bets. Wagman then sent $2,000 to his contact man, to be split evenly between him and the player. The player was also instructed to act out an agreed-upon signal just before the game started—say, bending over and tying his left sneaker—as final evidence that everything was set. By that time, Wagman and his gambler friend would have their bets down.

Some players indicted for dumping made little secret of it. Why, they even boasted that they were selling their skills to gamblers. There was one young fellow who agreed to take money for shaving points but found out later that the point spread was so slim he would actually have to throw the game to live up to his agreement. He discovered this too late to make telephone contact with his gambler. So he waited until he could meet him.

The meeting took place right on the basketball court as the player was warming up. While he took his practice shots, he spotted his man. "Hey," the player shouted. "I'm not dumping!" His teammates wheeled around. Then they began shooting again. Nobody spoke to him about it. "Hell, I wasn't worried," the player said later. "Not then anyway. I thought everybody on the team was doing business."

To understand how the betting took place, assume that the game Aaron Wagman fixed was between Team A and Team B. Team A was favored to win by 10 points. That meant bookies would accept your bet if you thought Team A would win by more than 10 points. Wagman had told his bribed player, on Team B, that his team must lose by at least 15 points. Therefore he could bet on Team A, giving 10 points.

As the money Wagman and his gambler friend bet on Team A poured in, the bookies would alter the line to protect themselves. Team A would become an 11-point favorite, then 12, then 13, until the bookies took the game "off the boards," which meant they would take no more bets. Wagman had made bets at all the point spreads. If the fix worked, as it usually did, he won them all.

The New York detectives were just completing their case against Wagman and another fixer named Joseph Hacken when they discovered something that forced them to act quickly. Wagman had applied for a passport, was obviously preparing to leave the country.

They arrested Wagman and Hacken immediately. At that time they had solid cases on only a few fixed games and bribed players. A player at the University of Connecticut took $750 to blow a Colgate game. At State College, Mississippi, a Mississippi State player took $1,500 to blow a game to Ole Miss. In Philadelphia, a La Salle player was to get $1,250 for messing up a game against Duquesne, but he didn't play that night and they gave him $750 for solace. Down at Chapel Hill, North Carolina, a member of the University of North Carolina team took just $75 as introduction money, but once he had it in his pocket he was through.

The scandal touched other places, too—the University of Detroit, and Tennessee, and St. Joseph's of Philadelphia. The story always was the same. Kids went for money and they went for it quickly and easily. The number who turned it down was small. The number who took it and weren't caught was staggering.

One solid case was Wagman's fix of the Connecticut-Colgate game played at Hamilton, New York. The other was Hacken's fix of a Seton Hall-Dayton game played in Madison Square Garden. Two Seton Hall players had agreed to lose the Dayton game by more than the six-point spread. They did; Seton Hall lost by 35 points.

There was an important difference between the Wagman-Hacken techniques and those used to fix games in 1951. Then the fixers and gamblers decided precisely which games would be manipulated and gave the orders to their bribed players. Wagman, contrarily, sat back and waited for one of his contact men to call. The contact man, in turn, waited for the player to come to him and say that he wanted to pick up some quick cash. This assured Wagman that any fix arrangement would be entered into eagerly and that he could count on a full "effort" by the player.

Wagman and Hacken worked independently of each other, as did a number of other fixers who were later arrested, but they exchanged information, and occasionally doublecrossed each other. Though both borrowed to finance their deals, neither was a small-time operator. They were the master technicians; they had the apparatus that made the fixes work.

Once the New York district attorney's men sensed it was 1951 all over again, it was a simple thing for them to figure out what was going on. So the check began. Wagman and Hacken and some of their contacts were questioned by New York authorities.

"We broke the thing open in the questioning," a DA's man said. "One of them told us everything. All we had to do was start working. We wound up with a list of players a foot long. We started calling them in. Two players from Seton Hall. Then one from Connecticut. Then another from NYU. They gave us information against Hacken and Wagman and the rest of them. That took care of the case."

With the previous scandals still fresh in everyone's mind, it was shocking that college athletes would yield to the temptation of a fast and easy buck. But the reasons were plain to any sophisticated observer. When a college used all manner of sly and under-the-table inducements to recruit a player, when it allowed him to slide through school on a ridiculously easy academic schedule, when alumni slipped him the money, bought him clothes and generally fawned on him to keep him happy, when, in short, a player realized that everyone around him was winking at the rules of proper behavior, he was prepared to take further steps in the wrong direction. As a matter of fact, by accepting the blandishments of college and alumni, he was already committed to wrongdoing—the only question remaining was how far he felt he could safely go along the path. Those players who accepted the bribes of gamblers obviously felt that shaving points was safe enough.

It was just as obvious that much of this corrupting atmosphere could be swept away by strict enforcement of recruiting rules and elimination of academic double standards—one for athletes, one for other students.

In a strong editorial, *Sports Illustrated* stated: "College athletics demand closer supervision. The NCAA, like supervisory bodies in various pro sports, should have a security arm whose members are perpetually on the lookout for possible trouble. The mere common knowledge that such a security force exists would have an inhibiting effect on youngsters tempted by an easy dollar . . ."

North Carolina State's Everett Case, who was generally credited with bringing big-time basketball to the Atlantic Coast Conference area by recruiting out-of-state players in 1946, decided that "New York talent" was responsible for all the crookedness. Two of his players charged with taking bribes were from Brooklyn, the third from Louisville, Kentucky.

"Maybe the sense of values of New York boys is all screwed up," he said at the time. "I don't know, but the North Carolina boys would certainly be loyal."

The *New York Herald-Tribune*'s Red Smith sprung to the defense of his town's basketball flesh.

"The poor, bewildered, unreasoning, mixed-up guy," he wrote of Coach Case. "After a lifetime in the dream-world of children's games, he has been hit in the eye by a fact and he doesn't know how to face up to it. He's got integrity confused with geography. If the sense of values of some New York boys is screwed up, not to mention some boys from Louisville and some from Philadelphia and some from Connecticut, then the important question is how it got that way. What standards of behavior do these young men have, and where did they acquire them?"

Smith pointed out that most kids of college age are idealists. "Any bonafide undergraduate—from the sandhills of Carolina or the streets of New York or the badlands of Dakota—who goes out for the team and makes it will play as well and honestly as he can for his personal satisfaction," Smith wrote. "He also plays for the good opinion of his schoolmates and for the honor of the school. He will, as Case says, be loyal. Anything else would be unthinkable.

"It is not the [young man's] fault that he is indoctrinated in a different code. Starting in his impressionable high school days, older and presumably responsible men representing reputable institutions have reminded him that he has something for sale, that his athletic skills have a cash value. 'You're a chump if you don't take the best bid,' the recruiters tell him, again and again. The same men who have hammered this cynical philosophy home are shocked when the kid accepts a higher bid from some punk named, say, Aaron Wagman. They wonder where the corruption started. Don't they realize that a boy who can be bribed to shoot baskets can also be bribed to miss them, if the price is right?"

Carolina high schools, Case said, did not produce the polished basketball players that had been coming to college from other regions. This, he explained inferentially, was why he had gone outside the state for his material. Now he was disillusioned.

"The recruiting is too vicious," he said. "The rivalry is too vicious. We're so close together in this state, and everybody wants to win . . . Basketball is meant to be a game. Down here it has turned into a war. I'm ready for a truce."

"After 15 years, he ought to know," Red Smith said. "Yet does he? He seeks refuge and solace in the Case Law: you can take the boy out of the city but you can't take the city out of the boy. He does not seem to realize that the seeds of corruption grow as readily in red clay as in asphalt."

In March of 1960, for example, New York

NYU's Ray Paprocky loses the ball (right).

University flew down to Charlotte, North Carolina, to face West Virginia in the opening game of a two-night program which would send the winner out to Los Angeles for the NCAA championship round. It was a tremendous game. The game ended with Jerry West of West Virginia driving toward the basket in a man-to-man, shoulder-against-chest duel with Tom "Satch" Sanders of NYU. This was in overtime and NYU had a one-point lead. Here came West, on the left side, and here was Sanders on him and then at the last second, just as West was going to try and shoot over Sanders' hands, Ray Paprocky of NYU cut across from under the basket and he went up, too, and now West could see nothing and he had to throw the shot up blind and he missed.

New York University was to play Duke the next night. The afternoon of the game, one of the New York writers called Manhattan to get the price on the game.

"What's doing?" he said to the bookmaker.

"Nothing," the bookmaker said. "That Sanders is too good for them kids, isn't he?"

"Yes. Is anybody making a move on the games?"

"Just normal stuff. Nothing's going on with these big games."

Now this was a big bookmaker, a guy who had been around for years. He should have known everything. But he didn't know the NYU game of the night before had been bought and paid for as a dump, but that the dump hadn't come off. The bookie didn't know anything about it. It gives you an idea of what the DA's men were up against trying to break open the scandal.

New York University beat Duke easily the next night and after the game there was a party. While everybody was around Lou Rossini, NYU's fine coach, and talking about how his team won, Bob Quincy, the sports editor of the Charlotte *News*, came over to have a drink and talk.

"We got a mess down here," he said quietly. "There's been something the matter here all season long. I just can't get at it yet. The state bureau of investigation is on it. They won't tell me anything. If you happen to hear anything up North you let me know and if I hear anything down here I'll let you know. Sure as we're standing here, there's trouble."

Among those from the New York press in attendance was Jimmy Breslin. The next morning he got on the plane back to New York and for a while during the trip he sat with a young man who was on the way to making a fine name for himself as a member of the NYU team. With a little work on his outside shot, scouts regarded him as a stout NBA prospect.

"How is everything?" Breslin asked him.

"I don't know," the player said. He was wearing a long frown. "When I got married I figured with the $150 a month my basketball scholarship pays me and my wife's salary, $75 a week, we could get by until I finish school. But now she's pregnant and I don't know what to do. I don't know how I'm going to make it. I'm in a jam. I don't have any money to pay the doctor for the baby."

"Well, whatever the hell you do," Breslin told him, "don't take any money on this basketball thing."

"What do you mean?"

"I mean," Breslin told him, "don't take any

money to blow a game. They're doing it, you know."

"Me?" the player said. "Never. I don't know anything about that stuff."

For such a young kid, the player was a good actor. Breslin wanted to believe him. But a week before, Joe Hacken had sat in a car in front of the boy's house and handed him $1,000 to guarantee that NYU would lose to West Virginia by more points than the line called for. The next season, the same player blew games to Wake Forest and St. John's.

One morning in April of 1961, he walked into District Attorney Alfred Scotti's office, sat down and listened to the rackets bureau chief tell him:

"It is five years for perjury every time you lie. You're going before a grand jury. Now what about you taking money to fix basketball games?"

"I don't know anything about it," the player said. "I haven't done anything."

"What about the thousand you took from Joe Hacken for the West Virginia game at Charlotte last year?"

Now the player knew it was all over. He talked. With him, he said, the basketball scandals started right in the hallways of his school between classes. He recalled that he had at least five guys come up to him and talk, guys who were also going to NYU. They talked rather generally, but the player said he got the message.

"God," he told Scotti, "it looked like everybody was trying to fix games."

Then before the St. John's game in March of 1960 somebody told him he could make some money selling tickets to it. It was an important contest, a sure sellout, just like the old days.

"Go see this fellow named Charley Tucker," the player was told. "Here's his address."

Charley Tucker was living in a one-room apartment up in the Bronx, on University Avenue. So the player took him some tickets for the St. John's-NYU game. Tucker was flopped out on a studio couch when the young man came in and he paid him $50 for them.

Then Tucker got down to business.

"Listen," he said, "do you want to make some real money playing basketball?"

Hesitantly, the fellow said, "I'm interested."

Several days later, Tucker called him on the phone and repeated the questioning. "Still interested?" he wanted to know. "Yes," the player said. "I'm interested." And Tucker said, "Okay, then. I'm sending a guy named Hacken around to see you."

At first, Hacken wanted the young man to do business on the St. John's game. "No good," was the reply. "That's too big a game for the school." Well, Hacken said, how about West Virginia. The player said sure.

"I got a thousand for it," the player confessed afterward. "Hell, I wasn't hurting my teammates or anything. I just wasn't scoring myself or taking care of my man right."

The 1961 fixers did it in the grand, take-chances style of the old fixers. If you can remember a member of the Bradley team in 1950 moving around the Convention Hall in Philadelphia in a pregame warmup and holding out his thumb and sticking it down so the fixers would know he was going under the points against Temple, then you can understand gambler Joe Green grabbing a member of the Columbia team as the kid came out of the locker room to start the second half against Pennsylvania in 1960.

This young fellow was the last player out of the room as the team headed up the stairs to go out on the floor of the small Columbia gym. Penn was leading by four. The player's agreement with Green said the Quakers should have been ahead by 13.

"What are you doing?" Green said nervously. "This is business. My guys are going to think I don't have you."

The player went back into the game and took his first shot of the second half against Penn. He just threw it up aimlessly. Somehow, it went in. He shook his head. In the stands, Green exploded. Then the player, still an amateur at dumping games, settled down. He didn't shoot any more that night and blew the game.

For ten years, people had been warning colleges that as soon as they started throwing airline tickets and money and attention on kids just because they could play basketball, then there would be 20 guys on the streets who knew how to get to them with more money to make them do tricks during a game.

"And the colleges didn't do a damn thing about it," Jimmy Breslin said. "Now they cry like suckers when they get jacked-in with a basketball fix. How silly can you get?"

Listening, you had to think of another name

player, one who let himself be swayed by money. This young fellow came out of a New York City high school and some people rated him the best basketball player at his stage they ever saw, outside of Wilt Chamberlain. Then the colleges got on him—Indiana, Iowa, Colorado, Michigan State, Ohio State, Illinois, Kansas, Northwestern and Seattle. In the spring of 1960 they all flew him out to their campuses to spend weekends.

"I was offered $250 a month to go to Seattle," he said.

He picked Colorado, at first. He went to summer school there in 1960, but the people of Iowa did not give up easily. There was a short, stocky little fellow in a blue suit who owned a feed business and he always had made a fuss when the young man visited Iowa City. The player was at Colorado when Iowa people got hold of him and took him back to Iowa.

"For money," he admitted. "I went for money."

What to do? Jimmy Breslin says that there is important money bet on basketball and as long as there is this betting there will always be a good economic reason for an Aaron Wagman or a Joe Hacken to go out and get a couple of players to do business.

"And there will be betting on college games for just as long as the colleges persist in playing a caliber of sports that establishes an importance to the public and a form on which prices can be drawn and bets made," points out Breslin. "If college games were played between teams that were comprised of students who just came to the schools on their own, the quality of play would be a mess by present powerhouse standards, the eight and ten-dollar a ticket crowds would dwindle and nobody in his right mind would take a bet on the games because they would be meaningless and erratic. Mention this at a big college convention and athletic directors would call for somebody to throw you out. Then they would resume their discussions on the evils of gambling. They would never mention that gambling is going to be a part of this country forever."

As for the honesty of modern athletes, all sorts of stories can be cited. There was one afternoon, some years ago, when Howard Hobson, who was coaching basketball at Yale after many years at Oregon, sat in an office in New York with a high school player and the player's father, both of whom came from only average circumstances. With them was a Yale alumnus, who set up the meeting.

The boy had grades and apparently fine character and the man from Yale kept saying what a great opportunity it was for the boy to attend a place like Yale.

The gentlemanly Hobson talked quietly about New Haven and the procedures the boy would have to follow in order to enter Yale. There was, of course, a scholarship involved. After all, the boy was one of the most sought-after basketball players in the country.

Both the boy and his father listened respectfully. When Hobson had finished making his pitch, the boy said, "This is fine. Now let's get down to business. How much am I going to be paid?"

The boy's father nodded his head.

"We have been offered as high as $100 a week," the father said.

Howard Hobson was on the next train to New Haven.

Everybody who heard the story said that the kid, unfortunately, was typical of the modern, money-hungry athlete. Nobody said anything about all the schools who had been offering him money. Nobody seemed to think that the schools and their money had anything to do with the values of the kid at all.

Twenty-five years ago, Grantland Rice, the best friend college athletics ever had, talked about the trapping and care and feeding of athletes, about slipping them through phony courses so they could make headlines and profits for the college with no danger of intellectual pursuits distracting them from the main job. He said that unless the colleges scrubbed up fast, there was sure to be a scandal so large that it would invite the reformers to abolish intercollegiate sports altogether.

"As a matter of fact," Red Smith wrote at the time, "who honestly believes it hasn't happened already?"

George Raveling, the coach at Washington State, once offered an alternative to the recruiting pressurecooker.

"I have the solution to heavy recruiting," he said.

"Oh?"

"Yes," he said. "Give the coach $10,000 for expenses and tell him he can keep for himself everything he doesn't spend."

Bearcats Prove They're No Fluke: 1962

For 12 months, the champion Bearcats of Cincinnati brooded and boiled because they felt their upset win over Ohio State in Kansas City the previous March was regarded by many as something of a fluke. They couldn't wait to prove it was not. And at the same time the Buckeyes from Columbus had been fretting about the overtime defeat that cost them membership in the select circle of teams—Oklahoma A. & M., Kentucky, and San Francisco—that had won NCAA championships two years in a row. They wanted to prove to the world Cincinnati *was* a fluke.

Only a mathematician knows what the odds are of the same two teams meeting each other in the NCAA finals two years in a row, but that was the way it was going to be in 1962 if Ohio State beat Wake Forest, the eastern regional winner, and Cincinnati got past UCLA, an upstart underdog from the West, in the semifinals at Louisville.

It was estimated that in the event Ohio State and Cincinnati won, thus setting up their "grudge match," some 100,000 tickets could have been sold to watch them play. Freedom Hall, the game site, seats 18,000, and 25,000 ticket orders were received the first day of sale in a flood of money and requests reminiscent of a football bowl game.

While Louisville's lucky ticket holders may have considered regional tournaments of the week before as nothing but routes to the finals, the regionals themselves offered plenty of drama and revelations of their own. Wake Forest, led by Coach Bones McKinney, its arm-flailing, coat-throwing Baptist preacher, had the devil's own time winning the eastern regional in College Park, Maryland. The tall and strong

Deacons had reduced McKinney to a nervous ruin four days before when they came from behind to beat Yale in an overtime. Now, against St. Joseph's, they set about torturing their coach again. Len Chappell, 6' 8", and Bob Wollard, 6' 11", the team's two biggest men, at times showed about as much life as a statue, and tiny St. Joseph's stole the ball and the action. With only two minutes to play, Wake Forest trailed, 72-66. McKinney, in and out of his seat like a jumping jack at every movement of the ball, tugged frantically at his bright red socks, tossed towels high in the air. He didn't have a prayer of winning at this point. In a final gesture of dismay, he peeled off his coat and threw that in the air, too.

So he threw all caution to the wind and did a stupid thing. He ordered Wake Forest into a full-court press. This was absurd because Wake Forest was neither fast nor agile, and St. Joseph's was both. But suddenly St. Joseph's normally smooth guards could not handle the ball. They threw away two passes and handed away a third. Now there were only 28 seconds left. Bill Packer, Wake's slick guard, sank a desperation set shot to come within two points of St. Joseph's, 74-72. There were only 13 seconds left on the clock. St. Joseph's called time out before attempting a free throw. McKinney uttered a small prayer, thanking the angels for St. Joseph's decision to stop play, because he had no timeouts left. He took advantage of the lull to give his team a play in case St. Joseph's missed the free shot.

St. Joseph's did miss, McKinney's strategy got the ball to the hot-handed Packer and, with four seconds to go, he threw in a long jump shot to end regulation play in a tie. In the subsequent overtime a rejuvenated Wake Forest closed out the season for St. Joseph's, 96-85.

It was an awakened Wake Forest that took on rugged Villanova the next night. Wollard and Chappell out-jumped and out-rebounded their opponents at both ends of the floor. This seemed to tire the Wildcats and weaken their vaunted zone defense. Wake Forest forged ahead with 14 minutes to go and held it from there. At the end of the game Bones McKinney waved the only piece of cloth he hadn't handled in two nights, a large Confederate flag. The Dixie fans roared, and the Deacons headed for Louisville and a date with Ohio State.

The NCAA's western regional tournament was played in Provo, Utah, on the austere campus of Brigham Young University. In spite of the fact, as one Utah reporter put it, that "the teams coming in here wouldn't excite your Aunt Abigail," Provo responded to the two-day tournament with two crowds of 10,000. The Utah writer, of course, didn't know about the nutsy bunch of UCLA Bruins, the team with the second worst record (16-9) in the entire NCAA tournament.

To the surprise of everybody but themselves, the sizzling Bruins literally ran away with the merchandise at Provo. On the first night, against Utah State, a team that preferred a deliberate style of play, UCLA displayed its blinding fast break at its best. Led by its polished sophomore guard, Walt Hazzard, the Californians moved so swiftly they forced Utah State into an early, desperate press. The Bruins countered with zinging passes to Center Fred Slaughter, who would then slip the ball to a guard driving for a layup. When State attempted to block the middle, frail Gary Cunningham (the same Gary Cunningham who was named head coach at UCLA in 1977) fired in shot after shot from the corner. The Bruins piddled away a 43-30 halftime lead, as it often did, and then joyously grabbed it back again, as it also often did. UCLA won, 73-62.

On Saturday night in the final game, UCLA took on Oregon State and its 7-foot center, Mel Counts. All year long the Beavers had been quietly knocking over all comers. Even Coach Slats Gill, an old hand at the basketball business (34 years), was ready to admit that this was his best team ever.

In the pleasant lumber and college town of Corvallis, Oregon, Slats Gill was a local basket-

ball legend. An All-American at Oregon State himself once, he had been an enormously successful coach since the days when he had to schedule 10 games in 12 days to break even on road trips. That was when his teams played on an auditorium stage in Los Angeles and in a warehouse in Astoria. Five times he won the old Pacific Coast Conference championship and he took OSU to the NCAA semi-finals in 1949.

When Oregon State built its 10,500-seat field house in 1949, authorities decided to name it Gill Coliseum. "You can't name a building for a living man," said the state's board of higher education.

"What do they want us to do?" demanded a Portland newspaperman. "Shoot Slats?"

After that no paper ever dared call the building anything but Gill Coliseum.

Venerable and philosophical Slats Gill was a stern, fair, fatherly man, with sad eyes and thick, gray-streaked hair who taught his teams a tough defense and what he called a "natural" offense. "There is no Gill offense," he explained. "I experiment until I find the offense that best suits the natural abilities of my boys. That's the one we use that year." He combined these strategic techniques with a demand for intense concentration. Only his captain, Jay Carty, was permitted to talk to an official. If further talk was necessary, Slats did it. He jumped off the bench so much that he finished one season with a total of $1,400 in fines, a West Coast record. To offset his nervousness, he drank salted tea by the gallon, chewed pocketfuls of mints and after especially bitter losses he went home and wrote poetry.

And that nickname?

"I like the name," he said one time. "If your first name was Amory and your middle name was Tingle, you'd like to be called Slats, too."

The floor leader of the team was Oregon State's famous football quarterback, Terry Baker, winner of the coveted Heisman Trophy nine months later. Six-foot-three and fast, he liked to drive with a basketball as much as he liked to run with a football, and his passes had the same jolting quickness in both sports.

At center was Mel Counts, a rare sophomore phenomenon, a solidly built, smooth-moving, seven-footer whose rebounding set up Oregon State's fast break. Helping with the rebounding was Captain Jay Carty, perhaps the best all-around player on the team, and 6' 6" Bob Jacobson, playing with only two fingers on his right hand, and Rex Benner, a sophomore guard who had lost the vision in one eye when somebody threw sand in his face at the beach.

It was this combination of talent and toughness that brought 16 straight wins and a sixth-place national ranking to Oregon State the latter part of the season.

But UCLA scouting reports had found a flaw. Los Angeles sleuths watched as both Seattle University and Washington beat the Beavers—teams that Oregon State had defeated earlier—and they saw what opponents saw—the OSU defense was not particularly strong, that it did not have a really good outside shot and that it might have trouble coping with a slowdown type of game.

"It's like going around a baseball league twice," confessed Slats Gill. "The first time you bat .400, but the next time the word is out that you can't hit an inside curve, so you bat .200."

In the final game at Provo, Oregon State followed Utah State's example and tried to press from the beginning, but Johnny Green and Hazzard always found room to get the ball upcourt, and every Oregon State mistake seemed to mean a basket for UCLA. Slaughter, only 6′ 5″ and no match for Counts in inches, showed Counts and the crowd that speed mattered more than height—Slaughter was a state 100-yard dash champion in high school. The Bruins were in front, 44-30, at halftime and midway through the second half their supporters smelled victory. "Louisville . . . Louisville . . . Louisville," cheered the UCLA partisans.

Coach John Wooden, staid as a conference of bankers, showed little emotion over having his first NCAA semifinalist in 14 years at UCLA. "I'm proud of all of you," he told his players in the dressing room after the game, going from man to man and patting each on the head. "And we're proud of you, too, Coach," said a player quietly. That coach-player closeness was a big reason why the team nobody heard of was off to Louisville.

There were no surprises about the winner of the midwestern regional, played in Manhattan, Kansas. What did emerge was an absolutely awesome picture of basketball defense by Cincinnati's Bearcats. On the previous Monday, Cincinnati won its way to Kansas by beating Bradley, 61-46, a team that had been averaging 80.6 points a game; on Friday night, the Bear-

cats allowed Creighton just 46 points while winning 66-46, or 30 points under Creighton's average; and then in Saturday's final against Colorado the Bearcats gave the Buffaloes that same total—46 points—to finish a remarkable week of defensive basketball.

"Defense is 80 per cent of the game," Ed Jucker said, and that was precisely the way his team played. Against Creighton the Cincy front line of Ron Bonham (6′ 5″), Paul Hogue (6′ 5″) and George Wilson (6′ 10″) destroyed the country's leading rebounder, Paul Silas. Three of the first four shots he tried were batted away by Hogue and Wilson. While the front line

Ed Jucker

controlled the boards, Cincy guards Tom Thacker and Tony Yates applied their usual pressure. The result was that Creighton took 41 shots in the first half and hit only eight. In the second half they scored only two baskets in 14 minutes.

"Has an NCAA tournament team ever been held scoreless?" Colorado coach Sox Walseth asked ruefully.

After shaking everybody up in Manhattan, Coach Jucker came to the point. "We're at our peak now," he said, "just as we were last year when we went to Kansas City for the NCAA finals. We're ready."

Meanwhile, in Iowa City, Iowa, Ohio State showed it wasn't quite that ready. On Friday night against Western Kentucky, the Buckeyes were cold. Jerry Lucas was held to nine points by the same sort of triple-teaming that gave him only nine against Louisville in the first NCAA tournament game in 1961.

"I have never been so tired," Lucas said. "Three times up and down the floor and I was done."

After 10 minutes the score was tied, 19-19, and Lucas picked up his third foul. At that point Coach Fred Taylor sent in Gary Bradds to replace Lucas and the sophomore played the rest of the half. Ohio State moved out to a 13-point lead and won going away, 93-73.

Kentucky beat Butler the same night to set up the most intriguing game in all the regionals: Ohio State vs. Kentucky.

"We're not going to challenge Ohio State's right to be No. 1," said Kentucky's wily old Adolph Rupp. "We'll let Cincinnati do that. But if Ohio State isn't hitting and we are lucky it might be a fair game. Now, if they are hitting and we aren't lucky I just might go home at half time."

"He's never gone home at halftime yet," said Fred Taylor, still wiping the sweat from his face after the Western Kentucky game.

Taking no chances, Coach Taylor put John Havlicek, his defensive ace, on Cotton Nash, the sensational scoring wonder for Kentucky. Havlicek ate Nash alive—Rupp benched him twice. Without scoring from the usually consistent Nash, Kentucky was virtually dead.

Jerry Lucas, meanwhile, was having a whale of a night. After seven minutes of play the score was tied, 8-8. In the next eight minutes he dumped in 23 of OSU's 25 points, and the

basket not credited to him was a debatable tip-in by a teammate after a Lucas hook shot. In one fantastic 60-second burst he made three straight three-point plays, being fouled each time as he hooked the ball in. The score was 41-35 as the first half ended, with Lucas having 25 of Ohio State's 41. That was as close as the Wildcats got, losing 74-64.

Harry Lancaster, Rupp's assistant coach, had a word of warning for the Buckeyes. Spotting the 16 errors they had made against his team, Lancaster said, "If they make as many mistakes against Cincinnati they'll get whipped good."

On the basis of their play in the regionals, most oddsmakers favored Cincinnati. Looking at the four teams realistically, they felt that the Bearcats would tower over John Wooden's pesky gnats, and though UCLA would delight the basketball-mad Louisville crowd, it was going to have fits running a successful fast break against Cincy. Ohio State, on the other hand, expected more trouble with Wake Forest. "If Wake's big men can control the backboards and if Packer is hitting, the game will be close," wrote one reporter. "But that's a lot of ifs."

The four regional winners all arrived on Thursday, at the start of the long-awaited basketball weekend, and at a press conference that afternoon Bones McKinney spoke convincingly of Ohio State, the overwhelming co-favorite and his semifinal round opponent. "I'd take most any player they've got and use him instead of mine," he said.

When Fred Taylor's turn came he said everybody was talking about a Cincinnati-Ohio State final.

"But what if my kids lose to Wake Forest?" he said. "Third place is for the birds."

Then Ed Jucker got up and said a few nice things about his next opponent, UCLA, but it was clear that his mind was on Ohio State.

John Wooden was the last to speak.

"I don't think we can beat Cincinnati at their slow-down game," he said, "and I don't think we can beat them at our fast one, either."

Later that evening, another coach said he wasn't buying any of that. "You get to the NCAA semifinals on talent," he pointed out. "But after that you are in the hands of God."

The Wake Forest-Ohio State game began to a crescendo of sound. The Southerners' drum-and-cymbal section sported a Confederate-type sign that read: "Yankee Go Home!" Bones

McKinney nearly fainted when he saw it. He would have been in a mess if the Yankees had gone home. All five of his starters were from north of the Mason-Dixon Line.

It took less than three minutes for Jerry Lucas to score six points, and Coach McKinney could have sent his Northerners home right there. All-American forward John Havlicek so thoroughly contained All-American Len Chappell that the broad-backed Wake Forest ace could put in only five of his 13 shots in the first half. At intermission, the Deacons were behind, 46-34, and they went to their dressing room to pray and talk things over.

It was with 6:19 to go in the game; Ohio State was struck with disaster. Lucas had gone up for a rebound of a missed Wake Forest shot and his left leg hit the calf of Bob Woollard, the Deacon center, causing Lucas to land on his heel instead of his toe. It was a harmless-looking collision, but when Jerry tried to get up he couldn't. He finally stood on one leg and hopped toward the bench in pain. Examination revealed that there was a strain of tissues in the left kneecap. Lucas limped to the dressing room.

Half an hour later Lucas was still stretched out on a rubbing table, a towel filled with ice cubes wrapped around his knee. A large crowd of hushed and sad-faced Ohio State sympathizers formed outside the dressing-room door.

"Will he be able to play tomorrow?" asked Treva Lucas, Jerry's pretty wife.

"Will the sun come up in the east?" answered her determined husband.

Meanwhile, UCLA, set to start against defending champion Cincinnati, made the mistake of turning to look at the Bearcats while they warmed up. The sight of mighty Paul Hogue, George Wilson, Tom Thacker and Tony Yates was too much.

After five minutes of play the Bruins were still watching Cincy warm up. The Bearcats had scored every time they brought the ball downcourt. Hogue took only two minutes to make his first three baskets. The Bruins had not picked off a single rebound. The numbers on the scoreboard: 18-4.

"The worst start I ever saw," said John Wooden later.

Then, unbelievably, Cincinnati began to blow its lead. With Gary Cunningham pumping in one long jump shot after another, and with guards Walt Hazzard and Johnny Green driving heretofore icy-careful Yates and Thacker to make mistakes, UCLA forced Cincinnati to squander a 14-point lead. By halftime the score was tied.

Some 19:50 minutes later it was still deadlocked, 70-70, when Ed Jucker called for a time-out. Except for Hogue, the Bearcats had been playing as though their hands were tied behind them. Hogue had kept them in the game by scoring their last 14 points.

During the breather, Jucker put in a play calling for Hogue to get the ball. Cincinnati was throttled, however, so it tried the first option off the play. Thacker drove to the right side, leaped and sank a 25-footer with three seconds left. That was the first outside shot of six tries that Tom had made all night—but he made it when it mattered. Cincinnati had been making the big play all season.

A relieved and wrung-out Ed Jucker told the press after the game that, except for Hogue's 36-point effort, 20 more than his average, the Bearcats had played poorly.

"But let's not take anything away from UCLA," he was quick to add. "That's a lot better team than anyone knows."

Now Cincinnati and Ohio State were at last officially matched in the NCAA finals. On Saturday morning the only question to be heard around Louisville concerned Jerry Lucas' knee. "He should be all right by game time," assured Robert Murphy, the OSU doctor. "I plan to tape the leg so that it will not quite be straightened out into its most painful position."

Lucas had limped through an eight-block morning walk.

"Feels fine, feels fine." he said to countless well-wishers as he strolled along.

"It hurts," he quietly told a close friend. "It hurts every time I straighten it." In his pocket was a small envelope of pills marked "PAIN."

When Lucas took the floor for the center jump against Paul Hogue on Saturday night he wore tape on his left leg, nearly from his shorts to his sock. Yet he moved without limping. Still, Hogue was moving with much more mobility. In the first two minutes he put in a hook shot, blocked a Lucas shot, then sank another hook shot. He played like a man possessed—out to show the world he was better than Lucas. He tore the ball off the backboards, and the ones

1962 NCAA finals at Louisville: Cincinnati 71, Ohio State 59.

he missed, an inspired George Wilson got. Lucas came back quickly, however, to score from 10, 20 and 12 feet. At the end of the first five minutes, Ohio State had the lead, 11-8.

But Cincinnati dominated the backboards. They wanted the basketball so badly they fought each other for it. Ohio State went one dry spell of several minutes where it got only one shot. Fred Taylor was to say later that it was "pathetic."

Slowly, inexorably, Cincinnati began to pull away. Thacker and Yates gave OSU room in the center but kept them from passing to the forwards in the corners. Soon the Buckeyes were doing what they had done against the Bearcats in the 1961 finals. Taylor had warned his players before the game that they had to have *movement* if they hoped to win but, thwarted and perplexed on offense, they gave up their own slashing style of attack and became hopelessly deliberate. In the last 10 minutes of the first half they scored only three baskets. Lucas, significantly, did not score at all in the final 15 minutes of the half.

The Cincy offense was operating crisply, however. It was getting good shots and a neat strategic move was paying off. John Havlicek, a strong rebounder, was kept away from the backboard because the man he was guarding, Ron Bonham, had been ordered by Jucker to stay well outside.

Cincinnati led at halftime, 37-29, with Hogue scoring 16 of his team's points.

Fred Taylor attempted some strategy of his own as the second half started. He sent in substitute center Gary Bradds, 6′ 8″, as a forward, and moved Lucas out past the foul line. Normally Lucas could drive to the basket if Hogue tried to play him closely out there. But now, with his knee killing him, he couldn't drive. When Hogue realized that, the game was over. Cincinnati continued to control the ball easily, pushed out to an 18-point lead and breezed to a 71-59 victory.

At the buzzer, Ed Jucker flung a single finger skyward signifying the magic No. 1. "Does this prove it?" he cried. "Aren't we the best? They can't overlook us anymore. They can't overlook the national champions two years in a row."

Coach Jucker, the masterful coach of defensive basketball who in his only two years as a head coach had now won two NCAA titles, had every right to be exuberant. The 700 basketball coaches who saw the Bearcats play said, yes, Ed Jucker's team was rightfully No. 1. Not even a healthy Jerry Lucas, on the last night of his college career, could have changed that.

Loyola Defies Detractors: 1963

Fred Taylor, a man who twice now had seen his top-ranked Buckeyes beaten in the NCAA final by Cincinnati, conceded that the Missouri Valley was the toughest basketball conference in the country. Adolph Rupp agreed with him.

"No question about it," said Rupp. "It's a very strong league."

Rupp found out just how strong in 1963 when St. Louis overwhelmed Kentucky, 86-63. It was one of the worst beatings ever given a Rupp team.

"The Big Ten has some real good teams," added Ray Meyer of DePaul, "but not as many as the Valley." Notre Dame's Johnny Jordan said much the same thing. "As an independent team, we play schools from all conferences," Jordan said. "The Valley is tops."

In spite of its status, the Missouri Valley Conference was something of an enigma. Even its own basketball followers were hard-pressed to name its schools. No wonder, for it was a hodge-podge league of seven teams from seven different states. It rambled west from Cincinnati to Peoria (Bradley), just south of Chicago, swung into the cornfields of Iowa (Drake), then south through St. Louis, the Kansas plains (Wichita), the oil fields of Oklahoma (Tulsa) and the North Texas cattle country (North Texas State). The name of the conference was a geographical absurdity, for not one of its seven schools was located in the Missouri River Valley, most of which is northwest of St. Louis.

Though the conference was ineptly named, there was nothing inept about its teams. Midway through the 1963 season, four of them were ranked among the nation's best. Cincinnati, undefeated, untied and practically unscored upon,

was an unanimous No. 1. Wichita was in the top 10, and Bradley and St. Louis were not far behind. Not many out-of-conference teams beat the Valley. The league's record against outsiders was 50-16 for a .758 percentage, easily the best in the country. The Southeastern Conference was a distant second at .694, followed by the Big Six at .643, the Big Ten at .556 and the Atlantic Coast Conference at a flat .500. At home, the Valley stood a remarkable 44-1 against outside competition.

In 1962, Ed Jucker was said to have remarked, more or less seriously: "After winning in the Valley, the NCAA was a breeze." Joe Swank, the peppery coach of Tulsa, said he wouldn't want to coach in any other league. "When you beat a Valley team, you can be proud," he said.

Almost everyone was ready with an explanation for the Valley's success. High-voltage recruiting, said some. "That's the tipoff," said Fred Taylor. "They go after basketball players like nobody else, believe me." Detroit's Bob Calihan talked like a man who had been done out of a few athletes by Valley coaches—and who hadn't been? "If they want a kid these days," grumbled Calihan, "you might as well forget him."

Everyone agreed that what really made the Valley the king of basketball was its top-notch coaching. Jack Gardner of Utah admired Ed Jucker. "Nobody wins two national titles unless he's a great coach," Gardner said.

Cincinnati was the favorite again to win the NCAA championship, symbol of basketball supremacy. By midseason the Bearcats had won 71 of 76 games for Jucker since 1961, and had the country's longest winning streak, 32. They had not lost at home since 1957.

No one expected Ed Jucker to win in such grand style when he was promoted from assistant to head coach three years before. Oscar Robertson had just graduated, removing in his own person a major part of the Cincinnati basketball team. Few people outside of Cincinnati had ever heard of Jucker. He had been a fine basketball and baseball player at the university in 1939-40 before starting a coaching career in both sports that led him to Batavia (Ohio) High School, the Merchant Marine Academy at Kings Point, Rensselaer Polytechnic Institute in upstate New York and finally, in 1953, back to Cincinnati as assistant basketball coach.

When Jucker took over the Bearcats, he made a bold, and seemingly suicidal, decision: to discard Cincy's popular run-and-shoot offense for a slower, more deliberate game accenting defense, a shift that was greeted by hoots and howls at home. The fans rode Jucker hard. "Let 'em run, you bum," they screeched. Jucker's mail carried the same sweet message. "I'll admit I had some doubts," he said, but Jucker never wavered. Cincinnati started to win, the hoots changed to cheers, and when the season ended the team had won everything possible, including the NCAA championship over upstate rival Ohio State. Ironically, Ohio State had already been voted the top team in the country, and its coach, Fred Taylor, had been selected as Coach of the Year, but Cincinnati won in overtime, creating a rather awkward situation for the pollsters. To compound matters, Ohio Governor Mike DiSalle released a proclamation immediately following Cincinnati's victory, congratulating Ohio State on being chosen the top team of the year and bringing glory to Ohio. Basketball fans take such slights seriously, and the catcalls from Cincinnati could be heard all the way to the State House in Columbus. Later, DiSalle ran for reelection and was defeated. He got little support in Cincinnati.

The year 1962 was a virtual duplication of the year before. Again, after losing a couple of early-season games, the Bearcats won the rest to reach the NCAA final. Again it met Ohio State, a team that had been ranked tops in the country from the very beginning of the year. And again Cincinnati won the championship.

The two Cincinnati-Ohio State finals, with one team getting the awards, the other the victories, created a certain amount of cross-Ohio tension. Fred Taylor insisted he was not bitter toward Jucker but was sure Jucker was bitter toward him. Jucker denied that, but he was obviously delighted at twice being honored as the Columbus Touchdown Club's Coach of the Year, right there in Taylor's own backyard.

By now, Jucker was under tremendous pressure to win. Ralph Miller, the Wichita coach, said that one loss for Jucker was probably equal to five or six for him at Wichita. "I heard that after Cincinnati lost to us in 1962 they got booed when they returned home," Miller said. "The people in Cincinnati expect to win, and the pressure keeps mounting on Ed."

"It's like being the last egg in an incubator," Jucker admitted. "Everybody's standing around waiting for you to crack."

But Jucker and his Bearcats did not crack. One by one, Missouri Valley teams learned there was just no way to stop streaking Cincinnati. Drake, for example, got off to an early lead but then Cincy got down to business and the Bulldogs faded like a thirsty man caught without water in the middle of Death Valley, losing 71-60. Next, Bradley's Chuck Orsborn tried to jam Cincinnati's inside shooters with both a zone and a sagging man-to-man. The only trouble was that it left Larry Shingleton, who almost never shot, free and willing. He sank seven of 11 shots. Still, Cincinnati led by only a single point, 60-59, with 58 seconds to play. Then Tony Yates dropped in two free throws, and the Bearcats went on to win, 65-61, their 37th straight and 69th in succession at home.

Ranked No. 1 all season, with a disciplined defense that held opponents to 52.3 points per game, when you talked of Cincinnati in 1963 you talked in superlatives: Tony (Gramps) Yates was the *best* defensive player in the country, Tom (Cobra) Thacker was the *tallest* 6' 2" man in the world, center George Wilson had the *sharpest* elbows. The team led the nation's colleges in total defense. They exasperated rivals with their canny stalls, their deliberations, their icy disdain—tactics that made them odds-on favorites to accomplish what no other team had ever done before: win the NCAA championship three years in a row.

The prospects of Cincy's continuing success

led the brothers of Alpha Epsilon Pi fraternity on the campus to start a frat house graveyard for Cincinnati victims, where the students played taps as the wooden markers were hammered into the ground—"Rest In Peace," with the date, score, name of opponent, etc. It was a depressing sight.

Ed Jucker summed up his own team best.

"I'm sorry," he said to St. Louis Athletic Director Bob Stewart after routing the well-regarded Billikens, 70-40, "I'm sorry we had to be so good."

There were three changes in the Cincinnati cast from 1962, but only one new face among the starters, Larry Shingleton at guard. In place of the graduated Paul Hogue, Forward George Wilson was moved to center and Thacker from guard to forward.

Talk of Cincinnati's weaknesses was often vague and wistful and ran to criticism of its bench strength. Nit-pickers could manage to find things about the Bearcats that warranted a little concern. With the 235-pound Hogue gone, their rebounding was not as overpowering, and the team was not as tall. It was not a great shooting team, so it had to work the ball in to score. It also had a distressing habit of getting behind early in games.

"When a team repeatedly falls behind, and when this is a radical departure from what has gone before," said one rival Missouri Valley coach, "you have to figure some element is missing—maybe timing, maybe morale—who knows?"

Duke, Loyola of Chicago, and Oregon State—teams that could shoot and run—joined Cincinnati in Louisville for the climax of the national championship tournament. The scouting report on Duke (W-24, L-2) was that it was big, strong and possessive under the boards, and would fast-break if permitted, or set up plays around Art Heyman and Jeff Mullins inside. Zone or pressing defenses did not bother them; they used several kinds themselves. Their only offensive weakness was that the guards did not score very much.

Like Duke, Loyola of Chicago was 24-2 and thrived on a helter-skelter fast break and peerless rebounding. Jerry Harkness, who was Loyola's all-time leading scorer, headed a well-balanced attack that averaged 93.9 points, best in the nation. The starters made 13 to 21 points

a game apiece. The Ramblers, however, were not too strong in reserves or on defense.

There were no believers far outside of Corvallis in Oregon State's chances against Cincinnati in the semi-finals. The OSU defense, mostly man-to-man, was tough, and football star Terry Baker, who directed the offense, was dangerous on drives up the middle. However, the attack often bogged down when 7-foot Mel Counts, a fine rebounder, had trouble shooting. The Beavers had looked good—and bad. What chance did Oregon State have against Cincinnati? Not a good one, really. To win, they would have to figure on the Bearcats having an off night offensively—and take it from the defending champions, there was no way they were going to have an off night.

Louisville was alive to the prospect of seeing favored Cincinnati match up with Loyola or Duke, the speed entries, in the title game. Scalpers were getting $100 a ticket. One Cincy rooter, a lady, walked around town with a sign draped around her neck: "Wanted, desperately, two tickets for tonight." A group of 13 from Cincinnati had reserved hotel rooms the year before—but didn't have seat one in Freedom Hall for Friday's game.

Loyola Coach George Ireland knew full well the only chance he had of ever getting a crack at Cincinnati would be in the championship game in Louisville. As early as the previous December he began sending his scouts to see the Bearcats play. To realize his dream, the Ramblers had to knock off the Southeastern Conference champion (Mississippi State), the Big Ten co-champion (Illinois) and, in their semi-final in Louisville on Friday, Atlantic Coast Conference champion Duke, 94-75. When Coach Ireland and his assistant, Nick Kladis, sat down to watch Cincinnati take Oregon State apart, 80-46, in the second game, it was the tenth time one or the other had seen the Bearcats play that season. By contrast, Ed Jucker had scouted Loyola only twice.

Loyola players called their coach "The Man," and they held him in awe. He was athletic director as well as basketball coach, and on busy days he was known to be quite grim. Other times he was animated and waggish. On basketball theory, however, Ireland was single-minded. He played to run and shoot. "The object of the game is to put the ball in the basket," he said, and Loyola did it with greater consistency than any team in America. He defied his detractors to say his attack lacked order. "Undisciplined? You called us undisciplined?" he roared, challenging a reporter who had unthinkingly used the word to describe the Ramblers. "Listen," he said, "When I tell my boys to sweat, they sweat.

"This is a good bunch of kids," he continued. "Relaxed but sensitive. Leslie Hunter gets tears in his eyes when you correct him. Of course, everybody says we don't play much of a schedule, and we've got a little guy (5′ 9″) at guard in Johnny Egan, and Jerry Harkness shoots two-handed foul shots. Nobody seemed to want him until he came with us and made All-American."

On Saturday morning, Ireland sat in a conference with his assistants at a downtown Louisville hotel.

"Can your kids out-rebound Cincinnati?" he was asked.

"I think we can," Ireland said.

"Can you press them?"

"I think we can. We'll drive on them, drive for the basket. We'll make them play our game instead of standing around like they do. I think we can make them foul, and I don't think their big boy, Wilson, is strong enough to handle ours, Hunter. But Vic Rouse will have to be alert when they start picking off for that Ron Bonham."

Over in the enemy camp, Ed Jucker depended on execution, and no one denied that his teams had been the best executioners in college basketball for three years. "He gives us three weeks of defense before we're allowed a shot in scrimmage," said Ron Bonham. "Even a lousy defensive player like me learned something."

After Duke squashed Oregon State in the consolation game, 85-63, the sellout crowd of 19,153 (including 750 coaches in town for their annual convention) settled back to watch a contest of offense against defense. The game had barely begun, however, when it appeared as if the fastest guns in basketball weren't going to fire on anybody but themselves. They missed 13 of their first 14 attempts, and Cincinnati compounded Loyola's frustrations by refusing to let the Ramblers run. The Bearcats quickly moved out to a 19-9 lead. By halftime it was 29-21. The

Ramblers had made only eight baskets in 34 attempts. All-American Yates had held All-American Harkness to zero points.

Coach Ireland refrained from bawling out his players. "You're still a better team than they are," he told them in the dressing room. "The ball's just not dropping for you. But it will. You're getting the shots and it will."

In the second half, Cincinnati came out to make it a rout, sinking five out of six shots in one stretch. Then Bonham hit three in a row as Wilson screened out Rouse, and, with 12 minutes to go, the Bearcats led by 15 points, 45-30.

Then, subtly, the tide started to change. With Loyola pressuring Cincinnati hard, the normally mistake-proof Bearcats began losing their cool, turning over the ball on errors. Even worse, they got into foul trouble.

Now the ball was dropping for Loyola. With the score 45-33 and 10:21 to play, Wilson was charged with his fourth foul, and Jucker sent in Dale Heidotting to replace him. Heidotting was the only reserve to get into the game, and then only for four minutes.

Here Cincinnati stopped shooting. In fact, Bonham, its leading scorer, played the last 17 minutes of the contest without taking a shot. Thacker, Wilson and Yates all had four fouls on them, forcing the team to become super-cautious and resort to stalling tactics, a pet ploy. The strategy was to provoke more Loyola fouls as they tried to get the ball, and foul they did, but now the Bearcats, who generally made their free throws, missed one foul shot out of every two. The once comfortable Cincinnati lead dwindled dangerously: 48-39, 48-43, 50-48.

With only 12 seconds left to play, Cincinnati desperately held a 53-52 lead when Harkness intentionally fouled Shingleton. The Cincinnati ace made the first free throw and grinned back at Yates. One more would clinch it. But the shot dribbled off the rim to Hunter, who quickly flipped the ball downcourt to Harkness, who stuffed it into the basket, tying the game at 54-all. With five seconds left in regulation play—time enough to set up one last shot—Jucker yelled to his players to call time out.

"But by this time the crowd was going wild," Jucker explained afterward. "I couldn't be heard above the noise."

In the overtime, the two teams traded baskets until the score was 58-58. With 2:15 to go,

Coach George Ireland, an advocate of run-and-shoot basketball, was held in awe by his players at Loyola of Chicago.

Loyola got possession of the ball, but Shingleton bottled up Egan and forced a jump. The Ramblers got the ball back and ate up the clock while playing for one shot. Their best shot was Harkness, who tried to get free of Bonham. Harkness had the ball, dribbled to the left corner, circled under and went up to shoot. Bonham, sticking to him like corn plaster, slapped at the ball—and Harkness suddenly slipped the ball to Hunter in the middle. Hunter shot and missed—right into the hands of Rouse on the right side. Rouse grabbed the ball, jumped for the sky and laid it in. He said later that he had missed several other layups earlier and wanted to be very sure he made the clincher.

"Oh, my, it felt good," he said.

After losing to Loyola, 60-58, Ed Jucker said that except for the fouls and the final score, he considered 60 points and 61 Loyola misses out of 84 shots a job well done. "We forced them to play our game," he said. "After all, they had been averaging 93 points a game."

He might have added, but didn't, that his team would have won easily had it not committed 16 turnovers, while Loyola lost the ball only three times on errors.

In his own analysis of the game, George Ireland gave no quarter. "We forced the action," he said. "We forced the fouls. We harassed

This shot won the 1963 national championship for Loyola of Chicago, with Vic Rouse (40) getting the honors. Defending champion Cincinnati forced the contest into overtime, but finally lost, 60-58.

Loyola of Chicago—1963 NCAA champs—the fastest guns in basketball. Front row, left: Coach George Ireland, Asst. Coach Jerry Lyne. Second row, left: Captain Jerry Harkness, John Egan, Chuck Wood, Vic Rouse, Les Hunter, Rich Rochelle, Jim Reardon, Dan Connaughton, Ron Miller, Mgr. John Gabcik, Asst. Mgr. Fred Kuehl, Trainer Dennis McKenna.

them into their mistakes and, ultimately, beat them with a stall right out of Ed Jucker's book."

While supporters for both teams crowded around the players after the buzzer and claimed with raised fists they were "No. 1, No. 1, No. 1," everybody agreed it had been a stirring contest of offense vs. defense. If this particular game belonged to the run-and-shooters, the final score wasn't nearly decisive enough to make Ed Jucker's publisher stop distributing his book.

The team honors went to the Midwest in 1963, but when it came to individual stars, pro scouts talked about the spectacular Gus Johnson, a 6' 6", 225-pound center at University of Idaho. Sportswriters fell all over their typewriters calling him "another Baylor," "another Russell," "another Lucas." But the fact was Gus Johnson was none of these. He was a unique basketball player. And he was rapidly becoming a local legend.

One morning he ate a breakfast of a stack of wheatcakes, three fried eggs, a double order of potatoes and a rasher of bacon, which he consumed slowly, steadily and joyfully. "I've got to take it easy," he said, downing a second glass of milk. "There's a game tonight."

The natives of Moscow, Idaho, loved to tell about the time Johnson stuffed a shot in the basket with one hand, caught it with the other and handed it to the startled referee.

After Idaho trounced University of Oregon twice to bring its record to 15-3, Steve Belko, the Oregon coach, shook his head sadly. "That Johnson jumps like he's sold his soul to the devil."

"I go up with him," an Oregon player protested. "But when I come down he just stays up."

When Johnson was asked if there wasn't something freakish about the way he got off the ground, he talked in the florid and didactic manner of a southerner. "Heck, no," he said. "I just say, 'Legs, jump,' and they say, 'How high, boss?' "

Joe Cipriano, who had been a nifty little backcourt man on the University of Washington teams in the early 1950s, was the Idaho coach.

"He's only a sophomore," Joe said. "He's still growing. Just watch him go next season."

Gangway for UCLA Dynasty: 1964

The nation was just chock full of growing boys in 1964, and coaches fell all over themselves to get 6' 5" guards, 6' 8" forwards and 6' 10" centers.

Walt Hazzard was asked how he would appraise Cazzie Russell, the Michigan guard. The UCLA guard thought a bit. He was a senior, 6' 3" and 188 pounds, which was a nice size for a guard, but Russell was a 19-year-old sophomore who was 6' 5½" and 220 pounds. "Well," Hazzard said finally, "it is a very good thing that I am getting out of college, because there isn't going to be much room for me if they start finding guys that size who play guard."

It was a distinct surprise, then, as well as an affront to the law of gravity, that the best team in the country in 1964 was Hazzard's UCLA Bruins, with not a starter over 6' 5". This turn of events was plainly pointed up in the Los Angeles Classic—the best of the season's holiday tournaments—when UCLA gave Cazzie Russell and his taller Michigan teammates their first defeat, 98-80, paving the way for the Bruins to take their second straight LA title and go on and capture their first NCAA championship at Kansas City. Unbeaten UCLA won with the perseverance and crisp execution that exemplifies the success of the good little teams. It showed that a well-coached squad with good personnel, regardless of its size, could win even when it was playing "under its heads," as sportswriter Frank Deford put it. Fred Slaughter, 6' 5" UCLA center, said there was no reason for him to get stage fright among all those goons. "I've been looking up to everybody I've played against for four years," he said. Slaughter survived against the giants because he got so much help from his teammates. Coach John Wooden

demanded, for example, that all his players work the backboards. The result was balanced rebounding that enabled the Bruins to win all their games against bigger opponents.

One of the reasons for UCLA's success in 1964 was Gail Goodrich, who was Hazzard's running mate in the backcourt. At a time when little men were assuming command in college basketball, Goodrich was no less than the prototype of them all. He barely topped 6', had a deadly left-handed jumper, and quick hands. Quickness was the quality that allowed UCLA to control a game and a bigger team with its tight zone press.

"When we do it properly," said Wooden, "our press sets a tempo for the whole game, and when we get the other team falling into our tempo we have gained a big advantage."

Goodrich, who manned the trenches, put it another way. "We're so little, we just have to press."

Wooden's Bruins were very well conditioned, which was particularly necessary in 1964, because the bench was so thin. To get his players in shape, Wooden's practices were highly organized and efficient. But he refrained from fiery, Rockne-type speeches before a game. "Quiet and businesslike," he said. "That's how I expect them to go into a game."

John Wooden was a seraphic gentleman who appreciated Kipling and Keats as much as he did a good hook shot. He didn't smoke, drink or swear at officials. He could not say "dad-burned" without cupping his hand over his mouth, and when he quoted someone else he carefully abbreviated to clean up the obscenities.

As the NCAA tournament time drew near,

opinion was divided over how far the Bruins would go. Dick Strite, a Eugene, Oregon, sports editor, got up at a luncheon in New York and said he didn't think they could possibly get past Oregon State in the West and therefore would never even see the lights of Kansas City for the finals.

"That might be true, all right," said NYU's Coach Lou Rossini, "but I have not seen a team that can run with UCLA. Believe me, that UCLA zone press is the exact equivalent of solitary confinement for a team with the ball."

Being puny, Rossini said, did not bother puny UCLA one bit. He was also very impressed with guards Hazzard and Goodrich. "An extraordinary pair of ball hawks," he called them. "And Coach John Wooden—whew. He's just great."

Aleksandar Nikolic, a compact man with quick eyes and thick accent, was the basketball coach of the Yugoslav national team. He had been darting around the U.S. for three months, cordially talking to college basketball coaches in hopes of picking up ideas that he could use against us in the Olympic Games in the fall. After watching the Bruins win their 20th and 21st games in a row, he said: "Is small team. No big man, no big score like Cotton Nash of Coach Roop team in Kentucky. But ziss is best I see. Because is *team*. All five." He held up five fingers. "Team. You understand? Is best."

Recently, Tacoma dentist Dr. Marvin "Tom" Tommervik, Jr., who played against UCLA for three years and captained Washington State University in 1965, recalled what it was like. Dr. Tommervik was one of those quick, sure-handed, solidly-built little (5' 10'') guard whom the Cougars' Coach Marv Harshman was always recruiting. Highly competitive, a team leader, Dr. Tommervik was not easily intimidated by the Uclans' growing reputation. On the contrary, he looked forward to the UCLA game.

"The Bruins were fun to play against," he said. "They appeared to be having fun themselves. They didn't play the game as if it was a big battle. I thought it was unique that John Wooden could take a group of outstanding athletes and let them run a free-lance offense, yet have enough discipline to keep from turning their attack into a rat-race. Wooden had a very

simple offense; scouting UCLA must have been the easiest job in college basketball, because its plays were so simple. Our preparations weren't really any different for UCLA than for anybody else. We went through a regular week's workout, running our offense against their defense. Physically, we matched up with UCLA as did just about all the other Pac-8 teams. They weren't overpowering in a physical sense, but they finessed you to death. The 1962 and 1963 Bruins, for example, let you do pretty much what you wanted; they never hounded you on defense, no pressure at all. They had tremendous poise; never got too rattled, never lost their control.

"It was always exciting to play the Bruins in Los Angeles. We knew we had to play a perfect game to be in any way competitive. Even when we played well, they always seemed to be ahead eight or 10 points. It was always catch-up ball. They could score so fast. We'd be hot on their heels for the first 18 minutes and then—boom—they'd be off on one of their famous two-minute spurts and we'd lost it all. The Bruins were like a time bomb. You could never tell when they'd explode. One minute you'd be in the game, and then out.

"Reporters often asked if Coach Harshman did anything special to get us up for UCLA. My answer was always the same: You don't have to say or do anything to get athletes excited about playing good players. It was always a big game. We always knew the nation was watching when UCLA was involved. One thing about playing UCLA—we never had anything to lose. The press, the fans, never expected much from us, so we always went into the UCLA game loose, relaxed. Coach Harshman was more positive. Even when we were badly outmanned, he told us we could win. He was *convinced* we could pull the upset of the year. And, finally, we did. In 1966, we upset the Bruins, 81-80. I saw a side of John Wooden that night that I came to admire more and more. After the game—hell, even before the clock had run out—he came over and congratulated Harshman and each of those sitting on our bench. 'Nice game, good game,' he said. John Wooden could take it as well as dish it out."

Of course, no coach with dreams of landing a spot in the NCAA tournament was willing to concede anything to UCLA. Even though his team was soundly beaten by 18 points by the Bruins in December, Michigan Coach Dave Strack remained unconvinced. "They don't look like a superteam," he said. "They were better on a better night, that's all. We must have missed 16 dead layups."

It was characteristic of Wooden's coaching that UCLA had great speed. "We run," he said, "though sometimes we don't take the ball with us." It was also a very intelligent team, self-confident, secure in the knowledge of having worked together as a unit two years in a row. It did not, however, have strength and height. "I have been asked," said Wooden, "whether I'd like taller boys. Goodness gracious sakes alive!"

The 1964 Bruins were not always precise. They did not have Villanova's smooth attack or Kentucky's polished ball handling. In a game against Washington they threw the ball away nine times in the first half. They gambled, sometimes too much, on the zone press, which had an uncommon feature in that center Slaughter played up on the front line with guard Goodrich, but more often than not they pressed a team into errors. "Pressure," said Wooden, "is the way to play basketball." Most opponents tried to slow UCLA down; most of them did not succeed.

Meanwhile, what about Loyola University, the defending national champions? Peppery George Ireland had discovered that there was not much breathing room at the top. Little Loyola did not sneak up on opponents anymore. Teams battled the Ramblers in play like it was Guadalcanal instead of basketball. For their kind of perilous living, they had not done badly—19-5. Yet Coach Ireland, who had been named Coach of the Year four times and Man of the Year twice since the victory at Louisville, said he was surprised his team lost five games.

"I am surprised we lost two to Wichita, surprised we lost to St. John's and Memphis State, and most certainly surprised we lost to Georgetown," he said. "But don't tell me 19 and 5 is a disappointing season, because I'll take that kind of disappointment any season."

"Is it possible Loyola can make it to Kansas City and win a second straight NCAA championship?" he was asked.

"Definitely," he said firmly. He then began to outline how he would play Michigan ("We'd

Marv "Tommygun" Tommervik scores for Washington State against California; Tommervik now has his own dental practice in Tacoma, Washington.

give Russell 25, and Buntin 25, too") or Ohio State ("That Bradds worries me, but he's the only one") in the regionals at Minneapolis.

In the final weeks of the season, no one was quite sure which team to worry about. UCLA had beaten everyone in sight, but the view was limited on the West Coast, where competition was not the keenest. Loyola came on strong after a slump. Michigan became sluggish at the finish. San Francisco looked third-rate, losing four of its first eight games, then won 18 in a row and gave Coach Pete Peletta a first-rate ulcer. At Lexington, Coach Rupp, uneasy, asked a reporter from New York: "Tell me the truth. How do we stack up against Michigan and UCLA and those people? Don't be afraid to hurt my feelings." An unoptimistic appraisal did not hurt The Baron's feelings nearly as much as the pairings hurt his chances for a fifth national championship. Kentucky was bracketed in the Mideast Regionals in Minneapolis—the one with Michigan and Loyola.

Coach Vic Bubas felt his Duke Blue Devils were good enough to win the national championship; this despite the fact they had been slammed by Michigan, 83-67, in December. They didn't have Art Heyman any more, and Heyman led them to the semifinals in 1963. But his leaving served to unleash Jeff Mullins, an All-American forward who averaged 23.5 points a game, led the team in rebounds and presided over the senior class. Duke was also playing some real defense, and there was no more compelling sight than 6' 10" Jay Buckley and 6' 10" Hack Tison on the court at one time. The Blue Devils averaged close to 50 percent from the field, and Buckley, the most improved, led with 58.1.

Teams chasing the favorites were Wichita, Creighton, Brown, Texas Western, Kansas State, and Oregon State. Perhaps the very best front-court player in the country would not be there, however. He was Miami's Rick Barry, a 6' 7", 19-year-old junior from Roselle Park, New Jersey who averaged 30.9 points and 16 rebounds a game, set a record of 50 points in one and was being called "magnificent," "exceptional," "mighty fine" and "better than Art Heyman" by rival coaches. Coach Bruce Hale's worry was that Barry could also equal Heyman's temper. He scored 35 points against San Francisco and then tried to throttle an opposing

player for what he thought was an indiscreet elbow. He went careening into the first row atop Florida's Dick Tomlinson in Gainesville. In the 1963 NIT against Providence he threw the ball into the stands when charged with a foul just when Miami had cut a huge Providence lead to two points. The result was a technical foul and the ball was given to Providence. The lead quickly shot up seven points, extinguishing Miami's chances. The NCAA tournament fans would not get an opportunity to see young Barry play.

John Wooden was not given to idle boasts, but there was nothing idle about what he was given to say a week before the NCAA regionals began. His was "a great team—a truly great team," he said. The prospect of a rematch with Michigan—in the finals in Kansas City—obviously did not frighten Wooden. Certainly it would delight Dave Strack. If that was to be the dream match, it was, after all, what KC was there for.

In the way of proving the pollsters correct, Duke swept through the tournament at Raleigh without missing a step, UCLA was still undefeated after 28 games and several miracle escapes, and Michigan, 22-4, was still the toughest bully on any block. "Everything we do," Dave Strack said, "is keyed on Cazzie Russell." And what the Wolverines had managed to do was join Duke, UCLA, and Kansas State in the semi-final round of the NCAA tournament in Kansas City. Kansas State was the only qualifier that did not figure.

None of the four had ever won a national basketball championship, and only Duke made it to the semifinals in 1963. UCLA, of course, was a semifinalist in 1962, Kansas State in 1958, and Michigan would rather not discuss it. The latter, nevertheless, had unequivocal credits in 1964: it knocked off defending champion Loyola, 84-80, in the regionals at Minneapolis, and Duke still remembered them from the December crushing.

What happened to Kentucky? The Wildcats got caught looking toward Kansas City, and were routed, 85-69, by unheralded Ohio. Rupp's 1-3-1 zone was shattered in the first half by excellent Ohio ballhandling, and All-American Cotton Nash was embarrassingly boxed out for the entire game.

Cazzie Russell came back to score 25 points

The 1963-64 Duke Blue Devils overwhelmed most opponents with their imposing height. In the NCAA playoffs, they finished third in 1963, and were runnersup to UCLA in 1964.

as Michigan beat Ohio in the final at Minneapolis, while Duke's only real competition at Raleigh was Villanova, and the magnificent Jeff Mullins, the Duke captain, took care of Villanova in 20 minutes. He made 18 of the Blue Devils' first 30 points. He stole the ball six times for easy layups, held Vallanova high scorer Richie Moore to eight points, wound up with 43 points himself and Duke won, 87-73. The next night Mullins scored 30 and Duke won by 47 over Connecticut.

Duke's opponent at Kansas City on the first night would be Michigan. Coach Vic Bubas, a vigorously positive thinker, admitted to a tactical error the first time Duke played Michigan. He ordered a slowdown. Michigan tore down the slowdown. "We ran and hid," Bubas said. "But not this time. This time we come out swinging."

Everybody had been swinging at UCLA all season long, but UCLA always hit back. In the Far West Regionals at Corvallis, the Bruins pressed from the opening tipoff and won over Seattle, 95-90. It was hardly one-sided, but it was typical UCLA—a lot of hands, hustle and too much Walt Hazzard, who scored 26 points.

UCLA had more trouble the next night against San Francisco, which was riding a 19-game winning streak. The Dons slowed the tempo, controlled the ball and as the Bruins missed their shots San Francisco twice pushed to 13-point leads. Wooden refused to panic. "We'll be all right as soon as our shots start dropping," Wooden told his players. Sure enough, they started finding the range, especially Hazzard, who scored 14 points in the last 14 minutes and UCLA won, 76-72. "They're the best," said Pete Peletta.

At Wichita, Don Haskins, the Texas Western coach, predicted that Wichita would cut Kansas State to shreds. Adding fuel to the fire was Wichita Coach Ralph Miller's claim that KSU had been ducking his team for years. But Wichita did not tear Kansas State to shreds. Not even a little. Tex Winter, expectedly, used his 1-3-1 zone and forced Wichita to shoot from outside. He countered the Wichita press with an unexpected and blazing fast break. At half time, Kansas State was ahead, 46-33, and then held on to win in a give-and-take finish, 94-86.

That gave Kansas State a winning streak of 13 straight, but it wasn't expected to reach 14. "My team lacks the playmaking and ballhandling abilities of UCLA," Tex Winter admit-

Quickness was the quality that allowed UCLA to win its first NCAA championship in 1964. Two of the quickest Bruins were running mates Walt Hazzard and Gail Goodrich. Hazzard (42) hits against Duke in National finals as Goodrich (25) looks on.

ted. The 1-3-1 zone that choked off Wichita was not going to bother the Bruins because Hazzard and Goodrich could ruin it from outside.

A contented amalgam as a team, Coach Wooden had to handle his individual players carefully. Forward Keith Erickson, a fine safety man in the 2-2-1 zone press and the team's leading rebounder, considered criticism subversive. Slaughter, the center, was a good student in the classroom but had to be prodded to be equally industrious on the court. Goodrich's passion was shooting. He once advised a high school group that "if your girl asks you to walk her home, tell her you're sorry, you have to go shoot baskets." Goodrich had to constantly remind himself that there was more than that to basketball. The champion hand-wringer, however, was forward Jack Hirsch, who also led the Bruins in solvency—he drove a blood-red 1964 Pontiac Grand Prix and owned a third interest in one of his dad's bowling alleys. The soft life notwithstanding, Hirsch developed into an excellent left-handed shooter, a tough rebounder and a dedicated defender. He limited Michigan prodigy Cazzie Russell to 11 points earlier in the season.

This was not an easy team for Wooden to coach, but he did not give up on his five starters. "Lately," he said as the Bruins packed for the trip to Kansas City, "we have not been going well, but somehow we keep our poise and get out of the jams we get ourselves into."

UCLA was a hard team to figure. It went for long spells at a time looking mortal and vulnerable. Then a certain mystical something would happen—UCLA coaches called it "the two-minute explosion"—and the Bruins would blow an opponent off the court. There was no predicting when it would happen, only that it would. At the Municipal Auditorium in Kansas City the two-minute explosion exploded on consecutive nights. In each case the explosion lasted a few seconds longer as UCLA beat Kansas State, a good team, 90-84, and then beat Duke, a better team, 98-83, and won the NCAA championship.

In the semifinal on Friday night, after Duke had taken Michigan impressively, 91-80, the Bruins, with their undersized, plain-looking players and a coach who did not smoke, drink, cuss or recruit very much, bumped around with

KSU and fell behind, 75-70, with seven minutes to play. There followed a flurry of hands and feet and—presto!—two minutes later UCLA was ahead, 81-75. And they stayed ahead.

The championship game on the final night was so attractive—big, resourceful Duke of the East against not-so-big, resourceful and unbeaten UCLA of the West, smackdab in the middle of America—that scalpers asked for and received three times the face value of tickets. The contest started briskly and for a time it appeared Duke, indeed, could defeat the UCLA press. The Blue Devils scored two quick baskets with ease and before long Wooden sent sophomore Doug McIntosh in for Slaughter; then another sophomore, Kenny Washington, appeared in the normally pat UCLA lineup. Both boys had performed well against Kansas State, and now, subtly, they began to make their presence known to Duke.

What made the Bruins so super was the deadly art of self-defense that Wooden taught, and basketball tacticians could not imagine how offensive defense could be until they had seen UCLA's busters gang up on the backboard or on some taller team, like Duke. UCLA pressed and UCLA converted—a stolen pass into a basket, a rebound, clearance and fast break into a basket, etc.—and the size disadvantage UCLA always faced was, always, negligible. "How do you look at Duke?" Wooden was asked before the game. "Up," he said. But despite Buckley and Tison and their five-inch advantage over any single UCLA player, the height difference was a paper difference. UCLA attacked not singly but in swarms, like gnats.

Lefthander Gail Goodrich, UCLA's leading scorer, was in top form with 27 points, his best production since the tournament began. Coach Wooden made it possible for Goodrich and Hazzard to drive to the basket by keeping his post man high, thus drawing Buckley out and clearing the middle. On defense, the Bruins nullified the Blue Devils' height advantage by pressing Tison in the high post. Keith Erickson, Hirsch, Washington and McIntosh all took turns making his life miserable for Duke. Pressed by the Bruins, the combination of Tison to Buckley did not have a chance. Even Mullins, despite his 22 points, was guilty of sloppy passing and seemed lethargic. Buckley got 18 points but only nine rebounds and Tison

The first of the UCLA dynasty—1964 national champions. Front row, left: Mgr. Dennis Minishian, Gail Goodrich, Jack Hirsch, Rich Levin, Walt Hazzard, Kent Graham, Mike Huggins, Chuck Darrow. Rear, left: Head Trainer "Ducky" Drake, Asst. Coach Jerry Norman, Steve Brucker, Fred Slaughter, Doug McIntosh, Vaughn Hoffman, Keith Erickson, Kim Stewart, Kenny Washington, Head Coach John Wooden.

grabbed only one, compared with McIntosh's 11 and Washington's 12.

Washington had the best shooting percentage in the game, hitting 11 of 16 for a total of 26 points. UCLA out-rebounded the taller Blue Devils, 43-35, and forced them to commit 29 errors. During the two-minute explosion, when the mistakes piled up more and more, the losers came so undone that they often had the wrong men with the ball in the wrong places. That was the kind of team UCLA was; it could rattle you to death.

After the game, when the Bruins were alone,

Coach of the Year Wooden spoke quietly to them. He told them, reverentially, how proud he was of them. They really were the best, he said. Their record of 30 straight victories proved that. But now, he said, came the hard part.

"Don't let the championship change you," he said. "You are the champions and you must act like champions. You met some people going up to the top—and you'll meet the same people going down."

Over the next dozen years, however, the Bruins wouldn't be touching the down button very often.

Bruins Cream of Crop: 1965

The new season came, but in college basketball the top of the Old Order remained pretty much the same. Bill Bradley of Princeton and the UCLA Bruins quickly established themselves as the cream of the crop for 1965. In the two best of many holiday tournaments, their spectacular successes differed from 1964 only in the numbers on the scoreboards.

It took Bradley exactly three minutes of Princeton's opening game with Syracuse in the Holiday Festival in Madison Square Garden to stake out squatter's rights as the nation's best college player. The Orange from upstate New York had set up a four-man box zone defense against the Orange from upstate New Jersey, with Sam Penceal assigned to guard Bradley. Penceal took the assignment literally, clinging to the Princeton star like lint on a blue serge suit. He clutched, he grabbed, he clawed. Then suddenly, fed up, Bradley rocked the stout Penceal with a well-planted elbow in the gut. There was a loud gasp from both Penceal and the overflow crowd. Then the fans cheered Bradley for his spunk. The referee was not so appreciative, however, and Penceal was awarded a ticket to the free-throw line.

Moments later Bradley broke loose from his shadow and got the ball for the first time. Immediately he took dead aim on the basket and hit a jump shot from 20 feet. That was just a sample of things to come. Before the half ended, he scored 21 more points, and by the end of the game there were 36 after his name. The final score, 79-69, earned Princeton the right to play Michigan, the country's No. 2-rated team behind UCLA, in the next round.

While Bradley was scoring 36 against Syracuse, Cazzie Russell matched that total against Manhattan in the same tournament, causing headline writers to label the Princeton-Michigan game "Bradley vs. Russell" and "Tigers vs. Wolverines," but as it turned out it was to be "Bradley vs. Michigan."

In the Michigan game, Bradley and his teammates were 12-point underdogs. But within minutes after play started, Bradley began to dominate all the action, not just for himself, but obviously inspiring his fellow Tigers. Soon the entire Garden came alive for him. "Go, Tigers, go!" they cheered. Near the end of the first half, Bradley caught fire and scored 12 straight points to give Princeton a 39-37 lead. Twenty-three of those points belonged to Bradley. Russell, bothered by the excellent defensive play of Don Rodenbach, had only six.

At the start of the second half, Rodenbach quickly was charged with two fouls, and Bradley was switched to the backcourt to fill the gap. This added to Bradley's burden. Now he was expected to do it all—score, ball-hawk, rebound and bring the ball upcourt. Whenever he got the ball the crowd chanted, "Go, Bradley, go!"

The heavy work load eventually took its toll. Bradley tired, missed two foul shots. Seconds later he was caught traveling, and then was called for checking Oliver Darden too closely and fouled out of the game. He walked off the floor to one of the biggest and warmest ovations ever given an athlete at Madison Square Garden. He had scored 41 points, gathered nine rebounds and four assists, but his playmaking and general floor skill (the man he guarded was held to one point and Bradley had several steals) was what captured the Garden audience.

Two-time All-American Cazzie Russell rallied Michigan to basketball heights in 1964 and 1965, as he averaged 33.2 points a game and earned national Player-of-the-Year honors in his senior season.

"I didn't think that any one player on any team could dominate a basketball game against another team," Dave Strack was to say later. "I knew Bradley was great—Russell had played with him in the 1964 Olympics and told me he was. We were willing to give him even 35 or 40 points, but I just never thought that one man could control a game like that."

When Bradley left the game, Princeton was in front, 75-63, and there was only 4:37 left on the clock. The fans sensed a major upset. Gary Walters, the Princeton guard, then drove through to make it 77-63. Now there was just 3:44 to go.

Then it happened. Princeton, without its star, suddenly collapsed. Bradley sat with a towel draped around his head and watched his accomplishment smashed to pieces. Michigan, which could be so overpowering, fought back savagely. In one stretch of 24 seconds, Russell, George Pomey and John Thompson each

Shoot, score, ball-hawk, rebound, bring the ball up-court—Princeton's Mr. Inspiration, Bill Bradley, did it all.

scored baskets, while shutting off Princeton with only one shot in the last three minutes of play. There were only 51 seconds left on the clock when Michigan tied the score, and only three seconds to go when Russell scored the winning basket from the left corner.

At the buzzer, Bill Buntin, the Michigan center, ran over to the Princeton bench and hugged Bradley—not in the exuberance of victory, but in admiration. Frank Deford, sitting at the press table, noticed that Bradley hardly sensed the gesture. "Bill hurried away, past where his mother sat and past where a few ordinary fans were crying for him," Deford recalled. "Michigan coach Strack came up in the gloomy hallway outside the Princeton locker room, where Bradley slumped against the wall, and put a hand on his shoulder and complimented him. 'We didn't deserve that,' Strack told him. As he walked away, he repeated it, louder, so anyone could hear: 'We didn't deserve that.' "

Bradley had nothing to prove after the Holiday Festival. Though Princeton won only the first round, he was chosen Most Valuable Player over Cazzie Russell. Against the best, before a basketball grand jury, he had answered all the questions, including some quibbles: great shooter, granted, but would he be strong enough under the boards, or tough enough? Only 205 pounds and not big in the shoulders— was he big enough? Ask Sam Penceal. The Syracuse star had no way of knowing that Bradley not only knew how to play a physical game, but within limits liked it that way. "I think there should be contact allowed," Bradley said. "Especially when a guy doesn't have the ball." Bradley encountered all the contact one man could use as opponents rigged defenses for him and many tried to jostle him into the retaliation that would hasten his exit.

"I learned a lesson about that when I was a freshman," Bradley said. "We were playing Manhattan, and we got ahead, 17-2. It got close later, about two points, and a guy did a real dirty thing to me. I lost my temper and really gave it to him—not anything dirty, but hard, you know? That was my fourth personal, and a little while later I fouled out. We lost by two points."

For the rest of his college career Bradley was "aggressive enough," but he never lost his head. He averaged 30.1 points a game, and his conduct against the gang jobs was more than adequate. After the Michigan game in the Holiday Festival, Bradley had nowhere to hide from reporters. The cult increased a hundredfold, and he became a household name. Whether the public wanted to know or not, it had to be told how many lefthanded hook shots Bradley took in warming up, how many inches behind his right foot he positioned his left for a foul shot and to what extent his jump shot was an imitation of Jerry West's. Bradley got through such interviews smoothly, because he liked to talk about basketball. A most coachable athlete, he spoke of his coaches gratefully and proudly. There was Arvel Popp in high school, who wouldn't use a 6' 5" kid up front because he wouldn't learn the whole game; Ed Macauley at summer camp, who taught him the set shot and something else—that when you aren't practicing, somebody else is; and Bill Van Breda Kolff at Princeton, who pretended Bradley was just another player and became "a guy we'll always want to go back and see."

It is not true that Bradley practiced two or three hours *every* day. In high school, at Crystal City, Missouri, there was baseball in April and May and he sort of fooled around in June, so he didn't get to serious basketball practice until July. As a sophomore at Princeton he was the first baseman, and he batted .316. "But I hadn't developed enough to make it worthwhile. I could concentrate on basketball, but baseball I just played."

So he concentrated on basketball.

"The weeks I missed a day of practice," he said, "I could count on one hand. Well, two hands."

During the summer of 1964 he developed a routine of persisting with each shot until he had made 10 of 13. "That was so I could get practice done in an hour," he explained. "When I had time I used to work on a shot until I'd made 25 in a row."

Meanwhile, 3,000 miles away . . .

While UCLA was scrambling to a perfect 30-0 season and the undisputed national championship in 1964, Pete Newell, the California Athletic Director, observed: "Whenever they're in trouble they go to the insurance man." In Newell's nomenclature the "insurance man" was the pressure player—the player he wanted to have holding the ball in tense situations. Walt Hazzard filled the bill for the Bruins in

1964, but now he was graduated. In his place as a 1965 model of the insurance man was Keith Erickson. Taking over Hazzard's role, he quickly became the offensive ignition of the team, its floor and inspirational leader, the steadying influence. He was cocky and given to drifting indifference in the tedium of practice, but the earnest, understated John Wooden admitted he could tolerate some insouciance as long as "Herc" Erickson rose to the occasion at game time. "And Erickson gets better as the pressure gets higher," Wooden said.

With Erickson acclaimed the tournament's Most Valuable Player, UCLA and its pesty zone press worked its way through Arizona (99-79) and Minnesota (93-77) and Utah (104-74) and set scoring records to boot to win the Los Angeles Classic for the third straight, embarrassing time. "UCLA simply destroys you—physically, mentally and morally," groaned Utah coach Jack Gardner. Erickson had been everywhere: sometimes on the prowl downcourt; sometimes picking up the first man loose on Utah's fast break; sometimes intercepting passes; and other times zooming up, up and away into the air around the baskets as if catapulted from a launching pad. Seeing the spring in his legs, it was easy to understand why he was a member of the 1964 U. S. Olympic volleyball team.

The Bruins opened the season with a loss to Illinois, their first defeat in 31 games. Everybody was sure they were not going to be as good as the 1964 edition. But then they ran away with the LA Classic, looking even better than they did when they won the NCAA championship, and the poll people changed their tune and installed them as the team to beat for the national title all over again.

After the Classic, a reporter talked to Jack Gardner, picking his brains, trying to make sense of the Bruins. After all, Utah battled UCLA practically dead even in the first half, behind by only three points. The score was tied 11 times. With that, John Wooden tightened his zone press and Utah, bending under the terrible weight, committed seven major ball-handling errors in the first six minutes of the second half. What had been anybody's ballgame was suddenly UCLA's all the way—by 30 points at the finish.

"What have they got?" the Utah coach was asked.

"What *haven't* they got?" blurted Gardner. "I'll tell you what they have. They have balanced board power. And great speed. Also great shooting. And fantastic jumping. Don't overlook great depth. And—and don't ever forget it—Keith Erickson."

It was enough for a rival coach to call off the 1964-65 season then and there.

With most teams settled down to battling for conference championships by mid-January, some semblance of form finally was visible in major-college basketball. Davidson, for one, threatened to turn the Southern Conference race into a runaway. Michigan was leading in the Big Ten, and Wichita State in the Missouri Valley. UCLA's powerful game was overwhelming the AAWU conference, and San Francisco had a piece of the lead in the West Coast AC. But there were surprises, too: North Carolina State was tied with Duke in the Atlantic Coast, Auburn led the Southeastern, and Oklahoma State was first in the Big Eight. Even more startling, SMU shared the lead with Texas Tech in the Southwest Conference.

Six weeks later there were 23 teams in the NCAA tournament. Surprisingly, the team to beat was not UCLA. According to the overwhelming opinion of the public and the polls, the favorite was *Michigan*. The Wolverines had not lost since January 2, when it was upset, 75-74, by St. John's in Madison Square Garden, although many of its victories after that appeared to be hairbreadth escapes. Close or not, they were victories, and against strong teams. "My team's pretty courageous," said Coach Dave Strack. "It didn't win all the close games, but most of them. That's the mark of a good team."

If beating Michigan was a requisite for winning the national championship, seven of the teams in the 1965 NCAA tournament had the personnel and the playing style to place first: St. Joseph's, Miami of Ohio, Notre Dame, Oklahoma State, Brigham Young, San Francisco and UCLA. Most compared favorably, as did Michigan, with the picture of the composite NCAA champion that grew out of a study made in 1951.

The ideal team, according to that analysis, had seniors on it but was not dominated by them. It had, in fact, nearly as many sophomores as seniors, and more juniors than either. The ideal team had a good bench, but not a deep one; depended on well-balanced, superior teamwork, with seven regulars carrying the load, led by an All-American, most often a center who played his best at tournament time. He was not a superstar, nor was he one of the nation's highest scorers. The ideal team, if not staffed by highly experienced players, was led by a coach with many years of college competition behind him. The ideal team was no surprise, having been ranked prominently by the wire-service polls, almost always in the top three, and nearly half the time as No. 1. The ideal team was a good road club, and almost never lost at home. It won a holiday tournament at Christmas. It was a member of a conference and won that race rather easily, without a pressure-packed struggle. It was a team with the killer instinct. It outscored opponents by an average of at least 12 points a game, and was not the least bit ashamed to run up the score.

Those were the qualities that turned up most often in the 14 NCAA champions since 1951, and only one—Kentucky's Fiddling Five of 1958—had less than half of them. By those standards, the 1965 St. Joseph's team stood out impressively. The Hawks lacked seniors, and did not have the stature of an outstanding center, but, otherwise, it matched the composite champion in every way, from coach (Dr. Jack Ramsey, 209-65) to record (25-1, no losses at home or on neutral courts) to average margin of victory (17.6). It ranked third in both major polls, was 12th nationally in offense, was undefeated in its conference and won the Quaker City Christmas tournament.

There were more good teams in the East, however, and St. Joe's was going to need luck. It didn't get it. So much for the Ideal Team theory. When wisps of smoke rose over what had been the Eastern Regional tournament at College Park, Maryland, it was Princeton's poor little rich boys, and not the Hawks, who would be representing the East in the NCAA semifinals at Portland, Oregon. The Tigers had been magnificent. They trounced favored North Carolina State, 66-48, and then absolutely ruined Providence, the No. 4 team in the polls, 109-69. Bill Bradley went on another of his typically hot-shooting sprees. He made 14 of 20 shots, all 13 of his free throws—41 points—and he had nine assists and 10 rebounds. Tom Jorgenson, who was scouting for Michigan, said after the tournament that he was going back to Ann Ar-

bor and just tell the team that Bradley was the best player in history. "Why tell them anything else?" he said. "They wouldn't believe me anyway."

It marked the first time in 21 years that an Ivy League team had gone so far in the NCAAs, and no Ivy team had ever won, though Dartmouth finished second in 1942 and 1944. Michigan won its regional title and would meet the Tigers in the NCAA semifinals, while defending champion UCLA and Wichita faced off in the second game.

In the shellshocked Princeton locker room after losing to Michigan in December, Bradley had stood up and told his teammates that it was no one-night stand, no fluke. "We must regroup," he reminded them. "We must win the league title, must win the regional—and then beat Michigan for the eastern championship." Old Nassau had now carried out two-thirds of the vow, so when the Tigers returned from College Park the normally blasé Princeton student body showed up 1,000 strong to welcome the team back to the campus. And it was the *whole* team they cheered. It was the *whole* team that shot 68.3 percent against Providence (while Bradley shot 70 percent) and 72.7 percent in the second half. In one stretch the Tigers went 12 minutes without missing a shot— 14 straight from the floor and the free-throw line. The crowd hoisted Bradley and the other players up on the top of the team bus. The band was there, and so were all those students. "We have been thinking of only one thing since December 30th," Bradley told them. Naturally, he remembered the date. "We have been thinking about beating Michigan." Then the band played *Old Nassau*, and the Tigers all sang, touching their right hands to their hearts and then extending their arms, as was traditional.

Against Providence, not a few experts felt Princeton was the best team in the country— better even than UCLA, which had regained its championship pace—better even than mighty Michigan, whose season's record indicated it should beat Princeton at Portland. Of course, such routine reasoning was meaningless if Princeton Coach Bill van Breda Kolff's blue-bloods maintained their momentum. They had a 13-game winning streak going because they were so improved. After Bradley, the best of the other Tigers was 6' 6"sophomore Ed Hummer, slow to develop, but now a topflight player.

Before the 1965 NCAA tournament began, some experts believed Princeton to be the best team in the country, better even than UCLA and Michigan. The Tigers finished third. Back row, left: Coach Butch van Breda Kolff, Gary Walters, Allen Adler, Ed Hummer, Robinson Brown, Bill Koch, Chris Chimera, Larry Lucchino, Bob Sinkler (trainer), Mgr. Stuart Ball. Front row, left: Don Rodenbach, Don Roth, Don Niemann, Captain Bill Bradley, Ken Shank, Bill Kingston, Bob Haarlow.

While not a starter, he was used primarily to come off the bench and stir things up. Playmaker Gary Walters, 5′ 10″, was an uncommonly poised sophomore who could beat the press. The center was 6′ 9″ Robby Brown, who had improved steadily all season and scored 14 points against Providence. Brown was an elbows-and-knees stringbean who should have been named Ichabod, not Robby. The other two starters were juniors—6′ 2″ forward Bob Haarlow and guard Don Rodenbach.

For two centuries Princeton was esteemed in the elite Ivy League. Now it had become a power in basketball, not only in its own academic community but nationwide. Much of the credit went to Coach Butch van Breda Kolff, a husky ex-marine with a voice that had been roughened and deepened by too many cigars. Before Princeton, he had served as lacrosse coach at Lafayette. "My first year we were 0-9," he said. "So the guy asked me, 'How will you do next year?' I told him, 'Can't do any worse.' So what does the guy do? He scheduled 10 games. And then we were 0-10!"

Butch van Breda Kolff's real given names are Willem Hendrik, but Butch seemed to fit him much better. He once attended classes in the neighborhood of Nassau Hall. The 1948 alumni directory listed him with "-45" after his name,

giving him a hyphen rather than an apostrophe because he did not get his degree. He left Princeton to be a defensive specialist for the New York Knickerbockers and earned his apostrophe at NYU. Princetonians did not hold that against him, however, when it came time to hire a basketball coach in the fall of 1962. After the Knicks he had gone to Lafayette and built a winning record when he was not moonlighting with lacrosse. Hofstra, a small college on Long Island, hired him away. He stayed seven years and had records like 20-7, 23-1 and 21-4 before moving on to Princeton. His teams won Ivy League titles the first three seasons. And he won with superior talent—most of which he recruited—and he won on his coaching ability, too.

Life on the Princeton campus was somewhat different from that at most American schools. With clubs and without coeds, the students, including the basketball players, studied hard. Robby Brown, the most articulate member of the team, liked to discuss Coach van Breda Kolff's freelance offense this way: "It's a sort of intellectual exercise, because you've got to see what everybody's doing and gauge your actions accordingly."

Recruits were surprised to discover that Raycroft Library was hidden at the end of an L-

Southpaw Gail Goodrich (25), deadly on the attack, also played a harassing role in the dreaded UCLA press.

shaped hall off the lobby of Dillon Gym. "A library in the gymnasium," cracked one Tiger. "That's typical of Princeton."

Princeton's sensational rout of the East in 1965 shoved the three other regional champions into the background, but now it was time for them to surface. Out on the Coast, everybody was talking about the UCLA press, a weapon of immense potency. It had made the Bruins famous and had brought Coach John Wooden inquiries from 700 other coaches, all of them anxious to learn how UCLA did it. It had turned up in countless variations across the U.S., but no one ran the press like the Bruins.

The press, á la Wooden, was really a fairly simple tactic. The more of the floor the Bruins used, the better chance they had to overcome their usually bigger, more powerful opponents. So they kept the action moving all around the court, counting on their speed and quickness. This forced the taller, slower team to play from one end of the floor to the other—and almost always to disastrous disadvantage.

UCLA's stifling press would begin after the Bruins scored and the other team took the ball out of bounds. McIntosh, for example, harassed the man with the ball, while Goodrich and Goss moved to guard against the easy inbounds pass. Because a longer pass was always risky, this occasionally led to a failure to put the ball into play within five seconds, and UCLA got possession. When the inbounds pass was successful, McIntosh joined Goodrich to double-team the receiver, either to tie him up or force him into a bad pass. Lacey and Erickson, meanwhile, shaded over to the side where the ball was. This action frequently induced a long pass to the free man upcourt, but because Goodrich and McIntosh had their hands up and were jumping, the pass had to be a soft lob. This allowed Erickson time to change direction and intercept the ball.

"All I am asked about is the UCLA press," said Michigan's Dave Strack shortly before the 1965 semi-finals began. "Well, anybody can press, but to make it work you need the personnel. The UCLA press is mostly the UCLA players."

John Wooden first used his zone press when he was a high school coach, but for a long time he felt that it could not succeed in college competition. He decided to take a chance with it in 1963 when he had what he thought was the right material.

The press is what UCLA used to beat Wichita State and Michigan to win its second NCAA championship in a row. Wichita, a gritty team that somehow made it to the semi-finals even after All-American Dave Stallworth ran out of eligibility at mid-year and center Nate Bowman flunked out, was no match at all for the Bruins. Powerful Michigan was something else, however. For a while, Cazzie Russell, Bill Buntin and Oliver Darden took command and controlled the rebounds, made shots from all over the court, and led, 20-13, after eight minutes. With All-American and floor leader Gail Goodrich missing his shots, the Bruins were tense. Then co-captain Keith Erickson injured his leg, forcing Lacey to play his safety man position on the press. Because of his size and mobility, Erickson was regarded as the most valuable man in the press—and now he was on the bench. On Wednesday, he pulled a muscle in his left leg, and aggravated it on Thursday and in pregame drills on Friday. He scored only two points in the Wichita State game, as compared with 28 and 29 in the regionals, and he limped noticeably. On Saturday morning he had ultrasonic treatment and he was determined to play against Michigan, but in the game he was bothered more by a tight bandage than by the injury itself. By the time

he had gone back to the bench and loosened the bandage, his substitute, Kenny Washington, had ignited a typical UCLA explosion. Jump shots by Washington, Fred Goss and Lacey made the score 20-19, followed by a Goodrich free throw. Now the Bruins took charge on the boards. In the midst of all this smoke Russell managed one basket for the Big Ten champions, but Washington and Doug McIntosh came swooping down like hawks out of nowhere to block other Michigan shots. And triggering it all, making this offensive charge possible, was the vaunted press. Suddenly, twice within 60 seconds, the Wolverines could not even get the ball upcourt. The more they fought to break through, the more the blocks and interceptions followed.

"The crowd was yelling louder and louder each time we did something," McIntosh recalled later. "But this one time I wasn't able to really put any pressure on Cazzie. Then I looked, and I saw the ball just dribble off his leg. I just watched that ball dribble off his leg, and all I could think was: 'Isn't this sweet? We're going to win.'"

Even though his team was trailing at the time, McIntosh's hunch was right. The tempo of the game had switched completely. The Bruins outscored Michigan, 10-1, in a three-minute burst just before the half ended, giving UCLA a 47-34 lead. Michigan was supposed to be the best rebounding team in college basketball, but UCLA was actually ahead in this department, 19-17, and continued to control all facets of the game in the second half as Goodrich gave the Wolverines a superb lesson in ballhandling. He scored on long lefthanded jumpers, he led the fast break, he twisted through a forest of tall defensemen to hook in layups, and with his teammates he smothered the Michigan attack mercilessly on defense. But when all was said and done, it was the UCLA press that won this game—as it had won virtually every game for the past two championship teams.

Russell made 28 points and played well as always, but the losers had a hard time getting the ball to him in close. As against Princeton on Friday night, there seemed to be no pattern at all to the Michigan offense. One coach described the UCLA-Michigan game as "a tag-team match between five matadors and five bulls," but Strack never abandoned the bulls,

UCLA's national champions, 1965 edition. Front row, left: Asst. Coach Jerry Norman, Gail Goodrich, John Lyons, John Galbraith, Mike Serafin, Brice Chambers, Larry McCollister, Freddie Goss. Rear, left: Coach John Wooden, Trainer "Ducky" Drake, Rich Levin, Edgar Lacy, Doug McIntosh, Vaughn Hoffman, Will Winkelholz, Mike Lynn, Keith Erickson, Kenny Washington, Willie Ureda.

even when it was obvious that they were being cut into hamburger while still on the hoof.

More than anything else, Michigan was betrayed by poor ballhandling and playmaking against both UCLA and Princeton. In the Princeton game, the Michigan power was more than sufficient compensation, however, and the Tigers were out-rebounded, 56-34. Still, it was the only game of the weekend that was close—until Bill Bradley, in foul trouble for all of the second half, fouled out with five minutes to play.

Bradley finished his college career on Saturday in what the romanticists would call "a blaze of glory." He was magnificent. In as satisfying a climax as could be hoped for in a consolation game, he set all kinds of records as Princeton routed Wichita State, 118-82. Bradley made 22 of 29 shots from the floor, and 14 for 15 from the free-throw line, for a total of 58 points. He

made sets, long and short, jumps, hooks with both hands. And there were others that defied description. With victory secured, Bradley expected to come out of the game. He lacked, he confessed later, the "killer instinct" and never had a taste for running up a score on an outclassed opponent. But Coach Bill van Breda Kolff would not shortchange the "Bradley cult," and when Bradley's teammates began returning the passes he gave them, he had little choice but to shoot. By the end of the game he had scored all those points and the NCAA tournament record book was out of date.

After that, Bill Bradley was no longer being compared to any of his contemporaries but only to the other legendary collegians of basketball and to the memories of their finest hours. "Hank Luisetti and Oscar Robertson were unbeatable," former All-Pro Carl Braun said flatly, "but Bradley is the greatest." Joe Lapchick was

Bill Bradley (No. 42) leaves a game for last time as a collegian after scoring 58 points against Wichita State to lead Princeton to third-place finish in 1965 NCAA tournament at Portland, Oregon. Note the standing ovation.

willing to go almost as far. "I always thought Oscar was the greatest, but Bradley is only a half-step behind him. Right now, if the Knicks could get him, he'd be worth $100,000 to them."

The Knicks were going to have to wait. Bill Bradley had committed himself to a Rhodes scholarship for two years at Oxford. The temptation to play pro ball dissolved when he was advised, just before Christmas, that he had been elected a Rhodes scholar. It was during the exhaustive interviews by the Rhodes screening committee that Bradley suspected he was going to like Oxford, an asylum of anonymity. In school, Bill always relished his privacy, was quite formal, and called everybody Mister.

"By the way, Mr. Bradley," asked a committee member at the end of one session, "have you ever played any sports?"

You could hear the laughter all the way from Old Nassau.

Defense Wins for Texas Western: 1966

At the end, there was Don Haskins, a young coach at a school that had never before even challenged for a national title in any sport, standing with defiance in the way of Kentucky and Adolph Rupp. It was a combination that bridged both the history and glory of college basketball.

Not that Texas Western had exactly been glorified. No Miner player had made an all-district team, much less an All-American selection, but the team just kept on winning and finally met Kentucky in the NCAA finals at College Park, Maryland. Kentucky '66 had been a team touched by fate, a team overlooked by nearly everyone before the season started, but everybody's favorite at the end. Yet instead of Adolph Rupp winning his fifth national title, Don Haskins won his first. "I'm just a young punk," Haskins said. "It was a thrill playing against Mr. Rupp, let alone beating him."

The beating was thorough as well as exciting. The Wildcats were a frazzled, feeble bunch of ballplayers when they faced Texas Western in the showdown, but that was no alibi, for the Miners had come through a tough season, too. Essentially, the championship contest matched Kentucky's offense against Texas Western's defense, and it was the defense that won.

The whole Kentucky team was tired. Only Rupp, a remarkable old man hungry for another championship, remained eager for the last two games of the season. At the age of 64, he continued to pursue the only challenge left—trying to top himself. And that was some tough act to follow. Rupp had won 23 Southeastern Conference titles and four NCAA national crowns, as well as enough acclaim—and cen-

sure—to serve most men for all their years. Yet his persistence in staying at his job had won him in 1966 something more than just another trophy or a few fresh statistics. He was threatening to become the grand old man of basketball.

For most of the season, Kentucky was ranked No. 1 in the polls. This moved Rupp into voluntary, eager praise of his team. "These boys are coachable," he said. "They listen and they do what they're supposed to. They're a pleasure and they're all regular. They are regular to the last man. It would be *mean* if they lost a game."

There was a great deal of speculation over the change in Rupp in 1966. Everyone's explanation for his new phase was that he had mellowed. One difference was that his sarcasm, which used to endanger sensitive eardrums, was held to a minimum. And, off the court, the players, a very intelligent and personable bunch, were accorded attention and solicitude that no other Rupp team had ever been granted. One day guard Tommy Kron heard him ask forward Larry Conley what he was going to do after graduation. "I never heard of that before," Kron said. "Coach Rupp always sort of found those things out. He was interested, but there was never anything like that."

The change in Rupp was not easily explained by his former players. "With us," said Alex Groza, All-American center on the Fabulous Five champs of the late 1940s, "there was no joking, no laughing, no whistling, no singing, no nothing. Just basketball. When we traveled, for instance, he often communicated with us through the team manager." But there was one time in Alabama in 1966 when Rupp positively enthralled his players with an enchanting story about how his mother used to prepare fried chicken. On another occasion, Louis Dampier, the little guard, walked up to Rupp before practice and said happily, "Hey, Coach, a professor told me a funny story about you today." Rupp was delighted. He asked to hear the tale, chuckled throughout it and then told Dampier, "It's absolutely true, too."

At times during the 1966 season Rupp solicited and then used advice on strategy from his players. He did it at halftime in the St. Louis game, when the Wildcats led by only two points. He even went so far on some occasions as to ask the players if they approved of his strategy, something practically unprecedented. "I can't ever remember us offering suggestions in a game," said Frank Ramsey, star of the undefeated 1953-54 team. "We did discuss things with him, but you have to remember that was a special situation. Since the NCAA suspension kept us out for that year, we could do nothing but practice, and three of us were five-year men. We'd known Coach Rupp for a long time."

One reason for the change in Rupp was his health. He had had trouble with his blood pressure for a decade. In 1965 he endured the worst record (15-10) of his career and was physically exhausted as well. "Why, I'd just be sitting there dictating a letter, and suddenly I'd be all dizzy," Rupp said. "Just to get on the floor was hard. I was breathing like a panther all the time." In 1966 he was 20 pounds lighter, the blood pressure was down, the dizziness was gone and he had never felt better.

"He's so loose now," said Harry Lancaster, Rupp's assistant and comrade for two decades. "I don't believe he's ever been so relaxed. I think this is important for this team, too. He's made it clear that it's their ballclub. He's given them the credit."

The 1966 Wildcats underwent a metamorphosis almost as pronounced as that of their coach.

"There was dissension on this team in 1965," Dampier confessed. "We were always bickering, and by the end of the season we knew we were holding onto the ball for ourselves instead of passing it."

The key to Kentucky was 6' 3" forward Conley, a frail and uncommonly perceptive young man who was that rarity, a playmaking forward. More accurately, he played smart and was what the NCAA meant when it used the term "student-athlete." Conley leaned toward becoming a dentist, but he majored in political science and took a curriculum that included Russian, art, music and most anything else he thought might be interesting. "I came to college," he said, "thinking that I should make it as broadening, as enlightening an experience as I could."

Oh, yes, about that story Louie Dampier heard from his professor and related to Rupp. It seems that Rupp, who was never encumbered by modesty, once taught a basketball class at University of Kentucky, and he would always give all of his students straight A's. Rupp's reasoning was simple. "No one," he explained, "can learn basketball from me and not get an A."

In the semi-finals at College Park, Texas Western played Utah, while Kentucky met Duke. Everyone presumed that the winner of the Kentucky-Duke game would have no trouble with the western contender on Saturday night. At the start Kentucky rushed to a 23-14 lead. Conley, who had been ill all week, hit his first shot, but in a few minutes he began to gasp and took himself out of the game. Bob Verga, Duke's star shooter, who just the day before had been released from the hospital, went to his own bench soon after and he was never himself in this game. His illness had robbed him of the spring in his legs, and the power for the jump shot that had made him Duke's 19.2 scorer over the season. He made only one jumper and had four points in the game. "No spring, no bounce, no life," he said later.

But Jack Marin and center Mike Lewis combined to move Duke back into the lead. Rupp tried to stop the Blue Devils with a one-three-one zone, but Duke quickly figured that out, forcing Kentucky back to a man-to-man.

Both teams traded the lead back and forth in the second half, until, with 3:31 left to go, Pat Riley (who came to the game wearing a fuzzy little shamrock in his lapel for luck), and Dampier put together a fast break that moved Kentucky ahead by four points. From there the battle was even until Duke missed a good shot. Now there was only a minute and a half to play. Tommy Kron picked off a rebound and pitched it out to Conley, who was moving up the middle on a three-on-two fast break. Seeing the Blue Devils flare out, he drove all the way in with virtually his last breath to give Kentucky a six-point lead. "That was the tough one," Duke's Vic Bubas said. Three times in four years he had led his Duke team to the NCAA semifinals, only to lose each time.

Texas Western, as expected, beat Utah, 85-78. All that kept Utah in the game was Jerry Chambers, just about the best player in the tournament. He scored 38 points against the Texans, the most scored against them in five years. When the Miners' four big men—Dave Lattin, Nevil (The Shadow) Shed, Harry Flournoy and Willie Cager—got into foul trouble, Coach Don Haskins brought in Jerry Armstrong, and Armstrong came closer to stopping Chambers than the regulars had. Texas Western won easily, but they were not happy.

"The officials called it like a girls' game," said Lattin, who fouled out.

"Baby fouls," said Shed. "They called baby fouls."

In the second game of Friday night's doubleheader, Don Haskins, whose team had no shooters in Duke's class, was the most interested observer as he watched the Blue Devils shoot Rupp's one-three-one zone to shreds quickly. Haskins figured—correctly—that if Kentucky won and the Miners won, Texas Western would see that one-three-one zone in the finals.

On Saturday morning, Haskins looked at the world through bloodshot eyes. He hadn't slept a wink. He sat in his room with Bill Cornwall, having a few beers. Cornwall was an El Paso construction-supply executive and the team's lucky charm. He had missed only one road trip in 1966—to Seattle—and that was the only game TW lost.

"Once in a lifetime," Haskins kept repeating. "You know, tonight's game is once in a lifetime."

"You're young yet," Cornwall reminded him. "You'll have another team in the championship."

"No," Haskins said. "No chance. Mr. Rupp is 64, and he made it a lot of times, but it's probably going to be just once in a lifetime for me."

Saturday was Texas Western's day. It was the one that counted. It was to end in El Paso with bonfires and orange bunting all over town and two riot squads to calm down the natives. In Maryland the band played *Miners Fight* over and over, and they all screamed "We're No. 1." Haskins had a splitting headache—frightful, bursting pains that seemed to cleave his brain—and chain-smoked cigarettes and said, "This may never happen to me again." The closer he got to game time, the worse the headache grew. Perhaps his suffering was attributable to the implausibility of it all, for now Haskins really began to wonder if maybe he wasn't knocking destiny just a little bit out of joint. He savored the situation, of course. He loved it. But now and then he would stop to muse on the "once in a lifetime" aspect, toying with the idea, mulling the whole incredible thing over in his aching mind. Did this happen to Arnold Palmer? Or Roger Maris? And, years ago, what was Gene Tunney thinking when he startled the world when he outsmarted Jack Dempsey in the prize ring?

Before the NCAA final, Haskins let his players do as they pleased—no chalk talks or strategy sessions. He had one surprise up his sleeve for Kentucky but planned to stick with his basic game, which was man-for-man on defense and a loose freelance attack. Dave "Big Daddy D" Lattin, Western's intimidator at center, slept most of the day, stirring only for meals and a chat with friends. Harry Flournoy, the team's top rebounder, nursed a sore knee.

The Kentucky players also lolled about, marking time.

As Haskins had anticipated, Kentucky planned to use the one-three-one zone. Haskins' surprise for Rupp was a three-guard lineup. Bobby Joe Hill, 5' 9", and 6' 1" Orsten Artis were the regular backcourt starters, and he decided to use 5' 6" Willie Worsley in place of big Shed, to get more speed in against the very speedy Wildcats. All three played the whole game.

Before the game, Rupp walked into the Kentucky locker room and asked his players to name a captain for the contest. Somebody said Riley. He was the logical choice, Conley said, because it was his birthday the next day. All right then, Rupp said, beating Texas Western would be a great birthday present for Riley.

Duke beat Utah by two in the consolation game, and the Wildcats jumped up from their benches in the dressing room and ran out on the floor to try to win a fifth NCAA championship for Adolph Rupp.

It was a disaster almost from the beginning. Kentucky's marksmanship failed in the face of the tight Miner defense, and even the shots the Wildcats made were individual tributes to Dampier's and Riley's skill. For weeks, Coach Haskins had been telling the press that his team was capable of better defense than it had shown. Now they proved it.

Early in the contest the two teams were tied, 9-9, when Texas Western broke the knot with a foul shot. Insignificant at the time, that free throw opened the way to the most important sequence of the playoffs. Bobby Joe Hill, who was positioned off to the right side of the court, suddenly swiped the ball from Kron, and dribbled half the length of the floor and scored. Undaunted, Dampier calmly brought the ball back upcourt, spotted Hill in his path at midcourt, swerved left—and there was Bobby Joe again, waiting. Magically, Bobby Joe picked the ball off Dampier's dribble and took it all the way in for another easy layup. That opened the floodgates, and the Wildcats spent the rest of the evening playing catch-up. As late as eight minutes into the second half they came within only one point of TW, but never could quite make it all the way. Once they had three straight shots at a tie—Dampier, Cliff Berger and Riley—and missed them all.

The Wildcats were no slouches on defense themselves, but the Texans demonstrated that they could control the ball even with a net over them. Their three small men—Hill, Artis and Worsley—broke Kentucky's tight zone with long baskets from outside. Those were the same kind of shots that Kentucky kept missing. When the Wildcats started to foul in desperation, TW made the free throws—in one 37-minute period, 26 of 27. At the end, with Bobby Joe and Worsley just dribbling around to kill the clock, it was Texas Western by seven, 72-65.

The Kentucky players took the defeat very hard. As soon as Tommy Kron, who had played his heart out, got inside the locker room, he sat down and began to cry. Louis Dampier came over and put his arm around him and hugged him.

Across the hall Don Haskins hugged the game ball. The splitting headache that had been cleaving his brain for weeks was gone.

Considering what loomed ahead for college basketball—three varsity seasons of Lew Alcindor at UCLA—it was safe to say that for 1966's losers, tomorrow was four years away. Indeed, the College Park playoffs was the Tournment of the Last Chance.

There was a movement afoot in 1966 to do something about basketball's biggest bugaboo: domination of the sport by the goons. John L. McHale was the master behind the plan. For 10 years he had been developing an idea called *balanced basketball*. Here is how it operated:

Every player belonging to a conference or other class of competition would be officially registered according to a precisely devised scale of numerical "height-units." For example, a man under 5′ 2″ would wear the height-unit "0" on his jersey. If he stood 5′ 2″ to 5′ 3″, his height-unit was "1"; 5′ 4″ to 5′ 5″, "2"; 5′ 6″ to 5′ 7″, "3", and so on up to "12", which was the designation for those 7-feet and up. Lew Alcindor, 7′ 2″, would be a "12."

"The team ceiling would total 30 height-units," explained the 6′ 3″ McHale, whose own height reflected personal frustrations in court duels with taller players. "Thus, a coach could use five 6-footers, or any other combination of players whose measurements added up to no more than 30. In my opinion, *balanced basketball* would end the giants' monopoly while still admitting any big man who is skilled. Sure, the extra-tall fellow has as much right to play as anybody else, but the whole idea is to have everyone competing under just one criterion—ability."

McHale believed that team ceilings would allow coaches an interesting degree of leeway. Should a 7-footer, a "12," be teamed with four men of average height, perhaps four "4s," for a total of 28? Or would it be wiser to unveil a combination of two men who were fairly tall, two fairly short, and one of average height?

"The best choice," McHale said, "would be dictated by the abilities of the available players, by matchups and whatever game strategy the coach favored. Here, again, a question arises: Would coaches be up to such challenges? Imagine the sleepless nights, the churning brains, the numerical gyrations, the suspicion of 'loaded' scales and the potentially ruinous effect of the difference of an inch. But the height crisis in basketball has mounted alarmingly throughout

Unheralded Texas Western came from out of nowhere in 1966 to upset favored Kentucky, 72-65, in the NCAA championship game at College Park, Maryland. One of its stars had the perfect name for a basketball player—Willie Cager, shown here controlling the ball against Adolph Rupp's Wildcats.

the country. Statistics back this up. The average height of American men is only 5' 9", and the proportion of giants—6' 6" or taller—is one in 1,000. Yet, in the NBA, most players are at least 6' 6". It's been four years since the league had a player of average height. This is obviously an astronomical degree of misrepresentation. Analyzed, it is more than a crisis; it's an emergency. Basketball is too great a game to be denied to so many people."

Joe Lapchick thought McHale's proposal was intriguing. Cliff Buck, president of the AAU, favored giving it a test. Adolph Rupp liked its potentialities. Bud Foster, chairman of the National Basketball Committee, the rules body, felt it was worth experimenting with.

John Wooden said he liked the game just the way it was, thank you.

At least for the next three years.

UCLA's Excellence Too Much: 1967

The Great Stall Debate, somewhat dormant since the college days of Wilt Chamberlain, was back again. It started one night in Los Angeles after USC Coach Bob Boyd decided his players were not going to be the hors d'oeuvres for undefeated UCLA and its ultimate weapon, Lew Alcindor. From the opening tipoff the Trojans went into a game-long stall, did not shoot for as much as two or three minutes at a stretch, led 17-14 at halftime, and forced the Bruins into overtime before losing, 40-35.

Boyd's tactics quickly spread. When the Bruins traveled north to Eugene two weeks later the Oregon Ducks refused to shoot unless they had easy shots. UCLA led 18-14 at the half, and Wooden decided to fight back with his own version of the stall. For the first time that he could remember in 32 seasons of coaching, other than end-of-game situations, he ordered his team to freeze the ball. The contest became about as exciting as watching grass grow. More than nine minutes went by without a shot fired. The game finally picked up tempo with five minutes to play, and UCLA won, 34-25. Big Lew Alcindor scored 12 points, his lowest production of the season.

UCLA was not the only target of hide-and-seek basketball. Princeton, a tall, hot-handed gang of run-and-gunners in the East, faced the stall twice in 1967. Early in the season the Tigers demolished Dartmouth by 74 points, so the Big Green stalled the second time the teams met, hoping to be within striking distance at the end. They lost by only 14, which was progress of a sort. Later Pennsylvania tried a freeze and was only one point behind, with 1:04 left, when Princeton pulled away and clinched the Ivy League title, 25-16.

Down South, Ken Rosemond, the Georgia coach, benched his second leading scorer for one game because the boy had told reporters that stalling hurt his chances to play pro ball.

Pro-, anti-, or neutral, everybody seemed to have an opinion about stallball. In some quarters the cry went up for a pro-type 24-second clock to compel action. "We need rules that will prevent inaction more than anything else," said UCLA's John Wooden, who indicated he favored a 30-second clock. But he added that any such rule change probably would not be passed while Alcindor was at UCLA. He was no doubt correct. Rules are passed to handicap basketball's giants, not to aid them. No other college coach had anyone as tall or as effective as Alcindor, yet Wooden was not alone in wanting a clock. Kentucky's Adolph Rupp did, too, but "only after a team has made no attempt to score within one minute. And the clock should stay in effect only until the last three minutes. That would give a team a chance to protect its lead."

"I'm certain some coaches use the stall merely to keep the margin respectable," said Fred Taylor of Ohio State, another advocate of the 30-second clock. "They know, going into certain games that they have little or no chance to win, and they further know that if they get into a baseline-to-baseline chase they'll get run out of the place."

After a particularly low-scoring contest against Connecticut, Boston College coach Bob Cousy said he was not completely against control tactics. "I'd use them myself if it was necessary," he said. "But there are degrees to everything. I think the difference tonight was that Connecticut didn't take the good shot even when they were presented with them. I believe in patient ballhandling under these circumstances, but you should be working for the good shot. This was a farce."

Cousy's star that night, Steve Adelman, said it a bit differently. "It's a funny feeling after playing a game—not even sweating or being tired."

In spite of the fact that some college coaches wanted to put some sort of antifreeze into the NCAA rules, the stall was destined to stay. A survey of officials, coaches and ex-coaches showed that there was overwhelming antipathy toward any kind of time limit on stallball. Villanova's Jack Kraft was the area representative on the rules committee for coaches, "and I can tell you now that of the 130 or so schools in the area there was only one coach who suggested a time limit."

One reason was that most coaches felt their shooters were too quick on the trigger as it was. A set of NCAA statistics going back to 1956 showed that at the college level the ball had changed hands within 10 seconds 94.3 percent of the time—backcourt, frontcourt, shots and turnovers. Within 30 seconds the ball had changed hands 99.68 percent of the time. The figures confirmed that since 1960 field-goal attempts were up two-and-a-half shots per game.

Most coaches did not want college basketball to emulate the nonstop NBA teams, which raced up and down the court and fired at will. The coaches wanted to keep the variety of defenses, including the zone, and they wanted to keep their own hands on the tempo of a game. "The pro teams play so much alike," said Houston's Guy Lewis, "that a player can be traded from one team to another between halves and never miss a pass."

"If they put the 30-second rule in, UCLA won't lose a game in three years," said Michigan State's John Benington. "Upsets would be something of the past. The teams with the big recruiting programs would win, and the little guy wouldn't have a chance."

While much was made of the fact in 1967 that UCLA was virtually an all-sophomore team—five of the first six; and no senior at all—a less publicized truth was that sophomores abounded in unusual numbers everywhere across the country. At the same time, only a few teams featured seniors. Late in the season, there were exactly 11 senior starters on the top 10

teams. UCLA, the best team in the land, was 80 percent sophomores. The five best were 48 percent sophomores, and all 23 teams going into the NCAA tournament field were 31 percent sophomores. How good were they? In the seven first-round games, the winners started twice as many sophomores as the losers. There had been tournaments before that starred sophomores and were notable for the absence of seniors—Indiana's 1953 champions played no seniors; Ohio State's 1960 winners were led by three sophs—but none had been so heavily populated by rookies.

The Biggest Sophomore of them all, of course, was Lew Alcindor, who stood 7' 0" by the time he was only 15. An opposing coach recalled the first time he saw Alcindor in a basketball uniform. "I watched him walk out for warmup, chewing a lollipop. Then he began striding down the court with those giant steps, flicking the ball into the basket, first with one hand, then the other—and I suddenly realized what we were up against. By the time the game started, half my team was in a state of shock."

Alcindor was 6' 10" by the time he enrolled at Power Memorial High School in midtown Manhattan, where he led the school on a 71-game winning streak in the next three years. In his last game as a high school player, he scored 32 points, had 22 rebounds and set the New York City record for career points (2,067) and career rebounds (2,002), as Power defeated Rice High, 73-41 for the Catholic league championship. "I'll trade two first-round draft choices for him right now," said Gene Shue of the Baltimore Bullets. But the pros would have to wait while Alcindor went to college. The importance of that decision was reflected in the number of newsmen (80) that appeared for his press conference in the Power gym, May 4, 1965, to reveal he was going to UCLA. It was the first time in anyone's memory that a high school basketball player had held a press conference.

Ignoring the pressure of his first college game while thousands looked on in Pauley Pavilion, Alcindor scored 31 points to lead the freshmen over the varsity, 75-60—the same UCLA varsity that had won two straight NCAA titles. "UCLA is number one in the country and number two on its own campus," wrote one reporter. The next season, in his first varsity game, Alcindor destroyed crosstown rival Southern Cal with 56 points, a school record. The usually

UCLA, the best college team in the country in 1967, was 80 percent sophomores—and the biggest sophomore of them all was 7-foot Lew Alcindor (33).

conservative John Wooden surprised newsmen by calling Alcindor awesome. "At times," Wooden said, "he frightens me."

In the 1967 NCAA tournament preliminaries, the four regional survivors were UCLA in the West, Houston in the Midwest, North Carolina in the East, and Dayton in the Mideast. The "Lew-CLA" Bruins, everybody's favorite, had it easy beating Wyoming, 109-60, and Pacific, 80-64, in Corvallis, Oregon, while Houston surprised Kansas, 66-53, and then Southern Methodist, 83-75, in Lawrence, Kansas. North Carolina defeated Princeton, 78-70, in overtime, and Boston College, 96-80, in College Park, Maryland. Meanwhile, Dayton barely got by Tennessee, 53-52, and Virginia Tech, 71-66, in Evanston, Illinois.

Basketball interest had never been higher in the NCAA, either despite or because of Lew Alcindor. The finals were billed for national television and regional telecasts had become routine. Live attendance was also establishing records. In 1962, the figure was padded to an impossible 187,000. The true count for 1967 was 175,000. That was quite an attendance for sophomores to play before and for coaches to annoy with their slowdowns. But even grander things were in store for the future, if Coach Johnny Dee of Notre Dame had his way. He suggested that the NCAA tournament format be changed to include every member school in the country—all 600 of them. They would start off playing in 64 sectionals and work down from there. Coach Dee figured that would bring $5 million in gate receipts even before the final round and before TV paid a penny.

When the four contenders arrived in Louisville for the final round of the NCAA, the air was filled with UCLA talk. "UCLA is the most impressive college team of all time," one correspondent wired his paper. At Corvallis the week before, Wyoming was behind, 30-6, almost before a breath was drawn. The Bruins used their old favorite, the full-court press, to best advantage in this game, causing 19 turnovers by Cowboys. Well ahead, the Bruins moved into a three-one-one zone that gave away corner shots but closed off nearly everything else. Alcindor played the last "one." Coach Wooden called that "a great psychological barrier."

The next night, against Pacific, which had put out defending champion Texas Western the night before, UCLA had one of its stronger tests of the year and still won, 80-64. This time the Bruins used a man-to-man in the first half, a two-one-two zone in the second. Lucius Allen started the scoring with a three throw and one UCLA fan yelled, "Game's over!"

UCLA's opponent on Friday night in Louisville was Houston, headed by All-American Elvin Hayes. Southern Methodist Coach Doc Hayes, whose Mustangs went down valiantly to Houston, 83-75, said afterward: "We faced Bill Russell and San Francisco in 1956 and we faced Wilt Chamberlain and Kansas in 1957, but I'm not so sure that this team isn't more powerful than either." The Cougars handled SMU off the boards, 52-38, held SMU to 41 percent from the floor and the Huge E took care of the rest. Elvin Hayes outshone Westley Unseld of Louisville and everybody else in this Regional, scoring 31 against SMU and 19 in a Friday-night win over Kansas. The Houston victory over the Jayhawks was as unexpected as SMU's last-second win over hightly-touted Louisville.

Houston's quandary was how to stop Alcindor. Seattle's Lionel Purcell said run on him. Bob Boyd of Southern California advocated the play he used: "Be ball-control conscious. And you must zone and double-team Lew." Pete Newell, the California athletic director, thought that was ridiculous. "What good does it do," he asked, "to put a man in front of Alcindor so he can play his belly button?" Newell also voted against a press, because the UCLA guards, notably Mike Warren, would break it in a moment. Offered Red Auerbach: "You might be able to congest the middle. On second thought, Alcindor is so big and strong, he'd still get the ball and you would be just fouling and fouling trying to keep him from getting it."

No matter how good so many of the Bruins were and how well they were coached, the heart of their game was still Lew Alcindor. As a sophomore, he dominated the college game much more than Bill Russell and Wilt Chamberlain did the pros—if only because collegians heretofore had not often encountered such a phenomenon. Of course, they learned fast enough. It did not take Houston long against UCLA to abandon its plan of attacking Alcindor and to move Elvin Hayes farther out for his shots. Some observers, watching Alcindor for the first

time, evinced disappointment in his performance. His languid, almost bored attitude toward overkill was misleading. His teammates suggested that this was simply his style, and that he was not only alert and ready to assume command when necessary, but that he was feigning indifference to lure the Cougars to him. He was not only a smart player but utterly selfless. "We play team," he said, succinctly. "We don't play one man. You lose playing one man." It was significant that when the huge Houston front line was collapsing all over him (when he was also supposed to be in a grudge duel with Hayes) that he still refused to accept such a meaningless challenge. Again and again, holding the ball high, poised, turning, looking, thinking, he would make the right play—shoot or pass to the open man.

The excellence of the UCLA team was perhaps best shown in the early minutes of the Houston game. With six players standing at least 6' 6" and Don Chaney a hefty 6' 5" guard, the Cougars were about the most massive team in the country. Powered by such muscle, they attempted to go strength for strength—right at Alcindor. It was no personal crusade by Hayes, as some people thought. "No," Coach Guy Lewis said. "All week we just said, 'Go to him.' All week that was it." Before the game Johnny Dee of Notre Dame, whose team played both Houston and UCLA, guessed the Houston strategy. "They've got to try to foul Alcindor out," Dee said. "The only way to beat him is to hope for the three Fs—Foreign Court, Friendly Officials and Foul Out Alcindor."

It was a good idea, but Alcindor had the fourth F—Forget It. Houston got Alcindor to foul—once, after 33 minutes. Still the Cougars played very well. They actually led the Bruins, 19-18, midway through the first half. They were holding their own on the boards, they had given Alcindor only one basket, and their overall floor game was crisp and together. Using their height, they stuck to sharp overhead passes to chop up and spit out the UCLA full-court press, which was, really, only a ghost of its former self. The Bruins were struggling. And yet, despite all their sputtering, UCLA trailed by only one point. Then Lynn Shackelford hit on a beautiful, long lefthanded jumper from the corner to put the Bruins ahead. Then they stole the ball off the press for the first time in the contest, Alcindor stuffed in a basket a few seconds later—and quickly it was 29-19. UCLA coasted on to win, 73-58.

Elvin Hayes, citing statistics, insisted afterward that his teammates had "choked" and that he had found Alcindor sadly lacking as an opponent. "He's not aggressive enough on the boards, particularly on offense," spoke Hayes unemotionally and with conviction. "Defensively, he just stands around. He's not all they really put him up to be." As Hayes talked to the press, patiently pointing out Alcindor's deficiencies, Big Lew moved through the crowd nearby signing autographs, expressionless and undisturbed. He was absolutely unmoved by Hayes' public criticism of him.

The next afternoon, Coach Mickey Donoher called his Dayton team together to talk of Alcindor and the Bruins. Donoher was nervous. Here was his team, unranked and untroubled by fame all year, suddenly about to play for the national championship. The night before, behind Don May, who had made 13 straight shots, 34 points and had 15 rebounds, the Flyers had upset favored North Carolina, 76-62. Dayton was behind, 9-2, when Donoher substituted Glinder Torain and Torain fired up the team's performance on the boards. May did the rest. At 13-13 he had eight points and so did Larry Miller of North Carolina. After that Miller made five, May 26, and eventually Miller himself had to sacrifice his fire power to guard May.

Donoher, a varsity coach for only three years, brought a team all the way to the national championship that had lost to the likes of Niagara and had been cut to bits twice by Louisville. After the Flyers won their 13th game, Donoher was heard to say wistfully: "Only one more to go." He was asked what he meant by that. "One more for 14," he said. "They always say if you win 14 they can't fire you. It guarantees you'll be over .500." Now the one more to go was for the national title.

As it turned out, Dayton held Alcindor reasonably well, but there were mismatches all over the court and expectable gaps in the Flyers' defense. Sophomore Dan Sadlier played against sophomore Alcindor, and Sadlier was 6' 6". He received help, and that was how the gaps opened. It took five and a half minutes for Dayton to score and it was 20-4 soon after. It was 70-46 when Wooden graciously removed Alcindor and Mike Warren with 5:17 still left, and there was a 29-point spread (76-47) just

after Allen, the last Bruin starter, went to the bench. The final score was 79-64.

Alcindor's influence was so dominant that it was difficult to determine how good his teammates really were. For instance: forward Lynn Shackelford made 16 baskets in 29 attempts in the two games against Houston and Dayton, most of them long lefthanded jumps. A great shooter? Who really knew? Shackelford rarely had to shoot with a hand in his face. The man guarding him was always hanging back, preparing to help out against Alcindor.

The other UCLA forward, Kenny Heitz, was assigned to Dayton's Don May. Against Heitz, May missed his first six shots and was only three for 12 in the first half. When the game was over, Heitz said, "May is just a terrific player. So strong—and, more than that, he knows how to use his strength. I know that he was trying to get inside on me, but I could tell all along that he wouldn't take me in as far as he would normally like to because Lew would be there."

Outside, Mike Warren and Lucius Allen gave appearances of being the best backcourt in the land. They whipped the ball around and popped in the shots, and Allen particularly moved down the middle without the ball for the easy pass and layup. But all that, too, they were able to accomplish without the close defense that other good guards had to face.

It all boiled down to the question of just how good Warren, Allen, Shackelford and Heitz were. Better than advertised? Overrated? It was impossible to tell. One thing was sure, however. Basketball fans had begun treating the Bruins like a bully on the block.

"We're not very popular, are we?" sighed Kenny Heitz, who had been booed and cursed early in the Dayton game for accidentally bumping May to the floor. Even May emphasized the collision had been clearly unintentional. Nevertheless, all the frustrations of dealing with UCLA, of seeing the Bruins win so effortlessly, poured out on Heitz, who wore glasses and was skinny and was an honors student.

"You know," he said, wanly. "we're even starting to feel hurt by all this crowd reaction. We are not a bully team at all. You practically have to smash Lew in the mouth before he gets tough." Pause. "Oh well," he shrugged, finally, "I'm learning to understand these things now. I used to root for all the underdogs myself."

4th Title in 5 Years for Bruins: 1968

All over the country college basketball teams were getting better and better and, with a few exceptions, approaching parity. So why, then, were the visiting teams winning only 30 percent of the games? Was there any significance in that old debate about the home-court advantage? After all, times had changed. Huge, clean field houses were replacing the tiny, cramped, dim gyms of the past; "homer" officials were gone in favor of referees chosen largely by neutral commissioners, not the coaches; and the general behavior of the fans, once a real menace to visiting teams, had greatly improved. So the question was why. Why was every college team worth at least five additional points when it played at home, as Jimmy "The Greek" Snyder claimed? The home-court advantage was no myth—right? Right.

"Anytime you win on the road it's an upset," said Marquette's Al McGuire.

In 1966, for example, Wichita State won all its Missouri Valley Conference games at home and lost all the others. "Since any two teams are likely to be extremely even," said Coach Gary Thompson, "those factors that, taken together, produce a home-court edge will usually determine the outcome of the game. I know that's true in the Missouri Valley, where even our last-place team, North Texas, can hold a team like St. Louis to a two-point margin on the North Texas court. But it isn't limited to the Valley. Six or seven years ago you could look down your schedule at the start of the season and pick half a dozen games you could count on winning. No more. Today, if each team plays its average game, the home team usually will win. Coaches understand this. The public doesn't."

Pete Newell, California's athletic director,

believed that a visiting team simply did not play as aggressively on defense as it did at home. "Many times violations are called because the home fans pointed them out to officials—like hacking or blocking," Newell said. "These are never called from the stands about the home team. Somebody will yell, about a visiting player, 'Watch Smith, he's always shoving,' and the official finds himself looking for shoving. The zone press is an intimidating kind of defense that requires aggression. It loses its effectiveness if Jones is reticent, and if early fouls are called on him, his aggressiveness is curbed."

With it's press UCLA did not lose a game at home in three years. Against Duke in North Carolina in 1966, the Bruins lost twice on successive nights, and in both games the press was used only sporadically ineffectively. UCLA clearly did not play the same kind of game it played at home. Few pressing teams did.

While most college coaches had cleaned up their act at home (they no longer did things like cutting off the heat in the guest locker room to make the visitors miserable) many of the old familiar handicaps still bedeviled the visiting teams. Arizona State's Ned Wulk said he tried everything to overcome the hazards. "Arrive a day early and get in two drills, change eating schedules, call meetings, do anything to keep the boys busy and not bored or tense," he said. "Nothing works. No matter what you do it still boils down to whether the ball goes into the hoop, and a boy doesn't have to be far off to be way off. Different lighting, different floor feel, the home crowd—they all add up to a couple of inches, and he won't hit anything. You can't psyche basketball players as you do in football;

The Big E—Elvin Hayes—carried Houston all the way to the NCAA semifinals in 1967 and 1968. The high-scoring Cougar was unanimous All-American both seasons.

there are too many games on the schedule."

On the theory that such talk made matters worse, many coaches preferred to ignore or at least soft-pedal the whole home-court controversy in the presence of their players. "Remember," said Ted Owens of Kansas, "a player will seldom appear on a so-called hostile court more than three times in his career. He rarely associ-

ates it with any special difficulties. It's the coach who remembers all the bad things that happened over the years."

"Many coaches get psyched," asserted George Ireland of Loyola. "They say, 'Gee, we just can't win at Wichita.' And that is the real reason they lose at Wichita."

Whether or not the home-court advantage had anything to do with it, the University of Houston's Big E, 6' 8" senior Elvin Hayes, hit 68 percent of his shots, scored 39 points, took 15 rebounds and made the two deciding free throws to upset UCLA, 71-69, before the largest crowd ever to see a basketball game in the U.S. (52,693), in Houston's famous Astrodome. It was not a case of the Cougars sneaking up on UCLA. The Bruins were ranked first in both wire-service polls, but Houston was ranked second and had won *48 straight games at home.* The Cougars had won 17 in a row since losing to UCLA in 1967's NCAA semifinal, and Hayes was the third leading scorer in the nation and certainly no stranger.

Hayes completely outplayed Alcindor, but it was noted that Lew had suffered a scratched left eyeball in the previous Friday night's game against California, forcing him to miss games against Stanford and Portland. He wore an eye-patch and stayed in bed part of the week; the inactivity no doubt affected his play. He made only four of 18 shots against Houston for one of his least impressive performances in his college career. Still, at halftime, Houston only led 46-43. In the second half, the Big E blocked two shots in a row (one by Alcindor), hit a jump shot and made Mike Lynn commit his fourth foul—all in the first few minutes. But then UCLA started double-teaming Hayes and he added only 10 points to his first-half total.

UCLA, which had been down by as much as nine points in the first half, battled back in the second half to tie the score, 54-54, and from then on it was a dogfight. Alcindor made it 65-all with a free throw, and two Lucius Allen free throws made it 69-all with time almost run out. Then, with only 28 seconds left, Jim Nielsen, who had come in for Mike Lynn and had been effective in cooling off the Big E, fouled Hayes, which could have been a disaster for Houston because Hayes was shooting only 60 percent of his free throws. But he regained his eye and put them both in for a two-point lead.

UCLA then had a pass intercepted, got the ball back because of a Cougar traveling violation and lost it again out of bounds with 12 seconds left. The Bruins never got the ball again. Final score: Houston 71, UCLA 69. Basketball's debut in the Astrodome was, indeed, a howling success—at least to Texans.

In the Houston locker room after the game, Coach Guy Lewis of the Cougars called the Big E's first-half heroics "the greatest I've ever seen in college basketball." In the subdued UCLA dressing room, John Wooden was free with praise of Hayes. But he wouldn't go so far as to say he was the greatest.

"As a matter of fact," he admitted, "I wouldn't trade Alcindor for two Hayeses."

Lucius Allen was thinking of a possible rematch in March in the NCAA tournament at the Los Angeles Sports Arena.

"I hope they come to L.A. undefeated," said Allen. "That would be very nice."

So would the hometown advantage.

While Alcindor and Hayes waited for a rematch, there was a sophomore down at Baton Rouge who was earning the title of college basketball's most prodigious scorer—Pistol Pete Maravich. *Marvelous* Pete Maravich, of Louisiana State, the coach's son. Dribbling, shooting, passing, rebounding, he was practically the teams' entire offense. He could go left or right with equal facility, he had every shot known to man—with both hands. Yet, remarkably, the strongest part of his game was his deft passing.

Always moving, always contemplating, that long, lean, macaroni body was a constant threat. He'd look the man guarding him in the eye and fire a push shot from 35 feet or give him the head fake for the push shot and then was quickly on the move with a crossover dribble under his leg, around the defender, to the left and up for his jump shot. If it missed, he was following, leaping, crashing over bigger and stronger players to tap the ball into the basket. No matter who LSU was playing, the zone defense was always there to plague Pistol Pete. Always the zone. And he was always there to challenge it. In a season loaded with the usual vicissitude and inconstancy, one unassailable certainty was that Maravich would be faced with the zone every time he held a basketball. An opponent's next line of defense was some variation of a gang-attack man-to-man that concentrated only on Maravich.

Joe Dean, an LSU star of the early 1950's and a big Maravich fan, lamented that just one time he wished somebody would play The Pistol honest, instead of ganging up on him. "I realize they've all got to do what's best to win," he said, "but just once it would be beautiful to see a team play this guy honest with just one man on him. Pete would be so great that night, he'd scare people."

Pete Maravich, the collegian, was that terrific. He was only a soph, and he made the mistakes of all sophomores—forcing shots, committing useless fouls and hotdogging it all over the floor. Moreover, his basic shot, released by hands that cradled the *sides* of the ball, was a strange and unattractive maneuver that had the ball spinning sideways rather than up and over, as basketball teaching usually dictates. But Maravich was the most exciting college basketball player of the day, and his dad, the coach, could be excused for overlooking these minor flaws.

In the early part of the season Maravich and Calvin Murphy of Niagara engaged in a long-distance duel that promised to produce the two best scorers major-college basketball had ever known—in the same season. Maravich scored 48 points against Tampa in his varsity debut, had the national scoring lead taken away from him by Murphy twice in the next four games and then regained the lead for good with a 46-point night against Mississippi. He was never behind Frank Selvy's record average of 41.7, set 14 years before at Furman, and, after LSU split with Tulane and Mississippi one week at the fag-end of the season, in which he scored 55 and 40 points, he had an average of 44.9 and a total of 1,079 points and was 219 points ahead of Murphy, whose average had fallen to 39.1. What did all those numbers mean? They meant that Pistol Pete Maravich, in his sophomore year, had all but wrapped up the title as college basketball's "most prolific scorer (per game) of all time."

By the time he was 20, all of Pistol Pete's tricks and his vast repertoire of shots had been made into a movie, "Homework Basketball," which never failed to amaze its viewers, including Carl Stewart, the coach of all-black McKinley High in Baton Rouge. "My god," he exclaimed after one viewing, "he's one of us!"

It was almost inconceivable that frustration and jealousy would not exist on a team when one player (Maravich), took 40 shots a game

1968—Louisiana State's Pistol Pete Maravich joined Oscar Robertson as the only sophomores ever to lead the nation in scoring. He averaged a record 43.8 points.

and scored more than half the points, but that seemed to be the case at Louisiana State. "We each have a job to do on this team," said Jeff Tribbett, who fed Rick Mount in high school and was now feeding, and rooming with, fellow sophomore Maravich. "It's very simple. Pete has to shoot 40 times a game in order for us to win. He just has to."

Maravich, himself, appeared surprised that the question even came up. "There might be some dissension if we were losing," he said at the time, "but we've been doing some winning. I'm conscious of what people say about my shooting so much, but there's a lot of difference between shooting 40 times a game and being able to shoot 40 times. I can get open that many times, I don't care who's playing. Some other people would have to start throwing over their heads to get it up there 40 times."

Despite a high regard for the coaching abilities of his father, Press, young Pete could not always control the sophomore in him. He admitted this, confessing that there were times when he gave his old man some backtalk, unmindful that his father was also his coach. In practice, Pete constantly mouthed off at his pop, sometimes to the point of being downright discourteous and flippant, and by debating strategy and suggesting that he, Press, didn't know what he was talking about. *Do it my way,* was the son's credo. Press usually allowed his boy some latitude, but one day father and son reached a point of no return. Then Press let Pete have it. "Dammit!" he roared. "I'm the coach here. I'll say who shoots, who passes and who rebounds. I don't need you to tell me what to do."

That cleared the air. The tension was short-lived. No harm was done. As one teammate put it, "When the son is leading us to the NIT with 45 a game, who really worries about a little family bickering?"

After Houston defeated UCLA in January in the Astrodome, establishing that the Bruins were less than immortal after all, the conjecture was that the two teams would meet again in the semifinal round of the NCAA tournament at the Sports Arena in Los Angeles. The way the draw was set up they could not meet in the finals. If the experts were correct, then the Bruins would be playing in *their* home town and in an arena thoroughly familiar to them. Not so long ago they played all their home games in the Sports Arena. Easily 90 percent of the crowd attending the NCAA playoffs would be rooting for the Bruins.

"I don't anticipate any real problem with the Los Angeles crowd," said Houston Coach Guy Lewis. "When you're going for the national championship, you aren't going to let the crowd bother you. I'm more worried about UCLA. They're the ones to worry about."

His fears were well founded. Since the Houston loss, the Bruins seemed hungrier and more aggressive. According to California coach Rene Herrerias, Alcindor, who shot poorly under the Dome because of a scratched eyeball suffered in an earlier game and was sluggish after several days in bed recovering, was "devastating" again. "Lew is the greatest I've ever seen, just fantastic," Herrerias said after Alcindor made 11 of 15 shots, in the first half of a game against his Bears.

Except for Alcindor's return to form, the UCLA attack had not changed much. But Coach Wooden had made the trap zone an important part of his defense. Now when Big Lew cleared the board the zone enabled UCLA's wingmen to take off more quickly on Wooden's pet fast breaks. Edgar Lacey was no longer with the team, but his quitting had not hurt the team appreciably; Mike Lynn was a better shooter, Jim Nielsen had more brawn and everybody was getting to play more, boosting morale.

Houston was also missing a man since January. George Reynolds, an excellent passer and all-court hustling guard, was ineligible for NCAA competition because he did not have enough credits when he transferred to Houston from a California junior college. "He meant a great deal to our offense," Lewis said. "In fact, he was leading the team in assists. But I think my son Vern will be able to replace George on defense all right."

The NCAA cast at Los Angeles was virtually the same as it was at Louisville in 1967: UCLA vs. Houston and North Carolina vs. Ohio State. The Buckeyes were something of a sleeper. A couple of weeks before, they themselves thought they were all washed up. Iowa, with a half-game lead in the Big Ten race, had only to beat Michigan at home to clinch the championship and move on to the Mideast Regional. Even Bill Hosket, the Ohio State captain, bought a ticket for the regional games, fully

The LSU Maravich's—Coach Press and son Pete— did not always see eye to eye.

expecting to be a spectator. But then Iowa lost, and OSU won the subsequent playoff on a neutral court.

It didn't make much difference. The regional was in Lexington, and home team Kentucky, the SEC champion, seldom lost basketball games in Lexington—not with Adolph Rupp at his end of the bench. What's more, the 1968 Buckeyes were not precisely reincarnations of the super Ohio State athletes of the early 1960s: Jerry Lucas, John Havlicek, Mel Nowell *et al.*, who won one NCAA title and finished second twice. In fact, a scout for one of their opponents who saw them play Georgia Tech earlier in the year said, "I thought then I'd like to make my living playing them."

But after OSU reached the NCAA semi-finals, he was not so sure. Ohio State rolled over East Tennessee in a so-what game while Kentucky was making mince meat of Marquette. The following night, everybody picked the Wildcats in a walk, looking ahead to UCLA and Houston. But when it was all over, Ohio State had whipped Kentucky in nearly every category, including points. The game was close all the way and the Wildcats had a one-point lead with 28 seconds left, but they made the mistake of not fouling in order to gain possession. The Buckeyes would have been allowed one free throw, so Kentucky would only have risked having the game tied in exchange for a chance at the last shot. Instead, Ohio State got it. Dave Sorenson, a muscular, 6'7" member of OSU's front line, hit a five-foot fallaway jumper with three seconds left to win the game, 82-81, and send himself and his teammates on an unexpected trip to Los Angeles.

North Carolina was a veteran, tournament-toughened team. The Tar Heels beat Oregon State in the Far West Classic in Portland, scraped through the annual Atlantic Coast Conference playoffs, easily took undefeated St. Bonaventure and then state rival Davidson in the East Regional. The Bonnies were the big disappointment of the tournament, but Davidson stayed with North Carolina right to the end, even without the injured Doug Cook, one of its best players. "I'm not but 35 years old and I'm going to be up there someday soon," said Davidson's Coach Lefty Driesell afterward. "I've got most of these boys back and some of them may be with me when we win this whole thing."

Right then, however, North Carolina was up there, led by All-American Larry Miller and Center Rusty Clark, the surprise of the team who had 22 points and 17 rebounds against Davidson and who did a fine defensive job on Bob Lanier, the St. Bonaventure whiz.

North Carolina, like Ohio State, had a proud basketball tradition, and the players bitterly remembered still being run off the floor twice the season before at Louisville, while their fans yelled, "We're No. 4, we're No. 4!" Larry Miller especially embarrassed himself in that tournament, making only five of 20 shots in each game. "I am going to have a good game the first night at Los Angeles," he vowed, "and then we'll worry about UCLA or Houston. Last year

we came out of the ACC tournament, played sloppily in the Easterns and felt lucky to even be in the final four. Then everybody said we didn't have a chance to beat UCLA and we just kept thinking about that. Dayton made us look terrible. This time nobody knows if UCLA is going to win against Houston. I don't know either. But the winner of that game is bound to have a letdown the second night. We may be in there to see just what happens."

Seeking its fourth NCAA title in five years on what used to be its home floor, UCLA won the West Regional at Albuquerque, but it looked flat in a 58-49 victory over slow-it-up New Mexico State and didn't have much competition from Santa Clara, leading by 17 points at half time and winning by 21. The Bruins were no doubt looking forward to Houston.

Critics of Houston made snide remarks about the quality of the Cougar's opposition. Perhaps they were dismayed at the prospect of a Texas team winning the NCAA championship for the second time in three years. It was true that in pounding such teams as Sacramento State, Lamar Tech and Centenary (twice), Houston played a schedule that did not match the prestige-conscious schools. But few good teams were willing to play the independent Cougars, and those that dared—Marshall, Brigham Young, Marquette—were beaten just like the Lamar Techs, although not quite as easily.

In the opening round of the Midwest Regional at Wichita, Houston took Missouri Valley champion Louisville apart like a Swiss watch, 91-75. The Cardinals, led by All-American Wes Unseld, had won their last 12 games and had good height and shooting, but they were held scoreless for more than six minutes of the first half as the Cougars dominated the backboards—and the game.

"I've never seen a team hit the offensive boards the way the Cougars do," said Louisville Coach John Dromo, "and I never want to see another one unless it's my own."

Hayes had a big night against Louisville, scoring 35 points and taking 24 rebounds (two more than Unseld). The next night, against Texas Christian University, he had 39 points and 25 rebounds, prompting Coach Johnny Swaim to say, "Of all the players I have ever seen, he ranks at the top. He is a panther."

Elvin believed he was a more settled player than he was the year before at Louisville, when

Alcindor forced him out of his normal game. "I won't be forced out of it this time even though I know Alcindor will be much stronger physically than he was at Houston."

The Big E was a man to speak his mind. He had a cocky, refreshing and sometimes shocking way of blurting out whatever happened to race through his mind. At the 1967 NCAA tournament he said his teammates had choked. Before the crucial showdown against UCLA at Los Angeles, he predicted that Houston would win by a bigger margin than in the Astrodome. At a breakfast in Minneapolis, honoring a small group of All-American basketball players, he asked the waitress for a bowl of Kellogg's Corn Flakes. There was nothing unusual about that—except that the breakfast was sponsored by *Wheaties*.

In the semifinals of the NCAA tournament Friday night against UCLA, evidence turned up just before the game that it would not be Houston's night. A Houston student who had contacts with the team was arrested outside the Sports Arena and booked on charges of scalping tickets. Scalpers were getting as much as $50 a ticket. To many the prices were not unreasonable, and a crowd of 15,742, plus thousands more watching closed-circuit TV in six locations, anxiously awaited the tipoff.

The Bruins got the tip and were never behind, but the contest was not a runaway—at first. UCLA spurted to a 12-4 lead, the Cougars worked their way back to within one point, 20-19, and the packed Sports Arena crowd hunched back to watch the two best teams in the U.S. battle it out to the bloody end. And then came the Bruins' dreaded spurt. Without warning, UCLA suddenly stomped on the gas and outscored Houston, 17-5, in the next four minutes. When Lynn Shackelford stole the ball and flipped it downcourt to Lucius Allen for a cinch layup to put their team ahead, 37-24, Houston called timeout and Don Chaney slammed the ball down hard in disgust.

Periodic consultations with Coach Guy Lewis did not help, not even at halftime when he appealed to their pride. "Don't quit, hang tough," he told them, in the best Knute Rockne tradition. "Don't give up those good ol' American principles we'll need if we ever fight the Russians or the Chinese."

UCLA kept tormenting Houston in the second half with its full-court press and scoring easily on fast breaks and accurate outside shooting. The lead grew to 28, to 39 and reached its peak at 44 late in the game. If the Bruins had not cleared their bench in the last five minutes, they would have won by 50 points. Guy Lewis confessed it was the greatest exhibition of college basketball he ever saw. The final score was 101-69. Shasta, Houston's pet cougar, was so bored he slept through the second half.

The vaunted Hayes vs. Alcindor duel failed to materialize. One reason for this was that Hayes reacted to the rematch roughly the way Shasta did. Hayes revealed that when something discouraged him, he became completely discouraged.

John Wooden and his assistant, Jerry Norman, came up with a diamond-shaped zone defense that put Mike Warren at the top of the key, Allen and Mike Lynn on the wings and Alcindor underneath the basket. That left Lynn Shackelford free to shadow Hayes, and he did such a competent job that there were moments when he and Hayes looked like identical twins. Much of the time Elvin was tied up in traffic and couldn't free himself. His play affected the whole team; it shot a miserable 28.2 percent from the floor. Theodis Lee made only two of 15 shots. UCLA, in contrast, hit better than 50 percent. Alcindor, Lynn and Allen each had 19 points. Allen dazzled the crowd with 12 assists, nine rebounds, and his dribbling. He seemed to dribble in and out of Houston's one-three-one zone whenever he felt like it. As for Alcindor, he was his old intimidating self on defense, and he made half his 14 shots from the floor, five of six free throws and took down 18 rebounds.

All the Cougars seemed to be flat, uninspired and too loose. "The guys seemed more worried about selling their tickets for $50 apiece than about the game itself," said one Houston player, in reference to all the pregame scalping. "In Houston, in January, we were *worried* about playing UCLA, but this time it seemed just like another game." Theodis Lee got more to the point. "We just weren't up for it," he said. "I figured before the game that the best we could shoot would be 35 percent. Our mental attitude wasn't right."

On the other hand, the Bruins were just the opposite. "We're a vindictive team," admitted Mike Warren afterward. "We've been looking forward to this game ever since they robbed us

Lew Alcindor was in great form as he scored 34 points, recovered 16 rebounds and blocked seven shots to subdue North Carolina here enroute to the 1968 NCAA championship at Los Angeles.

of our No. 1 ranking and a chance for a second straight undefeated season. And we're not looking past North Carolina. We'll run them back down South, too."

In the other semifinal game, North Carolina beat a surprisingly good Ohio State team, 80-66, as All-American Larry Miller scored 20 points.

Before the UCLA-Houston game started, Tar Heel Coach Dean Smith was asked which team he would rather play. Smith answered by quoting Coach Fred Taylor of the Buckeyes: "Getting hit by a train or a truck, it doesn't make much difference."

"If we don't control the tempo against UCLA, we'll be out of it by halftime," Smith said. "So I plan to use my four-corner offense, with Charlie Scott, Rusty Clark, Bill Bunting and Dick Grubar in the corners and Miller roaming around in the middle. Once we get through the press, we will set up carefully and look for the high-percentage shot. In this way, we might be within striking distance at the end. But I know it'll take a miracle; still I have confidence in my players."

The miracle did not occur. After Ohio State whipped Houston in the preliminary game for third place, UCLA confidently took North Carolina, 78-55, "running them back down South" as Mike Warren said they would. The Bruins discovered early in the game that only Miller and Scott appeared willing to shoot and concentrated on them.

Against North Carolina's man-to-man defense, Alcindor scored 34 points, recovered 16 rebounds and had at least seven blocked shots. He was named player of the tournament, and three teammates, Allen, Warren and Schackelford, joined him and Miller on the All-Tournament Team.

Immediately after the final buzzer, Alcindor carried a chair over to one basket and cut down the net—basketball's mild version of football's tradition of tearing down a goalpost. Big Lew had the net draped around his neck like a lei by the time the big NCAA trophy was presented to the Bruins. Warren wore the one from the other basket.

At the post-game news conference, Coach Dean Smith said the Tar Heels did not play a perfect game. "And you have to play a perfect game to beat UCLA," he declared. "Alcindor is the greatest player who ever played the game.

It was the Bruins again in 1968. National champions, front row, left, were: Mike Warren, Gene Sutherland, Lucius Allen. Rear, left: Coach John Wooden, Asst. Coach Jerry Norman, Kenny Heitz, Lynn Shackelford, Jim Nielsen, Lew Alcindor, Mike Lynn, Neville Saner, Bill Sweek, Head Trainer "Ducky" Drake, Mgr. Frank Adler.

And UCLA is the greatest basketball team of all time." He did not single out whether he meant the colleges or the pros. The Bruin basketball players tended to believe they were champions of all the world, college or pro. No one argued with them.

So where did they go from there?

"Our next goal is a third NCAA title next year," said Allen.

While no team in the history of the NCAA had ever won three basketball championships in a row, nobody was betting against the Bruins. Returning to the squad were Alcindor, Allen and Shackelford, plus Curtis Rowe, the star of an undefeated freshman team, and a couple of talented redshirts and an outstanding junior college prospect.

Despite UCLA's winning its fourth NCAA championship in five years, Houston was awarded most of the season's honors. Elvin Hayes was chosen player of the year, and his coach, Guy Lewis, was the choice as coach of the year. That was fair enough. What was ludicrous, however, was the fact that the Cougars also won the two national wire-service rankings. The weekly polls ended before the NCAA tournament began.

But anybody who saw what the Bruins did to the Cougars in Los Angeles knew that Houston was not No. 1—not by a Texas mile.

Bruins Roll On And On
And On . . . : 1969

By now, there was talk of reserving a niche— maybe even a whole room—for John Wooden in basketball's Hall of Fame. Consider his record: he was an outstanding professional player for six years. Before that he was a consensus All-American guard at Purdue for three straight seasons. And before that he starred on one of the finest high school teams ever to play in Indiana. As a coach, he had had only one losing season, his first. His UCLA teams won two national championships before Lew Alcindor, and they were likely to win some more after he left. Johnny Wooden belonged up there with the sport's all-time elite.

Actually, there were *two* Johnny Woodens. There was the soft-spoken Wooden with a trace of homespun Hoosier in his voice; the deacon-of-his-church, kindly grandfather Wooden who tucked in his wallet such inspirational sayings as "Make each day your masterpiece," or "Build a shelter for a rainy day," or "It's better to go too far with a boy than not far enough," or "Be true to yourself," or "It's the little things that count." On the wall near his office desk hung the building blocks of his personal *Pyramid of Success* formula: "Industriousness," "loyalty," and "self-control."

That was one side of him. Then there was the intensely competitive John Wooden of the UCLA bench whose incendiary, sometimes flaunting performances could burn the britches off a referee. He sat there wielding a rolled-up program like a Roman candle and, like most coaches, suffered while an entire year's work was compressed into an hour-and-a-half game. Tough Al Lightner, who used to officiate on the Pacific Coast, testified that he saw Wooden so mad at times he was afraid Wooden was going

to suffer a coronary during a game. "But I never heard him curse," Lightner said. "About the closest he ever came to swearing was to holler, 'Dadburn it' or, 'Goodness gracious sakes alive!' He was the Walter Johnson of roundball."

Wooden was a master psychologist. If you were a Wooden watcher, you knew that sometime during the first half of most games he chose one incident, a close call, to jump all over the referee. He only chewed him out in a gentlemanly manner, if there is such a thing, but he let him know that he, Wooden, had his scathing side. Then, during halftime, Wooden would seek out the referee and apologize to him. "I know I should have known it was a close call," Wooden would tell him. "I was wrong. It's just a job and you're doing the best you can." And then they would part, with Wooden walking away meek as you please. In the second half, if another close call arose, chances were the referee would call the play in UCLA's favor.

To make his full-court press as effective as possible, Wooden wanted referees to be acutely aware of the rule that gave a team only 10 seconds to get the ball across the mid-court line. Sometimes he carried a stopwatch to the bench. He would not say a word about it and seldom even bothered to check the second hand, but he made sure that the officials noticed the stopwatch.

Wooden insisted he knew what he was doing when he yelled about close calls. Often it was to show his players he was fighting for them. Obviously, he had a reputation as a referee-baiter, an image he felt was totally undeserved. In defense of himself, he said, "No official, no player has ever heard me use a word of profanity. I don't stand up and do anything to excite the crowd. That's one of the worst things coaches can do. You've never seen me throw a chair or a towel, or jump up and go down the floor yelling. I don't say, 'You're a homer!' I'll say, '*Don't be* a homer!' I'll say, 'See 'em the same way at both ends!' I'll say, 'Watch the traveling,' or some such, but no profanity and not personal. The thing I may be ashamed of more than anything else is having talked to opposing players. Not calling them names, but saying something like 'Keep your *hands* off of him' or 'Don't be a butcher' or something of that type."

Walt Hazzard, the star of Wooden's first NCAA champions in 1963-64, was a big admirer of his coach's needling. "He was one of the best bench jockeys in the world," Hazzard said. "He had an 'antiseptic needle'—clean but biting. I saw opposing players left shaking their heads, but there was nothing they could say."

In the final Pacific Eight game of the 1968-69 season, Wooden, himself, was left shaking *his* head—and there was nothing much he could say, except to admit that after 41 straight victories, the Bruins lost. And to the meek (15-11) Trojans from crosstown USC, who just the night before had lost in double overtime to UCLA. But, then, in the final Pac-8 game of the year, the Trojans froze the pants off the Bruins. With 19 seconds to play, it was USC 44, UCLA 44, when Ernie Powell passed the ball inbounds for the Trojans. With 15 seconds remaining, Powell and teammate Don Crenshaw maneuvered for position on the right side of the key. Five seconds later Powell took a pass, worked behind Crenshaw's screen and prepared for one last shot. With six seconds left his 20-foot jumper went up and then down through the net. UCLA, in a desperate race against the clock, got the ball to Sidney Wicks after two long passes. He arched a shot for the basket just as the buzzer sounded, but the ball caromed off the rim. And so ended UCLA's 41-game winning streak.

The upset ended a home-court winning streak at 85 and was only the fourth defeat for an Alcindor team in eight years of high school and college. UCLA and its agile 7' 1½" center were still favorites to win their third straight NCAA title—something no school had ever done—but not without a stiff struggle. Opti-

mists predicted that the 1969 NCAA semifinals and finals in Louisville, March 20 and 22, would become one of the most exciting tournaments since the whole thing started back in 1939. Southern California convinced everybody that the Bruins were human after all.

College basketball needed a spate of hard, clean competition right then, if for no other reason than to burn off the black clouds from the regular college season, which was scarred by such sidelights as All-American Spencer Haywood hitting a referee, Texas A. & M. fans working over a Baylor player while he was lying on the floor, and the president of Morehead State University stalking onto the court to berate an official. Brave partisans in Philadelphia's Palestra had thrown cans of beer and

There was no stopping UCLA again in 1969. About all Washington's Coach Marv Harshman could do was yell—but the Bruins rolled on to their fifth NCAA championship in six years nonetheless.

a whiskey bottle, bananas had been thrown in Colorado State's arena, hot pennies at Washington State, turkey eggs at Texas Tech and ice cubes at Mississippi State. Most of the fighting, of course, had been among the players, but the University of California and Stanford pep bands had a free-for-all. Even two mascots, students costumed as St. Joseph's Hawk and Villanova's Wildcat, went at it, Mr. Wildcat using his tail as a whip. Cheerleaders no longer cried, "Yea team!" Now they shouted, "Sic 'em!"

Even before the regional games were played, the speculators were betting that the championship game at Louisville most likely would be between UCLA and North Carolina for the second straight year, although the tall Tar Heels would have to fight their way through the toughest of the four regionals (Duquesne, Davidson and St. John's) and then beat the Mideast champion, probably Purdue but possibly Kentucky. Meanwhile, UCLA would have to get by a couple of hungry opponents, New Mexico State and once-beaten Santa Clara, a tall order, but the West Regional was in the Bruins' own Pauley Pavilion, which, now that the pressure of a 41-game winning streak was off the team, would again become the home advantage it had always been.

If Kentucky got into the final game against UCLA, coaches John Wooden and Baron Adolph Rupp had extra incentive: both would be aiming for a record fifth national championship.

"I don't honestly think we have the bench to go all the way in the NCAA," confessed Rupp. "Our bench is practically all sophomores and we'll just have to go into the tournament with our five starters and two reserves, and in a national tournament that just isn't enough bench."

Yet in 1958 a lightly regarded Kentucky team made it to Louisville, and in the finals faced a hero almost as magnificent as Lew Alcindor, Elgin Baylor of Seattle. Baylor got in foul trouble early and Rupp's Wildcats won.

There were more than 70,000 applications for tickets to the Louisville games. After UCLA lost to USC and proved itself fallible, the NCAA estimated it could have sold twice that many seats. The fact was there was a strong belief that the 1968-69 edition of the Bruins was not bound in the same rich leather of previous years, even if Big Lew was a year older and

wiser. Before the loss to the Trojans, UCLA already had played two difficult games against Washington, a so-so team with a smart coach, Tex Winter, who insisted all season the Bruins could be beaten and was finally proved correct. Coach Winter figured out UCLA this way:

"Patience is the first requirement. You can't play a definite delay game, but you must work for the high-percentage shot and pass up those tempting perimeter shots John Wooden's teams have always given you. You must force UCLA to play defense as long as possible. One good, quick guard is needed to get the ball up-court and control the tempo of the game. If the Bruins have a weakness this year it is the inability of the guards to apply proper pressure. Defensively, because the Bruins have too many good shooters, I think a pressure defense, man-for-man, all over the court, is the answer. You must press three-quarter court and force the forwards and Alcindor out to help get the ball up-court. Once the Bruins get in their offensive set you must go to a specially concocted defense to help out against Alcindor. You must gamble somewhere. I say play tight on Lynn Shackelford and John Vallely and give the other forward and guard the outside shot, using your defensive men to sag back on Alcindor. Under no circumstances do you get into a running game with UCLA. I don't think there is a college team in America capable of running with them."

The 1969 Uclans were quite a bit different from the national champions of 1967 and 1968. They shot better, for one thing. Sophomores Curtis Rowe, 6' 6", and Sidney Wicks, 6' 8", and Alcindor were the leading percentage shooters in the Pac-8, and Shackelford and Vallely, letting fly from greater distances, were not far behind—but they guarded less than former UCLA teams, mostly because Mike Warren and Lucius Allen were gone. Still, with their rebounding, speed, depth, the winning streak off their backs, a great coach and Lew Alcindor, a lot of folks were picking them to win it all at Lousville.

So it was on to Louisville. The distinguished company who would be fighting it out in the semifinals included Drake, Purdue, UCLA and North Carolina, the first team ever to win three straight East Regionals. No matter what was tried—triple-teaming Alcindor, freezing the ball, prayer—none of the other three opponents had much of a chance if UCLA played as it did against Santa Clara in Pauley Pavilion in the quarterfinals. The Broncos, a good team that had lost only once all season and had beaten stubborn Weber State in overtime to earn the right to play the Bruins, were so quickly overwhelmed that they were behind, 7-0, before anybody even got the ball across the mid-court line. In no time it was 11-2 and then 18-2, and any Santa Clara notions of trying to imitate USC's successful stall were obviously out of the question. Santa Clara did not get one shot for the first 3½ minutes and continually found itself snared in the UCLA zone press. It was the Bruins' most impressive victory since the one-sided drubbing of Houston in the 1968 tournament. The usually serious Wooden was so loose after the game he even smiled.

"We finally played our game," he said. "It was the first time we have in three weeks. The press did it. We worked extensively on it all season—the 2-2-1 zone—but we hadn't used it in a game."

Dick Garibaldi, the Santa Clara coach, agreed with Wooden's assessment. "The press tore us apart," he said. "That and their shooting blasted us completely out. We never got to play the game we prepared for. They took us out, hung us on a line. We had to play UCLA's game and, man, that's murder."

There was nothing as one-sided in the East and Mideast Regionals. The East final, in College Park, Maryland between North Carolina and intrastate rival Davidson, was close all the way; no more than five points separated the teams in the first half. In a classic battle between two black stars among all the white faces, the Tar Heels' Charlie Scott (who once signed a letter of intent with Davidson and then reneged) outplayed Mike Maloy and all the other Wildcats, totaling 14 of 21 shots from the floor, four of five free throws, six rebounds, four assists and 32 points. He scored 12 of North Carolina's last 17 points and flipped in a jumper with two seconds left to win the game, 87-85.

In the Mideast Regional played at Madison, Wisconsin, Purdue did not meet Kentucky in the finals as expected, because Adolph Rupp's Wildcats were beaten by Marquette, 81-74, in the opening round. Al McGuire made sure his players did not forget the 1968 regional in Lexington, Kentucky, when their star, George Thompson, was "Mickey Moused" out of the contest early with fouls and Kentucky won in a waltz. "I'm too old for feuds," Rupp insisted, but bad feeling was evident on the court and there were several near-fights.

Dean Meminger, a sophomore who scored 20 points, didn't even play in the controversial 1968 Marquette-Kentucky game, yet confessed after the '69 showdown: "This was for revenge. Our primary objective in this tournament was to beat Kentucky."

Mission accomplished. Marquette very nearly went on to win the tournament, falling to Purdue's depth and All-American Rick Mount's remarkable shooting. Playing without its starting center, 7-footer Chuck Bavis, who was out with an injured collarbone, and its best all-round player and leading rebounder, Herm Gilliam, who was available for only part-time service because of a bad ankle, Purdue was forced to go to its bench as Marquette battled it to a draw, 63-63, in regulation time. The Warriors might have won, but Meminger missed a free throw and Ric Cobb, with a chance to win the game by making two more foul shots, blew the second.

In the overtime the two teams exchanged baskets and free throws until it was 73-73 with 26 seconds left and the Boilermakers, with possession, took time out. Everybody in attendance knew who would take the last shot—Rick "The Rocket" Mount. When it was time to go into his act, Rick dribbled to the right side, lost his defender on Jerry Johnson's pick and suddenly found himself all alone 20 feet from the basket. His jump shot swished through—and for the 20th time in 31 tournaments a Big Ten team was in the NCAA semifinals.

In the Midwest Regional at Manhattan, Kansas, Drake was out to make a point. The Bulldogs felt slighted by the fact that they had received little attention despite their 23-4 record and a Missouri Valley playoff victory over Louisville. They hadn't made it into the AP poll until the final week. They took out their anger on Colorado State, 84-77. In the locker room after the game, Dolph Pulliam, Drake's star defensive forward, was undaunted at the prospect of playing UCLA as the Bulldogs' next opponent.

"We've won our conference and our regional and so we think we have a right to demand respect," he said. "If the pollsters don't give it to us they'd better look out. I can't think of a better way of getting our 13th straight than by beating UCLA."

Give Pulliam an A for self-confidence. In the semifinals, in Louisville's Freedom Hall, UCLA almost did not make it past Drake. Maurice John, the Drake coach, had said before the game that he would play the Bruins man-for-man, Lew Alcindor notwithstanding. That was what he did, too. Not only that, he started 6' 5" Al Williams on Big Lew—something like asking a banty rooster to roust Gargantua. The strategy worked. While Drake's excellent guard, Willie McCarter, and a substitute guard, Gary Zeller, were doing most of their team's critical scoring, Pulliam led a defense that so harassed the Bruins they could not see Alcindor well enough to get the ball in to him. Only guard John Vallely's hot shooting late in the game saved the victory for UCLA. With only 1:12 left to play, the Uclans still led, 83-74, but Drake scored eight straight points, cutting the lead to one point just before Lynn Shackelford was fouled and the buzzer sounded simultaneously. Shackelford's two free throws made it UCLA 85, Drake 82. Wooden admitted afterward that he felt like he'd had a reprieve.

In the surprise of the tournament, Purdue slashed its way into the final by shocking North Carolina, 92-65. This despite the Tar Heels' vaunted Four Corner delay offense and height advantage—6' 10" Rusty Clark, 6' 8" Bill Bunting and 6' 10" Lee Dedmon. North Carolina had the height, but Purdue had Rick Mount and the clever 5' 10" Bill Keller, who moved in and out of NC's pressure defense like a mosquito on water. When they finished overwhelming the Tar Heels, Mount had 36 points, mostly from long range, and their opponents had 26 turnovers. It was such a bad night for North Carolina that the newly installed blue-green Scor-Tron scoreboard, manufactured in North Carolina and featuring "metal ceramic electroluminescent panels" instead of bulbs, balked and sputtered and refused to show the score properly.

Because Purdue was much the same kind of team as Drake, some of the uninitiated thought the Boilermakers had a good chance of beating UCLA for the championship. Lew Alcindor brought them back to this planet in record time. Playing 36 minutes, he scored 37 points and took 20 rebounds. Purdue never was in the game. It did not have the quickness of Drake, and its man-for-man coverage of Alcindor was a total failure. The result was UCLA 92, Purdue 72. Rick Mount managed to score 28 points, but he hit on only 12 of 36 shots, and most of those came in the second half when the game already was out of control.

Almost as important to UCLA in this victory as Alcindor was the defensive play of Kenny Heitz, who guarded Mount. "I feel," Coach Wooden said, "that every point that Mount scored under his average, 33.8, before the game was decided should be counted for Kenny."

The third straight title, and fifth in six years, was a personal triumph for John Wooden. Five different schools, including UCLA itself, had won two NCAA titles in a row, but this was the first time anybody had made it three. And what about that Alcindor, Lew? For three varsity years at UCLA—with 56 points in his first appearance 90 games ago and with more than 2,300 points in all—he helped draw the biggest indoor basketball crowd in history, led the Bruins to 88 victories against two losses, and was down in history as the first "big man" Wooden ever had.

Looking back over the Alcindor years, Wooden reflected, "It was not as easy an era as it might have seemed to outsiders. But it's been a tremendous era, I think. I've heard it said that any coach would have won championships with Lewis. That might be true, it really might. But they'll never know. I do."

For the third straight year, Alcindor was named the Most Valuable Player in the NCAA championship. Nobody before him had ever won the honor three times; perhaps no one ever will again.

"I'll just say it feels nice," Lew said later. "Before that final weekend of play, everything was up in my throat. The strain of the final week was terrible. I could see ahead to the end, but there was apprehension and fear. Fear of losing. I don't know why, but it was there. Before the other two tournaments it didn't feel that way. This one did. But, wow, after I knew Purdue was beaten I came back to the bench yelling. Wow, I was excited."

"Yes, yes," Lynn Shackelford said. "A long time from now we can look back and hold our three straight championships over all the teams to come along. 'What have they done?' we'll say. 'Have they done what we did?' The yoke is removed now. Let them try and match us."

DYNASTY: THE SEVENTIES

Blue-and-Gold-Buttons Say It All: "We're No. 1": 1970

A coach was now faced with a new kind of nightmare: the "mood" of his athletes and how it might affect their game. Not only were they bigger; they were brighter, more independent. "All I know is, you can't talk to athletes like you once could," one mentor in the Midwest said. "You can't sit on them. They're exposed to too many things. They're too smart, too aware. If they're not convinced that self-discipline is for their own good, they're not going to perform like you want them to."

A good example of the problem was Louisville's Coach John Dromo, who refused to let Joe Sigur, a 6′ 6″ transfer student, suit up because of his long hair. Dromo said he didn't mind if his boys let their hair grow a little long in the back or if they wore sideburns, but damned if he was going to have them looking like Saint Bernards.

"I just don't see any correlation between my hair and how I play basketball," Sigur said. "I've always wondered what God said a basketball player was supposed to look like."

While God remained silent on that subject, college teams cranked up their best Sunday punch to stop UCLA. After 14 games, the Bruins, with a vastly dissimilar style of attack, led all the national polls. To accentuate the positive, UCLA students wore blue-and-gold buttons with the words, "We're No. 1." And indeed they were.

Because the Uclans were shooting better, rebounding better and scoring more points than the year before, comparisons with the Blue and Gold champions of the Alcindor years were inevitable. Since Big Lew dominated the stage almost every game, all his teammates had had

an obsession with playing time, how much time they spent in games.

Every season, all the time, the problem was always a glut of stars and who got to play. The only thing they aimed for was not so much winning—they *knew* they'd win—but getting into a game. If a Bruin had a good game he got playing time the next game. There were disappointments. Morale was often low. "A lot of it was boring, sitting on the bench or even playing when the other team was obviously weaker," Lynn Shackelford admitted after graduation. "From the very start everybody said we would win three championships. That took a lot out of the actual accomplishment. I think that was one reason for our businesslike manner on the court. We were only doing what we'd been expected to do."

John Vallely, the Uclans' steadying influence in the 1970 backcourt, spoke for everybody on the team when he said it was like they were playing real basketball now, the way they grew up playing it. "It's difficult to make comparisons because Big Lew was such a great player," Vallely said. "But we all agree it's a lot more fun now. I mean, we must be more fun to watch. With Lew, the way he is, once you've seen him hook two or three times, it's over. He used to hook it in a few times and we'd win by 30. What a drag. Now we're running and pressing and all of us are getting into the act—you know, just like in regular basketball. It's funny, though. People still ask about the challenge of playing without Lew and about the pressure of winning. I've never really thought of it in terms of pressure. Not winning just has never occurred to me. We've always been winners here, all of us from high school on. Winning is the only thing we know. There are no other options."

The 1970 Bruins had their work cut out for themselves. Over the past 3½ seasons, UCLA had won 102 of 104 games. Despite such imposing numbers, Coach Wooden believed his current team had certain attributes above and beyond those of his former champions. Included among them were the brilliant long-range shooting of 6' 1" Henry Bibby, whose all-around generalship reminded UCLA watchers of Walt Hazzard and Gail Goodrich; and team rebounding, a chore that was the vested responsibility of Wooden's tough front line of Steve Patterson, Sidney Wicks and Curtis Rowe: the college game's answer to the Three Musketeers.

Another thing different about the 1970 Bruins was that they were more relaxed, laughed a lot more. The team comedian was Sidney Wicks. He almost never felt anger or frustration, and whenever winning became too routine and basketball a drudgery, the kid from the West Los Angeles ghetto would lift the spirits of his teammates with his imitation of *Midnight Cowboy*'s Ratso Rizzo or of his idols—Butch Cassidy and the Sundance Kid. He knew by heart all the dialogue between Butch and Sundance during their flight through South America, and he'd do the whole number, complete with fast draws and facial expressions.

Other times, he would trail, at a safe distance, a somber John Wooden through airports, concocting loud but imaginary conversations with his coach, saying all those things that no teammate ever dared to tell Wooden to his face.

Arrogant. That's what critics called Sidney Wicks. He had a glare as intimidating as a mugger's. A sociology major, he was bright (he graduated a quarter *ahead* of his class), knew basketball tactics and strategy, and was never reluctant to share that expertise with the Bruin coaching staff.

"Sidney is definitely the fastest, quickest big man I ever coached," John Wooden said.

Henry Bibby called him a super player.

"The first time I saw him play, he was a sophomore and I was a freshman," Bibby recollected. "I was impressed by his strength and the way he moved. After playing with him for a couple of years, I knew he'd have no trouble

playing in the NBA." (After Wicks graduated from UCLA the following year, 1971, he signed with the Portland Trail Blazers for $1.5 million over five years.)

Although UCLA's starters (with the exception of Rowe and Vallely) had to wait until 1970 to earn playing time of any consequence (Bibby was a sophomore), the quintet appeared to get along marvelously in the high post offense that was the hallmark of the pre-Alcindor days. It was an attack that afforded equal shooting opportunities for all but Steve Patterson at center, and it put a premium on balanced scoring, screens, cuts and teamwork. With it, all five averaged in double figures and shot, as a group, almost 53 percent.

Early in the season, however, UCLA deprived itself of its set plays simply by being so proficient in another phase of its offense: the fast break. The Uclans won six of their first eight games by 25 points or more, running their opposition ragged. Paradoxically, the other two wins were one-pointers over Minnesota and Princeton, and it suddenly dawned on people that to beat the Bruins all you had to do was to slow the tempo and control the ball. As a consequence, Wooden reached back and resurrected, piece by piece, his devastating zone press, still another strategic UCLA ploy that Alcindor, by his very presence, had transformed into a useless relic. The zone press, the way Wooden taught it, forced a control team out of its patterns, made it get moving to survive and, as the creator of chaos, was the fastest way to send a team unprepared for such tactics to the funny farm.

Before the season began, it was generally assumed that UCLA would have a strong first five and no depth, but in two of the Uclans' early close games it was a substitute coming off the bench who played a major role. Against Princeton, 6' 4" swingman Kenny Booker, a defensive whiz, came in with 12 minutes left for the express purpose of stopping the Tigers' Jeff Petrie, who had poured in 26 points up to that time. Booker shut out Petrie from the floor as UCLA won on an acrobatic shot by Wicks just before the game ended. Moreover, against Oregon State, John Ecker, a willowy forward without much varsity experience, was sent in for a jump ball when Wicks fouled out with 16 seconds to go and the Bruins were trailing the Beavers by one point. Ecker not only controlled the tip but got loose underneath and converted a perfect pass from Patterson for the basket that won the game.

More than anything else, that play was the one final stroke that brought the 1970 Uclans together as a unit in the largely esoteric terms of identity, morale and relationships. It also served as the force that separated the team from the unsettling rumors and whispers of dissension that surrounded the three Alcindor seasons. Vallely said that when Ecker won the Oregon State game, it gave his teammates a special lift because he was a substitute who did it. It meant he contributed something that none of the starters could.

"It was better that way," Vallely said. "I remember our 1969 championship, and a lot of guys didn't feel anything about it because they didn't think they had contributed. And they hadn't—it was all so easy. But now everyone is helping each other a lot more—not just saying 'too damn bad' if another guy makes a mistake—and, if we win again, they're all going to have contributed. I want us to win the NCAA again for guys like Booker and Terry Schofield and Bill Seibert. We'll all be a part of it this time."

Steve Patterson agreed with Vallely's assessment.

"The *esprit de corps* was, frankly, not good last year," Patterson said. "This wasn't because of Lew. He wasn't a detriment; there will never be a better team player than Lew. But we were all too concerned with points and playing time, not with winning. We would win. The main thing was contending with each other to get into games. We're so much more together this year."

"We are much more open this year," added Sidney Wicks. "There is more joviality, laughter. We smile a lot more."

All of this spiritual uplift was not lost on Wooden, a considerate man who seemed to be enjoying his team after three years of storm and controversy that took its toll on his health, if not his peace of mind. At 59 and the only man to win five NCAA basketball titles, he was in his 22nd season at UCLA and enjoying every minute of it. "It's more fun now," he admitted. "I'm even enjoying the tight games. It used to be that in close ones, well, we'd be okay. Lewis

was there, and we'd work things out. There didn't seem to be much to it. Now I feel like I have something to *do*. I feel more alive. It's been a long time."

The season was not without its vexations for UCLA. Toward the end, the Bruins traveled to Eugene to play Oregon and during a timeout with two minutes to play and the Ducks ahead by 15 points, Wooden found himself strolling over to the Oregon bench to shake Coach Steve Belko's hand. "It's going to be a little wild at the end, Steve," he said. "So I thought I'd say congratulations now. You beat us every way you could." In handing UCLA its first defeat of the season and breaking the Bruins' winning streak at 25 games, the Ducks outshot the Bruins, 43 to 34 percent, outrebounded them, 56 to 52, and outscored them, 78-65. Forward Rusty Blair broke the tide of a UCLA rally early in the second half with five straight field goals. The Ducks' win left the country without an undefeated major college team.

Both Oregon and then Southern California in UCLA's own league proved the Bruins could be beaten. But after a grueling season, UCLA was the champion of the Pac-8 once more and primed for the "whittling process" of NCAA tournament play. The various regionals were scheduled for Columbia, South Carolina; Columbus, Ohio; Lawrence, Kansas; and Seattle. The finals would be played in College Park, Maryland. The Las Vegas bettors figured UCLA would win—for the sixth time in seven years. They were picking the Bruins, they said, because of the team's experience, quickness, discipline, a powerful and high-scoring front line and perhaps the most accurate-shooting pair of guards in the college game. If there were any reservations about UCLA, it was that it had better opposition waiting in the wings than Bruin teams of the past, and winning the NCAA this time around was not going to be routine.

In the Western Regional at Seattle, UCLA's first opponent, Cal State at Long Beach, came to town acting very much like a new kid down the block just itching to clean the local bully's clock. Coach Jerry Tarkanian counted on Sam Robinson and George Trapp, both 6' 8", to neutralize UCLA's big men inside a 1-2-2 zone, but admitted he was scared out of his pants at the prospect. From the start, the contest was a backyard ruckus in more ways than one—many of the Long Beach players had faced the UCLA players during summer games at 109th Street in Watts—but the 49ers, who had the nation's longest winning streak (19) were never really in it. Henry Bibby made five long baskets over the zone while the Bruin defense cut off Cal State's heralded board game, and the Uclans won in a waltz, 88-65.

In the other half of the Seattle twin bill, Utah State got past Santa Clara by the skin of its teeth, 69-68, and was given no chance against UCLA two days later. "The task is Herculean," wrote one Seattle reporter. "In fact, Hercules himself might blanch at the assignment." Coach LaDell Andersen's Aggies did not blanch, but when it was all over the scoreboard read UCLA 101, Utah State 79.

A few weeks before the playoffs began, John Wooden sat at his desk on the UCLA campus fingering a sealed envelope. Inside were his predictions, made at the beginning of the season, on the outcome of all UCLA games. It was a little game he played with himself each season, not opening the envelope until the NCAA tournament was concluded.

"In the three years Lew Alcindor was here, did you pick any losses?" a reporter asked him.

"Yes," he said.

"How many?"

"Not many."

"Did you pick the Houston loss in the Astrodome?"

"No," he smiled.

"Did you pick the Southern Cal loss?"

"Anybody who predicts an undefeated season is a fool," Wooden said.

The thought prevailed that Wooden picked UCLA to lose a few in 1970—but it was safe to say he did not predict that any of those would happen in College Park.

Joining the Bruins for the finals of the NCAA tournament were Jacksonville, St. Bonaventure and New Mexico State. At first, there were those who suspected—with reason—that this was going to be the closest competition among the final four in years. Unlike most other seasons, this one had surfaced with championship contenders that had size, speed, good shooting, individual stars, team play and fine coaching. There wasn't a dark horse or a fluke among them. The Eastern final especially was to be an intriguing matchup of towering post-

men, 7' 2" Artis Gilmore vs. 6' 11", 265-pound Bob Lanier.

Teams that had been destroyed by Jacksonville were rapturous about Gilmore. "I have never seen a player—and I've seen Lew Alcindor several times—dominate a game like Gilmore," said Coach Bill Harrell of Morehead. "He has a variety of shots, the most impressive being a left-handed jump-hook-dunk. The only time he ventures more than a few feet away from the basket is when he is fouled and has to go to the free-throw line. At the other end of the court he has that same shot-blocking ability that served Alcindor so well at UCLA. His timing is good, and he has a good sense of where the hoop is so that he can avoid goaltending calls. His mere presence in the key forces opponents to shoot from longer distances and with a much higher arc than normal."

Gilmore, the collegian, was not a skinny, gawky freak. He had a good athlete's physique—with muscular thighs and arms—and his coaches insisted he could play for them if he were a mere 6' 5" or so. He did, in fact, take a P.E. course with a 6' 5" teammate whom he often out-performed on the trampoline.

Bob Lanier was so large he was called The Buffalo. Nobody in America, and that included a lot of the pro teams, had a more talented or intimidating center than this fun-loving, friendly man-child whose most memorable dimension was neither his height nor his weight but his feet. "They're really size 19," he confessed, "But sometimes I tell people they're size 30, just to get them off my back. Some of them believe me." Guard Billy Kalbaugh, his roommate and best friend, was a 5' 10", 150-pound chatterbox, and when he got to mouthing off at Buffalo Bob, the biggest Indian of them all threatened to shut him up by sticking him in one of his shoes.

The Gilmore vs. Lanier collision in College Park was publicized as a veritable Thunder Road—but then suddenly it was not. St. Bonaventure's graceful, ubiquitous center, with 9:39 to go in the Bonnies' 97-74 rout of Villanova in the Eastern regional final, was accidentally hit from behind by the Wildcats' Chris Ford, who had tripped going for a loose ball, and Buffalo Bob crashed to the floor in sections. He got up and continued to play, but after a half-minute he called time out and limped to the bench, where he told Coach Larry Weise, "I can't run." Lanier had torn the medial collateral ligament in his right knee. Ironically, his college career had come to an end on a meaningless play, long after the Bonnies had wrapped up the regional title. That night he went home to Buffalo on crutches for surgery.

Before his premature end, Lanier was asked how he would go about beating his own team. "I'd front me, surround me and gamble on us missing from outside," he said. "When you cut off the pass to the corners and collapse inside, we're hurting."

In the Mideast Regional at Columbus, Ohio, Gilmore contributed 54 of the 848 total points scored by Jacksonville, Kentucky, Iowa and Notre Dame. Though Jacksonville won the strongest regional, the Dolphins did it by the skin of their teeth. Sparked by Chip Dublin, who came off the bench to score 19 points, they held a comfortable 72-60 lead over Kentucky, before the Wildcats' 6' 8" star, Dan Issel, began to assert himself with nine straight points. But as Issel moved down the floor to set up on offense with 10 minutes to play, Issel slammed into Vaughn Wedeking for his fifth foul and went to the bench in tears. Kentucky gamely fought back to within two points with only about a minute to go, but Rex Morgan's one-hander and his two free throws saved the game for Jacksonville, 106-100.

Earlier, Jacksonville barely escaped from the clutches of Iowa when Pembrook Burrows rebounded Wedeking's 25-footer with three seconds left to win, 104-103. Though the Dolphins had earned a ticket to Maryland, they had yet to face a good defensive team in the NCAA tournament, and their inability to protect the ball at the end of both victories in Columbus had a lot of experts saying it was going to be UCLA again in the final four.

UCLA's opponent in the semifinals was New Mexico State. The scouting report on the Aggies claimed that their backcourt was quicker than the Bruins'. "If their guards can withstand what certainly will be some sort of pressing game by UCLA and not fold up their gun arms at the same time, they can win," stated one report. History, however, dictated that the big games were won underneath, and there the Uclans were too strong and swift for even such a physical aggregation as the Aggies, who won the Midwest Regional championship with victories over Kansas State, 70-66, and Drake, 87-78.

All through the season, the legend of the Jacksonville Dolphins had been growing. They had not one but two 7-footers, plus a super scorer with a name right out of the funny papers: Rex Morgan. They were free spirits with no training rules and a young unorthodox coach, Joe Williams, who kept track of his scouting reports by scribbling notes to himself on the backs of envelopes. The team's magic carpet was supposed to go flat in the tough Mideast regional round, but the experts had not reckoned with the hot hand of Artis Gilmore and the Dolphins beat Western Kentucky, Iowa and Kentucky.

But somewhere between Columbus, Ohio, and College Park, Maryland, something happened to Jacksonville's sorcery. The something, of course, was UCLA. After getting by St. Bonaventure in the semifinals in a victory described as "flat, unimpressive," the Dolphins found themselves paired against the Bruins in the NCAA finals. Out of 225 teams eligible for the championship, it was UCLA once again, without Lew Alcindor this time, but still with the best team and the best coach, John Wooden, 23 years older than Joe Williams. Wooden had already been named Coach of the Year by AP, UPI, the Coaches' Association and the basketball writers.

To get to the finals, UCLA had to get through what was supposed to be a difficult semifinal against New Mexico State. As far as the Aggies were concerned, the game was a grudge match—the previous two years NMS had been eliminated by UCLA in the West Regional—and Guard Jimmy Collins felt they had their momentum going. "Maybe it's our turn to win," he told reporters before the game. It wasn't. Collins bucketed 28 points, but his teammates stood around picking their noses and the Aggie front line lacked UCLA's quickness. At the final buzzer it was UCLA 93, New Mexico State, 77.

Lou Henson, the Aggie coach, was frustrated. "You get a complex after a while," he said. He had plenty of company. Yet he could comfort himself a little by noting that Wooden's teams down the years lost nine of their first 12 NCAA tournament games. As recently as 1963, Arizona State beat the Bruins by 14 points. Of course, they didn't lose many after that.

To bolster their confidence, the Dolphins looked for omens. For example, the last time

All-American Forward Sidney Wicks is a textbook example of what a jump shot is all about; here he scores for UCLA on way to 93-77 victory over New Mexico State in 1970 NCAA semifinals at College Park, Maryland.

the NCAA finals were held in College Park, a little-known independent, Texas at El Paso, beat Kentucky, a prestige basketball school. Now Jacksonville was assigned to the same motel where UTEP once slept, just up the street from the Maryland campus.

It would take more than omens to sink the Uclans. The Bruins not only had 1,000 fans cheering for them, but they also had all the rooters from St. Bonaventure, who felt their team, without the services of injured Bob Lanier, had been gypped by the officials in the game against Jacksonville and who persisted in calling the Dolphins tunas. "You're a tuna, Gilmore," they shouted. "You're a stiff."

Sidney Wicks didn't know until just before the game that he was guarding Artis Gilmore, who at 7' 2" was six inches taller than Wicks. Gilmore was so tall he could stand flatfooted and touch the rim with the ball. "I thought I was going to guard anybody but him," said Sidney.

"The original strategy was for Sidney to stay close to Gilmore, at his side, while our other four pressured the passers," Wooden explained later. "It didn't work."

Gilmore scored three times from near the basket and Jacksonville quickly led, 14-6, when UCLA finally woke up enough to call a time out.

"During the break," Wooden recalled, "I moved Sidney around behind Gilmore and had Patterson and others ease off their own men a little to help out. If Gilmore did get the ball inside it would be in close quarters and difficult for him to get a shot. With men all around you with their hands up, it's just not that easy."

The busiest, most intimidating hands belonged to Wicks. Giving away six inches in height, he still managed to block Artis' shots four times. "I couldn't move him no kinda way," said Sidney. "So I tried to make him get the ball six or seven feet from the basket and I'd back off him. Then I had room to jump between him and the hoop."

The result was that Gilmore suffered a horrific shooting night—nine for 29—and trailed Wicks, 18-16, in rebounds.

Meanwhile, the Bruins played better defense and flashed more poise than the Dolphins and fought back to a small lead on clever fast breaks and the shooting of Vallely and Rowe. Despite

14 turnovers and a super defensive job on Bibby by little Vaughn Wedeking, UCLA managed a sudden spurt just before the halftime buzzer to walk off the floor with a 41-36 lead.

Steve Patterson, 6′ 9″, said later that he and his teammates agreed in the locker room that the outcome of the game was going to be determined by what happened in the first several minutes of the second half. The Dolphins were down by only five points and could still catch the Bruins, or UCLA could quickly move out by 10. UCLA moved out. Jacksonville wasn't used to playing *behind* teams—it hadn't played a schedule as rough as UCLA's. "I think Gilmore was surprised to see a 6′ 8″ guy go up and block his shot," Patterson said, "but I've never seen anybody better than Sidney."

In the second half, Gilmore missed his first five shots and UCLA steadily increased its lead to eight, 11 and 16 points. Coach Joe Williams calmly took what was obviously a lost cause. The Dolphins would have to settle for second place. When Gilmore fouled out with 1:50 left, Wooden substituted freely and the final margin was 11 points, 80-69. UCLA not only won the point battle against college basketball's tallest team but the rebound contest as well, 50-38.

For the Bruins, the victory marked their fourth NCAA title in a row and their sixth in seven years. Would this domination end? Hardly likely. Only Vallely would be missing from the 1971 defending champions.

The juniors on the team—Wicks, Rowe and Patterson—were bursting with confidence after beating Jacksonville. They felt they had proved themselves.

"Everybody was looking forward to playing without Big Lew this season," Rowe said. "Until now, every time somebody mentioned the three in a row they said Lew did it. Well, we just proved that four other men from that team could play basketball, too—with the best of them."

It may not have been a typical season for college basketball in America, but never mind. These things happen. Kentucky State's Travis Grant broke his school's scoring record by 30 points in a 141-93 victory, hitting a whopping 70 percent of his field goal shots for 75 points—and hurt his accuracy average (73 percent) for the season.

The brilliant all-around generalship of 6′ 1″ Henry Bibby (No. 45) reminded UCLA watchers of Walt Hazzard and Gail Goodrich. Here "King Henry" lofts a jump shot over Jacksonville Center Artis Gilmore for two more points as UCLA romped, 80-69, to another NCAA title.

The 1970 UCLA National Champions. Front row, left: Henry Bibby, Terry Schofield, Andy Hill. Middle row, left: Mgr. George Morgan, Asst. Coach Gary Cunningham, Coach John Wooden, Asst. Coach Denny Crum, Trainer "Ducky" Drake. Rear, left: Kenny Booker, Rick Betchley, John Ecker, Sidney Wicks, Steve Patterson, Jon Chapman, Curtis Rowe, Bill Seibert, John Vallely.

In a tight contest between Eastern Kentucky and Murray State, the former apparently won, 79-78, but then Murray claimed the clock had flipped at the end of the game and ended 10 seconds too soon. An examination of the clock supported Murray's charge. Art Guepe, Commissioner of the Missouri Valley Conference, ruled that the missing 10 seconds would have to be played. So at the end of the season, Murray State traveled 600 miles round trip from Paducah to Richmond to play 10 seconds worth of losing basketball.

Finally, Mississippi College, loaded with the runningest, gunningest hombres since Butch and the Kid, gained the reputation as basketball's most prolific loser in NCAA history. The predominantly white, Baptist-supported school of 2,300 students began the season, averaging 112 points a game, leading the nation in scoring and sporting an 0-5 record. The Choctaws opened the season losing to Livingston (Alabama) University, 160-146. They followed this

with a 135-131 defeat at the hands of Southeastern Louisiana. Among other frustrations MC had to endure was the old long net trick. To hold down the scoring, rivals tightened the nets with a drawstring at the bottom. Every time the ball went through, the ball stuck, killing time. Mississippi College started carrying a pocketknife. During warmups when the other side wasn't looking, the Choctaws sent a boy in for a layup and he'd cut the string.

Poor old (sob) MC. Against Northeast Louisiana State it scored 27 points in the last three minutes—and still lost, 112-100.

The coach of the "Chocs" was an optimist named James Q. Allen. His basketball philosophy became ingrained around 1929 when, as a 6' 4" guard for Mississippi College, he helped beat the original New York Celtics in Meridian, Mississippi.

"We just kept forcing and forcing 'em," Allen remembered. "That made 'em mad, and they beat us by 25 points the next night."

No End in Sight for UCLA: 1971

Optimists were saying that this was going to be the year. "This is the season we stop UCLA," they said, though not too loudly. Down in Dixie many experts believed that South Carolina, led by brilliant All-American John Roche, was the only team with an even chance to defeat UCLA in the final playoffs. "I wouldn't trade the dirt under his fingernails for anyone else's soul," said Coach Frank McGuire of Roche in a phrase and manner that their Irish forefathers would know and love. "I'm not Jesus. Roche is the best I've ever seen at controlling a game. While I have him, we have to take advantage of that." In the Gamecocks' intrasquad games, the first team won by 20 points with Roche and lost by 20 when he switched sides.

Another giant killer for UCLA to think about was Marquette. Opponents were being left openmouthed and frustrated by the dipping, rolling, bippety-bopping moves of All-America Dean (The Dream) Meminger and a center who was really a center this time, 6' 11" Jim Chones. Midway through the season, the Warriors had run off the nation's longest winning streak—25 games over the past two years—and had won 51 straight games in the Milwaukee Arena. Still Coach Al McGuire (no relation to Frank) refused to think about Houston, the site of the NCAA playoffs in March. "I can't think about the championships," he said. "Houston is for dreamers, and dreamers usually are asleep.

Al McGuire had paid his dues. He came out of the 108th St. playground in Rockaway, New York in the footsteps of his brothers, Dick and John, who starred at St. John's. "When I was in high school and college coaches came to recruit," Al recalled recently, "they'd run about 20 prospects into the woods. The kids that ran *through* the trees went out for college football. The ones that ran *around* the trees went out for basketball." Al played basketball at St. John's under Frank McGuire and later made the NBA where, he confessed, "I was the worst player ever to last three years in the big time." He played with broken jaws, broken noses and once was charged with eight fouls in a single game— the six that eliminated him plus two technicals for attempting to dislodge the referee's head from the rest of his body. Remembering some of the wild ones he had coached and seen, Frank McGuire shook his head with the memory of Al. "He was my all-timer," said Frank.

After his wars in the pros, Al went into coaching. His first head coaching job was at little Belmont Abbey College, in North Carolina, in 1957. Belmont fans would have loved McGuire's teams—if the teams stayed home long enough to be seen. One year, Coach McGuire scheduled 22 of their 25 games *on the road*.

In 1964, Al was offered a chance to rescue the floundering basketball fortunes of Marquette. Looking back on those years, he admits now, "I was not the average coach. I said things I shouldn't. I went berserk. If I had been a university, I'd never have hired me."

McGuire's success at Marquette was built largely on his relationships with his players, his use of psychology, passion, loyalty and especially a realistic treatment of the black-white factor, or what he preferred to call "the checkerboard problem."

The first player McGuire recruited for Marquette was 6' 3" Pat Smith out of Harlem, a center who could not see and could not shoot but who used what talents he did have to acquire a distinguished nickname: "The Evil Doctor Blackheart."

"Coach McGuire understands our background and environment, and he forces us to remember," said Smith. "He keeps reminding us we have nothing to go back to and he's right. Men from the ghetto shape up here."

Meminger said, "Coach tells Lackey, 'Hey, you haven't passed to a white man in four days.' He tells Brell, 'Goose, don't you see any brothers open?' I mean, he comes out and lays it on the line. We try not to get into cliques. If we do, there's trouble."

"Why not be frank?" McGuire said. "We talk about differences, and we don't stop when practice ends. I don't want my guys going back to 1870 as soon as 5 o'clock comes."

Author Jimmy Breslin grew up near the McGuires on Long Island and was close to Al during the Marquette years. He remembers how Al came to get Jim Chones, who was sought by every major college in the country when he played on the basketball team at St. Catherine's High School, Racine, Wisconsin. Every college, that is, except Marquette. He had not received anything—not a phone call or even a letter—from this basketball power in his own state.

In April, Coach McGuire showed up in the athletic office at St. Catherine's High School. Jim Chones was summoned from class. The athletic director told him, "Jim, this is Al McGuire."

McGuire spoke with big, brown eyes locked on the 6' 11" Chones. "I wanted to talk to you for a long time," Al said. "But we heard your father was sick and we didn't want to bother you." Only recently the father, J. W. Chones, had died of lung cancer, after 22 years of working as a moulder in a steel plant. McGuire then invited young Chones to come down to a basketball banquet at Marquette. When Chones came, McGuire spoke to him again. Those big, brown eyes, serious, never left Chone's eyes once during the conversation. When Al McGuire talks to you he looks you straight in the eye.

"There is no money here," he said.

Chones mentioned some of the things other schools had offered him to play basketball for them. A nice house for his mother. A bright new, shiny car. Spending money. New clothes. His own apartment.

"That's fine," McGuire told him. "You'll be just another hired hand for them. A field hand." Chones knew what the coach meant. "You listen to me—you can do it differently. You're big, you've got reactions, good speed. With hard work you have a chance to develop here and later make big money as a pro. Big money for yourself. Once you make it for yourself it's clear sailing. Then you can do whatever you want with your life. You can be anybody you want, do anything you want. But make it on your own. You'll never get anything if you're just a hired hand for somebody."

He also told Chones that if he decided to come to Marquette there was one important promise he was expected to keep: "You've got to get a degree."

"So Chones came to Marquette in September, 1969," Jimmy Breslin said. "He found out a little bit more about his coach in the dressing room before a game with Creighton. One of the varsity players, Hugh McMahon, arrived late. McGuire began screaming. McMahon started screaming back. McGuire was all over him so fast nobody knew what was happening. But Chones, hunched in a corner of the dressing room in terror, saw it clearly. McGuire kneed McMahon in the groin. Then he hit him in the face. He threw McMahon against the wall and was about to kick him in the groin. McMahon suddenly turned and started walking out of the dressing room, forever. It was one of the great goodbye scenes in sports. Then an arm came out and grabbed McMahon's collar and McMahon came yanking back into the middle of the room. 'All right,' Al McGuire said to McMahon, 'now get dressed and let's play.'"

Breslin remembers another afternoon when the Warriors were practicing and Coach McGuire decided Gary Brell, 6' 6", wasn't in very good shape. He had Brell running wind sprints from wall to wall in the gymnasium. Brell stopped in the middle of one of the sprints and just stood there, bent over, his wind spent. "Hey, Coach," he panted, "why don't you make some of the black guys do some of the running, too?" McGuire said nothing. He walked out to where Brell was stooped over and spoke to him. He spoke to him by *hitting him in the face*. Brell, blood trickling down his lip, began running again.

People called Brell a flake, a hippie, for the way he dressed. "Goose," McGuire told him, "you look terrible. I don't mind you in Hipsville, I just don't want to see you in Tap City."

Brell protested.

"You're always getting on me for the guys I hang out with, calling them undesirables," he told the coach. "They want you to come over to meet them. They're peaceful. You'll dig."

"Goose," said McGuire, "you think you're telling me something? Well, I was the *original* flower child. I didn't call them undesirables, anyway. I called them jerks. Like that Mafia-type jerk who picked you up the other day. Him. Who was *that* jerk?"

"That," said Gary (Goose) Brell, "was my *brother*."

The only ones tall enough to guard the 6' 11" Chones when the Warriors practiced happened to be white players. Chones, irritated at all the arms and elbows, pushed back. In the middle of the scrimmage Coach McGuire walked onto the floor.

"Dammit," he shouted at Chones, "why don't you swing for once at a black guy? Are you afraid one of them will pick up something and crack your head?"

After practice, Chones was still thinking about what the coach had said. He never had heard a white man talk like that to him before. Totally uninhibited. By golly, he said to himself, his coach was the fairest white man he ever had heard of.

Judged on its regular-season play, there were suspicions that the 1971 Bruins were not up to their immediate predecessors. No longer did the once expertly programmed machine grind down opponents. The cold efficiency was gone. They had even grown used to close calls. Why, they even lost once, to Notre Dame by seven points. The latter was simply a case of too much Austin Carr—a 46-point wrecking job that fired the Irish to an 89-82 victory over towering, supposedly omnipotent, No. 1 UCLA. "We really had UCLA scouted," said Carr after the upset in South Bend. "They did all the same things we thought they were going to do. Our

fans helped, of course. They whip it up pretty good." Carr did much of the whipping-up on his own, and did it with a touch of everything: breaking the fearsome UCLA zone press, hurling baskets in from outside, flipping them up from inside, throwing some while turning and falling out of bounds, driving for others through the trumpeted UCLA front line, hitting open men when he himself was covered. He got rebounds, made steals, embarrassed four defenders, fouled out Sidney Wicks and finished with 15 of the last 17 Irish points. What Austin Carr did to UCLA on national television was "wake up the echoes and shake down the thunder all by himself."

Before the Notre Dame game, UCLA had won 14 straight games, 19 in a row over two years, 48 consecutive non-conference battles and, of course, those four NCAA championships in a row. "Ours is a veteran team, and with so much success it's hard to talk to them about winning more," John Wooden said before the Bruins played the Irish. "I feel like I'm talking to a stone wall. We're not sharp and we're not hungry."

Notre Dame was not UCLA's only problem during the season. Playing in one of the toughest major conferences in the country, the Bruins beat Stanford by only five points. They beat USC, after trailing by nine points with only 9½ minutes to go. They trailed Oregon by one point with less than a minute to go when Bibby stole the ball and drove in for the winning basket. Wicks hit a 20-foot jump shot in the final seconds to beat Oregon State. Two foul shots with seven seconds to go were the margin over Washington State. Rowe's jump shots with less than a minute left beat Washington.

Though it looked pretty bad at times, UCLA gradually got its act together. It anesthetized California and Stanford by more than 30 points apiece, and defeated USC with ease, 73-62, to serve notice on all survivors of league races and qualifying rounds that it fully intended to be in the NCAA final at Houston for the fifth straight time.

There were not many demurs. UCLA was back. Once more, that awesome front line of 6' 7" Curtis Rowe, 6' 8" Sidney Wicks and 6' 9" Steve Patterson ruled the backboards at both ends; the guards had steadily improved; and the defense was very tough, as always. It was just the sort of team to give all tournament challengers fits, with plenty of movement in its attack and ample rebounding strength.

The trip to Houston was not without its heart-in-the-throat moments for the Bruins. After disposing of Brigham Young, 91-73, in the West Regional in Salt Lake City, they were forced to prove worthy of their steel against Long Beach State, Jerry Tarkanian's team. Defense was the Pumas' game, and they gave UCLA all the defense it could handle as the Bruins narrowly escaped from an embarrassing 29 percent shooting performance to win, 57-55. The defending champions managed only eight field goals in the first half. Later, Coach Wooden confessed he thought about leaving early for Houston with his wife and enjoying the coaches' convention.

Tarkanian said afterward that Long Beach State did everything it had to do—except win.

"We stopped their inside game, we shut 'em off outside, we kept our hands in their faces," Tarkanian said. "We stayed close. We scored as much as we gave 'em. We did everything we wanted to do to win."

But with two more points than Long Beach, the Bruins were there at the end. They were now a problem for Kansas, which had beaten Houston (78-77) and Drake (73-71) at Wichita for the championship of the Midwest. Big, bold and brutish, Kansas carried as its standard a fantastic tendency for victory in close games. After their two squeakers at Wichita, a Kansas fan boasted, "Forget UCLA. Forget everybody. We're the best team." If they were, they had a heart-stopping way of showing it, for the Jayhawks won seven games by five or fewer points in winning 25 of 26 games during the regular season.

The other two schools comprising the final four at Houston were Western Kentucky and Villanova. The Hilltoppers were a surprise entry. No one had expected them to win the Mideast Regional at Athens, Georgia. It had been the norm of recent years for the Mideast to have the strongest and best-balanced tournament and 1971 was no exception. All four participants—Western Kentucky, Kentucky, Ohio State and Marquette—achieved Top Ten status. Most of the rooters in attendance were from Kentucky, including Governor Louie Nunn, resplendent in blue jacket ("for Ken-

tucky"), red shirt ("for Western") and white tie ("I come in peace"). All those bluegrass folks were there to watch Adolph Rupp's Wildcats clash with Johnny Oldham's Hilltoppers. They had waited forever for a meeting between the intrastate schools. Western had been fielding basketball teams for 52 years, Kentucky for 68—and yet they had never played each other. The main obstacle was Adolph (The Baron) Rupp, who had an aversion to putting his imposing reputation on the chopping block against smaller schools. The last time he did it he lost to Louisville in the 1959 Mideast Regional.

The Westerners were in tough. Despite a season of crippling injuries and nagging illnesses, including the hospitalization of Rupp, Kentucky won the SEC title as usual and coasted into the playoffs for the 19th time. The Wildcats had balance, depth, eight men who were shooting better than 50 percent, and a greatly improved big man in 7' Tom Payne.

Whichever team won, the oddsmakers figured it probably would be too emotionally drained to beat the winner of the Marquette-Ohio State game—most likely Marquette. Lame or healthy, 27 straight had fallen to the Warriors, 39 over the last two seasons. The Warriors qualified for the regionals by taking out Miami of Ohio, 62-47, largely on the strength of an excellent second-half comeback. "We're a second-half team," said Coach Al McGuire. "We won and we're going down South again. I spent six years down there, at Belmont Abbey, and all I can remember is Coca-Cola bottles, gas stations and red clay."

His memories were destined to be more vivid after Athens. Marquette rejected an NCAA bid in 1970 and won the NIT at Madison Square Garden, so it was tournament-toughened, and it had since added 6' 11" sophomore Jim Chones, possibly the best center in college basketball.

The Kentucky-Western Kentucky contest did not live up to its buildup. From the opening whistle it was evident that the Wildcats, lacking guards who could get the ball past midcourt, were not prepared for the quickness and speed of their neighbors. The Hilltoppers pressed like a cidermill. Aided by the deft passing and ball control of his crew of black henchmen whose time had been long in arriving but who now looked like a team with perhaps the best chance of any in recent seasons to topple UCLA, Big Jim McDaniels scored seven of Western's first 16 points. After that, the Westerners ran the score to 24-12, to 51-38 at the half, to 70-47 with 13 minutes left, and finally to 107-83.

In the other half of the night's doubleheader, Ohio State shocked everybody by beating Marquette, 60-59. With a 13-point lead and only nine minutes left in the first half, Coach McGuire made himself vulnerable for the inevitable second-guessers by switching to a zone from an airtight press, which had been working. Both his forwards, Bob Lackey and Gary Brell, were plagued with injuries, and the move was fashioned to give them assistance. The strategy backfired. The highly disciplined Buckeyes fought back as though their lives depended upon it, and at the half they trailed by only four points. Even more important, their tenacity got Dean Meminger, the Warrior ace, into foul trouble early in the second half.

With five minutes left in the game, Marquette was still up by five points. Then it happened. Meminger crashed into Ohio State's Captain Jim Cleamons and was flagged out of the game on fouls. He spent the waning moments trying to cool off Coach McGuire, who threatened to take a poke at the referees. Without Meminger's steadying influence, the Warriors fell apart and died.

Ohio State appeared to be on its way to a second straight upset within 24 hours when it calmly went out in front of Western Kentucky in the final, 38-24. McDaniels and Clarence (Big C) Glover got the Hilltoppers moving late in the first half, however, and with Jim Cleamons benched for 12 minutes with fouls, Western sunk Ohio State spirits with a dazzling spurt to tie the score late in the game and send it into overtime. Then after some big mistakes by both teams, Glover found the range to win it for Western, 81-78. "I'm not responsible for anything Clarence does," remarked Coach Oldham after the game. What Big C did was merely take 17 and 22 rebounds in the two tournament games. McDaniels scored 35 and 31 points.

Western's opponent in the NCAA semifinals in Houston was Villanova, a team with some pretty imposing credentials of its own. Down at Raleigh, North Carolina, the Wildcats had put on quite a production of their own, first elim-

inating Fordham, 85-75, by lobbing passes over the Rams' version of the full-court press. Then, in an all-Philadelphia shootout, they absolutely devastated Pennsylvania, 90-47—those same undefeated Quakers of the Ivy League who had previously won 45 of 46 games over two seasons. Earlier Penn had outclassed vaunted South Carolina, 79-64, by hitting 19 straight free throws in the second half. Before meeting Villanova, Guard Dave Wohl of Penn described his team's play as "basically dull, methodical, efficient, mechanical." The Wildcats proved him right.

Penn had beaten Villanova by eight points earlier in the season and had not lost to the Wildcats in three straight games, but the Wildcats were aroused at Raleigh and didn't give the Quakers a chance.

When the UCLA basketball team arrived in Houston it carried with it a won-lost record of 143-5 for the past five seasons and an NCAA tournament performance of 26 straight victories. Untypically, the usually low-key John Wooden forewarned everybody: "I think we have as good a chance as any team here." Typically, UCLA then went out and beat Kansas, 68-60, in the semifinals Thursday night with their usual businesslike precision, then flattened enthusiastic Villanova, 68-62, in the finals on Saturday. The Bruins' NCAA record then read: five straight championships and seven of the last eight.

If the story of UCLA's continued dominance of college basketball was familiar, the setting at least was different in Houston. The playing court in the Astrodome was a four-foot-high platform squatting in the middle of all that covered acreage, with an 80-foot-high NBC camera crane poised above it at one end. Joe Jares, the magazine writer, was there and he said later that "the spectators at ground level needed periscopes, while the spectators in the stands needed telescopes." A lot of the customers were unable to see the games. The press corps suspected all along that the Astrodome was not suitable for basketball, and they told the NCAA just that. But the NCAA chiefs ignored this unsolicited advice. Reason: the potential payoff was too fat to resist. The two sessions drew 63,193 people, adding up to $60,000 take-home pay for each of the four semifinalists.

For the millions of viewers who watched the Houston games on TV, it was easy to see that the players had a problem, too. There were only about 10 feet between the sidelines and the edges of the raised floor. "Here's my first prediction," said Coach Johnny Oldham, stepping up on the raised court for the first time. "I predict Clarence Glover goes over the side." Western's Rex Bailey promised he would go after the ball, no matter what. He said he didn't want to, considering the consequences, but with the national championship at stake he wasn't going to hold back. "Of course," he said, "I'll probably land on somebody's head."

A couple of hustling players did overshoot the runway in the four games—Glover was not among them—but nobody was hurt. (Outside the Dome, however, a Western Kentucky student was killed trying to jump from a motel balcony into a swimming pool.)

In the opening semifinal game between Villanova and Western Kentucky, the Wildcats were appearing in their 10th postseason tournament in the 10 years Jack Kraft had been coaching. This was not to be the Hilltoppers' night. Big Jim McDaniels, perhaps bothered by news reports that he had already signed a pro contract with the ABA (along with Villanova's 6' 8" Howard Porter he signed an NCAA affidavit, swearing to the amateur code), was a patsy on defense against Hank Siemiontkowski. Even though his shooting and aggressiveness on the boards was largely responsible for Western Kentucky getting 32 more shots and 11 more rebounds, McDaniels' ineptitude on defense cost Western where it hurt most: points. Villanova won in double overtime, 92-89. At that, Western might have pulled the game out of the fire before the end of regulation play had Jerry Dunn not missed a free throw with only four seconds to go.

UCLA didn't know what to expect from Kansas in the semifinal windup. The Jayhawks defied tradition. They started a center at forward, a forward at guard and a guard at the other forward. They also played two 6' 10" men who, despite their height and limited traction, were ordered by their bright young coach, Ted Owens, to press all over the floor on defense. Once upon a time Kansas relied on big, slow men to get the job done; now they actually ran.

"Kansas is better disciplined and a better team than most," said Oklahoma City's Abe Lemons, "but the Big Eight Conference destroys its members. Everybody stalls and packs around. The result is that Kansas is not free and easy like you have to be."

Yet a lot of people liked the Jayhawks' chances against the Bruins. Their frontcourt of Dave Robisch, Roger Brown and Pierre Russell was one of the most fearsome physical trios in college basketball, limiting opponents to a paltry 38 percent shooting average. Offensively, Kansas averaged 82 points a game, easily a school record.

The last time Kansas had as good a team was in 1966, and they lost to the eventual champion, Texas Western, 81-80, in two overtimes. That was in the NCAA Midwest Regional, when Jo Jo White stepped out of bounds as he tossed in what would have been the winning points.

A lot of Big Eight followers believed Kansas was the best college team in the country in 1966, but there were no questions left unanswered in the Astrodome after UCLA took out the Jayhawks. The contest was hard-fought but not especially exciting. UCLA led at halftime, 32-25, before Kansas made a run at them early in the second half. Trailing by only two points, 6' 10" Dave Robisch hit a jump shot to tie the score at 39-all, only to be called for traveling. "That turnover was the changing point of the game," Coach Ted Owens said later. "It cost us our momentum; we never regained it." UCLA gradually moved out into the lead, forged ahead by as much as 15 points and won by eight.

Meanwhile, a drama brewed up on the UCLA bench. John Wooden, the master tactician, uncharacteristically got into a shouting match with, of all people, Denny Crum, one of his assistant coaches. Crum wanted to send Guard Terry Schofield into the game. Wooden said no. Crum motioned for Schofield to take off his jacket and go in anyway. Wooden threatened to banish Crum to the end of the bench. Crum refused to sit there. Henry Bibby, one of the Bruin starters, tried to serve as peace-maker. No sooner had he cooled them off than Wooden and Crum were bickering again.

"Listen," Wooden told his assistant, "I'm the coach of this team. Don't tell me how to coach my team."

While Crum sometimes went too far, Wooden confessed afterward that he liked high-spirited aides. "I detest yes-men," he said. One of the secrets to his success, actually, was that after considerable prodding and debate an assistant could sometimes get Wooden to accept new ideas.

With the elimination of Kansas and Western Kentucky, Villanova hoped to become the second team in history with six losses on its record to win the national championship. Kentucky was the other, in 1958.

"The whole East Coast will go up in flames if we win," said Hank Siemiontkowski. "The school would be unbelievable. They'd burn it."

Back in Philadelphia, the Villanova campus was really psyched up. A group of the students marched about 11 miles to the University of Pennsylvania campus to crow some more over the fact the Wildcats had murdered Penn by 43 points in the East Regional. Adding to their zeal, Jack Kraft had just been named university division Coach of the Year by the National Association of Basketball Coaches.

"The season already is a big success," Kraft said, "but we don't intend to stop playing basketball just yet."

UCLA saved the East from burning.

Villanova opened against UCLA in a two-three zone, the defense that had given the Bruins headaches against Long Beach State in the West Regional tournament. Sidney Wicks and Curtis Rowe were contained fairly well, but Steve Patterson, the 6' 9" UCLA center, made nine of 13 shots, inside and out, and by half-time was credited with 20 points. With five minutes left in the first half, the Bruins were in front, 39-32. A furious pressing defense and some torrid shooting from long range kept up the pressure. Suddenly UCLA changed strategy, going into a stall to force the Wildcats out of their zone. The tactic worked just well enough to enable the Bruins to go ahead by 11 points.

In the second half, the Bruins went back to the spread again. Wooden explained that he was afraid the long shots, so necessary against the zone, would stop dropping and he was confident that his players could score against a man-to-man defense—something Villanova seldom reverted to. As it turned out, Wooden was wrong. The Wildcats played man-to-man as if they had invented it and the contest turned into wild thunder to the final buzzer. With 4:53 remaining, the Uclans held a precarious four-point edge and called timeout to talk over strategy. Villanova's new-found toy, the man-to-man, had them clearly confused. They had scored only three field goals, all layups, against it. Individually, the battle had narrowed down to a brilliant duel between All-American Wicks and All-American Howard Porter. Twice Porter closed the gap to three points with jump shots, but that was as close as he could get the Wildcats. Then Patterson, a great clutch player, put UCLA out of reach with a layup, helped along by a goaltending call, to make the score 66-60 and only 38 seconds to play. That brought Patterson's total for the night to 29, a career high. To Porter's credit, he scored 25 points and was named the tournament's outstanding player.

This was the first time in years that the Bruins were forced to work up perspiration in the NCAA finals. The final score was 68-62 as the two teams traded baskets in those last 38 seconds. Afterward, as Wooden stood holding his seventh NCAA championship wristwatch, he admitted it had looked dark at times. "But somehow we didn't give up," he said. "Except for the Notre Dame game, we always ended up where we wanted to be at the end."

UCLA's record for the past five years was now 145-5 and it had won 28 straight NCAA tournament games. And still no end was in sight.

The question of elegibility popped up again following the NCAA tournament. Two news correspondents with 20-20 vision insisted they saw ABA contracts signed by Howard Porter and Western Kentucky's Jim McDaniels. Both players swore they were untainted, and were allowed to participate in the NCAA playoffs. Then early the following Monday the Pittsburgh Condors made it official. It was true, they had indeed signed Porter. The upshot was that the NCAA decided to find both Porter and McDaniel guilty of signing pro contracts—thus forcing the NCAA to "vacate" runner-up Villanova and third-place Western Kentucky from the final tournament standings.

The Walton Gang: 1972

This was supposed to be the season that the country's collegians began antitrust action against UCLA's monopoly in basketball. This was supposed to be the New Look season. Gone were the big Bruin frontline pickets responsible for the last two championship teams. Gone, even longer, was the Alcindor era.

Elsewhere, Tom McMillen was to be the new star of the college game in the East, and Jim Chones was gathering support in the Midwest. Maryland would by No. 1—no, make that Marquette. No matter. All the chickens were coming home to roost. Somebody was going to get UCLA this time around.

Then, all of a sudden, a red-haired, freckled-faced sophomore who looked like an elongated Tom Sawyer came bursting onto the scene. Only an inch under 7', Bill Walton scored, rebounded, blocked shots, directed traffic like a cop and started the fast break faster and better than anybody else in the college game. He was an original, with his own style. He was the one who made the Bruins go. "His presence is worth 40 points," said the Lakers' Keith Erickson. "You play him with a box and one," said Washington State's Bob Greenwood. "Four guys on Walton and one on the rest." Loyola's George Ireland called the NCAA tournament the "UCLA Invitation."

It was mainly because of Walton's many talents why UCLA destroyed its opposition by a national record average of 32 points a game, and no one came closer than six points, by which Oregon State fell in Corvallis, until the championship tournament finals at season's end.

The only starter back from the 1971 Bruins was Henry Bibby, the team's steadying influence. The sophomores joining Walton in the starting lineup were 6' 6" Keith Wilkes, 18, a smooth, willowy forward, and 6' 4" Greg Lee, 20, the floor leader who ran the point offense that Wooden dreamed up specially for this team. Junior Larry Farmer, 6' 5", was the fifth starter. He had spent most of the previous season on the bench watching Sidney Wicks and Curtis Rowe play.

The team ran the fast break and Wooden's patented full-court zone press better than any UCLA team since the era of Goodrich-Hazzard-Erickson. But what set the Walton Gang apart from other UCLA teams was that the new group exuded so much more energy and charm. Even Wooden was captivated by them. He admitted it was fun to coach them. "They're exciting even when they make mistakes," he told a reporter. "And being so young, they make a lot."

Early in the season, unbeaten and ranked No. 1 in all the polls, UCLA met sixth-ranked Ohio State in the final of the Bruin Classic in Pauley Pavilion. The Buckeyes came to town with a 6-1 record and seemed worthy challengers. The game was never close. When the score got to be 30-10, Ohio State Coach Fred Taylor said he felt like "getting up and going to Disneyland." The rout ended, 79-53. With Wooden substituting freely, the Bruins proved to be so deep that there were those who believed the UCLA second team probably could have won the championship in the Big Eight or SEC. Wooden said that Walton's understudy, 6' 11" Swen Nater, could be better than Steve Patterson, 1971's center. After the Ohio State game, Walton was asked if Luke Witte, the Buckeyes' 7-foot center, was the best defensive center he had yet played against.

"No," Walton said.

"Then who?"

"Swen Nater," Walton replied. "It really helps me to play against him every day in practice."

The 1971-72 Bruins began to take shape during the summer. Wooden said he spent countless hours and several dozen notebooks dreaming up an offense tailored to his new players' abilities. It was not completely different, he said. It was something he actually borrowed from his Alcindor teams, plus what he was forced to do when Big Lew was on the bench, plus a few wrinkles. Generally, it was a modified 1-2-2 setup with Lee playing the point, Bibby and Farmer spread out on the wings and Wilkes and Walton setting up under the basket on opposite sides of the foul lane. Often it quickly became a 1-3-1 arrangement with Wilkes breaking out to set up a high post at the foul line. Wooden explained that his idea was to put each player where he could work to maximum efficiency. He knew that Walton would accept it because the principal feed was to him. "We needed a quick kid who is a good shooter for the high post, and that was Wilkes," Wooden said. "Lee has strong hands and he is an unselfish passer, so he was our point man. And it suits Bibby to a T because he does not have to bring the ball up the floor, as he did last year; he is getting his shots from the side, where he hits best."

To take advantage of the team's overall quickness and, primarily, Walton's uncommon ability to dominate the defensive boards and throw quick outlet passes, Wooden revived the fast break. Walton loved to leap high to grab rebounds, spin in mid-air and whip the ball to a teammate racing madly up the floor. Nobody was better than Walton at throwing the outlet pass. Between his freshman and sophomore years in high school he had cartilage removed from his left knee, and it was then that he learned how to get rid of the ball.

"I couldn't run very well," he said. "So there was no way I could stay with everybody in our fast break. All I did was get the rebound, make the quick pass and watch everybody go. I got pretty good at it because I did it so much. And

Only an inch under seven feet, All-American Bill Walton, a junior here, was the one who made UCLA go in 1972–73.

I sort of enjoyed standing back there watching our guys destroying everybody at the other end."

That Walton became a superstar was all the more remarkable when you considered that he had a serious condition known as tendinitis in both knees. He played with a good deal of pain in his first season with the UCLA varsity, especially when the team played a lot of games in a row.

Wooden's only serious criticism of Walton was that he was sometimes "too emotional." Bill had a tendency to hang his head or give up momentarily after making a mistake, habits Wooden tried hard to break. "Sometimes he expects too much of himself," said Wooden.

As if scoring, rebounding, blocking shots, directing traffic and starting the fast break weren't enough, Walton also ran the team's 1-2-2 zone press. As the deep man, he could see the entire floor and made it his responsibility to tell his teammates where to go and what to do. It was a role that delighted Walton. He towered over the action, waving, pointing, always on the move, always talking. "High post, Keith, high post," he'd scream, when Wilkes was in danger of running into a pick, or, "No fouls, Henry," if he thought Bibby was being too aggressive. Sometimes Walton got so carried away with his traffic cop's role that he lost sight of his own man. Then there was a flurry of red hair and waving arms as he hurried to catch up.

Bill Walton was easily the No. 1 big man in college ball now, the most talked-about player of the season. Already he was being mentioned in the same breath with such dominant figures of the past as Bill Russell, Wilt Chamberlain and the former Lew Alcindor (now Kareem Abdul-Jabbar). Walton, himself, shied away from such comparisons, preferring instead to give most of the credit for UCLA's success (26 straight wins) to his teammates.

"It hurts me when people talk as if I'm the only player on the team," he said. "I wish reporters wouldn't ask me anything personally at all. I would like to see them get the whole team together to talk. I don't like to be singled out as an individual because we don't play as individuals, we play as a *team*."

While his attitude was admirable, and while it did a lot to promote harmony on a team of great talent, it also was true that everything UCLA did well on the court stemmed directly from Walton. His statistics were impressive enough—21 points a game, 15 rebounds, a 63 percent shooting average—but they did not tell how Walton so completely dominated a game. Said Guard Greg Lee, a fellow sophomore and the team's playmaker: "I think you have to be a real student of the game to appreciate the way Bill plays. We are only now beginning to realize how good he is. With Bill back there on defense, the rest of us can afford to gamble, and we can cheat getting out on our fast break."

Wooden saw even more. "He does so many things that don't show up in the box score. Like intimidation. How do you measure that? I know that when we had Lewis, the other teams had a lower shooting percentage. It went back up during the next couple of years but now, with Bill, it will go down again. Our opponents for the year are hitting in the high 30's and he is greatly responsible for that. Not only because of the shots he blocks but because they are always looking for him, just as they used to for Lewis all the time."

As hosts of the 1972 NCAA tournament finals, the Bruins were expected to present the 61-year-old Wooden with his sixth straight championship and eighth in the last nine years. Such anticipated challengers as South Carolina, Penn, Marquette and Southwestern Louisiana came down with crippling cases of Upset Blues on their way to Los Angeles and had to cut out, but the North Carolina Tar Heels would be there. And so would cocky young Denny Crum, Wooden's former assistant, with a veteran Louisville team. Rounding out the final four were the most unlikely guests of all, the Florida State Seminoles, fresh out of the NCAA's jailhouse, having just completed a three-year sentence for various recruiting violations.

"Everybody talks about UCLA, North Carolina and Louisville," complained Otto Petty, Florida State's 5' 7" playmaker. "They're overlooking us, but we're going to show 'em."

The Seminoles zipped through the Mideast Regional and into the title round at LA before anybody even knew they were there. But once they surfaced, they weren't buying all "that bull" about UCLA having a lock on the championship. For Coach Hugh Durham it was the stuff of dreams. "Every year when we were on probation I would dream about getting to the finals," he said. "Now—boom—I'm there."

Florida State got to the semifinals by beating some very good teams. After ousting Minnesota, 70-56, in a dull game in Dayton, the Seminoles met Kentucky for the Mideast Regional championship. The Wildcats had upset Marquette, 85-69, in what was by far their best showing of the season. Often referred to by the caustic Adolph Rupp as "a bunch of clowns" and "the worst varsity I've ever had," Kentucky on that night was a smooth, poised team that outrebounded, outshot, outhustled and even outquicked the favored Warriors.

Because Rupp had been talking retirement most of the season, a lot of people were saying how nice it would be if he could beat Florida State and take his "last" Kentucky team out to the coast to play in the NCAA finals. Even Coach Hugh Durham, a native of Louisville who grew up cheering for Rupp's teams, seemed embarrassed to have to try to beat Kentucky. But once the game started his Seminoles showed no mercy. Little Otto Petty and the Florida State defense were the difference. Together they forced the Wildcats into turnover after turnover and pulled into front at halftime, 34-28. In the second half they stopped Kentucky's offense cold, something few teams had done, and even KU's fans were booing out frustration and screaming "shoot it!" By the time 5' 10" Ronnie Lyons hit a jump shot, Florida State had the game well in hand, 57-45. After the game, Rupp, who at 70 had reached the mandatory retirement age, hedged when asked if he would go on coaching.

"Is this your last game?"

"When I have an announcement to make," Rupp said, "it will come out of Lexington, not here."

"When?"

"Oh, maybe six or eight years from now. Then again, maybe I'll announce it on the way home so they can broadcast it all around the world."

One thing was certain, however: Kentucky would not be going to Los Angeles this year.

Meanwhile, at Morgantown, North Carolina performed so superbly in back-to-back victories over South Carolina and Pennsylvania that many people were beginning to wonder if, finally, a serious challenger to UCLA had been found. As the strongest team to come out of the East in years, the Tar Heels were so impressive—and so beautifully coached by the chain-smoking Dean Smith—that the odds-makers made them a good bet to pop Florida State's bubble and earn a spot in the final against UCLA, a big favorite over Louisville in the semifinals. The Tar Heels banked heavily on their four-corner offense, a pressure defense and their towering center, 6' 9" Bob McAdoo.

Going into the playoffs, the Bruins were unbeaten. If they went all the way, they'd become the first undefeated national champions since the Bruins were the undefeated national champions five years before in Lew Alcindor's sophomore season.

Bill Walton said he didn't think much about win streaks, but he confessed he'd hate to be a member of the first UCLA basketball team that finally lost in the NCAA tournament. "Then nobody will remember that you had a good season," Walton said. "They'd forget we had a 30-1 season. They'd remember only that we were the UCLA team that didn't go all the way. I wouldn't like that."

Louisville won its trip to Los Angeles by beating Kansas State, 72-65, in the final of the Midwest Regional at Ames, but that game was anti-climactic. In reality the Cards won their place among the final four several days before, when they came from behind to shoot down Dwight Lamar, leading scorer among the major colleges, and his fellow teammates from Southwestern Louisiana, 88-84.

Playing in the West Regional at Provo, Utah, UCLA turned in a couple of typically lopsided scores. The Bruins crushed little Weber State, 90-58, the first night, and then destroyed highly heralded Long Beach State, 73-57, two days later. For Coach Jerry Tarkanian, the pressure began building early for Long Beach State. By some freaky twist of fate, the team shared the same motel with the UCLA band. Long Beach fans claimed that the Bruin tootlers practiced their sharps and flats all night. Tarkanian confirmed that its rehearsing awoke him at 8:30 a.m. "I don't care," he said, "I'm not playing the band." Soon afterward Tarkanian had his athletes out in the motel parking lot working on its defense against the Walton Gang. "I wish I had more time to prepare," he said. He didn't. The Bruins won the game in typical cold-blooded fashion.

It was business·as usual in the Los Angeles Sports Arena when UCLA came face to face with the three challengers from the South. Against Louisville in the semifinals, Bill Walton dominated everything right away. On defense he harassed marvelous Jim Price the first time the Louisville guard drove the lane. Price stayed away after that. Then Walton intercepted Al Vilcheck's first pass and blocked his first shot. He also took away the inside moves of Ron Thomas, forcing Thomas to go outside, where he was no threat. After nearly 10 minutes into the first half, Walton had outscored Louisville, 16-14, by himself and UCLA was in front, 20-14. In the first 20 minutes of play, Louisville beat the UCLA press nine times to earn a two-on-one situation against Walton and an open shot from the corner—and nine times they missed. In frustration, the Cards became quite physical with Walton, provoking several angry exchanges. At one point Mike Lawhon, who was shut out on seven straight floor shots, stormed at Walton: "You big crybaby! What a candy you are." To punctuate his message, he let Walton have two shots to the body. Foul.

On the free-throw line, Walton fumed. "These are for you," he snarled at Lawhon as he sunk two free throws. "And I'll see you behind the gym after the game."

With the help of Larry Farmer's 15 points in the second half, the Bruins banished Louisville to the consolation round as Walton finished the night with 33 points and 21 rebounds. As for Vilcheck and Thomas, both fouled out of the game. Afterward, they were still steaming. "Walton is strong, but you can't touch him," said Vilcheck. "The officials put him in a cage. He cries a lot, constantly. He's too good a player to beef so much."

Coach Dean Smith did everything possible to keep his players' minds on the semifinal game against Florida State and not have them looking ahead to UCLA. The Tar Heels kept their watches set on Eastern Standard Time, they ate the right foods, drank lots of liquids—only to lose to Petty and the Seminoles. The little Florida State guard entered the contest with 10 minutes gone and, zipping in and out of heavy traffic with the speed of a gnat, proceeded to tear North Carolina apart. He took his lanky and mobile teammates from a one-point lead to a 45-32 halftime advantage. When he wasn't

deflating the NCU pressure defense, he was feeding Ron King and Reggie Royals for baskets. Soon the Seminoles were out in front by 23 points.

Suddenly the Tar Heels changed the tide. Bob McAdoo, playing the game of his life, started the rally only to foul out on a controversial call. Still NCU refused to quit. Dennis Wuycik picked up where McAdoo left off and swished them in from all over the floor, closing the gap to 70-65 and forcing the Seminoles to call time with 5:13 to go. There the Seminoles switched into a zone. Still North Carolina had four different opportunities to catch up but blew them all. When Kim Huband, the Tar Heels' best clutch shooter from long range, popped off the bench and missed an open 15-footer, they knew it would be Louisville and not UCLA they'd be meeting on the last day of the tournament. Final score: Florida State 79, North Carolina 75.

And so there was Florida State and Coach Hugh Durham in the NCAA final championship game against UCLA. A former girls' school, the Seminoles were the dark horses of the tournament. There were some coaches who resented the fact that they were even there. Bill Wall, the president of the National Association of Basketball Coaches, was the most outspoken. He referred to Durham as the coach who "has been caught with his hand in the till twice," in reference to the recruiting violations that had put Florida State on probation the previous three seasons. "They shouldn't even be here," said Wall, who coached at tiny MacMurray. "The coaches are amazed, disgusted and disillusioned."

Durham's only response was to say that he would not "get down to Wall's level." As for his school, it was considering a lawsuit.

Before the UCLA-Florida State game, John Wooden consoled Durham. "I'm sorry about all this," the UCLA coach said. "I want you to know we don't feel the same way."

Saturday afternoon, with Wall's comments still ringing in their ears, the Seminoles made a gallant and thrilling stand against the Bruins. After missing twice to open the game, they hit their next seven shots and led UCLA, 21-14. It was the only time during the season that UCLA had trailed by more than four points. Unfortunately, FSU, especially 6' 11" center Lawrence McCray, was getting in foul trouble. Quickly, Bibby and Walton tied the score, and then Tommy Curtis got hot to spark the defending champions to a 50-39 halftime lead.

In the second half, Walton got into foul trouble (4) and went to the bench. With Walton warming his pants, Ron King began hitting baskets for the challengers and cut UCLA's lead down to 79-72 toward the end of the game. Then Walton came back in and FSU was so busy swarming around him that they forgot Keith (Silk) Wilkes, who got free enough to finish with 23 points and make the plays that smothered FSU's last-gasp surge. The Seminoles became so flustered they turned over the ball three times, once when Wilkes blocked a pass. With 1:05 left, he also controlled a crucial jump ball and clinched the title with UCLA's final layup. Who said freshmen were too young for varsity competition? Wilkes was only 18.

Bill Walton's reaction to UCLA's sixth championship in a row, their eighth in the last nine years, was puzzling. It was a Bill Walton that the public would hear much more about in his junior and senior seasons. At a post-game press conference he told reporters he was "not elated" over his team's victory. "I feel as though we lost the game," he said disdainfully. To questions he did not like, he replied, "No comment." He was sarcastic, tart, defensive. When he grew bored, he stomped off, mumbling under his breath, "No more questions, I've answered enough."

It turned out that Walton was not pleased with UCLA's final margin of victory, 81-76. "We don't like to back into things," he scoffed. "We didn't dominate Florida State the way I know we can." For most people, however, a perfect 30-0 season and 45 wins in a row would have been enough.

Later, Walton relaxed and talked more freely about his basketball philosophy. "I enjoy basketball," he said. "But it's not always fun. When some people act like we have no right to win, it's no fun. When my knees are acting up, it's no fun. And I wonder about the fans. I wonder why they'll stand outside for hours to get into the pavilion, and then, once inside, they go crazy over us. I laugh at them. I can't believe them. What's so important about a basketball game? Why shouldn't they take all that money it took to build all those big sports arenas and use it to feed hungry people? Sports are fine, but why do they have to be blown out of proportion?"

Walton said money didn't mean anything to him. (Perhaps, but he later signed a multi-million dollar pro basketball contract with Portland.) "Money can't buy happiness, and I just want to be happy. I'm built for basketball, and I have the potential to be a star, but I'm not sure yet that I want it for a profession. I want to do more with my life than win a few games."

In an article in the *Los Angeles Times West Magazine*, Walton confessed to author Bill Libby that he resented being called a superstar. He said it was just not right. He felt that his teammates deserved more attention. "Without them," he told Libby, "I'd be nothing. This is a *team* game, and I'm just one of the guys on our team." He believed he was the center of so much attention because he was the "Great White Hope" in a game that was dominated by blacks. "If I were black," he said, "I'd be just another center who plays well. I want to be judged for my play, not my color."

The spirit of rebellion simmered deeply inside of Bill Walton. It was a part of his personality that the sporting public was going to find hard to get used to.

One Bruin Title at a Time: 1973

The trick to keeping dynasties alive is finding new motivations. UCLA had them in 1972-73. Early, it was going to need three consecutive victories for a school record. Midway, it needed 16 wins to break the all-time record of 60 straight set by Bill Russell's teams from San Francisco. And later there would be another NCAA tournament.

"I hope I never get to the position of thinking just in terms of records," Wooden said. "I don't want to think about 60. I want to win the next one—what is it? No. 46. I want to win 46 in a row."

John Wooden was unique. He played them one national championship at a time.

By now, many analysts felt that the Bruins had destroyed enthusiasm for college basketball elsewhere by becoming so much better than everyone else. In their desperate desire to beat UCLA, opponents frequently put two or three men on Bill Walton and cuffed him around until he was black and blue. When he complained he was called a "crybaby." Walton said, "It's not up to us to lose. It's up to other teams to beat us. That doesn't mean they're supposed to use ball bats on us."

Wooden said Walton's only weakness was that he let his emotions "get away from him."

"I don't try to stifle my emotions," Walton said. "My complaints are justified, too. I think that officials sometimes feel that because we win so much, and because I'm big and don't play a rough game, it's all right for others to foul me without being called for fouls. I don't think I'm a crybaby."

Walton was optimistic about the 1972-73 sea-son. He said he believed he was going to be better because he was getting better each year and because the Bruins would be better as a team. They lost only starter Henry Bibby and reserves Jon Chapman and Andy Hill, and added a trio of supersophs: Pete Trgovich from Indiana, Dave Meyers from La Habra and Andre McCarter from Philadelphia. The Bruins insisted they were not even thinking about equaling the three straight titles of Alcindor's UCLA teams in the 1960s. "We're not living in the future," Walton said. "All that really counts is *now*."

At the outset, what really counted was The Streak—achieving victory No. 61—passing the record of Bill Russell and San Francisco. This was accomplished midway in the season when John Wooden and Bill Walton and all the rest beat Loyola, 87-73, and Notre Dame, 82-63, in the Chicago Stadium in two nights of basketball that also featured Illinois. Loyola was the school San Francisco beat in 1956 for its record 60th straight win and the Ramblers were coached by George Ireland, who was playing at South Bend when Wooden coached at a South Bend high school. And Illinois? Well, the Fighting Illini was the team that stopped USF's streak 16 years before. As for Notre Dame, it was the last school to defeat the Bruins in basketball.

UCLA took The Streak in stride. After beating the Irish for No. 61, there was no noise, no jumping for joy in the dressing room. Walton, who had played with all the fervor of a river-boat pirate, calmly undressed and took a shower. Larry Hollyfield opened a can of soda pop. Tommy Curtis untied his shoelaces. Greg Lee, under orders to shun reporters, looked in a mirror and interviewed himself:

"Mr. Lee, how does it feel to win No. 61? Is it the ultimate?"

"No," Mr. Lee told Mr. Lee.

"Well, then, is it the pinnacle?"

"Not that either," said Mr. Lee to Mr. Lee.

"Then how do you describe it?"

"Just another ballgame."

The truth was that the UCLA players, having won so often and so much until there were no new worlds to conquer, had finally reached that inevitable point—winning had become a *bore*. It was no longer news to read about another UCLA basketball victory. The challenge, the fun, the celebration had gone out of it. Predicting a UCLA championship was about as risky as saying the sun shines in San Diego.

While The Streak went on, Bill Walton pleaded to be left alone. He craved for his privacy with a passion and longed to be recognized as a human being rather than a basketball superstar. "I can't go anywhere without being looked at as a freak," he lamented to a reporter. "People don't really know me—and they won't for a long time." He was shy around strangers, suspicious of them; he thought they were insincere.

But with his fame came a certain mellowing: "Last year I didn't understand the reactions to me," Walton said. "Fans made a fuss, a hassle, and I didn't like it. I was hostile, I admit that. I also confess I was antagonistic, sometimes downright rude. Well, I'm not looking at them so smugly anymore. I understand the role reversals, the hero-worship deal. I now understand people for what they are rather than for what they think I am."

Involved politically, sensitive to racial issues, disdainful of being tagged basketball's "Great White Hope," calling himself " a student of life," Walton shocked the establishment by joining a peace protest march and lay down in the middle of Wilshire Boulevard, marched through classrooms on the UCLA campus, barricaded doors with wooden horses, rode a janitor's scooter up the hill by the administration building and decried loud and long the government's mining of Haiphong Harbor. After he was arrested and was charged on five different counts, Walton pleaded *nolo contendere* in court, paid a $50 fine and was put on conditional probation by the university for two years. The penalty could have been harsher. As he was being hustled away from the protest demonstration in a Los Angeles Police Department bus, Walton spotted Chancellor Charles Young on the sidewalk and called him a bloody this and a bloody that. It was feared that the chancellor was going to expel Walton from UCLA, but no action was taken. Perhaps Chancellor Young was remembering that Bill Walton had been acclaimed Player of the Year in 1972 and would continue to be player of every year that he stayed at UCLA. About Walton, the eminent philosopher Hot Rod Hundley, who had seen all the recent great ones, said: "Surround Bill Russell or Kareem Abdul-Jabbar or Nate Thurmond or Wilt Chamberlain with the same teammates and none of them would win as many games as Walton does. Walton is the best white man ever to play the black man's game."

By now, the pros were all over Walton to get him to sign one of those trillion-dollar contracts, or whatever. But materialism—clothes, cash, real estate—meant nothing to him; friendship and privacy, everything. Walton refused to discuss whether he would leave UCLA after his junior season. But you knew which way he was thinking when he said: "I couldn't look forward to tomorrow if I deserted my teammates," and he was devoted to Wooden, who had been hospitalized with heart trouble in December. When Walton heard of his coach's sickness, his first reaction was "that so-and-so, he better get back here fast. We need him."

On the other hand, Walton admitted to more and more disgust at the college basketball rules—that he could not dunk, that opponents could stall and, moreover, that "the best players are restricted." He said he was zoned, triple-teamed and frustrated to pieces.

Meanwhile, the UCLA win streak went on and on and on.

Down South, the talk was about the Tigers of Memphis State. Over the past three seasons there was not one team—not even Alabama, Minnesota or Maryland—that had improved so much or so fast as the one coached by Gene Bartow. After it concluded the home portion of

The rejuvenation of Memphis State basketball in 1973 unified race relations in the city of Memphis as never before. Here the fans mob the Memphis Airport, waiting for their triumphant Tigers to arrive home from the Midwest Regionals.

its schedule by wiping aside Wichita State, 99-77, and West Texas State, 116-79, Memphis State had a 19-4 record and a commanding two-game lead in that strange and puzzling conference known as the Missouri Valley. The Tigers were aptly prepared and peaking to go on and win their first outright league championship and a place in the NCAA playoffs.

That was the dream that Bartow, a scholarly-looking fellow who was called Clean Gene by his admiring players, had nurtured since going to Memphis in 1970. Upon arrival from his previous head coaching position at Valparaiso, Bartow encountered a program that had fallen on hard times, racial turmoil, losing steaks and knife fights. The Tigers had lost 56 of 76 games

and finished last for three straight years in the league they had recently joined.

In the beginning Bartow opened up the Memphis attack. Larry (Little Tubby) Finch was given his head outside and Ronnie (Big Cat) Robinson ate up everything inside and the Tigers raced to records of 18-8 and 21-7. That first season Bartow had his team playing for a share of the Valley championship on the final day. The next season Memphis defeated Louisville twice only to lose the title in a playoff.

The rejuvenation of Memphis State basketball hit the metropolis at an opportune time, coming as it did after the murder of Martin Luther King tore the city apart on that terrible afternoon in 1968. A dangerous polarization of the races followed, and it was only after the growing success of the Tigers took hold of the populace that the deep wounds began to heal.

"This team has unified the city like it's never been unified before," said Mayor Wyeth Chandler. "Black and white, rich and poor, young and old are caught up in its success. Memphis is a better city now, thanks to the Memphis State team."

Significantly, Memphis State's enrollment was 13 percent black, the largest percentage of blacks at any major university in the country. As Finch and Robinson received accolades for bringing togetherness to the campus, so did they endure responsibility for the Tigers becoming the nation's mystery college team of the season. On some nights they were absolutely awesome, with 6' 10" JC transfer Larry (Dr. K) Kenon, a marvelous rebounder who was certainly the MVP in the Missouri Conference, doing his thing and Finch and Robinson functioning at top form. They could also be underwhelming—as they were in an 83-69 loss at Louisville late in the season when they shot 23 percent in the first half, and as they were at the start of the season when they lost three of their first five contests. They then went on a 14-game winning spree, during which Bartow installed a zone-trap defense employing three substitutes, freshmen Bill Cook and Clarence Jones and another JC transfer, 6' 7" Billy Buford.

While UCLA and Memphis State thought about St. Louis, where the final four NCAA teams would play for the championship, North Carolina State could think only about next year. Unquestionably at least the second-best team in college basketball, Coach Norman Sloan's crew lived in purgatory all season long, knowing it could not compete for the national title. The Wolfpack was on probation for recruiting violations. In such a situation it would have been very easy for the NCS players to be indifferent, to take it easy, play half-heartedly, to sit it out. But with the brilliant sophomore David Thompson, the elongated Tommy Burleson and peewee guard Monte Towe, the Wolfpack mowed down 27 straight opponents and lost none. And they did it against teams from the most harshly competitive league in America. They did it with everyone pointing for them. They defeated Top 10 teams a total of six times.

Before the season began, it hardly seemed likely that Indiana or Providence or Memphis State would still be playing basketball in late March. But there they were, joining UCLA in St. Louis for the NCAA title round, three verdant challengers bent on shooting down mighty UCLA, which was hunting its seventh straight championship and ninth in 10 years.

In truth, the championship series went pretty much the way the Las Vegas betting line said it would go. UCLA's semifinal opponent was Indiana, a team that looked like a bunch of well-muscled guys who would have trouble beating your local YMCA, and they got out of the first half on guts alone. They trailed, 40-22. With 17 minutes left and a 20-point lead, the Bruins let their guards down. Walton committed two quick fouls, his third and fourth, and was given a rest. Minus their star, the Bruins then proceeded to play some of the worst basketball any UCLA team ever played. They lost their vaunted poise, they forced shots, they incurred three-second violations and they committed a throw-in penalty and a technical foul. In short, they came dangerously close to blowing themselves right out of the tournament. At the same time they were failing to score, Quinn Buckner, John Ritter and Steve Downing combined to score an astonishing 17 straight points to bring the Hoosiers to within three points of the Bruins, 54-51.

There were only 9:24 minutes left in the game when Walton, back in the game and wheeling across the lane, collided with Downing. Referee Joe Shosid blew his whistle. Was it Walton for charging or Downing for blocking? Shosid pointed his finger at Downing, his fourth foul. Shortly afterward, with 7:57 remaining, Downing was banished to the Indiana bench for his fifth foul and the thunder went out of the Hoosiers. UCLA pulled away to win, 70-59.

On my last trip to Bloomington, in 1977, some of the Hoosiers still wondered what would have happened if Shosid's call had gone against Walton, if he had left the contest and Downing had stayed. "We would have won anyway," John Wooden said. Bobby Knight, the flamboyant Indiana coach, was unconvinced. "We took 14 more shots than UCLA, committed six fewer turnovers—and Downing outscored Walton, 26-14," Knight pointed out.

Memphis State's Larry Kenon shoots over Providence's Fran Costello (31) and Ernie Digregorio as Tigers win semifinal match, 98-85, at the 1973 NCAA championship playoffs.

Larry Finch, Memphis State University, shoots over UCLA's Tommy Curtis as Bill Walton moves in for the rebound. Action was during 1973 NCAA final; Bruins won, 87-66, for their ninth national championship in 10 seasons.

Memphis State earned its way into the final matchup with UCLA by trouncing Providence, 98-85, in a game marked by drama, intrigue, heartbreak and the nifty play of Ernie DiGregorio, the jump shot marvel. Ernie D, who had whiplashed the Friars from New England to a 27-2 record and confidently predicted that his team would be the one to finally knock off UCLA, nearly ran Memphis State out of St. Louis in the first half with an assortment of quick shots, lob bomb passes and behind-the-back assists. At the half, Providence held a 49-40 lead. Ernie D had scored 18 of his team's 22 baskets. But the Friars were in trouble. Bad Marvin Barnes, their dominating post man, had injured his knee before the half ended and was likely not to see further action. When play resumed Kenon and Robinson, seeing Barnes on the bench, staked out the boards for themselves and controlled the rebounds. Finch started scoring more and soon the aroused Tigers passed the Friars.

DiGregorio, who had to do everything now

and got scoring help only from Fran Costello, rushed his shots, tired and soon was gasping for breath. Though the scorebook credited him with 32 points, Ernie D missed 12 of 19 shots in the last 20 minutes and despite his reputation as one of the best playmakers in the country, failed to record a single assist.

Barnes finally talked Coach Dave Gavitt into letting him return to the action 14 minutes into the second half—and he did score an admirable fast-break basket to cut the lead to one point—but his knee was hurting him too much to deal with Kenon and Robinson.

After the game, as he walked slowly back to the Friars' dressing room with tears streaming down his cheeks, DeGregorio said, "We can't run without Barnes. But who knows? Even with him, maybe we'd get beat."

"Barnes' dislocated knee isn't the kind of break we like to get to win," said Robinson, who with Kenon combined for 52 points and 38 rebounds, "but we have to take it. Boy, we never thought we'd get *this* far."

1973 National Champions—UCLA, again. Front row, left: Bob Webb, Tommy Curtis, Gary Franklin, Casey Corliss. Middle row, left: Larry Hollyfield, Mgr. Les Friedman, Coach John Wooden, Asst. Coach Gary Cunningham, Trainer "Ducky" Drake, Greg Lee. Rear, left: Larry Farmer, Keith Wilkes, Dave Meyers, Bill Walton, Ralph Drollinger, Swen Nater, Vince Carson, Pete Trgovich.

After their showers, Robinson and Kenon accompanied Barnes out of the arena. Graciousness was served.

Early in the championship game, the reality of Bill Walton as the supreme player of college basketball struck Memphis State, especially Kenon, Robinson and Finch. The tall redhead totally dominated the inside play, as the Bruins built a 33-24 first-half lead. But the Tigers refused to quit. Kenon kept coming at Walton, until Walton found himself in foul trouble. Going into a zone, Memphis State roared back to tie the score at 39-39 at the half and even forged into the lead shortly after play resumed. But Walton, in spite of three fouls—and eventually a fourth—kept scoring basket after basket on lob passes from Greg Lee. "Our eyes meet and I just put it up there," Lee explained. Relentlessly, Walton savaged the defensive boards as the score moved from 45-45 to 57-47, UCLA. With 12 minutes to go, it was all over for Memphis State. When Walton limped off the floor on a hurt ankle with only three minutes left, the UCLA lead was 15 points. Memphis State's Billy Buford, displaying warm sportsmanship, helped Walton back to the bench. Finch, who had played a whale of a game himself, embraced Walton, and a once hostile crowd roared in appreciation.

What the whole thing boiled down to, however, was that the Bruins had just won their ninth national championship in the past 10 years. This was their seventh in a row. "Just another UCLA bullfight," said Oklahoma City's Abe Lemons. "You gore the matador all night. In the end he sticks it in you and the donkeys come out and drag you to the meat market."

UCLA might have been the greatest dynasty in all college basketball, but Abe Lemons was the funniest man in the whole sport. Part Choctaw Indian and head coach at Oklahoma City University, he picked up enough smarts and paleface one-liners to endear himself to after-dinner speakers and sports columnists forever. He had had several NCAA tournament teams and a couple of NIT appearances, always achieving humorous mileage out of the Indians ("Endins") on his team and its defensive shortcomings. Once, at halftime in New York after a particularly embarrassing exhibition, he scrimmaged his Chiefs against each other. "Couldn't even win the scrimmage," he said. He said he always had to remember not to puff his cigar around his players. "Ah might be cussin' in smoke signals," he drawled.

In New York, he told a press conference, "We're 7-1. Ah wish we was a football team. We'd be in a damn bowl."

The Streak Ends at 88: 1974

Bill Walton was staying at UCLA. As a matter of fact, even before he had blown apart the NCAA record book in the Bruins' 87-66 victory over Memphis State in the 1973 playoffs, even before he made 21 of 22 shots in that contest, scored a record 44 points and gorged on 13 rebounds, Walton had pretty much made up his mind about pro ball.

"I am not playing pro basketball next season," he had said. "I have decided there's plenty of time left to earn a living, but now is my time to be a young man. I don't want to worry about the other things. All the attention and the publicity and financial rewards are not for me or my life."

He called it a "non-decision" and said he would remain at UCLA through graduation in the spring of 1974. He said he didn't need any reasons for coming back. "I'm here and that's it," he said. He said money was never a factor. "I wish people would understand that."

The Walton Gang did not have to wait long for its first big test of the 1973-74 season. Thousands of fans packed into the St. Louis Arena, and millions watched via network TV as the No. 1 and No. 2 teams, UCLA and North Carolina State, fought for first place in the national polls. The contest was played on Saturday, December 15, and David Thompson, the Wolfpack's jumpin' jack, never forgot it. The game meant more to him than the chance to prove that his team was No. 1. It meant that NCS people were right when they said that "UCLA was champion of only 49 states" in 1973, when the NCAA Rules Committee kept the Wolfpack, 27-0, from playing the Bruins in the national finals because of recruiting charges.

As a sophomore in 1972-73, Thompson was a marvel. He led North Carolina State to its undefeated status, and in August of '73, in the World University Games, he devastated the USSR to gain revenge for what happened to the Americans at the Munich Olympics. A great natural shooter, Thompson had the spring of a high-jumper in his legs. His vertical leap was measured at 42 inches—from a standing position and going straight up. By comparison, Bob McAdoo, the former University of North Carolina star, jumped 34 inches, and Sidney Wicks, the one-time UCLA All-America, jumped 38.

"I jump pretty high," Thompson said. "I credit that to playing against taller boys and good players."

The UCLA vs. NCS game was advertised simply as David Thompson vs. Bill Walton. Midway of the first half, Thompson lived up to his advance notices, flying high above the backboard to slam the 6' 11" Walton's shot back into his teeth. The crowd went wild. This was what they had come to see, and they wanted blood—Bruin blood. They were due for a disappointment. UCLA forward Keith Wilkes, with the help of his teammates, concentrated on Thompson enough to stifle his shooting and backboard play. Wilkes rarely even let Thompson get the ball in position to take a jump shot. When Thompson got a rebound under the UCLA basket, he found several Bruins between himself and the hoop and was forced to pass. For the night, Thompson converted only seven of 20 shots and was outscored by Wilkes, 27-17. UCLA won easily, 84-66,

Despite the lopsided score, North Carolina State was convinced it could beat UCLA. To do it, the Wolfpack would have to be one of the final four in the NCAA championship round. Forgetting UCLA for the time being, NCS went back and won all its Atlantic Coast Conference games. When the ACC staged its annual tournament in Greensboro, the Wolfpack was there, too, winning the title and an NCAA berth by beating Maryland, 103-100 in overtime, making it the third straight year the Terrapins had been runner-up. The game was a barnburner. N.C. State shot 55 percent from the floor while Maryland hit 61. Monte Towe, at 5' 5½", was the shortest man on the floor, but with six seconds to play he proved to be the little big man, sinking two free throws to put State ahead to stay by three points. It was the 26th victory for the No. 1-ranked Wolfpack, which by now had lost only once in 54 games in two seasons.

The victory climaxed a personal vendetta for Tommy Burleson, the occasionally maligned, frequently gawky 7' 4" N.C. State center who was so thin that he wore a wrist band up near his elbow. Tall Tommy scored 38 points, grabbed 13 rebounds and blocked a handful of shots.

The N.C. State victory was not to be taken lightly by upcoming NCAA enemies. Three ACC teams—North Carolina State, Maryland and North Carolina—were ranked in the Top Ten.

As college basketball's best teams dwindled down to the final four—UCLA, N.C. State, Marquette and Kansas—it became abundantly clear that UCLA was a mystique as much as a team. The critics were on the Bruins. "The offense is too predictable," wrote one reporter. "The press is a fraud and doesn't work anymore," charged another. The guards could not shoot or penetrate. Walton was bothered by a back injury, had become passive from transcendental meditation and weak and docile because of his vegetarian diet.

Midway through the season it was discovered that Coach John Wooden was not born in an Indiana manger after all. UCLA dropped from No. 1 after Notre Dame ended the Bruins' 88-game winning streak, and later in the season two mediocre teams, Oregon and Oregon State, upset the defending champs within 19 hours. For the moment, anyway, the UCLA magic was gone.

Then they found it again. In the last Pac-8 game of the season, the Bruins came out snort-

North Carolina State's human jumpin' jack, David Thompson, averaged 29.9 points a game in 1974.

David Thompson and 5' 5½" Monte Towe of North Carolina State were pals on and off the basketball court.

in' and snarlin' and snappin' all over USC, leaving little doubt that they were ready for the ultimate challenge. UCLA held the Trojans to four baskets in the first half and roared to a 47-13 advantage as Walton, in full battle cry, had 20 points and 16 rebounds. The rest of the 82-52 victory was practically as fierce, and if it did anything besides sewing up another Pac-8 championship and embarrassing USC, it was serving notice on NC State that UCLA had its act together again.

Since East met West in the NCAA's restructured alignment, North Carolina State would get UCLA first in the semifinals at Greensboro, March 23-25. The advantage clearly was with the Wolfpack, which would be on home territory playing before more than 15,000 wild partisans for whom a national title was what life was all about. This time NC State was ready.

David Thompson said he was too high for UCLA the first time the teams met in December. "I started poorly, then just shot to get my touch back," he said. He never found it. Even though the Bruins were amazed by his talent, Thompson considered himself a failure in that initial meeting with UCLA.

But this was a different Wolfpack. State Coach Norm Sloan's team had shored up its weaknesses by experience. "We're more versatile than UCLA," he said. "And we have something left to prove. And we still have Thompson. I like the odds."

UCLA's Tommy Curtis said he looked forward to playing against David Thompson. Remembering the first game, Curtis said, "I couldn't believe what the dude was able to do. It's going to be a thrill to walk onto the floor with him again."

For the Bruins, they were seeking their eighth straight championship and their 10th in

11 years. This time they would find a more formidable trio of challengers. N. C. State, Marquette and Kansas all had the tools and skills to take the wind out of the defending champs' sails. No one gets to the final round of the NCAA tournament on a fluke. All four teams were blessed with talented big men in the middle, some superstars and good coaching. N. C. State was ranked as the best. Marquette banked largely on its stubborn defense, and Kansas had tradition behind youthfulness that had peaked just at the right time. UCLA was, of course, the defending champion, perhaps less reliable than some of the Bruin champions of the past, but a contender all the same.

And so there they were, N.C. State against UCLA in one semifinal contest on Saturday afternoon, Bill Walton on Tom Burleson, Keith Wilkes guarding David Thompson. The memory of St. Louis still burned in Wolfpack minds.

"I want North Carolina State to remember that we beat them by 18 points on a neutral court," John Wooden said after the Bruins won the Western Regional. "I want *them* to think about who has the psychological advantage." Looking for even more advantages, Wooden sent assistant coach Frank Arnold to scout State in the Eastern Regional in Raleigh.

North Carolina State had revenge on its mind. Monte Towe, the team leader, admitted he was humiliated by UCLA's wide margin of victory over the Wolfpack in December. Added teammate Thompson, "I was not only humiliated, I was *embarrassed*. Wilkes really gave me the business, but I do not feel it was a true test. We are the best team in the country and we'll prove it. We love each other as people and we respect each other as athletes."

Against a very good Providence team, N.C. State certainly lived up to its No. 1 spot in the polls, 92-78. While that was going on, UCLA got more reprieves than a cat in its 111-100 triple overtime victory over Dayton in the Western Regional, at Tucson. The Bruins then destroyed San Francisco, 83-60, in the regional title game.

The big loser in the regionals was No. 3 Notre Dame in the first round of the Mideast in Tuscaloosa. Whether the Irish took Michigan too lightly only their team could say, but they appeared listless early in the contest, and

they fell far behind the Wolverines, 28-8, as 6' 8" Campy Russell hit consistently from the inside and 6' 2" forward Wayman Britt banged away from the outside.

Notre Dame did manage to squeeze ahead, 54-52, early in the second half, but not for long. Russell dazzled the crowd with a series of sensational shots that took the fight out of the Fighting Irish and Michigan had its victory, 77-68.

Since Al McGuire first came to Marquette, the Warriors had never gotten beyond the NCAA regionals. To get there this time, they had to beat Vanderbilt, 69-61, and then Michigan. Against the Wolverines, the emotional McGuire was as upset by the officiating as by his uptight players. The upshot was an explosion and McGuire was charged with two quick technical fouls. An antagonistic crowd that had been reacting wildly to McGuire's sideline antics broke into derisive song, but Coach McGuire had the last laugh. Throwing a tight net around Campy Russell, the Warriors forged ahead, 63-62, on a three-point play and assist by reserve Rick Campbell. Then after a brief tie they went ahead to stay on freshman Bo Ellis' 10-footer. Final score: Marquette 72, Michigan 70. No one got more fun out of the victory than Al McGuire. At a post-game press conference, he joked, "If I'd seen Bo play this well before I would've given him more money."

There were fireworks aplenty at Tulsa, too, where Kansas won the Midwest Regional but was pushed into the background by the remarkable events surrounding Oral Roberts University and Ken Trickey, its lame-duck coach. In midseason, after a run-in with school president Oral Roberts, Coach Trickey resigned, then came back and coached his team into an NCAA at-large bid. But after beating Louisville, 96-93, in the first game of the regional, he was arrested for drunken driving by a state trooper. Once again he was suspended by President Roberts, who then prayed with him and decided every sinner deserved another chance. Trickey was reinstated in time for the Kansas game on Saturday night. "Ken told me he thought God wanted him to coach," explained Roberts. With only 2:50 to go against the Jayhawks, Trickey appeared to have redeemed himself. His team led, 81-74. But instead of putting the ball in deep freeze, Oral Roberts kept running—and a minute and a half later

Kansas had tied it. Kansas went on to win in overtime, 93-90. "We expected a miracle, and we got it," said Roger Morningstar, the Kansas forward.

On to Greensboro. The only teams in the final four who had played each other during the season were UCLA and N.C. State, and the situation had changed since they met. One big change was the locale. North Carolina partisans had been itching to get the Bruins down in their part of the country. Now they had their chance. If you listened closely, you could hear the Battle Hymn of the Confederates, with Stonewall Jackson at the head of the parade.

Whether Kansas or Marquette faced the winner was a tossup. The Jayhawks had shown a tendency to turn the ball over under pressure, as they did earlier in the season at Indiana. If the Jayhawks got nervous and butterfingered, the Warriors would steal them blind. At any rate, all four teams had a chance at the 1974 title, a refreshing situation for the NCAA in recent years.

If staging the NCAA finals for the first time in the heart of the South seemed the obvious plot for an ambush of UCLA, it must be remembered that Greensboro was selected four years before. In their separate ways both Coach Sloan and Coach Wooden ignored any hidden meanings attached to the site. "You know," Wooden pointed out, "we've had the finals in Los Angeles, too." And Sloan was heard to remark, "We're just visitors. After all, the host university is North Carolina, our chief rival, and a lot of Tar Heels will be rooting for UCLA."

He was right. "I hope," said one Tar Heel screamer, "that State gets beat by a thousand."

The magnitude of the UCLA-North Carolina State rematch so overshadowed the Marquette-Kansas game that even McGuire felt dwarfed by it. "I'm just glad to be playing in the B Class division," he said, tongue in cheek, while Coach Ted Owens of Kansas referred to the Marquette game as the "Preliminary." Sadly, that's the way their teams played, too, with the Warriors winning, 64-51.

By contrast, the second semifinal more than lived up to expectations. Not only did it bring together teams No. 1 and 2 in the national polls, but it matched Burleson against Walton, and Thompson against Keith Wilkes, four of the best players in college basketball. Adding zest to these main matchups was the bad blood remaining from UCLA's 84-66 victory over NC State in St. Louis. "We know they aren't 18 points better than us," said State Forward Tim Stoddard. "Now we're going to prove it." To which Bruin Andre McCarter replied, "The possibility of UCLA's losing just doesn't fit into history." Oh, yeah?

How NC State succeeded in doing the impossible was simple enough. It forced UCLA to start its offense farther out than it liked, and State stopped the backdoor plays as Thompson held Wilkes to five baskets in 17 shots while scoring 28 points himself. Towe frustrated the Bruin guards to death, causing turnovers, and Burleson was all over Walton.

It was probably demeaning State when UCLA's Dave Meyers said after the game, "We beat ourselves," but the truth of the matter was that early in the second half the Bruins rushed to a 49-38 lead, and later, with 11 minutes to go, were out in front, 57-46. But State refused to give up. As little Towe cracked the whip, shouting orders to his teammates, firing long, looping passes to them from midcourt, State kept closing the gap. Scoring 10 straight points, the Wolfpack closed to within one, 57-56, then to 61-60. When Thompson went high in the sky to score a three-point play, the scoreboard suddenly read, 63-61, and the partisan crowd went wild, smelling victory.

With 51 seconds remaining and the score tied 65-all, Walton missed a hook shot and Burleson rebounded. Going into a delay offense, State let the clock wind down to the last five seconds, when Stoddard let fly from the corner and missed. The shot could have ended the game.

In the first overtime, it was State's game to win after Stoddard picked off a pass intended for Walton. With the ball in Wolfpack possession once more, Thompson drove for the basket with 10 seconds to go. Instead of taking the shot himself, however, he suddenly twisted in midair and passed off to Burleson, whose short spin flip whirled around the rim and fell off.

After Walton and Wilkes took UCLA to a 74-67 lead with 3:27 remaining in the second overtime, the Bruins seemed well on their way to being the other team in the finals against

Marquette. But there was still plenty of bite in the Wolfpack. Pressing ever tighter, the Wolfpack opened up the floor, caused turnovers and got every rebound it needed. Six straight points set up a bank shot by Thompson that put State in front, 76-75, with only 53 seconds left. Thompson's two free throws and a pair of foul shots by Towe, the hero of all little guys, clinched it. Walton made a meaningless jump shot with five seconds to go, and that ended the scoring, 80-77. The UCLA dynasty was broken. The crowd of 15,829 in old Greensboro Coliseum went wild. Bring on Marquette.

As they had done earlier in the season, the Bruins played erratically, even foolishly, twice blowing big leads. After the game, Wooden agreed that his players had let State off the hook. "We made too many critical mistakes," he said. "We took shots I didn't think we should have. North Carolina State took advantage of them and had the poise to come back. We've had trouble holding leads this season. But we knew the string of titles had to end. It couldn't go on forever. I'm happy we had it as long as we did. We were close again today, but not close enough."

In the UCLA locker room, Bill Walton slowly dressed in silence, stuffed his soggy uniform into a bag and then went outside to sign autographs for some children. On his way out of the Coliseum a gray-haired man in overalls, a janitor, tugged at his arm. "Mr. Walton," the man said, "I work here, and I just want to shake your hand. You're a credit to basketball."

"Thanks," Walton said. "And thanks for all you've done for us." And then Bill Walton walked away from the NCAA basketball championship forever, and, after one more game, into pro ball.

On the night of March 25, 1974, North Carolina State officially won its first national basketball championship by the score of 76-64 over the Warriors. The contest was virtually decided late in the first half with a play on which, ironically, Marquette took the lead. When Marcus Washington drove into Thompson and was charged with a foul after his driving basket put the Warriors ahead, 28-27, Coach McGuire went into his act in front of the scorer's table and was hit with a technical foul. Thompson sunk three straight free throws, Burleson added

In the crucial 1974 NCAA semifinal, North Carolina State's Tommy Burleson (24) predominated in a personal battle with UCLA's No. 32, Bill Walton.

North Carolina State had Marquette down at halftime, 39-30, then went on to win 1974 NCAA title, 76-64. Here Maurice Lucas battles Tommy Burleson for the ball.

Coach Norm Sloan ordered the Wolfpack into a "tease delay" after charging ahead of Marquette by 19 points at one stage of the 1974 NCAA final.

a layup, and suddenly State had the lead, 32-28. Tall Tommy dunked another less than a minute later, and when Bo Ellis of the Warriors was called for goaltending, McGuire gave N. C. State another big lift by being zapped with his second technical foul for screeching too loudly at the referee. "The technicals sure helped us," Thompson said later. The Warriors were thus down 39-30 at halftime.

Five minutes into the second half the game really got out of Marquette's reach as State built up a 19-point lead. From that point on State Coach Norman Sloan ordered the Wolfpack, the most explosive team in college basketball, into what he called a "tease delay." It was not a tactic favored by many coaches. Sloan almost succeeded in turning a rout into something of a sick joke. With 10 minutes to play, Marquette cut the deficit to nine points. There

State's defense stiffened, and while the Warriors concentrated on Thompson, Towe and Moe Rivers slipped into the clear enough times to score to keep Marquette from drawing any closer.

From the gangling Tom Burleson, who held UCLA's Bill Walton to a draw and denied Marquette shooters access to their basket, to Monte Towe, that gnat of a guard with his adept ball control and sharp passes, the North Carolina State heroes would not be soon forgotten. Above all, there was the human jumpin' jack, David Thompson, literally above all—6' 4" in the Wolfpack guidebook but 8' 4" off the backboards. Years later, when fans would find it difficult to recall the team State beat in the 1974 finals to win its first national title, Thompson would still be up there, magically floating in to take a pass, and dropping it in for two.

The Wolfpack, 1974 National Champions. First row, left: Mgr. Mike Sloan, Steve Smoral, Craig Kuszmaul, Mark Moeller, Monte Towe, David Thompson, Greg Hawkins, Moe Rivers, Bruce Dayhuff. Second row, left: Asst. Coach Eddie Biedenbach, Asst. Coach Art Musselman, Steve Nuce, Dwight Johnson, Jerry Hunt, Tim Stoddard, Steve Smith, Ken Gehring, Asst. Coach Sam Esposito, Coach Norman Sloan. Third row, left: Bill Lake, Tommy Burleson, Phil Spence, Mike Buurma.

Wooden's Retirement Gift: 1975

In the grill of The College Inn at N. C. State, Monte Towe talked about the upcoming 1974-75 basketball season. With a bright choir-boy's face under a shaggy mushroom-cap of hair, his wide flashing grin suddenly turned serious.

"It's going to be different from last year, we know that," he said. "We won the NCAA championship, and now the only one who isn't back is Burleson, which means we'll have to be hustling the ball a lot more, a lot faster, to get it to the basket. Last year, Burleson was always there. But the difficult thing facing us is that everybody expects us to win again. In a way, we'll really be playing against our record of last season—playing who we were last year."

No bigger than a 15-cent sack of popcorn, Towe said he always had this driving need to win. He said he didn't know why, he'd never sat down and tried to figure it out, but it had always been there, gnawing at his insides. Maybe, he said, his lack of size had something to do with it.

"Ever since I can remember," he said, "I've been in the midst of people who were always taller than me. Lots of times, referees will come up to me during a game and say, gee, what a shame it is that I'm not a foot taller. But I don't know. Maybe if I was 6' 5" I wouldn't be like I am. Maybe in that foot's difference is where it's all happened. There's just this certain line between winners and everybody else, and I think it has to do with how much you want it. I mean, I *really* want it; harder than anybody else can even dream they want something. Maybe it's been the challenge of always being that foot shorter than everybody else that made up that line for me. People tell me I ought to read about Napoleon. Maybe so, but with me, I

don't want to conquer continents and become a monument in history—I just want to win another national basketball championship."

Early in the season, during the holidays, the Wolfpack had pushed their winning streak to 36 and were No. 1 in the polls. Coming up was Wake Forest, a Baptist stronghold better known for its golf teams, the place that invented Arnold Palmer. The basketball Deacons enjoyed a reputation of knocking the pride out of somebody each season. And so Wake Forest hustled the tail off N. C. State, 83-78. It was a marvelously executed conspiracy that was no fluke. It was the Deacons' tight, unnerving 1-2-2 zone and their jamming underneath to force the Pack shooters far outside that decided the game. Towe, Phil Spence and David Thompson were all challenged to fire from long range. This trio had been averaging 58 percent from the floor, so this strategy seemed implausible. It worked perfectly. Thompson missed 15 of 20 shots and Towe 15 of 22. Spence had to muscle inside for his eight baskets.

"A man is entitled to a bad game," said Thompson in the subdued locker room. "My trajectory was right, but everything else went wrong. I hate zones."

That was an understandable prejudice, except that State used exactly that defense the next night to trounce North Carolina, 82-67, with Thompson scoring 26 points and looking like an All-American all over again. The Pack was back, of course. The question was, for how long?

In the week of the wipeout—six Top 10 teams fell, including unbeaten Providence, Alabama and Southern Cal—Coach Bo Brickles, whose Davidson team was zapped by UCLA,

91-64, said, "If UCLA played North Carolina State now, they'd beat them badly." Two weeks earlier he had lost to the Wolfpack, 95-79. Oklahoma Coach Joe Ramsey was no less impressed. His Sooners had been shellacked by the Bruins, 111-66. "They have the greatest bench Wooden has ever had," he said.

Insiders were also high on the Kentucky Wildcats. They were running again. The Wildcats had squarely faced the challenge of a rejuvenated Southeastern Conference and had moved in alongside Tennessee as the No. 1 challenge in the SEC to favored Alabama. They were averaging 94 points a game. "Kentucky has, by God, the best talent since the Fabulous Five of 1948," said Adolph Rupp, who had been forced into retirement two years previously.

Unlike The Baron, Joe B. Hall was a Kentucky original, a child of the soil who was born in nearby Cynthiana, went to school at the university, traveled the area for Heinz' 57 Varieties, married a farmer's daughter, jumped into coaching and in 1965 became Rupp's assistant. Now he was the Boss Man and a lot of people liked his chances in the NCAA sweepstakes.

As time would tell, Indiana University was still a year away, but after 18 games the Hoosiers were undefeated and were solid residents of the No. 1 spot in all the polls. Individually, they enjoyed very little personal fame, but they did possess the widest average victory margin in the country: 27 points per game. They also had the sixth best offense, the 12th best defense and a .520 shooting percentage, and were ranked high in rebounding, yet their leading scorer was only 12th in the Big Ten and their top rebounder stood 10th. Indeed, the Hoosiers had balance.

Coach Bobby Knight, that mellowing martinet, coped with being No. 1 by playing inspirational tapes by legendary figures and reading biographies to his players. Literature included Pete Newell, Jack Nicklaus and Rudyard Kipling. "Kipling's my favorite," said substitute Steve Ahlfeld. "He's no sports guy."

Coach Fred Taylor of Ohio State said it was wise to play Indiana cautiously, "like making love to a porcupine."

What sort of man was Bobby Knight? One writer referred to him as "an eccentric genius." Knight had no curfew, no training table and hardly any rules. He demanded silence and total obedience at practice, then smartly kept his distance from his players off the court. He had a fiery temper and often erupted at the slightest provocation. During a heated exchange at courtside, he suddenly slapped Kentucky Coach Joe Hall on the head. Afterward, Knight said it was only a "friendly pat," claimed it was just a normal, meaningless gesture for him. "If it was meant to be malicious, as Hall suggested," Knight said, "I would have blasted the bastard into the seats."

Another of the endangered species on Knight's list were sports writers. He had nothing but disdain for the media. He was fond of telling journalists, "All of us learn to write by the second grade, then most of us go on to other things."

College basketball had found its answer to Woody Hayes.

It also had its court jester, Abe Lemons, whose Pan American University Broncs, of Edinburg, Texas, ran off with 18 wins in a row at one point in the season. The incomparable Abe was a man of many theories.

"They're always talking about cutting down the big man by raising the basket," he said. "I tell 'em they ought to bore a hole in the floor and change the rules so you have to drop the ball through. Then there'd be cheating to sign up little fellers. Everybody'd be chasing after guys two feet tall." Lemons stooped over, picked a tiny imaginary recruit, looked him squarely in the eye and said, "I'll give you a car."

For the first time in years, the final round of the NCAA championship shaped up as the most evenly matched tournament since John Wooden invented the zone press. Any one of the four finalists—Kentucky, Louisville, Syracuse or UCLA—had the horses to go all the way. Though the Wildcats and the Orangemen hardly figured to be in San Diego, site of the playoffs, when the season began, there were no cardboard entries in the finals. UCLA had long experience in tournament competition and pressure situations; Louisville was deep in reserves; Kentucky had more quick shooters than a John Ford epic; and gutty Syracuse had a hawking defense and fate working for it.

One thread ran throughout the regional playoffs. Each of the winning schools had won with teamwork. There were no superstars to dominate the scene, no Bill Waltons or David

All-American Forward Dave Meyers (34) was a fierce competitor.

Thompsons; just heroes with names like Trgovich and Bridgeman, Lee and Phillips, Johnson and Bond, Hackett and Flynn.

On the way to San Diego, Kentucky became something of a Cinderella by going hammer and tong at No. 1 Indiana in the Mideast Regional and coming away bruised and battered but the winner, 92-90. The loss ended the Hoosiers' 34-game win streak and ruined Bobby Knight's championship dreams. For the Wildcats, victory had never been sweeter. Earlier in the year Indiana had blasted Kentucky by 24 points in a contest surrounded with controversy. Joe Hall was embarrassed, especially by the well-publicized rap on the head given him by Bobby Knight. "All I want is another chance to play them," Hall said. "Knight personally humiliated me, and I'll never forget it."

Kentucky also never forgot the lesson it learned from the Hoosiers. After that onesided loss the Wildcats became a combative team. The turnaround was most evident at center, where Indiana's Kent Benson had intimidated UK freshman Rick Robey. "I found out a lot from Benson," said Robey later. "I learned not to give a lot of little cheap shots but to save up for one big one."

After the Mideast Regional the tone was conciliatory between the Wildcats and Hoosiers. Knight congratulated Hall and praised the Kentucky victory. The Wildcats followed Knight's lead. Benson walked up to Rick Robey with tears tumbling down his cheeks and said he hoped Kentucky went all the way in the NCAA tournament. "It takes a real man to do that," said Robey. "He gave me his best shots and I gave him mine, but we're not enemies."

Everybody was ready to take UCLA apart like a Swiss watch after the Bruins played one of their worst games in decades in defeating Montana, 67-64, in the West Regional. About the only thing the contest proved was that UCLA could win even when it did not play well. Not surprisingly, John Wooden decided it was time for a fireside chat with his players. He told them they were in sudden death now and that they had to show much more intensity. "The only fierce competitor on the team is David Meyers," he told them. "The rest of you are all kind people."

Kentucky's opponent in the NCAA semifinals in San Diego was Eastern winner Syracuse, which battled the clock to beat both heavily favored North Carolina, 78-76, and surprising Kansas State, 95-87. In the other half of the doubleheader, Wooden was matched against his former assistant, Louisville's Denny Crum. The Cardinals had wandered aimlessly most of the season, but they found themselves in the Midwest Regional, destroying Cincinnati, 78-63, and Maryland, 96-82. And UCLA played its finest game of the season against Arizona State to win the West tournament, 89-75, after the Montana scare.

According to insiders, the rivalry between Wooden and Crum, who had played for UCLA, dated back to the NCAA finals in Houston in 1971. Crum served as Wooden's assistant then and they got into an argument on the bench, supposedly over strategy. But that was only part of it. The rest of the story was that Wooden was mad because Crum had failed to give him a ride to the arena. Wooden had had to walk. Now here their teams were, matched against each other in the NCAA semifinals.

Despite a shallow bench, UCLA had a solid nucleus, headed by Meyers, Marques Johnson and Richard Washington. Wooden had taken to referring to Pete Trgovich and Andre Mc-Carter as "my much maligned guards," but in the latter part of the season they had not deserved the description. UCLA's most serious problem was Meyers' physical condition. He was bothered all season by leg injuries. "I've been taking a beating this year," he said. "The referees don't like me. Guys hit me and nothing gets called."

Louisville's answer to Meyer was Wesley Cox, who, despite a hamstring pull, scored 15 points and had nine rebounds in the Midwest final to help defeat Maryland. "He played with a lot of pain and a lot of painkiller," said Crum.

The Cardinals attacked in the same way the Marines used to take beaches. Crum sent in waves of reserves and they were good ones. At any rate, the UCLA-Louisville and Kentucky-Syracuse games figured to be horse races—and not one of the teams was a long shot.

Down home in Lexington, Kentucky, the Syracuse game posed a problem for Tommy Puckett, a local policeman. Tommy was scheduled to marry Julie Gaskin at 3 P.M. on Saturday, the day of the game. The invitations were already in the mail when Tommy realized to his dismay that the Wildcats would be starting their game at the very same time. With Julie's consent, he sent the wedding guests postcards bearing a picture of a basketball player, changing the time to 2 P.M.and adding the postscript: "UK is No. 1, Puckett-Gaskin Wedding No. 2. See you at the church and tipoff, too. Julie and Tommy."

Because of the presence of the Kentucky and Louisville teams, San Diego was overrun with Kentuckians. Arriving by plane, bus, auto and motorcycle, they took up lodging in neighboring hotels on Harbor Island and, depending on which side they were rooting for, argued that Kentucky was too timid to schedule games with Louisville, or acted as though they had never heard of Louisville. "Louisville *who?*"

Governor Julian Carroll of the Commonwealth lost a lot of Louisville votes when he phoned the NCAA and asked if he could present the championship to Kentucky in the event the Wildcats went all the way. "Hell," grunted one disgruntled Cardinal supporter, "the governor didn't even mention Louisville."

The Kentucky-Syracuse contest was anything but stylish. Sixty-one personal fouls were called. The Wildcats led at halftime, 44-32, and then

Richard Washington (31) gave the 1975 Bruins scoring and board strength.

increased the margin to 22 points early in the second half as the Orange went more than four minutes without scoring. Though Syracuse recovered to make the final numbers respectable (95-79) they left the floor afterwards looking like they had just lost a knife fight. The battle set a new record for rabbit punches.

Only a few close friends knew the feelings that boiled inside John Wooden during this final week of his 40-year coaching career. There had been rumors that he was retiring after the NCAA tournament. "This will be Wooden's last tournament," reported Washington State Coach George Raveling, who wrote a weekly syndicated column. Another Pac-8 coach revealed that Wooden had told him that he was stepping aside. Though appearing to be fit, Wooden had not been sleeping well, and his personal physician had advised him not to coach the 1976 U.S. Olympic team.

On the morning of the UCLA-Louisville semifinal, the Los Angeles *Herald-Examiner* confirmed the rumors that Wooden was stepping down. The story was given the bannerline treatment. An unmistakable look of resignation crossed Wooden's face as he read the articles, and he said he would like to go out a winner.

Even news of Wooden's retirement could not diminish the drama of UCLA's 75-74 overtime victory over Louisville. The game was not won in the trenches but on the backboards. That was where UCLA's Marques Johnson went to contribute two brilliant defensive plays that saved the game in regulation time and where Richard Washington arrived to score the last two of his 26 points and the winning basket with two seconds left in overtime.

From the very beginning, it was a struggle of fierce intensity. Louisville held early nine-point leads four times as the result of 18 points from Ulysses (Junior) Bridgeman and Allen Murphy. But hounded by the UCLA press, both men cooled off. Bridgeman, as a matter of fact, did not score a basket in the final 37 minutes of the game.

With 48 seconds to go, Louisville was ahead, 65-61. Two free throws by Washington and a desperate jumper by Johnson tied the score as time ran out and for the second straight year the Bruins found themselves in a semifinal overtime. "Nobody was thinking back," said Meyers, remembering UCLA's loss to N. C. State in 1974. "Against Louisville, we were just super lucky.

Then it was time for bread and butter."

In the overtime, Murphy scored seven points to run his total to 33, high for the game, and put Louisville in front, 74-73, with only 20 seconds to play. UCLA was forced to foul. Terry Howard stepped to the line and needed only to make both ends of his one-and-one to cement the victory. During the season, he had made 28 free throws in a row. But now he missed. UCLA quickly called for a timeout. When the Bruins returned to the floor the Cardinals settled into a zone defense. The ball went to Johnson, who waited for Washington to fake toward the foul line, then drift out along the baseline, and slipped him the ball. The 6' 9" Washington lifted off, cocked and fired. Right on target. The easy-going sophomore had cut the Cardinals to pieces.

After the game, Meyers said he hadn't been in such a shooting match in a long time. "Both gangs flailing away, no moaning, no messing around," he said. "It seemed like two UCLAs out there, one and the same."

Then Wooden called his players together in the Bruin locker room. He said he was retiring after one more game. The room went still. "I don't want to," he said. His eyes went around the room, his voice cracked. "I have to. Doctor's orders." Then he left the room.

Monday night in the San Diego Sports Arena brought together two teams, UCLA and Kentucky, which had won more than a third of all the NCAA basketball titles every played. The matchup evoked memories of Hagan and Ramsay and Issel, of Goodrich and Alcindor and Walton and all the rest. And there was Wooden one-on-one with destiny. Adolph Rupp, retired, sat next to the Kentucky bench and said, "It will be sad if he [Wooden] loses, but he's got enough of those darn trophies. Johnny's in against me tonight."

The Bruins also were in against a snarling squad of Wildcats that had reached this night on the strength of muscle, manpower and the sharpshooting of freshman Jack Givens. But if the Bruins were intimidated they didn't show it. Ralph Drollinger, showing some musclepower of his own, snared 13 rebounds and scored 10 points in 16 minutes, while Washington, dividing his time between the pivot and forward, scored 28, got 12 rebounds and found the time to hold Kentucky's three ponderous freshman centers to eight points. Washington,

After winning seven NCAA titles in a row and 10 in 12 seasons, college basketball's most successful coach, John Wooden, retired in 1975. He is shown here with his last national championship team. Front row, left: Marvin Thomas, Gavin Smith, Jim Spillane, Raymond Townsend, Pete Trgovich, Andre McCarter. Rear, left: Coach John Wooden, Asst. Coach Gary Cunningham, Marques Johnson, Dave Meyers, Richard Washington, Ralph Drollinger, Brett Vroman, Wilbert Olinde, Casey Corliss, Asst. Coach Frank Arnold, Mgr. Lenny Friedman.

the tournament MVP, said he even surprised himself.

The hectic tempo of the first half, in which there were 15 lead changes and five ties, continued in the second half until the Bruins broke away to a 66-56 lead with 12 minutes left to play. During the UCLA surge, Captain David Meyers put a net over Kevin Grevey, whose 18 points in the first half had made a contest out of it. But then Grevey suddenly came alive again, scoring 10 points, and Jimmy Dan Conner, the Kentucky quarterback, finally broke away from the defensive clutches of Pete Trgovich. With 6:49 remaining, the Wildcats trailed by only a point. At that point the Wildcats had a chance to take control, but the uncanny luck of the Bruins refused to give ground. Still ahead, 76-75, the Bruins' Captain Meyers went up for a jumper but crashed into Grevey and was charged with a foul. Meyers lost control of himself and was hit with a technical. Wooden screamed at Referee Hank Nichols, "You crook!!" and charged onto the court. Now the Wildcats had a possible five-point play—a maximum of three free throws followed by possession of the ball. But Grevey, who finished

with 34 points, missed the technical and then the first of his one-and-ones. Then James Lee, a Kentucky sub, was called for setting an illegal pick on the next play, and the Wildcats had come up empty.

Meyers then hit on two free throws that were matched by Bob Guyette's bank shot, but the busy Washington tipped in Marques Johnson's miss for an 80-77 lead. Kentucky never got closer. Final score: 92-85, UCLA.

After the game, Andre McCarter, the UCLA guard who had made 14 assists and a key late basket, hugged the 64-year-old John Wooden and said, "Coach, I hope you have a nice life." There were tears in Wooden's eyes.

Except for an emotional outburst or two during a very emotional game, John Wooden remained true to his image to the end. Having arrived in California 27 years before, he said, "I didn't really feel differently about this game. Just very proud."

He had much to be proud about. Of the last 12 NCAA championships, his teams had failed to win only two of them. Now there were no more games to go. Clearly, UCLA basketball would never be the same again.

The Hoosiers of Bobby Knight: 1976

The worst news for UCLA opponents was that the Bruins felt they had something to prove—that they could win without Johnny Wooden.

"Coach Wooden was the master," said Andre McCarter, the quarterback on the defending champions and one of only two seniors. "He proved his greatness. Now we have to prove ours."

UCLA was a team with a new coach, 45-year-old Gene Bartow, via Memphis State and Illinois. He affected a scholarly, fatherly attitude to match Wooden's, but he was contemporary. He said he was going modern and loosen the reins on his players. "There will be more freedom," he said. "I'll allow them a bit more one-on-one out on the floor."

Coach Bartow had the horses from top to bottom to do pretty much what he wanted. The UCLA bench was so deep that several potential stars drowned in obscurity at the far end of it. Only five players could be on the floor at once, and after Richard Washington, Andre McCarter and Marques Johnson (called Stalin, Churchill and Roosevelt by Bartow), the talent leveled off to just below world class. In a preseason interview, Bartow's candor was refreshing.

"We have as good a chance as anybody to win a national championship," he said. "Nobody else has any better players than we do. But we don't have the big man who can dominate; if you don't have the big man, you don't always win. And I'm on the spot. I have to win and win now. I am following a pretty tough act. I know that. So what are the odds against winning 10 championships in the next 12 years? About 100 million to 1!"

George Raveling, the Washington State coach, pointed up Bartow's dilemma perfectly: "If Gene wins the next four NCAA titles in a row, he'll still be six down."

Coach Bartow was not alone. His players shared the pressure with him. "Nobody else faces the kind of pressure we do," McCarter said. "Every year we're expected to win it. If we don't, people say what's wrong with UCLA?"

Yet while the Bruins knew they were under the gun to maintain Wooden's level, they were well aware that they had a winning tradition on their side. "When I was in high school and being heavily recruited," said 6' 10" freshman David Greenwood, "college coaches said to me, 'Come to our school and start your own dynasty. We can do what UCLA has done.' I told them to be serious. 'Listen,' I said, 'if you're a basketball player, UCLA is where you go to play basketball.' "

While a lot of people picked UCLA, Marquette Coach Al McGuire said he had to go along with Indiana. "Indiana has the best team with the best players and the best coach," he said. Even Bobby Knight admitted, "We have great senior leadership. Our players are as aware of how hard they should be working as any I've had." Obviously there had been no ill effects from the previous season, when the Hoosiers swept to a 31-0 record before suffering a 92-90 loss to Kentucky in the NCAA Mideast Regional. "Indiana will be almost impossible to stop," wrote one reporter. "Steve Green and John Laskowski have graduated and will be missed, but 6' 7" forward Tom Abernethy and 6' 3" Wayne Radford, a clutch performer who can play either guard or forward, will more than bring up the slack." There were four starters coming back: guards Quinn Buckner (6' 3") and Bob Wilkerson (6' 7"), forward Scott May (6' 7") and center Kent Benson (6' 11")—all prospective first-round pro draft picks. Buckner had come on strong since giving up football.

For years, everyone in Indiana knew how basketball should be played: run and shoot, run and shoot. That was the kind of basketball they grew up with. They weren't happy unless the ball was in the air. But after Bobby Knight arrived in Bloomington from West Point in 1971 and took command of the Hoosiers, he changed the cry to "dee-fense, dee-fense." His tank-trap tactics quickly caught on with the fans. "When we went into a late-game stall to protect a lead against Minnesota, the fans responded with a standing ovation," remembered Tom Miller, the IU sports information director. "A few years ago they'd have been screaming for 100 points."

Defense had been Knight's game ever since he was a sub on Fred Taylor's celebrated Ohio State teams of the early 1960s. Slow afoot and with people like John Havlicek, Larry Siegfried and Jerry Lucas as teammates, Knight, in spite of a keen shooting eye, did not play much. But he absorbed everything Taylor taught.

When he graduated, Knight was thinking of a career in law but gave himself a year to decide. He took a job as assistant coach at Cuyahoga Falls High School in Ohio. The next year he wound up serving as an assistant to Tates Locke at West Point. Coach Locke was another big advocate of defense.

When Locke left Army to coach at Miami of Ohio, Knight was given the head job. In six seasons under him the Cadets won 102 and lost but 50; beat Navy all six years; had the most victories for an Army team (22) in a season; played in four NITs; had a team defense that three times led the nation; and once Army finished 16th in the final national polls, the only time West Point has been in the top 20.

But as Army rolled to new heights, so did Knight's reputation as the *enfant terrible*. He drew so many technical fouls they began to call him Bobby T. Once he splintered a chair at the scorers' table. "When I started it was always a battle between me and the officials," he said. "But you can't coach like that. It just took me a while to learn."

Knight arrived in Bloomington with a reputa-

Fiery Bobby Knight reminds Indiana U. partisans of another hollerin' Hoosier of another era—the late Branch McCracken.

tion for winning, for outstanding defensive teams and for a hair-trigger temper. At a place that was somewhat diffident about his hiring, he started with a bang—one that made him a

While a lot of people picked UCLA in 1976, Marquette's Coach Al McGuire favored Indiana. "The Hoosiers have the best team with the best players and the best coach," he said. The "best coach," Bobby Knight, is shown here in a thoughtful moment.

lot of enemies among the alumni. At the first practice a large allotment of Old Grads gathered as always in the gym and Knight threw them out. They went away cussing under their breath. "All practices are closed," Knight said. "I want nothing to distract my players. When we are practicing, I want total quiet." He was

known to upbraid the hide off people for talking. "Basketball practice is my classroom and you don't talk in the classroom; you *listen*," said Knight.

The first year Indiana supporters hoped for a 12-12 season. Knight gave them 17-8, including nine of 10 victories in Indiana's last Big Ten games and a third-place finish in the conference. Whatever howls there had been against Knight from the Indiana alumni had long since quieted.

Behind Indiana and UCLA in the preseason polls was Marquette. For a change the Warriors were 10-strong in players and almost certain to go to a postseason tournament for the 10th year in a row. After nine seasons of routine success, they appeared to have the talent now to be a serious contender. There were four tall reasons for optimism: 6' 8" Bernard Toone, 6' 6" Ulice Payne, 7' Craig Butrym and 6' 10" Jerome Whitehead. But the apple of Coach Al McGuire's eye was Butch Lee, who had played well in a Puerto Rican League during the summer. McGuire was simply dotty about his star guard's carefree behavior during the heat of competition.

"I'd take him out of a game," McGuire said, "and he'd be up and down the bench slapping hands with guys. I'd say, 'Hey, Butch, what are you doing? We're down by nine points.' It's tough to get players like Butch to realize this. They're so used to playground games. Everybody just comes and plays. The game is just for the joy of playing. Somebody beats somebody else, and then they all go down to the corner and have hot dogs and a Coke."

Ranked No. 5 in the December polls was Maryland. It was still a long, long way to Philadelphia, site of the 1976 NCAA finals, but a lot of folks liked the Terps' chances. They were 24-5 in 1974-75 and won the ACC regular-season title. Fans were saying that Coach Lefty Driesell's club finally had arrived as the "UCLA of the East." Lefty had had more teams (seven) ranked in the Top 10 than any *active* coach. The Terps set an NCAA shooting percentage record last season when they hit .547 from the floor. The leading scorer per game (19.5) and team leader was John Lucas, called by many "the top sparkplug in college basketball."

A 6' 3½" senior guard, Lucas was so quick he had not had to bother learning to shoot a jump shot; he was tenacious on defense; his passes seemed always on target. On defense, Driesell often put Lucas on the opposition's best player, usually a forward much taller than he was, like Notre Dame's Adrian Dantley, although, as Lucas said, "Coach tells me I have a white man's disease. I can't jump. I'm probably a step away from being just another guy on the street."

Lucas entered Maryland as a member of the first wave of freshmen eligible under a new NCAA rule to play varsity sports. Back then few people thought that freshmen could crack a college lineup, much less be a star. Lucas made nine of 10 shots in his first game and was a distinguished starter all year for a team ranked among the nation's top five.

In 1975, Moses Malone made a brief appearance on the Maryland campus before he signed a pro contract with the Utah Stars. While Moses was deciding whether to take a million dollars or go to school, Lucas called a team meeting. Under his direction, the Terps agreed to donate their $15-a-month laundry money to a Save Moses Fund. Lucas told Moses they'd give him the money each month and he could lead them to the NCAA championship. At those prices, Malone said no. "I'm out of here," he told Lucas. Even without him, Maryland still won the Atlantic Coast Conference regular-season crown before losing to Louisville in the NCAA playoffs. Now Lucas was back for one more shot at the NCAA title. A realist, he knew the odds against his team. "You got to be 15 to 20 percent better the next year just to be the same," he said. "Everybody is gunning for you. It's easy to say, 'I don't have to play as hard because I know what I'm doing now.' You'll be good. But it depends on what you want to be, good or great."

Lucas was raised in a pleasant middle-class section of Durham, North Carolina. His father, John Sr., was the principal of nearby Hillside High School (enrollment 1,450). He was Durham's Father of the Year in 1972. His mother, Blondola, was assistant principal at Shepard Junior High School. She was the city's Mother of the Year in 1975. "All the stories about blacks are the same," said Lucas Jr. "They all come from the ghetto. They all grew up with roaches and rats and pimps and pushers. Well, all blacks *aren't* like that, and my family back-

ground is not like that. I had to be home when the streetlights came on. The first time I didn't, I got whipped."

From the very start, you had the feeling this was going to be the year of the Hoosiers. Around the end of November they made UCLA look like its numbers were on backwards. In their first game under new coach Gene Bartow, the Bruins went into the game all sunshine, and came out of it all frowns. Final score: Indiana, 84-64.

In midseason the Hoosiers struggled a bit through a series of games, but at the end they were still unbeaten and extolling the virtue of positive thinking. They beat their last four Big Ten opponents by an average of 23 points and coasted to their fourth straight league title.

Despite an undefeated record, a couple of All-Americans, a coach who acted as if he knew all the answers, Indiana knew it had some major hurdles in regional play to overcome before it could think about an NCAA championship. If you believed their all-conquering record made them a shoo-in, then consider the cold fact that history disagreed. Unbeaten UCLA teams won the NCAA crown four times, but only two other teams—San Francisco (1956) and North Carolina (1957)—ever entered the tournament undefeated and exited with the championship. Indiana was one that didn't. In 1975, the Hoosiers also were undefeated, although in the NCAA they had an excuse, specifically the cast on Scott May's broken arm.

In the opening playoff round in March, Indiana befuddled St. John's in an easy victory that hardly caused Coach Bobby Knight to leave his seat, much less throw it. To reach the NCAA semifinals in Philadelphia, the Hoosiers still had to win the Mideast Regionals at Baton Rouge, Louisiana, and that could pose all sorts of trouble for the undefeated. Mideast opponents had a combined won-lost record of 74-7, and two of them, Alabama and Marquette, were the kind of teams you'd expect to meet in the NCAA finals.

Indiana had it when it needed it and in winning the Mideast Regional proved it could play more than one kind of basketball. First the Hoosiers choked off Alabama with defense, 74-69, and then they went on the attack and riddled No. 2-ranked Marquette, 65-56. Both games followed the same pattern. Indiana broke on top each time and led most of the way, although its stars were in foul trouble: Kent Benson against Alabama, Scott May against Marquette. Whenever the enemy mounted threats Indiana turned it away with plenty of firepower. Indiana was a team that refused to beat itself. Neither Alabama nor Marquette could penetrate this aura of invincibility. In the Marquette game, for example, the Hoosiers simply ate up the Warrior defense, hitting eight of their first 10 shots and 14 of 18 for an early 30-19 lead. Marquette's Lloyd Walton said it all when he came off the floor: "They say you can zone Indiana, but when we do they make everything anyway."

And so the Hoosiers kept knocking opponents down as fast as schedule-makers could set them up, just as they had been doing all season. Only two more remained—UCLA and Michigan.

The NCAA West Regional was held in UCLA's Pauley Pavilion, where the Bruins had lost only three games in 11 years. And so they went right on piling up impressive records: led by juniors Marques Johnson and Richard Washington, they won their 167th and 168th victories at Pauley, their 12th Regional out of the last 13 and, most phenomenal of all, their 45th and 46th NCAA-tournament games out of their last 47. The victims: Pepperdine, 70-61, and Arizona, 82-66.

The happiest Bruin was Andre McCarter, who, after Notre Dame had beaten UCLA in late January, began a rite of rededication—dribbling a basketball to classes, to the store, to the Forum for pro games, to the bathroom, on dates—practically everywhere he went. Philadelphia was his home town and he had never played there as a collegian. He said he was willing to follow the bouncing ball the 3,000 miles between LA and Philly—on foot. "I told my teammates that if they'd get me home," he said, "I'd try to take care of everything else for 'em." Trouble was, the "everything else" included beating Indiana.

Located only a mashie shot from Philadelphia, Rutgers took a detour to Greensboro, North Carolina, where the Scarlet Knights dashed past Connecticut, 93-79, and Virginia Military Institute, 91-75, with scarcely a passing glance to win the East Regional. The burning question was not whether they could handle the Huskies and the Keydets. What the fans in that part of the country wondered was how Rutgers would have done against such preseason-rated powers as North Carolina, Virginia or Maryland. The unbeaten Scarlet Knights found it hard to believe that the defense of Dixie against invaders from the north had been left up to VMI.

So Rutgers was now 31-0. In other years 31-0 would have been good enough to win an NCAA title. Yet Rutgers could not afford to rest on its laurels. In previous seasons 13 teams had entered the NCAA tournament undefeated. Only six survived. Nothing less than 33-0 would do if the kids from New Jersey wanted to make it No. 7 on the survival list. Nobody had ever won 33 games in one college season. Rutgers co-captain Phil Sellers said he had looked at the team's schedule the previous summer and he told fellow teammate Eddie Jordan right then that he thought they could win all their games. "But you just can't expect that to happen," he corrected himself in March, after reality set in. "You've got to keep that kind of confidence tucked up your sleeve until it actually happens."

Skepticism over Rutgers' lightweight schedule followed the Scarlet Knights to Philadelphia. Indeed, with a genuinely tested Michigan squad awaiting them in the semifinals and, if they got by the Wolverines, either UCLA or Indiana after that, the Knights were still only a third, probably even a fourth, choice in the final four.

"That doesn't surprise me," said Rutgers publicist Bob Smith. "I know there were times this season when we were, say, 15-0, that some of the New Jersey papers covering us were just hanging around so they could be there when we got beat."

It's more than just a cliché—basketball is a team game. And at the Midwest Regional in Louisville the best team won. Until then, no one outside the Big Ten really knew—or cared—how good Michigan was. Notre Dame and Missouri should have listened to Northwestern Coach Tex Winter when he said, "I wouldn't be surprised to see Indiana and Michigan both in the NCAA finals."

The Wolverines were small and young. But they were also quick, well balanced, determined and not easily intimidated. They sometimes blew big leads as routinely as they built them, but they had an amazing ability to recover. Against Notre Dame, for example, they fell behind by 11 points in the first half and eight in the second but came on to win, 80-76. While All-American Adrian Dantley nearly collapsed from exhaustion underneath with 31 points, five Wolverines scored in double figures. The victory was especially pleasing to Michigan Coach Johnny Orr, who now was 4-0 against Notre Dame's Digger Phelps and had taken the Irish out of the NCAA tournament twice in the last three years. Orr complained that Notre Dame and the ACC stole national acclaim that rightfully belonged to himself, the Wolverines and the Big Ten. "If I were coaching an independent," he said, "I'd be in the NCAA tournament every year."

Coach Orr's kind of scoring balance made his Wolverines a formidable entry in Philadelphia. But there was no cause for overconfidence. Beside Michigan, there were those other three entries—two of them unbeaten, and the other merely the defending national champion.

Against UCLA in the semifinals, Indiana faced not only the defending champion but an opponent with a score to settle—20 points worth. After that humiliation, the Bruins had regrouped, won the Pac-8 and then moved easily through the West Regional. Now they were in Philadelphia and in no mood for brotherly love. Ray Townsend, one of the starting guards, was so high he broke out in a rash. Townsend was one of two new faces in the UCLA lineup since the teams last met. The other was David Greenwood, a freshman center as cocky as Muhammad Ali. "Lonnie Shelton of Oregon State is the best center I've guarded," said Greenwood, in an obvious attempt to rile All-American Kent Benson. "Benson's not even in his class." Benson made no reply.

With surprising ease, Indiana knocked off UCLA, 65-51. Along the way the Hoosiers conducted a clinic in all phases of the game, neatly snapping around their passes, controlling the boards, exposing UCLA's weakness in the backcourt, and just making the Bruins feel very helpless, just like North Carolina State had done two years before. And the cocky Greenwood? He played so poorly in the opening half he had to be benched, but did return in the

second half to grab every rebound in sight and force the Hoosiers to take a timeout to talk things over. When play resumed, Indiana slowly and patiently worked the ball around, running the Bruins through a maze of screens before Tom Abernethy broke loose under the basket for an easy two points. That took the life out of the Bruins. At the far end of the press table John Wooden stared in silence. He could do nothing to help his old team.

If Indiana's victory over UCLA was easy, Michigan's 86-70 triumph over Rutgers was a little sad. The Scarlet Knights from up the Jersey Turnpike arrived in Philadelphia proud of their 31 victories in a row, proud of their exciting, racehorse style, proud of their coach, Tom Young, proud of their All-American candidates, Ed Jordan and Phil Sellers. Before the game, Rutgers reserves Mark Conlin and Steve Hefele mused about what they would do if they won the NCAA championship. Conlin said he didn't know. "I'd probably just go to sleep," he said. Which was what the Scarlet Knights did. From the very beginning, they shot miserably, played a holding defense that leaked layins, and never found a way to stop the Michigan shooters. In the first 10 minutes Rutgers missed a half-dozen easy close-in shots. Everyone got anxious, everyone fell apart. A minute before halftime they trailed by 17 points. The second half wasn't any better. The margin became 23 before the Wolverines eased off, winning 86-70. Thus the Rutgers' bubble burst. "We're just back to being normal citizens again," said Mike Dabney.

Two days afterward, Michigan knew exactly how Rutgers felt.

The Hoosiers finally reached the end of its rainbow the following Monday night by using a harrowing defense and an excellent offense to wear down combative Michigan, 86-68. And they did it without their tall starting guard, Bobby Wilkerson, who was knocked senseless in the early minutes of the game and had to be carted off to the hospital.

The Hoosiers waited until the second half to turn the tide, denying the Wolverines the open space they needed, and ultimately taking the heart out of them. For Bobby Knight, who at 35 became one of the youngest coaches ever to win the NCAA crown, the victory was vindication for the way his Hoosiers lost to Kentucky

1976's Hoosier hotshots, front row, left: Bobby Wilkerson, Jim Crews, Scott May, Quinn Buckner, Tom Abernethy, Kent Benson. Second row, left: Mgr. Tim Walker, Rich Valavicius, Mark Haymore, Scott Eells, Wayne Radford, Bobby Bender, Mgr. Chuck Swenson. Third row, left: Coach Bobby Knight, Asst. Coach Harold Andreas, Jim Roberson, Jim Wisman, Asst. Coach Bob Donewald, Asst. Coach Bob Weltlich.

in the finals of the 1975 Mideast Regional.

"This was a two-year quest," said Knight after the Michigan game. Even in victory he did not smile. He already had his mind on next year. "I'm not paid to relax," he said. "I'll be on the train tomorrow morning. Recruiting."

Though twice beaten by Indiana during the Big Ten schedule, Michigan was not intimidated by the Hoosiers' undefeated record. From the opening tipoff, the Wolverines clawed and scratched and harried the Hoosiers, forcing them into turnovers. Led by Guard Rickey Green, they took a 35-29 lead to the dressing room at halftime, secure in the knowledge they had shot 61.5 percent and outplayed the Hoosiers on the boards.

Before the game, Bobby Knight asked the Boston Celtics' John Havlicek, a teammate of his on Ohio State's 1960 NCAA champions, to visit the locker room and say a few words to his Hoosiers. Now at halftime it was Knight's turn

to address the players and whatever he said moved them enough to go back out and tie the score five minutes into the second half. When Indiana went up 69-59 with only five minutes to play, Michigan crumbled. It was all over.

Indiana won because of the big things, such as Scott May's 26 points and MVP Kent Benson's 25. Benson's inside domination completely wrecked Michigan. The Hoosiers also won because of the little things—hours of practice endlessly polishing the gritty but important fundamentals. "You don't know what we go through in practice," testified Indiana freshman reserve Rich Valavicius. "We work so hard. Coach Knight is the boss here."

"But it's well worth it," said senior Quinn Buckner. "He's made us all better people."

Scott May, also a senior, agreed. He said, "The first time we met I saw in his eyes that this guy is all right."

And Kent Benson said, "Without him, we'd

never be champions of college basketball."

Between 1960 and 1976 Ohio State had gone from NCAA champion to last in the Big Ten. From SRO crowds to sparse attendance—and from three straight appearances in the national championship finals to low team on the totem pole.

Now Fred Taylor, 51, was quitting. In 18 years at Ohio State, he had won the Big Ten title seven times, the Mideast Region four times and the NCAA once—in 1960, when he was 35 years old. He coached four all-Americans, was twice Coach of the Year and was elected by his peers as president of the National Association of Basketball Coaches.

But all that was in the past. Now Taylor, a superb teacher of basketball, had come to the end of his patience. He had lost his taste for recruiting. He was frustrated by his inability to get along with Athletic Director Ed Weaver who, he felt, never gave him proper support, particularly in matters relating to the hiring and firing of assistant coaches, and disillusioned by the infamous 1972 brawl that occurred in a Minnesota-Ohio State game. That incident resulted in two Minnesota players being suspended and two Buckeyes being injured. It also left Fred Taylor badly scarred. He wasn't the same after that. The world he knew just wasn't the same. It troubled him deeply that there seemed to be more concern among Buckeyes over an opponent cheating in football than the fact that two of their basketball players had to be scraped off of a basketball floor and wheeled off to the hospital for major repairs.

Even if there had been no fight, Taylor's decline was probably inevitable. What it all boiled down to was that Fred Taylor was done in by the changing currents of the game itself—not by coaching mechanics but by the nature of modern day recruiting. Taylor was sickened by both the direction and speed of the recruiting madness. At a lot of campuses, college basketball had become a monster of bribery. What, after all, was a basketball scholarship but a bribe? Eventually, someone was driven to define an amateur athlete realistically. An amateur would not accept a check. A man of integrity, Taylor regarded recruiting as the least enjoyable of all his duties. It was a brutal, full-time job; much more time-consuming than coaching. It meant a coach had to get up earlier, stay at it later, get there first and get there last.

So Fred Taylor resigned to go to work for Ohio State's physical education and intramural athletics department. Although Bobby Knight of Indiana, Lefty Driesell of Maryland and Gale Catlett of Cincinnati all showed interest in succeeding Taylor, the Buckeyes ultimately chose Eldon Miller, 38, who had once been a star guard at Wittenberg University and a successful coach at his alma mater and Western Michigan.

McGuire's Last Hurrah: 1977

The season was only eight games old and already Indiana's dour Hoosiers, the defending national champions, were adrift in turbulent waters. Temperamental Bobby Knight was turning gray wondering when his team (3-5) was going to start playing ball. All but one of the stars from the championship team were graduated, and a string of other players had left Bloomington to work for less demanding coaches. One of them, Mike Miday, a starter who seemed ideally suited to Indiana's style, quit the team because of a conflict with the coach. The university's official announcement stated that Miday felt that he had made the wrong choice of school, but in an interview with the student newspaper the 6' 8", 215-pound Miday admitted that the real problem had been with Knight.

"I think my high school record speaks for itself," Mike said. "I could've helped the team here. But that's not the reason I'm leaving. I couldn't stand the way Knight treated me. I felt that as a player on the NCAA championship team I deserved better than to be treated as an object and demeaned in public. When he recruits you, you don't see him in a tense situation. In a game, he just goes bananas. I could take the tough practices, but it was the mental pressure. I'm terrified of the guy."

For the Hoosiers, it was to be a season of recrimination. When Cincinnati's Bearcats, for example, rollicked to a 52-43 win over Indiana at the Superdome in New Orleans during the Sugar Bowl championship game, the Hoosiers lost with star Center Kent Benson, among others, being punished on the bench, while at least one player, freshman Glen Grunwald, dabbed

at tears on his cheeks. Afterward, there were reports of team meetings without Coach Knight and general unrest.

A young team, the defending NCAA champions were seeded no higher than No. 13 in the pre-season polls. Everybody liked Michigan, North Carolina, Kentucky and UCLA. They saw Indiana as a one-man team—Kent Benson, who at 6' 11" and 255 pounds was 10 pounds heavier than a year ago. He also was two inches wider around the chest. "He's so big that whenever he yawns," quipped a reporter, "windows rattle all over the Midwest." The critics were anxious to see if Benson liked his star billing. Previously, he had co-starred with the likes of Scott May, Quinn Buckner, Bob Wilkerson and Tom Abernethy. Now they all were gone, leaving Benson with an unknown supporting cast.

The critics felt that if anybody could win an Oscar with this young bunch, it was Knight. But they hadn't reckoned with his young players' defiance of his never-ending quest for perfection and his brooding intensity. Rumors were rampant that even All-American Benson, a devout young man, was upset over Knight's incendiary language and that some of his teammates were rebelling over being ordered around as if they were in the Marines. Against Cincinnati in the Sugar Bowl, Indiana's mood was quite obvious when, with 10 minutes left and the Hoosiers behind by six points, Knight ordered Benson off the floor. Then the coach got down on one knee and loudly chewed out his captain. "Your play is a disgrace," he shouted. "We may lose the game, but not with you. You're done. If we're going to go down, we're going to go down with guys who are busting their asses." Indiana finished out the game playing four freshmen and a sophomore.

Afterwards the fans taunted Knight with cries of "You quitter," and then Knight herded his team into the locker room and kept the door shut to the press for 45 minutes.

Hearing about it later, Gary Yoder, the Bearcats' senior playmaker, shook his head. "Indiana wouldn't be enjoying themselves right now, even if they had won," he said. "The fun is gone from the game for them."

And so went the Hoosiers of Knight—champions yesterday, also-rans today. It was not going to be one of those seasons in which the sun shone on them.

Time to look in on Abe Lemons, the game's No. 1 laugh-maker. He had moved on. Abe had been hired to transform the Texas basketball team into the sort of exciting, high-scoring teams he had coached at Oklahoma City University and Pan American for the past 26 years. In 18 seasons at OCU, his teams won 308 games (and lost 179), led the country in scoring three times, produced seven authentic All-Americans, competed in seven NCAA playoffs and twice went to the NIT.

The last time Abe had been involved in a basketball game in Austin was when he was the coach at OCU. In that one, Oklahoma City had rushed to a 3-17 deficit and Abe had been hit with a third technical foul and ordered off the floor. So Abe went out to a local Mexican restaurant and ordered the No. 1 Combination Dinner. He was still there, his mouth full of beans, when he learned OCU had won the game.

If a team could win games while its coach was eating Mexican food, it followed—at least in Abe's mind—that a team had its own makeup and didn't need a lot of advice from him on how to behave. On the road, his teams had no curfew, no blackboard meetings and no required meals. He told them at what hour they were to be suited up and in warmups he let them practice whatever the players decided they wanted to. If Abe was really bored or frustrated, he'd skip practice. He said, "I tell my players, 'Listen, if you miss practice tell me the truth. Don't tell me you had swine flu or were trapped in an elevator. Tell me you were sick of basketball for a day, or were swamped by life, or

whatever the truth happens to be. I understand those things.' "

Abe was introduced at his first Texas alumni dinner as "the man who's gonna turn our basketball program around." Then he got up and told about the night he asked a basketball official, "Is it a technical if I go on the court and punch my player in the nose?" He said the official replied, "If I was you, I'd lure him over to the sideline. But I'd sure do something to him."

Modern college players, Abe said, had changed since he started coaching. "It's got to where now if you say hello to a player he's liable to show up the next day in your office with his feet on your desk. He's 19 years old and he says, 'Coach, I'm not happy.' I wave my hand at him like it's magic and say, 'Happiness to you.' This kid grew up on Walt Disney. He's looking for a shortcut. Sometimes it'll happen that a kid'll want to know why you're not playing him, and you'll have to say, 'Well, the truth is I don't like you, don't like your parents, don't like your hometown. I thought I did but I don't.' "

A man of uncommon candor, Abe once told one of his players who'd been dogging it on defense, "Congratulations. In the first half you got one more rebound than a dead man would have gotten."

Today, Abe Lemons is known as "the man of one-liners." Sample: "A couple of alumni came by to see me the other day and offered to buy up my contract, but I didn't have change for a $20 bill."

"I have a perfectly good explanation why I don't have curfews: It's always your star who gets caught."

On his part man-to-man, part zone defense that allowed 52 points in one half: "I call it The Sieve."

Unlike years past, there was no overwhelming favorite to win the NCAA championship. Any of 10 teams were grouped together, with Michigan given the best chance to go all the way after a season in which it was all-runnerup—in the NCAA, in the Big 10, even in a holiday tournament in Las Vegas. But the Wolverines were returning with a cast that included Rickey Green, Olympian Phil Hubbard, and rugged Steve Grote.

Before the season began, Al McGuire said,

"This year the ball goes to Bo. That's my whole recruiting philosophy. We decide who gets to star."

The designated star was Maurice (Bo) Ellis, a

Marquette's Bo Ellis (31) was one big reason why the Warriors won the 1977 NCAA championship.

6' 9" forward who was the first four-year starter in modern Marquette history. The previous season, when the Warriors were 27-2, Bo played a supporting role behind seniors Earl Tatum and Lloyd Walton, who by now had moved on to the pros. Now it was Bo's turn.

"I've paid my dues," Bo said. "I'll continue to get my four or five assists and 14 or 15 rebounds, but I'm not going to pass up as many shots as I did last year."

Ellis would have plenty of help on the boards. There was 6' 10" Center Jerome Whitehead, for example. "He'll dominate most people he faces this year," said McGuire, "and he'll hold his own with the super centers." At the other forward was 6' 9" sophomore Bernard Toone. When Ellis, Whitehead or Toone needed a breather, Ulice Payne, a transfer from Ohio U., was ready to come in; so was Bill Neary, a walk-on who didn't even start in high school; and freshman Robert Byrd, who could soar like his surname. Then, of course, there was Guard Alfred (Butch) Lee, the star of the Puerto Rican Olympic team at Montreal who scored 35 points in a one-point loss to the United States; and Jim Boylan, Gary Rosenberger, 7-foot backup center Craig Butrym, and 6' 6" transfer from Michigan State, Jim Dudley. McGuire needed all that talent for the simple fact that his schedule included nine games vs. 1976 tournament teams.

In the preseason polls, UCLA ranked as high as No. 4; three months later it had dropped four notches to No. 8, with a 16-2 record. But then the Bruins crushed seventh-ranked Tennessee, 103-89, at the Omni in Atlanta, site of the NCAA finals in March, and Gene Bartow started thinking about another championship.

"I'll be back at the Omni in March," he said. "I hope our team will be back, too. I think we have a chance. But there are a lot of great teams in the West. They talk about all the great teams in the East and Midwest, but they better think about some of those in the West."

It was the sixth straight win for the Bruins and their second in a row on national TV following a 70-65 victory at Notre Dame. Ray Mears, the Tennessee coach, said the Vols had not played anyone as "awesome as UCLA." He hadn't seen, he said, a better team than the Bruins. "They are great athletes, and their abilities didn't surprise me at all," Mears said. "When UCLA is fired up, it is a great basketball team. And it was fired up against us."

Ray Mears could not have put the curse of death more surely on the Bruins had he put rat poison in their cereal. They returned to Los Angeles and won the Pac-8 championship, all right, but then amid the raw and wild mountains of Utah, in an atmosphere fairly dripping with virtue, the Bruins were ambushed. For the first time in 28 games and 11 years, the Bruins were beaten in the West Regional, this time by Idaho State, 76-75.

UCLA asked for it. They ignored Marques Johnson, who had 19 points in the first half but took only four shots in the second half, shooting away at the basket recklessly and playing defense as if the Idaho State players had potato disease. With less than two minutes to play, the Bruins trailed Idaho State, 71-63, as the IS rooters stood shoulder to shoulder in Provo's Marriott Center and chanted, "Idaho State, Idaho State."

The Bruins waited too long to make a run for it. Even then, however, they almost came back, forcing three turnovers and sinking five of their last six shots, and though Idaho State sank 11 of 12 free throws down the stretch, the Bengals almost let the game get away from them. But when the buzzer sounded, UCLA was still one point shy of paradise and was being branded as "just another team that won't play for its coach."

"Gene Bartow deserves better than pettiness," said Idaho reserve Center Stan Klos. "His players came in fat-headed."

Just as certain as there was a big loser at Provo, so also was there a big winner. Idaho State's opponent in the West Regional finals was Jerry Tarkanian's University of Nevada at Las Vegas, and the Runnin' Rebels thoroughly dominated the West tournament with a bizarre, inexorable attack that totally destroyed the Bengals, 107-90, on Saturday night. That victory, coupled with an 88-83 win over Utah in the semifinals, raised Vegas' tournament scoring average to 105 points a game.

The dream was over for Idaho State, but for Las Vegas, a team that had now won 57 games in the last two seasons, the dream went on—all the way to Atlanta. Rebel Reggie Theus said he could smell victory in the air.

Al McGuire

The real star of the Midwest Regional in Oklahoma City was Al McGuire, 48, who had already announced he was retiring after 20 years of coaching. After victories over Kansas State, 67-66, and Wake Forest, 82-68, the Marquette coach had only one more week to go. He admitted he would like to go out a winner. The Warriors got to the final four largely on the strength of their usual stingy defense, and Butch Lee's ball handling and accurate jump shots. Butch also won the Midwest tournament's MVP award.

So Al McGuire's coaching career was extended to one more trip, possibly two more big games. It was obvious that his players had a special motivation for winning. Guard Jim Boylan said no one had expressed it openly, "but it would be nice for Coach McGuire to end up his career with an NCAA title."

A month before the East Regional in College Park, Maryland, North Carolina's Coach Dean Smith said he didn't know if the Tar Heels could beat Kentucky, a rough-and-tumble outfit with serious designs on the NCAA championship. But that's what North Carolina did, dispose of the Wildcats, 79-72. And they did it without their two injured starters, Phil Ford and Tommy LaGarde. Ford was forced off the floor because of foul trouble and an aching right elbow, a souvenir of a last-minute collision during NC's exciting victory over Notre Dame, 79-77, in the opening round of the East Regional. Ford had won that game by picking himself up off the floor to sink his 28th and 29th points to win the game in the last two seconds of play. At one point in the Notre Dame game, North Carolina trailed by as much as 14 points.

Kentucky had reached the East finals by disposing of VMI, 93-78.

In the North Carolina shootout, the Wildcats trailed at halftime, 53-41, but they came out smoking with Forward Jack Givens scoring 18 of his game-high 26 points in the last 20 minutes. Coach Dean Smith said he saw that the Wildcats had fire in their eyes. "I don't know what it is about the ACC that makes people want to beat us so badly," Smith said.

The second half was only five minutes old when the Tar Heels went to the old reliable—a four-corners offense, gambling that a slowdown would protect a diminishing 59-53 North Carolina lead. It worked. The Wildcats spent the rest of the night trying to catch up. When it was all over, John Kuester, Ford's running mate, was named the East Regional's outstanding player.

This was an especially bad month for the nation's top three teams in the rankings. Both UCLA and Kentucky had been ambushed, and Michigan was to follow. North Carolina-Charlotte made a mockery of the Wolverines' No. 1 status by beating them, 75-68, in the Mideast Regional in Lexington. All season the 49ers had played in the obscurity of something called the Sun Belt Conference, in the shadow of their famous neighbors from Chapel Hill, and at the bottom of the weekly polls. Every time that Coach Lee Rose tried to convince the public that his team was real or that star Center Cedric (Cornbread) Maxwell was legitimate

A great clutch performer: North Carolina's Phil Ford.

North Carolina Coach Dean Smith

All-America timber, the reporters yawned.

Now here they were, conquerors of mighty Michigan, and on their way to Atlanta, where they were bound to be fan favorites. How could Atlantans resist an underdog team from the South with a star named Cornbread? Now all the 49ers had to do was beat Marquette and all that Al McGuire sentiment. "Oh, Lordy," said one Charlotte fan, "I don't even want to think about it."

Actually, Marquette had the worst record (23-7) of the final four. One reason for this was that it had played fitfully much of the season. So before the opening tipoff, McGuire went up to the 49ers' Coach Lee Rose and said, "There are 100 schools in the country with names like yours and I can beat them all. But I'm not sure I can beat yours."

It appeared to some that McGuire's expression of concern was nothing more than a smoke screen, a psyche act, because the Warriors started right off as though they intended to humiliate North Carolina-Charlotte. The nervous 49ers had more turnovers (7) than field goals (3) and were behind, 23-9, after 13 minutes into the first half. Still Marquette was not able to run away from the 49ers. With Cornbread Maxwell blocking shots and picking up some timely baskets, Charlotte came on strong near the end of the first half, and when the buzzer sounded it had closed the gap to 25-22.

With Coach Rose whistling encouragement from the bench, he ordered his and ordering the 49ers into a zone press that clearly bothered the Warriors at the start of the second half. Then, with 2½ minutes gone, Lew Massey put his team ahead for the first time with a jumper and the battle was on. The score seesawed back and forth, neither team able to put the other away. Then Massey hit another jumper to put Charlotte up by one and only four minutes left to play. Marquette brought the ball slowly downcourt, shot, missed, and the 49ers controlled the rebound. With an eye on the clock, Charlotte fell into a deliberate stall, whittling away the seconds, and forcing the Warriors to foul Melvin Watkins with only 1:41 left. Watkins sunk both free throws and now UNCC led, 47-44.

Marquette fought back. Guard Butch Lee chopped Charlotte's lead to a point with a 22-foot jumper from the top of the key. Maxwell

was fouled with less than a minute to play and missed. Marquette got the ball back, worked it to Lee, who put his team back in the lead with another clutch jumper. Then Massey missed an 18-footer and in the crush for the rebound Marquette came up with the ball. Suddenly Gary Rosenberger broke for the basket, missed the layup, but was fouled. Only 13 seconds remained and here was a big opportunity for the Warriors to put the game out of reach. UNCC called time in an obvious strategic move to shake up Rosenberger. The tactic proved half fruitful—Rosenberger missed his first shot but made the second, and now the Marquette lead was two points. Only 10 seconds remained on the clock.

North Carolina-Charlotte brought the ball across the mid-court, worked it around to Max-

Marquette's Butch Lee

well, who drove to the top of the circle, lost his balance, somehow managed to get his shot off. Swish! That tied the score, 49-49. Marquette quickly called time. Only three seconds remained.

During the rest period, Al McGuire marched onto the court. He explained later that he went out there only to check the height of the Omni's huge clock-and-scoreboard above midcourt. McGuire was concerned that Butch Lee's inbound pass from the baseline might hit it, giving Charlotte, according to the rules, the ball back under the Marquette basket, with three seconds still to go. McGuire was also worried that Lee might make a bad pass downcourt.

But Lee hurled a perfect pass to Bo Ellis. The ball glanced off Bo's fingers at the foul line, sailed through Maxwell's hands and into the arms of Whitehead. Whitehead lunged for the basket. Maxwell partially blocked the shot. But the ball whirled around the rim and finally dropped in. The arena burst into tumult and confusion. What everybody wanted to know was, had the basket beaten the clock? Referee Paul Galvan hurried over to the scorer's table. "Score the goal," ordered the official timekeeper.

The Marquette fans among the capacity of 16,086 at the Omni went wild. Butch Lee put an arm around McGuire and hugged him.

"I know Coach Rose has to be heartbroken," McGuire said. "I'd be heartbroken, too."

Lee Rose was philosophical about the defeat.

"I learned a long time ago you don't change an official's judgment," he said. "You don't belabor the point. I admire the man who had to call it."

For a while it appeared that North Carolina, who was in the final four for the fifth time in 11 years, never would make it to the championship game. In its semifinal pairing against Nevada-Las Vegas, Guard Phil Ford, the only official All-American on the four semifinal teams, appeared tired and committed seven turnovers in the first half, and only Mike O'Koren, a 6′ 7″ freshman who scored 31 points on the night, most of them from close in, kept the Tar Heels in the contest. North Carolina made 15 baskets underneath but trailed, 49-43. Coach Dean Smith was dumbfounded by the accuracy of the Vegas shooting. "I didn't think their long jump shots could keep going in," he said later.

Shortly after the second-half tipoff, Vegas moved ahead by 10 points, but then Center Larry Moffett suffered a serious crack on the nose, forcing him to the bench. That seemed to rattle Vegas. Led by O'Koren and Rich Yonakor, the opportunistic Tar Heels scored 14 of the next 16 points to forge ahead. With 4:60 gone in the second half, North Carolina had a two-point lead. From the bench Dean Smith signaled for his team to go into its vaunted four-corner offense. Ford responded with a drive down the middle, and Las Vegas was playing catch-up the rest of the night.

Forward Eddie Owens admitted that Las Vegas was very unorganized at the end. "Whoever got the ball, shot it," he lamented. "We knew if they got a point lead they'd go into that four-corner offense."

North Carolina showed signs of crumbling near the end when Tony Smith's jumpers brought Las Vegas to within two points with a minute to play. Then senior guard John Kuester sank five free throws in a row and Walt Davis picked off a pass under the basket. North Carolina finally won, 84-83, Vegas cutting the lead to one with a basket just as the buzzer went off.

Ford, who was still hurting from a hyperextended elbow and had not practiced much in nine days, finished the game with nine assists, more than half North Carolina's total of 16. O'Koren hit 14 of 19 field goal attempts. Davis hit all seven of his field goals and Yonakor was five for seven from the floor. Top rebounders for the Tar Heels were O'Koren and Yonakor, both freshmen, with eight.

In a game as close as this, the difference came at the free-throw line, where North Carolina made 18 of 28 attempts. Las Vegas made only one of five attempts.

"We caused enough turnovers to win it," said Rebel Coach Jerry Tarkanian. "We just didn't play with patience, but that's not the way we generally play. We took some bad shots."

"It was like a schoolyard game," said O'Koren. "Except they weren't crackin' heads on defense. They'd lunge one way, I'd be gone back door the other."

After slowing down Nevada-Las Vegas, Dean Smith's plan on Monday night was to speed up Marquette. Al McGuire's game plan was much simpler: go for the head. "You've got to cut off the head for the body to die," McGuire said. Translation: decapitate Phil Ford. "Ford's dynamite," McGuire said. "No one will ever know the full value of North Carolina's four-corner offense until Ford leaves. We'll have to shortstop him. We'll have to be very patient." Ford said his elbow felt great. "I thought that after the Las Vegas game I'd wake up the next morning with some pain. But I didn't. It seems to be okay."

The Warriors' style was to play painstaking basketball, calculating each move with computer-like efficiency. It was this tedious, deliberate method that got them to the finals. Dean Smith was cognizant of the Marquette tempo. He said he was very concerned about it. "I don't want to force the tempo," he said. "I'd much rather slow down a team than speed it up. You can't force a team to play. There's no 30-second clock in college basketball. There is, however, the fast break, and we like to do that a lot. As for my four-corner offense, people have misconceptions about it. They think it's a stall. It isn't. It's designed to get easy layups, draw fouls and tire out the other side's defense, as well as run out the clock. Marquette's defense? They're probably the best rebounding team in college ball this season—maybe the best in any season. They also have another edge on us, an emotional one. They're going to be sky-high for Al McGuire's last game."

In my pregame notes of the 1977 NCAA championship game, I have the following: "Al McGuire's final game . . . North Carolina is trying for its second national title . . . Dean Smith believes in substitutions, playing 'em fresh . . . McGuire goes the other way, does not believe in substitutions—go with his best and stay with 'em . . . McGuire, who has hurt his team with technical fouls the past two years, has promised no T fouls in his final game . . . If game is close, North Carolina has tradition going for it: in 1957, the Tar Heels engaged in two triple overtimes on way to NCAA championship . . . In 11 seasons at Marquette, McGuire had one star each year. This year it's Bo Ellis. 'He's my star,' McGuire said . . . Ironically, Jimmy Boylan wanted to go to North Carolina. Dean Smith told him, 'Why don't you call Al McGuire?' Which is how Jimmy wound up at Marquette . . . Dean Smith and Al McGuire are close friends. This is the first time their teams have ever played against each other . . . The total margin of victory in this year's NCAA semifinals (3 points) was the closest in the history of the tournament."

During 1977 National Championship final against North Carolina, Marquette's Coach Al McGuire, in fit of anger, kicked scorer's table with such force he was in pain for the rest of the game.

On the night of Al McGuire's last game as a college coach, he and his Warriors arrived at the Omni only 45 minutes before the tipoff—hardly enough time to get into their work clothes. Only minutes after the ball was put in play, McGuire inexplicably kicked the scorer's table with such force that he hobbled for the rest of the game. Then early in the second half, Mike O'Koren scored the first four baskets for North Carolina to close a 39-27 Marquette lead, provoking a lot of ranting and raving from McGuire on the sideline.

"For God's sake, Al, sit down!" shouted someone in the stands. It was Pat McGuire, the coach's wife. Al sat down. He did not want to blow this one.

With 13:48 left, North Carolina squeezed into the lead, 45-43. The Tar Heels went into their four corners offense. Marquette had been waiting for the tactic. The Warriors sagged underneath to take away the back-door play and, spearheaded by Lee, who scored 19 points and was named the game's outstanding player, were patient on offense. The result was that North Carolina scored only four points over the next 12 minutes. Part of the demise could be blamed on NC's own slowdown tactics. Once the Warriors regained the lead with only six minutes to go, they taunted North Carolina with *their* delay game, and hit on 16 of 17 free throws while the Tar Heels committed turnovers

Coach Al McGuire's Last Hurrah—Marquette's 1977 National Champs. Front row, left: Mgr. Greg Stack, Ulice Payne, Gary Rosenberger, Butch Lee, Jim Boylan, Robert Byrd, and student managers Tom Hayden and David DuChateau. Back row, left: Asst. Coach Rick Majerus, Bill Neary, Jim Dudley, Bernard Toone, Craig Butrym, Jerome Whitehead, Bo Ellis, Asst. Coach Hank Raymonds, Trainer Bob Weingart. Coach Al McGuire is shown in inset.

and failed to take advantage of open shots.

There were less than two minutes to play and the Warriors were on top, 53-49, when O'Koren accidentally punched Bernard Toone in the eye. Thinking it was intentional, Toone gave O'Koren an elbow. A near free-for-all broke out. When calm returned, Toone was given one free throw for O'Koren's foul, which he missed, and was charged with a technical foul—two free throws—which Walter Davis took and made. Now Marquette's lead was cut to 53-51 and there was a jump ball. It was an uneasy moment for the Warriors, but they controlled the tip. The Tar Heels started fouling in pursuit of the ball, and McGuire's ultimate victory was secure.

With 62 seconds left, Marquette's Jim Boylan was fouled and went to the line. He calmly sank both shots. All told, in the final two minutes Marquette hit 14 foul shots, four in a row by Bo Ellis. As Gary Rosenberger sank the final two free throws to make the score 67-59, Al McGuire, ending a 20-year coaching career with his 404th victory, the full realization he'd won his first NCAA championship sweeping over him, began to sob on the bench. When the buzzer sounded, he remained seated. The tears flooded his eyes and he bowed his head. He did not bother to wipe the tears, for, as the poets might put it, they were like slow blood from his soul.

"I'm not afraid to cry," he said.

Later, McGuire regained his composure and talked about his team. "For a team that was going nowhere earlier this season, I honestly don't know what happened to our guys," he said. "Maybe they stopped listening to the coach. While North Carolina seemed to fall apart in the second half, we hung in there. Then they made that spectacular rally and tied us and I called some timeouts trying to stop their momentum. Normally we try to do it with contact-lens timeouts or something like that. You have to stop the momentum, no matter what. Then they went into their four-corner offense and I had to find something else to strangle it. I kept my big men around the basket so they wouldn't be able to score anything easy inside. But outside of my lucky suit, the thing that really got us to the top of the mountain was our subs coming through. Subs win tournaments for you. The subs must always play over their capabilities."

After the game, Jim Garretson, a fan from Jackson, Tennessee, talked about the style of the man. "At one point in the game," Garretson pointed out, "North Carolina's Phil Ford drove for a layup and wound up deep in the seats behind the basket. As Marquette brought the ball up, McGuire rose from the bench and told the referees to halt play until Ford could get back on the floor. I have seen a million games, but never do I recall a coach exhibiting that type of sportsmanship."

Al McGuire indeed went out in style.

Wildcats Untamed: 1978

Joe Hall, the former soup salesman, said it had been a very tough season. He was damn glad the pressure was off him, at last. Everybody had picked Kentucky to win the NCAA championship even before the season began, he said. "From the very first game we had no place to go but down," he said. "We *had* to win the championship. Our fans wouldn't have settled for anything less."

Joe Hall, an unsmiling man, was in his sixth year as head coach at Lexington. He had the misfortune of following a legend, Adolph Rupp, who died during the season. Haunted by The Baron's four national championships, the only way Hall could get the monkey off his back was to lead the Wildcats to their fifth NCAA title.

The year of '78 was never easy for Hall. There was never any time for small talk. He was forced to drive his players mercilessly week after week. Despite the fact that Kentucky was No. 1 in the polls all season except for two weeks, the fun of success had to wait until Monday night, March 27th, in St. Louis, where the Cats fought a gutsy young Duke team for the championship. Even then, UK supporters wouldn't let up on Joe Hall. With the whole season coming down to that one game, some of them paraded a bedsheet in front of the Kentucky bench, with the words: "Win one for Rupp." The Baron would have loved that, but someone in the Kentucky cheer section gaped at the message and snapped, "To hell with Rupp! Win one for Joe Hall!"

The last time the Wildcats won a national basketball title was 1958. Even while winning 102 games in their last four seasons, Hall and his players might have been shot at dawn had they come up short in St. Louis, such was the manic fervor of Kentucky fans. After all, the Wildcats had the highest ranking (No. 1), the best record (28-2) and the most experience of the final four teams. They had won the most demanding regional, defeating three regular-season conference champions. And, historically, Kentucky had won more games and played in more NCAA tournaments (24) than any other.

Looking forever like the Boston Marathon, there were 32 teams at the start of the NCAA playoffs; by Sunday, March 19th, they were down to four. Then it was on to St. Louis and the semi-championship playoffs: Kentucky, Arkansas, Duke, and Notre Dame.

"When you get to the final four, it is all butterflies," Al McGuire said. "This is St. Louis—this is the NCAA semi-final—this is the final four—this is what college basketball is all about. The Mecca of all college coaches is getting here. The four best teams in the nation, playing off in one afternoon."

Some of the best teams were conspicuously missing. UCLA. North Carolina. Defending champion Marquette. New Mexico. San Francisco. Victims of that old nemesis—the upset.

While Kentucky came to St. Louis with all the grimness of a machine on a mission, Duke (the youngest team in NCAA history to get that far—two freshmen, two sophomores, and one senior), Arkansas (the first time a Southwest Conference team had made the semi-round since Southern Methodist in 1956), and Notre Dame (after four consecutive years of losing in the opening round of the regionals, Digger Phelps finally got his alma mater into the final four for the first time) were thrilled just to be part of the show. No one had to remind them that they were the survivors of the closest tournament games in the history of the NCAA playoffs.

"I can't tell you what it means to me just to come to St. Louis and practice," said Duke's Co-Coach of the Year Bill Foster, whose Blue Devils had finished last in the previous four years before vaulting to second and winning the league tournament in 1978. Digger Phelps (his dad was a mortician, hence the nickname) of No. 6 Notre Dame and Eddie Sutton of No. 5 Arkansas felt pretty much the same way. At a Friday night meeting of Coaches and NCAA representatives, Phelps looked over at Sutton and, smiling, said, "Isn't it great to be here?" Sutton grinned. "It sure is," he said. Unfortunately, neither was able to enjoy himself for very long. The following afternoon both the Irish and the Razorbacks got behind and couldn't catch up, despite dramatic comebacks, Notre Dame losing to Duke, 90-86, and Arkansas to Kentucky, 64-59.

For the first 36 minutes, the Blue Devils played as though they had a pact with the devil, leading by as much as 16 points. Near the end of the first half, Al McGuire said that if Duke got a 14-point lead by intermission, it would be all over for Notre Dame. So by outscoring the Irish, 16-4, in the last five minutes, Duke *did* get a 14-point halftime lead, 43-29. As the teams went to their locker rooms to talk over tactics, McGuire said he felt that Digger Phelps stayed with his original game plan too long. "He should have scrapped it when the Irish started dropping far behind," Al said.

With a chance to become the only NCAA school in history to finish No. 1 in both football and basketball the same year, Notre Dame waited until the last four minutes of the contest to make its move. Duke turnovers and sloppy rebounding and accurate outside shooting by Notre Dame cut the lead to two. But it wasn't enough. Duke saved its scalp at the free-throw line. It didn't score any field goals in the last 3:55 minutes, but as the country's leading free-throw shooter (78%), Duke sank 10 straight in a final flourish, 32 of 37 overall, to hold off the Irish rush. At that, Notre Dame had a chance to tie the game in the last 18 seconds, but Duck Williams' 22-footer missed by a fraction, and Duke was in the final.

Digger Phelps was philosophical about the loss. "It was a helluva try," he said of the comeback, "but when you get as far behind as we did you have to play near-perfect basketball to catch up."

You would have thought that Duke won the national championship. The victory over Notre Dame seemed enough for the season. "We're No. 1 for sure next year," an exuberant Gene Banks, only a freshman, said in the shower. He was the game's leading rebounder who also scored 22 points. Captain Jim Spanarkel, who was no slouch himself with 20 points, overheard him. "Listen," he said. "We're not done with this year yet."

Before the St. Louis shootout began, Michigan State Coach Jud Heathcote, whose Spartans lost gallantly to Kentucky, 51-48, in the Mideast regional final, said, "Kentucky has no weaknesses. They go to the boards the way a team is supposed to. They want the ball. I believe they will win the national championship."

Compared to Notre Dame and Duke, teams that loaded the floor with sophomores and freshmen, the second semifinal was a match of senior citizens. Seniors dominated both Kentucky and Arkansas. Between them, they had lost a combined total of five times while winning 59 for the best records over the last two years.

It was quickness (Arkansas) against muscle (Kentucky). Eddie Sutton said that in spite of the scare Michigan State threw into Kentucky with a zone defense, he was not going to use it. "At this point of the season," he said, "I don't think anybody's going to put any tricky plays in or just ditch what has gotten them this far. We're basically a man-to-man team. What's going to be a key is defensive board play. That's going to be our biggest problem against a team as muscular as Kentucky."

Joe Hall said he planned nothing new.

"There are things I feel are effective against Arkansas that we're just not capable of doing," he said. "Quickness has been a problem for us. We usually make a substitution when we need more quickness, but we don't always solve that problem. So we'll go with what we do best regardless of what we think upsets the opponent."

Neither Kentucky nor Arkansas played anywhere near perfection in a ragged game that was marked by too much fouling and poor officiating. The constant whistling hurt the Hogs the most. Steve Schall, 6′ 11″, and Jim Counce, 6′ 7″, the biggest starters on the Arkansas team, both had four fouls apiece by halftime, and Kentucky was in front to stay, 32-30.

In the end, it was Kentucky's bench that turned the tide. Its reserves outscored the Hogs, 19-3. Among the starters on both teams, only Jack Givens played to form, with 23 points and nine rebounds.

Despite Coach Sutton's pregame promise to go with a man-to-man defense, Arkansas spent most of the contest in a zone. Ironically, it was not until the Hogs went back to the stingy man-to-man they played so masterfully that they closed the gap. In the remaining 3:31 minutes they came from nine points behind to only one. That was as close as they got, however. When the game was over, the Wildcats felt more relief than satisfaction.

In the Kentucky locker room, 6′ 11″ center-forward Rick Robey was excited. "One more, one more—just one more to go," he shouted. As freshmen, Robey, Mike Phillips, Jack Givens and Jim Lee were with the Wildcats when they lost to UCLA in the 1975 NCAA championship game, 92-85; as sophomores they won the NIT title in New York; as juniors they got as far as the East Regional final. But the NCAA crown kept eluding them, and, now, the game against Duke was their last chance to win it.

Joe Hall was worried sick. The possibility that his seniors might muff their last opportunity to be national champions haunted him. He was concerned about their attitude. He didn't want them believing all those exaggerations being said about them—that they could win the NCAA title with one arm tied behind their backs. "To hear some people tell it," Joe Hall said, "we could even win the NBA. I had to go into my players' heads and change their thinking so they wouldn't get too cocky."

In the consolation game, Arkansas won a "white knuckler" from Notre Dame, 71-69, as Ron Brewer sank a 25-foot jumper at the buzzer. That gave the Hogs a 32-3 record, the best ever by a team from the Southwestern Conference.

The championship game boiled down to a contest that Duke *wanted* to win and one which Kentucky *had* to win. Whatever, it was

sure to be an old-fashioned street fight, with the side that won the war on the backboards winning the game.

Jack Givens, the most versatile of the Cats, made the difference. He was magnificent, scoring 41 points, his career high and just three points under the championship-game record set by Bill Walton in the same St. Louis arena in 1974. It was as though Duke was matched against five Givenses as Goose seemed to be everywhere at once. One moment he'd be circling around the baseline—then he'd swish one from the corner—then he was at the key—now he was banking another from close in—swishers, dunkers, jumpers, tips, layins and free throws. He swept the boards, fed off, screened, blocked. He was a perpetual man in motion. He scored the last 16 points of the first half as Kentucky stretched a one-point margin to seven.

"Givens beat us in every conceivable way," Bill Foster said after the game. "He made everything he threw up. He just had a fantastic game."

"I took one shot in the second half, it hit the side of the backboard and went in," Givens recalled. "That's the kind of night I was having."

Duke trimmed the lead to one point five times during the last seven minutes of the first half. But Givens responded with two baskets and two free throws in the final 29 seconds to give Kentucky its seven-point bulge at halftime.

Captain Jim Spanarkel and John Harrell hit the first two baskets of the second half to pull the Blue Devils within three points of the Wildcats. But Kyle Macy's conversion of two free throws following a technical foul against the Duke bench sparked a 9-2 surge and Kentucky was suddenly ahead, 60-48, with 14:26 remaining. Duke's last burst came during the final 2:30, when the Blue Devils sliced a 13-point deficit down to four, 92-88, at the expense of Kentucky's reserves. Joe Hall quickly returned his regulars to the court, and Jim Lee made a slam dunk with four seconds left to seal the victory for Kentucky, 94-88.

Givens, voted the tournament's Most Valuable Player, scored 23 of his total points in the opening 20 minutes, and 18 more in the last half. When Kentucky saw how open Duke was leaving the middle, Hall junked his game plan and told his players to get the ball to Goose.

For some unknown reason, Duke did not come out of its zone defense until it was too late. Givens so dominated the contest, making 18 of 27 shots, that Rick Robey, who shot eight for 11 for 20 points and was Kentucky's leading rebounder with 11, was the only other Wildcat to break double figures.

Givens made a big impression on the Blue Devils.

"I've never seen anyone play so well," Captain Spanarkel said after the game. "I guess we played him on a night we shouldn't have played him."

Bill Foster didn't hesitate to label Kentucky "a great team." Duke made it close at the end, he said, but the Blue Devils simply couldn't make it all the way back. "But give us a lot of credit," he told reporters. "We've had a lot of fun and accomplished more than most people thought we could."

Duke once more relied on its big three—Gene Banks, Mike Gminski, and Spanarkel—but they were not enough to offset the play of Givens. Banks, who received two telephoned threats on his life prior to the game, scored 22 points. Spanarkel added 21 and Gminski 20.

With the music of "My Old Kentucky Home" ringing in his ears, Joe B. Hall finally was able to relax now. That damned monkey was off his back. The ghost of Baron Rupp had gone back to sleep.

The last time Abe Lemons was mentioned in this book, he had just become the new basketball coach at Texas and was being introduced to Longhorn alumni as the man who was going to turn their basketball program around. So what happened? So, in 1978, Texas shared the Southwest Conference championship with Arkansas, won its first NIT crown in history—and old Abe, himself, was named Co-Coach of the Year with Bill Foster. "I think we've got a guardian angel," Abe said. "I just hope he doesn't fly away."

If he does, Abe, there's always television. Abe had his own show on local TV and one night it opened with him lying on the floor in a dark suit, his hands folded on his chest, clasping a carnation. An organ was playing funeral music. Then, in slow motion and on cue, Abe rose to a sitting position, turned to the camera and shouted, "We're not dead yet!" It was scenes like that that killed horse opera.

THE RECORDS

Scores of All NCAA Tournament Games

1939 TOURNAMENT

FIRST ROUND
Villanova 42, Brown 30
Ohio State 64, Wake Forest 52
Oklahoma 50, Utah State 39
Oregon 56, Texas 41

CONSOLATION
Utah State 51, Texas 49

SEMIFINALS
Ohio State 53, Villanova 36
Oregon 55, Oklahoma 37

CHAMPIONSHIP
Oregon 46, Ohio State 33

1940 TOURNAMENT

FIRST ROUND
Duquesne 30, Western Kentucky 29
Indiana 48, Springfield 24
Kansas 50, Rice 44
Southern California 38, Colorado 22

CONSOLATION
Rice 60, Colorado 56

SEMIFINALS
Indiana 39, Duquesne 30
Kansas 43, Southern California 42

CHAMPIONSHIP
Indiana 60, Kansas 42

1941 TOURNAMENT

FIRST ROUND
Wisconsin 51, Dartmouth 50
Pittsburgh 26, North Carolina 20
Washington State 48, Creighton 39
Arkansas 52, Wyoming 40

CONSOLATIONS
Dartmouth 60, North Carolina 59
Creighton 45, Wyoming 44

SEMIFINALS
Wisconsin 36, Pittsburgh 30
Washington State 64, Arkansas 53

CHAMPIONSHIP
Wisconsin 39, Washington State 34

1942 TOURNAMENT

FIRST ROUND
Dartmouth 44, Penn State 39
Kentucky 46, Illinois 44
Stanford 53, Rice 47
Colorado 46, Kansas 44

CONSOLATIONS
Penn State 41, Illinois 34
Kansas 55, Rice 53

SEMIFINALS
Dartmouth 47, Kentucky 28
Stanford 46, Colorado 35

CHAMPIONSHIP
Stanford 53, Dartmouth 38

1943 TOURNAMENT

FIRST ROUND
Georgetown 55, New York University 36
DePaul 46, Dartmouth 36
Texas 59, Washington 55
Wyoming 53, Oklahoma 50

CONSOLATIONS
Dartmouth 51, New York University, 49
Oklahoma 48, Washington 43

SEMIFINALS
Georgetown 53, DePaul 49
Wyoming 58, Texas 54

CHAMPIONSHIP
Wyoming 46, Georgetown 34

1944 TOURNAMENT

FIRST ROUND
Dartmouth 63, Catholic 38
Ohio State 57, Temple 47
Iowa State 44, Pepperdine 39
Utah 45, Missouri 35

CONSOLATIONS
Temple 55, Catholic 35
Missouri 61, Pepperdine 46

SEMIFINALS
Dartmouth 60, Ohio State 53
Utah 40, Iowa State 31

CHAMPIONSHIP
Utah 42, Dartmouth 40 (ot)

1945 TOURNAMENT

FIRST ROUND
New York Univ. 59, Tufts 44
Ohio State 45, Kentucky 37
Arkansas 79, Oregon 76
Oklahoma State 62, Utah 37

CONSOLATIONS
Kentucky 66, Tufts 56
Oregon 69, Utah 66

SEMIFINALS
New York Univ. 70, Ohio State 65 (ot)
Oklahoma State 68, Arkansas 41

CHAMPIONSHIP
Oklahoma State 49, New York Univ. 45

1946 TOURNAMENT

FIRST ROUND
Ohio State 46, Harvard 38
North Carolina 57, New York Univ. 49
Oklahoma State 44, Baylor 29
California 50, Colorado 44

CONSOLATIONS
New York Univ. 67, Harvard 61
Colorado 59, Baylor 44

SEMIFINALS
North Carolina 60, Ohio State 57
Oklahoma State 52, California 35

THIRD PLACE
Ohio State 63, California 45

CHAMPIONSHIP
Oklahoma State 43, North Carolina 40

1947 TOURNAMENT

FIRST ROUND
Holy Cross 55, Navy 47
CCNY 70, Wisconsin 56
Texas 42, Wyoming 40
Oklahoma 56, Oregon State 54

CONSOLATIONS
Wisconsin 50, Navy 49
Oregon State 63, Wyoming 46

SEMIFINALS
Holy Cross 60, CCNY 45
Oklahoma 55, Texas 54

THIRD PLACE
Texas 54, CCNY 50

CHAMPIONSHIP
Holy Cross 58, Oklahoma 47

1948 TOURNAMENT

FIRST ROUND
Kentucky 76, Columbia 53
Holy Cross 63, Michigan 45
Kansas State 58, Wyoming 48
Baylor 64, Washington 62

CONSOLATIONS
Michigan 66, Columbia 49
Washington 57, Wyoming 47

SEMIFINALS
Kentucky 60, Holy Cross 52
Baylor 60, Kansas State 52

THIRD PLACE
Holy Cross 60, Kansas State 54

CHAMPIONSHIP
Kentucky 58, Baylor 42

1949 TOURNAMENT

FIRST ROUND
Illinois 71, Yale 67
Kentucky 85, Villanova 72
Oklahoma State 40, Wyoming 39
Oregon State 56, Arkansas 38

CONSOLATIONS
Villanova 78, Yale 67
Arkansas 61, Wyoming 48

SEMIFINALS
Kentucky 76, Illinois 47
Oklahoma State 55, Oregon State 30

THIRD PLACE
Illinois 57, Oregon State 53

CHAMPIONSHIP
Kentucky 46, Oklahoma State 36

1950 TOURNAMENT

FIRST ROUND
CCNY 56, Ohio State 55
North Carolina State 87, Holy Cross 74
Baylor 56, Brigham Young 55
Bradley 73, UCLA 59

CONSOLATIONS
Ohio State 72, Holy Cross 52
Brigham Young 83, UCLA 62

SEMIFINALS
CCNY 78, North Carolina State 73
Bradley 68, Baylor 66

THIRD PLACE
North Carolina State 53, Baylor 41

CHAMPIONSHIP
CCNY 71, Bradley 68

1951 TOURNAMENT

FIRST ROUND
North Carolina State 67, Villanova 62
Illinois 79, Columbia 71
St. John's 63, Connecticut 52
Kentucky 79, Louisville 68
Washington 62, Texas A & M 40
Oklahoma State 50, Montana State 46
Brigham Young 68, San Jose State 61
Kansas State 61, Arizona 59

SECOND ROUND
Illinois 84, North Carolina State 70
Kentucky 59, St. John's 43
Oklahoma State 61, Washington 57
Kansas State 64, Brigham Young 54

CONSOLATIONS
St. John's 71, North Carolina State 59
Washington 80, Brigham Young 44

SEMIFINALS
Kentucky 76, Illinois 74
Kansas State 68, Oklahoma State 44

THIRD PLACE
Illinois 61, Oklahoma State 46

CHAMPIONSHIP
Kentucky 68, Kansas State 58

1952 TOURNAMENT

FIRST ROUND
Kentucky 82, Penn State 54
St. John's 60, North Carolina State 49
Illinois 80, Dayton 61
Duquesne 60, Princeton 49
Kansas 68, Texas Christian 66
St. Louis 62, New Mexico State 53
Santa Clara 68, UCLA 59
Wyoming 54, Oklahoma City 48

CONSOLATIONS
North Carolina State 69, Penn State 60
Dayton 77, Princeton 61
Texas Christian 61, New Mexico State 44
Oklahoma City 55, UCLA 53

REGIONAL CHAMPIONSHIPS
St. John's 64, Kentucky 57
Illinois 74, Duquesne 68
Kansas 74, St. Louis 55
Santa Clara 56, Wyoming 53

SEMIFINALS
St. John's 61, Illinois 59
Kansas 74, Santa Clara 55

THIRD PLACE
Illinois 67, Santa Clara 64

CHAMPIONSHIP
Kansas 80, St. John's 63

1953 TOURNAMENT

FIRST ROUND
Notre Dame 72, Eastern Kentucky 57
DePaul 74, Miami (Ohio) 72
Holy Cross 87, Navy 74
Lebanon Valley 80, Fordham 67
Seattle 88, Idaho State 77
Santa Clara 81, Hardin-Simmons 56

SECOND ROUND
Notre Dame 69, Pennsylvania 57
Indiana 82, DePaul 80
Holy Cross 79, Wake Forest 71
Louisiana State 89, Lebanon Valley 76
Kansas 73, Oklahoma City 65
Oklahoma State 71, Texas Christian 54
Washington 92, Seattle 70
Santa Clara 67, Wyoming 52

CONSOLATIONS
Pennsylvania 90, DePaul 70
Wake Forest 91, Lebanon Valley 71
Texas Christian 58, Oklahoma City 56
Seattle 80, Wyoming 64

REGIONAL CHAMPIONSHIPS
Indiana 79, Notre Dame 66
Louisiana State 81, Holy Cross 73
Kansas 61, Oklahoma State 55
Washington 74, Santa Clara 62

SEMIFINALS
Indiana 80, Louisiana State 67
Kansas 79, Washington 53

THIRD PLACE
Washington 88, Louisiana State 69

CHAMPIONSHIP
Indiana 69, Kansas 68

1954 TOURNAMENT

FIRST ROUND
LaSalle 76, Fordham 74

No. Carolina St. 75, Geo. Washington 73
Navy 85, Connecticut 80
Notre Dame 80, Loyola (La.) 70
Penn State 62, Toledo 50
Bradley 61, Oklahoma City 55
Idaho State 77, Seattle 75
Santa Clara 73, Texas Tech 64

SECOND ROUND
LaSalle 88, North Carolina State 81
Navy 69, Cornell 67
Penn State 78, Louisiana State 70
Notre Dame 65, Indiana 64
Bradley 76, Colorado 64
Oklahoma State 51, Rice 45
Southern California 73, Idaho State 59
Santa Clara 73, Colorado State 50

CONSOLATIONS
North Carolina State 65, Cornell 54
Indiana 73, Louisiana State 62
Rice 78, Colorado 55
Idaho State 62, Colorado State 57

REGIONAL CHAMPIONSHIPS
LaSalle 64, Navy 48
Penn State 71, Notre Dame 63
Bradley 71, Oklahoma State 57
Southern California 66, Santa Clara 65

SEMIFINALS
LaSalle 69, Penn State 54
Bradley 74, Southern California 72

THIRD PLACE
Penn State 70, Southern California 61

CHAMPIONSHIP
LaSalle 92, Bradley 76

1955 TOURNAMENT

FIRST ROUND
Marquette 90, Miami (Ohio) 79
Penn State 59, Memphis State 55
LaSalle 95, West Virginia 61
Villanova 74, Duke 73
Canisius 73, Williams 60
Bradley 69, Oklahoma City 65
Seattle 80, Idaho State 63
San Francisco 89, West Texas State 66

SECOND ROUND
Marquette 79, Kentucky 71
Iowa 82, Penn State 53
LaSalle 73, Princeton 46

Canisius 73, Villanova 71
Bradley 81, Southern Methodist 79
Colorado 69, Tulsa 59
Oregon State 83, Seattle 71
San Francisco 78, Utah 59

CONSOLATIONS
Villanova 65, Princeton 57
Kentucky 84, Penn State 59
Tulsa 68, Southern Methodist 56
Utah 108, Seattle 85

REGIONAL CHAMPIONSHIPS
LaSalle 99, Canisius 64
Iowa 86, Marquette 81
Colorado 93, Bradley 81
San Francisco 57, Oregon State 56

SEMIFINALS
LaSalle 76, Iowa 73
San Francisco 62, Colorado 50

THIRD PLACE
Colorado 75, Iowa 54

CHAMPIONSHIP
San Francisco 77, LaSalle 63

1956 TOURNAMENT

FIRST ROUND
Connecticut 84, Manhattan 75
Temple 74, Holy Cross 72
Dartmouth 61, West Virginia 59
Canisius 79, North Carolina State 78 (4 ot)
Wayne State 72, DePaul 63
Morehead State 107, Marshall 92
Seattle 68, Idaho State 66
Southern Methodist 68, Texas Tech 67
Oklahoma City 97, Memphis State 81

SECOND ROUND
Iowa 97, Morehead State 83
Temple 65, Connecticut 59
Kentucky 84, Wayne State 64
Canisius 66, Dartmouth 58
San Francisco 72, UCLA 61
Utah 81, Seattle 72
Southern Methodist 89, Houston 74
Oklahoma City 97, Kansas State 93

CONSOLATIONS
Morehead State 95, Wayne State 84
Dartmouth 85, Connecticut 64
UCLA 94, Seattle 70
Kansas State 89, Houston 70

REGIONAL CHAMPIONSHIPS
Temple 60, Canisius 58
Iowa 89, Kentucky 77
San Francisco 92, Utah 77
Southern Methodist 84, Oklahoma City 63

SEMIFINALS
Iowa 83, Temple 76
San Francisco 86, Southern Methodist 68

THIRD PLACE
Temple 90, Southern Methodist 81

CHAMPIONSHIP
San Francisco 83, Iowa 71

1957 TOURNAMENT

FIRST ROUND
Syracuse 82, Connecticut 76
Canisius 64, West Virginia 56
North Carolina 90, Yale 74
Pittsburgh 86, Morehead State 85
Notre Dame 89, Loyola (La.) 55
Oklahoma City 76, Miami (Ohio) 77
Idaho State 68, Hardin-Simmons 57

SECOND ROUND
Syracuse 75, Lafayette 71
North Carolina 87, Canisius 75
Kentucky 98, Pittsburgh 92
Michigan State 85, Notre Dame 83
Kansas 73, Southern Methodist 65 (ot)
Oklahoma City 75, St. Louis 66
San Francisco 66, Idaho State 51
California 86, Brigham Young 59

CONSOLATIONS
Canisius 82, Lafayette 76
Notre Dame 86, Pittsburgh 85
Southern Methodist 78, St. Louis 68
Brigham Young 65, Idaho State 54

REGIONAL CHAMPIONSHIPS
North Carolina 67, Syracuse 58
Michigan State 80, Kentucky 68
Kansas 81, Oaklahoma City 61
San Francisco 50, California 46

SEMIFINALS
North Carolina 74, Michigan State 70 (3 ot)
Kansas 80, San Francisco 56

THIRD PLACE
San Francisco 67, Michigan State 60

CHAMPIONSHIP
North Carolina 54, Kansas 53 (3 ot)

1958 TOURNAMENT

FIRST ROUND
Dartmouth 75, Connecticut 64
Manhattan 89, West Virginia 84
Maryland 86, Boston College 63
Miami (Ohio) 82, Pittsburgh 77
Notre Dame 94, Tennessee Tech 61
Oklahoma State 59, Loyola (La.) 42
Idaho State 72, Arizona State 68
Seattle 88, Wyoming 51

SECOND ROUND
Dartmouth 79, Manhattan 62
Temple 71, Maryland 67
Notre Dame 94, Indiana 87
Kentucky 94, Miami (Ohio) 70
Oklahoma State 64, Arkansas 40
Kansas State 83, Cincinnati 80 (ot)
California 54, Idaho State 43
Seattle 69, San Francisco 67

CONSOLATIONS
Maryland 59, Manhattan 55
Indiana 98, Miami (Ohio) 91
Cincinnati 97, Arkansas 62
San Francisco 57, Idaho State 51

REGIONAL CHAMPIONSHIPS
Temple 69, Dartmouth 50
Kentucky 89, Notre Dame 56
Kansas State 69, Oklahoma State 57
Seattle 66, California 62

SEMIFINALS
Kentucky 61, Temple 60
Seattle 72, Kansas State 51

THIRD PLACE
Temple 67, Kansas State 57

CHAMPIONSHIP
Kentucky 84, Seattle 72

1959 TOURNAMENT

FIRST ROUND
West Virginia 82, Dartmouth 68
Boston University 60, Connecticut 58
Navy 76, North Carolina 63
Louisville 77, Eastern Kentucky 63
Marquette 89, Bowling Green 71

DePaul 57, Portland 56
Idaho State 62, New Mexico State 61

SECOND ROUND
West Virginia 95, St. Joseph's 92
Boston University 62, Navy 55
Louisville 76, Kentucky 61
Michigan State 74, Marquette 69
Kansas State 102, DePaul 70
Cincinnati 77, Texas Christian 73
St. Mary's 80, Idaho State 71
California 71, Utah 53

CONSOLATIONS
Kentucky 98, Marquette 69
Navy 70, St. Joseph's 56
Texas Christian 71, DePaul 65
Idaho State 71, Utah 65

REGIONAL CHAMPIONSHIPS
West Virginia 86, Boston University 82
Louisville 88, Michigan State 81
Cincinnati 85, Kansas State 75
California 66, St. Mary's 46

SEMIFINALS
West Virginia 94, Louisville 79
California 64, Cincinnati 58

THIRD PLACE
Cincinnati 98, Louisville 85

CHAMPIONSHIP
California 71, West Virginia 70

1960 TOURNAMENT

FIRST ROUND
Duke 85, Princeton 60
West Virginia 94, Navy 86
New York University 78, Connecticut 59
Ohio 74, Notre Dame 66
Western Kentucky 107, Miama (Fla.) 84
California 71, Idaho State 44
Oregon 68, New Mexico State 60
Utah 80, Southern California 73
DePaul 69, Air Force 63

SECOND ROUND
Duke 58, St. Joseph's 56
New York University 82, West Virginia 81
Georgia Tech 57, Ohio 54
Ohio State 98, Western Kentucky 79
Kansas 90, Texas 81
Cincinnati 99, DePaul 59

California 69, Santa Clara 49
Oregon 65, Utah 54

CONSOLATIONS
West Virginia 106, St. Joseph's 100
Western Kentucky 97, Ohio 87
Utah 89, Santa Clara 81
DePaul 67, Texas 61

REGIONAL CHAMPIONSHIPS
New York University 74, Duke 59
Ohio State 86, Georgia Tech 69
Cincinnati 82, Kansas 71
California 70, Oregon 49

SEMIFINALS
Ohio State 76, New York University 54
California 77, Cincinnati 69

THIRD PLACE
Cincinnati 95, New York University 71

CHAMPIONSHIP
Ohio State 75, California 55

1961 TOURNAMENT

FIRST ROUND
Princeton 84, George Washington 67
St. Bonaventure 86, Rhode Island 76
Wake Forest 97, St. John's 74
Louisville 76, Ohio 70
Morehead State 71, Xavier 66
Houston 77, Marquette 61
Arizona State 72, Seattle 70
Southern California 81, Oregon 79

SECOND ROUND
°St. Joseph's 72, Princeton 67
Wake Forest 78, St. Bonaventure 73
Ohio State 56, Louisville 55
Kentucky 71, Morehead State 64
Cincinnati 78, Texas Tech 55
Kansas State 75, Houston 64
Utah 91, Loyola (Calif.) 75
Arizona State 86, Southern Califronia 71

CONSOLATIONS
St. Bonaventure 85, Princeton 67
Louisville 83, Morehead State 61
Loyola (Calif.) 69, Southern Calif. 67
Texas Tech. 69, Houston 67

° St. Joseph's participation in 1961 tournament voided.

REGIONAL CHAMPIONSHIPS
°St. Joseph 96, Wake Forest 86
Ohio State 87, Kentucky 74
Cincinnati 69, Kansas State 64
Utah 88, Arizona State 80

SEMIFINALS
Ohio State 95, °St. Joseph's 69
Cincinnati 82, Utah 67

THIRD PLACE
°St. Joseph's 127, Utah 120 (4 ot)

CHAMPIONSHIP
Cincinnati 70, Ohio State 65 (ot)

1962 TOURNAMENT

FIRST ROUND
Wake Forest 92, Yale 82
New York University 70, Massachusetts 50
Villanova 90, West Virginia 75
Butler 56, Bowling Green 55
Western Kentucky 90, Detroit 81
Texas Tech 68, Air Force 66
Creighton 87, Memphis State 83
Oregon State 69, Seattle 65
Utah State 78, Arizona State 73

SECOND ROUND
Wake Forest 96, St. Joseph's 85
Villanova 79, New York University 76
Kentucky 81, Butler 60
Ohio State 93, Western Kentucky 73
Colorado 67, Texas Tech 60
Cincinnati 66, Creighton 46
Oregon State 69, Pepperdine 67
UCLA 73, Utah State 62

CONSOLATIONS
New York University 94, St. Joseph's 85
Butler 87, Western Kentucky 86
Creighton 63, Texas Tech 61
Pepperdine 75, Utah State 71

REGIONAL CHAMPIONSHIPS
Wake Forest 79, Villanova 69
Ohio State 74, Kentucky 64
Cincinnati 73, Colorado 46
UCLA 88, Oregon State 69

SEMIFINALS
Ohio State 84, Wake Forest 68
Cincinnati 72, UCLA 70

THIRD PLACE
  Wake Forest 82, UCLA 80

CHAMPIONSHIP
  Cincinnati 71, Ohio State 59

1963 TOURNAMENT

FIRST ROUND
  New York University 93, Pittsburgh 83
  West Virginia 77, Connecticut 71
  St. Joseph's 82, Princeton 81
  Bowling Green 77, Notre Dame 72
  Loyola (Ill.) 111, Tennessee Tech 42
  Oklahoma City 70, Colorado State 67
  Texas 65, Texas El Paso 47
  Arizona State 79, Utah State 75
  Oregon State 70, Seattle 66

SECOND ROUND
  Duke 81, New York University 76
  St. Joseph's 97, West Virginia 88
  Illinois 70, Bowling Green 67
  Loyola (Ill.) 61, Mississippi State 51
  Colorado 78, Oklahoma City 72
  Cincinnati 73, Texas 68
  Arizona State 93, UCLA 79
  Oregon State 65, San Francisco 61

CONSOLATIONS
  Mississippi State 65, Bowling Green 60
  West Virginia 83, New York University 73
  Texas 90, Oklahoma City 83
  San Francisco 76, UCLA 75

REGIONAL CHAMPIONSHIPS
  Duke 73, St. Joseph's 59
  Loyola (Ill.) 79, Illinois 64
  Cincinnati 67, Colorado 60
  Oregon State 83, Arizona State 65

SEMIFINALS
  Loyola (Ill.) 94, Duke 75
  Cincinnati 80, Oregon State 46

THIRD PLACE
  Duke 85, Oregon State 63

CHAMPIONSHIP
  Loyola (Ill.) 60, Cincinnati 58 (ot)

1964 TOURNAMENT

FIRST ROUND
  Villanova 77, Providence 66
  Connecticut 53, Temple 48

  Princeton 86, Virginia Military 60
  Ohio 71, Louisville 69
  Loyola (Ill.) 101, Murray State 91
  Creighton 89, Oklahoma City 78
  Texas El Paso 68, Texas A & M 62
  Seattle 61, Oregon State 57
  Utah State 92, Arizona State 90

SECOND ROUND
  Duke 87, Villanova 73
  Connecticut 52, Princeton 50
  Ohio 85, Kentucky 69
  Michigan 84, Loyola (Ill.) 80
  Wichita State 84, Creighton 68
  Kansas State 64, Texas El Paso 60
  UCLA 95, Seattle 90
  San Francisco 64, Utah State 58

CONSOLATIONS
  Villanova 74, Princeton 73
  Loyola (Ill.) 100, Kentucky 91
  Texas El Paso 63, Creighton 52
  Seattle 88, Utah State 78

REGIONAL CHAMPIONSHIPS
  Duke 101, Connecticut 54
  Michigan 69, Ohio 57
  Kansas State 94, Wichita State 86
  UCLA 76, San Francisco 72

SEMIFINALS
  Duke 91, Michigan 80
  UCLA 90, Kansas State 84

THIRD PLACE
  Michigan 100, Kansas State 90

CHAMPIONSHIP
  UCLA 98, Duke 83

1965 TOURNAMENT

FIRST ROUND
  Princeton 60, Penn State 58
  St. Joseph's 67, Connecticut 61
  Providence 91, West Virginia 67
  DePaul 99, Eastern Kentucky 52
  Dayton 66, Ohio 65
  Houston 99, Notre Dame 98
  Oklahoma City 70, Colorado State 68

SECOND ROUND
  Princeton 66, North Carolina State 48
  Providence 81, St. Joseph's 73 (ot)
  Vanderbilt 83, DePaul 78 (ot)

Michigan 98, Dayton 71
Wichita State 86, Southern Methodist 81
Oklahoma State 75, Houston 60
UCLA 100, Brigham Young 76
San Francisco 91, Oklahoma City 67

CONSOLATIONS
North Carolina State 103, St. Joseph's 81
Dayton 74, DePaul 69
Southern Methodist 89, Houston 87
Oklahoma City 112, Brigham Young 102

REGIONAL CHAMPIONSHIPS
Princeton 109, Providence 69
Michigan 87, Vanderbilt 85
Wichita State 54, Oklahoma State 46
UCLA 101, San Francisco 93

SEMIFINALS
Michigan 93, Princeton 76
UCLA 108, Wichita State 89

THIRD PLACE
Princeton 118, Wichita State 82

CHAMPIONSHIP
UCLA 91, Michigan 80

1966 TOURNAMENT

FIRST ROUND
St. Joseph's 65, Providence 48
Davidson 95, Rhode Island 65
Dayton 58, Miami (Ohio) 51
Western Kentucky 105, Loyola (Ill.) 86
Texas El Paso 89, Oklahoma City 74
Houston 82, Colorado State 76

SECOND ROUND
Duke 76, St. Joseph's 74
Syracuse 94, Davidson 78
Kentucky 86, Dayton 79
Michigan 80, Western Kentucky 79
Texas El Paso 78, Cincinnati 76 (ot)
Kansas 76, Southern Methodist 70
Oregon State 63, Houston 60
Utah 83, Pacific 74

CONSOLATIONS
St. Joseph's 92, Davidson 76
Western Kentucky 82, Dayton 62
Southern Methodist 89, Cincinnati 84
Houston 102, Pacific 91

REGIONAL CHAMPIONSHIPS
Duke 91, Syracuse 81
Kentucky 84, Michigan 77

Texas El Paso 81, Kansas 80 (2 ot)
Utah 70, Oregon State 64

SEMIFINALS
Kentucky 83, Duke 79
Texas El Paso 85, Utah 78

THIRD PLACE
Duke 79, Utah 77

CHAMPIONSHIP
Texas El Paso 72, Kentucky 65

1967 TOURNAMENT

FIRST ROUND
Princeton 68, West Virginia 57
St. John's 57, Temple 53
Boston College 48, Connecticut 42
Dayton 69, Western Kentucky 67 (ot)
Virginia Tech 82, Toledo 76
Houston 59, New Mexico State 58
Texas El Paso 62, Seattle 54

SECOND ROUND
North Carolina 78, Princeton 70 (ot)
Boston College 63, St. John's 62
Dayton 53, Tennessee 52
Virginia Tech 79, Indiana 70
Houston 66, Kansas 53
Southern Methodist 83, Louisville 81
Pacific 72, Texas El Paso 63
UCLA 109, Wyoming 60

CONSOLATIONS
Princeton 78, St. John's 58
Indiana 51, Tennessee 44
Kansas 70, Louisville 68
Texas El Paso 69, Wyoming 67

REGIONAL CHAMPIONSHIPS
North Carolina 96, Boston College 80
Dayton 71, Virginia Tech 66 (ot)
Houston 83, Southern Methodist 75
UCLA 80, Pacific 64

SEMIFINALS
Dayton 76, North Carolina 62
UCLA 73, Houston 58

THIRD PLACE
Houston 84, North Carolina 62

CHAMPIONSHIP
UCLA 79, Dayton 64

1968 TOURNAMENT

FIRST ROUND
St. Bonaventure 102, Boston College 93
Columbia 83, LaSalle 69
Davidson 69, St. John's 70
Marquette 72, Bowling Green 71
East Tennessee 79, Florida State 69
Houston 94, Loyola (Ill.) 76
New Mexico State 68, Weber State 57

SECOND ROUND
North Carolina 91, St. Bonaventure 72
Davidson 61, Columbia 59 (ot)
Kentucky 107, Marquette 89
Ohio State 79, East Tennessee 72
Houston 91, Louisville 75
Texas Christian 77, Kansas State 72
UCLA 58, New Mexico State 49
Santa Clara 86, New Mexico 73

CONSOLATIONS
Columbia 95, St. Bonaventure 75
Marquette 69, East Tennessee 57
Louisville 93, Kansas State 63
New Mexico State 62, New Mexico 58

REGIONAL CHAMPIONSHIPS
North Carolina 70, Davidson 66
Ohio State 82, Kentucky 81
Houston 103, Texas Christian 68
UCLA 87, Santa Clara 66

SEMIFINALS
North Carolina 80, Ohio State 66
UCLA 101, Houston 69

THIRD PLACE
Ohio State 89, Houston 85

CHAMPIONSHIP
UCLA 78, North Carolina 55

1969 TOURNAMENT

FIRST ROUND
Duquesne 74, St. Joseph's 52
Davidson 75, Villanova 71
St. John's 72, Princeton 63
Marquette 82, Murray State 62
Miami (Ohio) 63, Notre Dame 60
Texas A & M 81, Trinity (Tex.) 66
Colorado State 52, Dayton 50
New Mexico State 74, Brigham Young 62
Weber State 75, Seattle 73

SECOND ROUND
North Carolina 79, Duquesne 78
Davidson 79, St. John's 69
Marquette 81, Kentucky 74
Purdue 91, Miami (Ohio) 71
Drake 81, Texas A & M 63
Colorado State 64, Colorado 56
UCLA 53, New Mexico State 38
Santa Clara 63, Weber State 59

CONSOLATIONS
Duquesne 75, St. John's 72
Kentucky 72, Miami (Ohio) 71
Colorado 97, Texas A & M 82
Weber State 58, New Mexico State 56

REGIONAL CHAMPIONSHIPS
North Carolina 87, Davidson 85
Purdue 75, Marquette 73 (ot)
Drake 84, Colorado State 77
UCLA 90, Santa Clara 52

SEMIFINALS
Purdue 92, North Carolina 65
UCLA 85, Drake 82

THIRD PLACE
Drake 104, North Carolina 84

CHAMPIONSHIP
UCLA 92, Purdue 72

1970 TOURNAMENT

FIRST ROUND
St. Bonaventure 85, Davidson 72
Niagara 79, Pennsylvania 69
Villanova 77, Temple 69
Notre Dame 112, Ohio 82
Jacksonville 109, Western Kentucky 96
Houston 71, Dayton 64
New Mexico State 101, Rice 77
Long Beach State 92, Weber State 73
Utah State 91, Texas El Paso 81

SECOND ROUND
St. Bonaventure 80, North Carolina State 68
Villanova 98, Niagara 73
Kentucky 109, Notre Dame 99
Jacksonville 104, Iowa 103
Drake 92, Houston 87
New Mexico State 70, Kansas State 66
UCLA 88, Long Beach State 65
Utah State 69, Santa Clara 68

CONSOLATIONS

North Carolina State 108, Niagara 88
Iowa 121, Notre Dame 106
Kansas State 107, Houston 98
Santa Clara 89, Long Beach State 86

REGIONAL CHAMPIONSHIPS

St. Bonaventure 97, Villanova 74
Jacksonville 106, Kentucky 100
New Mexico State 87, Drake 78
UCLA 101, Utah State 79

SEMIFINALS

Jacksonville 91, St. Bonaventure 83
UCLA 93, New Mexico State 77

THIRD PLACE

New Mexico State 75, St. Bonaventure 73

CHAMPIONSHIP

UCLA 80, Jacksonville 69

1971 TOURNAMENT

FIRST ROUND

Pennsylvania 70, Duquesne 65
°Villanova 93, St. Joseph's 75
Fordham 105, Furman 74
°Western Kentucky 74, Jacksonville 72
Marquette 62, Miami (Ohio) 47
Notre Dame 102, Texas Christian 94
Houston 72, New Mexico State 69
Brigham Young 91, Utah State 82
Long Beach State 77, Weber State 66

SECOND ROUND

Pennsylvania 79, South Carolina 64
°Villanova 85, Fordham 75
°Western Kentucky 107, Kentucky 83
Ohio State 60, Marquette 59
Drake 79, Notre Dame 72 (ot)
Kansas 78, Houston 77
UCLA 91, Brigham Young 73
Long Beach State 78, Pacific 65

CONSOLATIONS

Fordham 100, South Carolina 90
Marquette 91, Kentucky 74
Houston 119, Notre Dame 106
Pacific 84, Brigham Young 81

REGIONAL CHAMPIONSHIPS

°Villanova 90, Pennsylvania 47

°Villanova's and Western Kentucky's participation in 1971 tournament voided.

°Western Kentucky 81, Ohio State 78 (ot)
Kansas 73, Drake 71
UCLA 57, Long Beach State 55

SEMIFINALS

°Villanova 92, °Western Kentucky 89 (2 ot)
UCLA 68, Kansas 60

THIRD PLACE

°Western Kentucky 77, Kansas 75

CHAMPIONSHIP

UCLA 68, °Villanova 62

1972 TOURNAMENT

FIRST ROUND

South Carolina 53, Temple 51
Villanova 85, East Carolina 70
Pennsylvania 76, Providence 60
Marquette 73, Ohio 49
Florida State 83, Eastern Kentucky 81
°SW Louisiana 112, Marshall 101
Texas 85, Houston 74
Weber State 91, Hawaii 64
Long Beach St. 95, Brigham Young 90 (ot)

SECOND ROUND

North Carolina 92, South Carolina 69
Pennsylvania 78, Villanova 67
Kentucky 85, Marquette 69
Florida State 70, Minnesota 56
Louisville 88, °SW Louisiana 84
Kansas State 66, Texas 55
UCLA 90, Weber State 58
Long Beach St. 75, San Francisco 55

CONSOLATIONS

South Carolina 90, Villanova 78
Minnesota 77, Marquette 72
°SW Louisiana 100, Texas 70
San Francisco 74, Weber State 64

REGIONAL CHAMPIONSHIPS

North Carolina 73, Pennsylvania 59
Florida State 73, Kentucky 54
Louisville 72, Kansas State 65
UCLA 73, Long Beach State 57

SEMIFINALS

Florida State 79, North Carolina 75
UCLA 96, Louisville 77

°SW Louisiana's participation in 1972 tournament voided.

THIRD PLACE
North Carolina 105, Louisville 91

CHAMPIONSHIP
UCLA 81, Florida State 76

1973 TOURNAMENT

FIRST ROUND
Syracuse 83, Furman 82
Pennsylvania 62, St. John's 61
Providence 89, St. Joseph's (Pa.) 76
South Carolina 78, Texas Tech 70
°SW Louisiana 102, Houston 89
Marquette 77, Miami (Ohio) 62
Austin Peay 77, Jacksonville 75
Long Beach St. 88, Weber St. 75
Arizona State 103, Oklahoma City 78

SECOND ROUND
Maryland 91, Syracuse 75
Providence 87, Pennsylvania 65
Memphis State 90, South Carolina 76
Kansas State 66, °SW Louisiana 63
Indiana 75, Marquette 69
Kentucky 106, Austin Peay 100 (ot)
San Francisco 77, Long Beach St. 67
UCLA 98, Arizona State 81

CONSOLATIONS
Syracuse 69, Pennsylvania 68
South Carolina 90, °SW Louisiana 85
Marquette 88, Austin Peay 73
Long Beach St. 84, Arizona 80

REGIONAL CHAMPIONSHIPS
Providence 103, Maryland 89
Memphis State 92, Kansas State 72
Indiana 72, Kentucky 65
UCLA 54, San Francisco 39

SEMIFINALS
Memphis State 98, Providence 85
UCLA 70, Indiana 59

THIRD PLACE
Indiana 97, Providence 79

CHAMPIONSHIP
UCLA 88, Memphis State 67

°SW Louisiana's participation in 1973 tournament voided.

1974 TOURNAMENT

FIRST ROUND
Providence 84, Pennsylvania 69
Pittsburgh 54, St. Joseph's (Pa.) 42
Furman 75, South Carolina 67
New Mexico 73, Idaho State 65
Dayton 88, Los Angeles State 80
Notre Dame 108, Austin Peay 66
Marquette 85, Ohio 59
Oral Roberts 86, Syracuse 82 (ot)
Creighton 77, Texas 61

SECOND ROUND
North Carolina State 92, Providence 78
Pittsburgh 81, Furman 78
San Francisco 64, New Mexico 61
UCLA 111, Dayton 100 (3 ot)
Michigan 77, Notre Dame 68
Marquette 69, Vanderbilt 61
Oral Roberts 96, Louisville 93
Kansas 55, Creighton 54

CONSOLATIONS
Providence 95, Furman 83
New Mexico 66, Dayton 61
Notre Dame 118, Vanderbilt 88
Creighton 80, Louisville 71

REGIONAL CHAMPIONSHIPS
North Carolina State 100, Pittsburgh 72
UCLA 83, San Francisco 60
Marquette 72, Michigan 70
Kansas 93, Oral Roberts 90 (ot)

SEMIFINALS
North Carolina State 80, UCLA 77 (2 ot)
Marquette 64, Kansas 51

THIRD PLACE
UCLA 78, Kansas 61

CHAMPIONSHIP
North Carolina State 76, Marquette 64

1975 TOURNAMENT

FIRST ROUND
Syracuse 87, LaSalle 83 (ot)
North Carolina 93, New Mexico State 69
Boston College 82, Furman 76
Kansas State 69, Pennsylvania 62
Central Michigan 77, Georgetown 75
Kentucky 76, Marquette 54
Indiana 78, Texas El Paso 53

Oregon State 78, Middle Tennessee 67
Cincinnati 87, Texas A & M 79
Louisville 91, Rutgers 78
Maryland 83, Creighton 79
Notre Dame 77, Kansas 71
Arizona State 97, Alabama 94
Nevada Las Vegas 90, San Diego State 80
UCLA 103, Michigan 91 (ot)
Montana 69, Utah State 63

SECOND ROUND
Syracuse 78, North Carolina 76
Kansas State 74, Boston College 65
Kentucky 90, Central Michigan 73
Indiana 81, Oregon State 71
Louisville 78, Cincinnati 63
Maryland 83, Notre Dame 71
Arizona State 84, Nevada Las Vegas 81
UCLA 67, Montana 64

REGIONAL CONSOLATIONS
North Carolina 110, Boston College 90
Central Michigan 88, Oregon State 87
Cincinnati 95, Notre Dame 87 (ot)
Nevada Las Vegas 75, Montana 67

REGIONAL CHAMPIONSHIPS
Syracuse 95, Kansas State 87 (ot)
Kentucky 92, Indiana 90
Louisville 96, Maryland 82
UCLA 89, Arizona State 75

SEMIFINALS
Kentucky 95, Syracuse 79
UCLA 75, Louisville 74 (ot)

THIRD PLACE
Louisville 96, Syracuse 88

CHAMPIONSHIP
UCLA 92, Kentucky 85

1976 CHAMPIONSHIP

FIRST ROUND
DePaul 69, Virginia 60
Virginia Military 81, Tennessee 75
Rutgers 54, Princeton 53
Connecticut 80, Hofstra 78 (ot)
Michigan 74, Wichita State 73
Notre Dame 79, Cincinnati 78
Missouri 69, Washington 67
Texas Tech 69, Syracuse 56
Alabama 79, North Carolina 64
Indiana 90, St. John's (N.Y.) 70

Marquette 79, Western Kentucky 60
Western Michigan 77, Virginia Tech 67 (ot)
Pepperdine 87, Memphis State 77
UCLA 74, San Diego State 64
Arizona 83, Georgetown 76
Nevada Las Vegas 103, Boise State 78

SECOND ROUND
Virginia Military 71, DePaul 66
Rutgers 93, Connecticut 79
Missouri 86, Texas Tech 75
Michigan 80, Notre Dame 76
Indiana 74, Alabama 69
Marquette 62, Western Michigan 57
UCLA 70, Pepperdine 61
Arizona 114, Nevada Las Vegas 109 (ot)

REGIONAL CHAMPIONSHIPS
Rutgers 91, Virginia Military 75
Michigan 95, Missouri 88
Indiana 65, Marquette 56
UCLA 82, Arizona 66

SEMIFINALS
Michigan 86, Rutgers 70
Indiana 65, UCLA 51

THIRD PLACE
UCLA 106, Rutgers 92

CHAMPIONSHIP
Indiana 86, Michigan 68

1977 CHAMPIONSHIP

FIRST ROUND
Virginia Military 73, Duquesne 66
Kentucky 72, Princeton 58
Notre Dame 90, Hofstra 83
North Carolina 69, Purdue 66
UCLA 87, Louisville 79
Idaho State 83, Long Beach State 72
Utah 72, St. John's (N.Y.) 68
Nevada Las Vegas 121, San Francisco 95
Michigan 92, Holy Cross 81
Detroit 93, Middle Tennessee State 76
N. Caro. Charlotte 91, Cent. Mich. 86 (ot)
Syracuse 93, Tennessee 88 (ot)
Marquette 66, Cincinnati 51
Kansas State 87, Providence 80
Wake Forest 86, Arkansas 80
SIU Carbondale 81, Arizona 77

SECOND ROUND
Kentucky 93, Virginia Military 78

North Carolina 79, Notre Dame 77
Idaho State 76, UCLA 75
Nevada Las Vegas 88, Utah 83
Michigan 86, Detroit 81
N. Carolina Charlotte 81, Syracuse 59
Marquette 67, Kansas State 66
Wake Forest 86, SIU Carbondale 81

REGIONAL CHAMPIONSHIPS
North Carolina 79, Kentucky 72
Nevada Las Vegas 107, Idaho State 90
N. Carolina Charlotte 75, Michigan 68
Marquette 82, Wake Forest 68

SEMIFINALS
Marquette 51, N. Carolina Charlotte 49
North Carolina 84, Nevada Las Vegas 8

THIRD PLACE
Nev. Las Vegas 106, N. Caro. Charlotte

CHAMPIONSHIP
Marquette 67, North Carolina 59

1978 CHAMPIONSHIP

FIRST ROUND
Michigan State 77, Providence 63
Western Kentucky 87, Syracuse 86 (ot)
Miami (Ohio) 84, Marquette 81 (ot)
Kentucky 85, Florida State 76
UCLA 83, Kansas 76
Arkansas 73, Weber State 52
San Francisco 68, North Carolina 64

Fullerton State 90, New Mexico 85
Duke 63, Rhode Island 62
Pennsylvania 92, St. Bonaventure 83
Indiana 63, Furman 62
Villanova 103, LaSalle 97
Utah 86, Missouri 79 (2 ot)
Notre Dame 100, Houston 77
DePaul 80, Creighton 78
Louisville 76, St. John's 68

SECOND ROUND
Michigan State 90, Western Kentucky 69
Kentucky 91, Miami (Ohio) 69
Arkansas 74, UCLA 70
Fullerton State 75, San Francisco 72
Duke 84, Pennsylvania 80
Villanova 61, Indiana 60
Notre Dame 69, Utah 56
DePaul 90. Louisville 89 (2 ot)

REGIONAL CHAMPIONSHIPS
Kentucky 52, Michigan State 49
Arkansas 61, Fullerton State 58
Duke 90, Villanova 72
Notre Dame 84, DePaul 64

SEMIFINALS
Kentucky 64, Arkansas 59
Duke 90, Notre Dame 86

THIRD PLACE
Arkansas 71, Notre Dame 69

CHAMPIONSHIP
Kentucky 94, Duke 88

NCAA Tournament Sites, Coaches, and Outstanding Players

	NCAA SITE OF FINALS	COACHES OF TEAM CHAMPIONS	OUTSTANDING PLAYER AWARD
1939	Evanston, Ill.	Howard Hobson, Oregon	None Selected
1940	Kansas City, Mo.	Branch McCracken, Indiana	Marvin Huffman, Indiana
1941	Kansas City, Mo.	Harold Foster, Wisconsin	John Kotz, Wisconsin
1942	Kansas City, Mo.	Everett Dean, Stanford	Howard Dallmar, Stanford
1943	New York City	Everett Shelton, Wyoming	Ken Sailors, Wyoming
1944	New York City	Vadal Peterson, Utah	Arnold Ferrin, Utah
1945	New York City	Henry Iba, Oklahoma State	Bob Kurland, Oklahoma State
1946	New York City	Henry Iba, Oklahoma State	Bob Kurland, Oklahoma State
1947	New York City	Alvin Julian, Holy Cross	George Kaftan, Holy Cross
1948	New York City	Adolph Rupp, Kentucky	Alex Groza, Kentucky
1949	Seattle, Wash.	Adolph Rupp, Kentucky	Alex Groza, Kentucky
1950	New York City	Nat Holman, CCNY	Irwin Dambrot, CCNY
1951	Minneapolis, Minn.	Adolph Rupp, Kentucky	None Selected
1952	Seattle, Wash.	Forrest Allen, Kansas	Clyde Lovelette, Kansas
1953	Kansas City, Mo.	Branch McCracken, Indiana	B. H. Born, Kansas
1954	Kansas City, Mo.	Kenneth Loeffler, LaSalle	Tom Gola, LaSalle
1955	Kansas City, Mo.	Phil Woolpert, San Francisco	Bill Russell, San Francisco
1956	Evanston, Ill.	Phil Woolpert, San Francisco	Hal Lear, Temple
1957	Kansas City, Mo.	Frank McGuire, North Carolina	Wilt Chamberlain, Kansas
1958	Louisville, Ky.	Adolph Rupp, Kentucky	Elgin Baylor, Seattle
1959	Louisville, Ky.	Pete Newell, California	Jerry West, West Virginia
1960	San Francisco, Calif.	Fred Taylor, Ohio State	Jerry Lucas, Ohio State
1961	Kansas City, Mo.	Edwin Jucker, Cincinnati	Jerry Lucas, Ohio State
1962	Louisville, Ky.	Edwin Jucker, Cincinnati	Paul Hogue, Cincinnati
1963	Louisville, Ky.	George Ireland, Loyola (Ill.)	Art Heyman, Duke
1964	Kansas City, Mo.	John Wooden, UCLA	Walt Hazzard, UCLA
1965	Portland, Oreg.	John Wooden, UCLA	Bill Bradley, Princeton
1966	College Park, Md.	Don Haskins, Texas El Paso	Jerry Chambers, Utah
1967	Louisville, Ky.	John Wooden, UCLA	Lew Alcindor, UCLA
1968	Los Angeles, Calif.	John Wooden, UCLA	Lew Alcindor, UCLA
1969	Louisville, Ky.	John Wooden, UCLA	Lew Alcindor, UCLA
1970	College Park, Md.	John Wooden, UCLA	Sidney Wicks, UCLA
1971	Houston, Texas	John Wooden, UCLA	Vacated
1972	Los Angeles, Calif.	John Wooden, UCLA	Bill Walton, UCLA
1973	St. Louis, Mo.	John Wooden, UCLA	Bill Walton, UCLA
1974	Greensboro, N.C.	Norm Sloan, North Carolina St.	David Thompson, No. Caro. St.
1975	San Diego, Calif.	John Wooden, UCLA	Richard Washington, UCLA
1976	Philadelphia, Pa.	Bobby Knight, Indiana	Kent Benson, Indiana
1977	Atlanta, Ga.	Al McGuire, Marquette	Butch Lee, Marquette
1978	St. Louis	Joe Hall, Kentucky	Jack Givens, Kentucky

NCAA Division I Champions

Years Champion	Years Champion	Years Champion	Years Champion
1939—Oregon	1949—Kentucky	1959—California	1969—UCLA
1940—Indiana	1950—CCNY	1960—Ohio State	1970—UCLA
1941—Wisconsin	1951—Kentucky	1961—Cincinnati	1971—UCLA
1942—Stanford	1952—Kansas	1962—Cincinnati	1972—UCLA
1943—Wyoming	1953—Indiana	1963—Loyola (Chi.)	1973—UCLA
1944—Utah	1954—La Salle	1964—UCLA	1974—No. Carolina State
1945—Oklahoma A&M	1955—San Francisco	1965—UCLA	1975—UCLA
1946—Oklahoma A&M	1956—San Francisco	1966—Texas Western	1976—Indiana
1947—Holy Cross	1957—North Carolina	1967—UCLA	1977—Marquette
1948—Kentucky	1958—Kentucky	1968—UCLA	1978—Kentucky

NCAA Division I Records

(RESTRICTED TO GAMES BETWEEN 4-YEAR COLLEGES.)

Career Scoring Averages

Player, team	Last Year	Games	FG	FT	Pts	Avg
Pete Maravich, LSU	1970	83	1,387	893	3,667	44.2
Austin Carr, Notre Dame	1971	74	1,017	526	2,560	34.6
Oscar Robertson, Cincinnati	1960	88	1,052	869	2,973	33.8
Calvin Murphy, Niagara	1970	77	974	654	2,548	33.1
Frank Selvy, Furman	1954	78	922	694	2,538	32.5
Rick Mount, Purdue	1970	72	910	503	2,323	32.3
Darrell Floyd, Furman	1956	71	868	545	2,281	32.1
Nick Werkman, Seton Hall	1964	71	812	649	2,273	32.0
Willie Humes, Idaho St.	1971	48	565	380	1,510	31.5
Elgin Baylor, Col. Idaho-Seattle	1958	80	956	588	2,500	31.3
William Averitt, Pepperdine	1973	49	615	311	1,541	31.4
Dwight Lamar, SW Louisiana	1973	112	1,445	603	3,493	31.2
Elvin Hayes, Houston	1968	93	1,215	454	2,884	31.0
Bill Bradley, Princeton	1965	83	856	791	2,503	30.2

Season Averages

Player, team	Year	Games	FG	FT	Pts	Avg
Pete Maravich, LSU	1970	31	522	337	1,381	44.5
Pete Maravich, LSU	1969	26	433	282	1,148	44.2
Pete Maravich, LSU	1968	26	432	274	1,138	43.8
Frank Selvy, Furman	1954	29	427	355	1,209	41.7
Johnny Neumann, Mississippi	1971	23	366	191	923	40.1
Billy McGill, Utah	1962	26	394	221	1,009	38.8
Freeman Williams, Portland State	1977	26	417	176	1,010	38.8
Calvin Murphy, Niagara	1968	24	337	242	916	38.2
Austin Carr, Notre Dame	1970	29	444	218	1,106	38.1
Austin Carr, Notre Dame	1971	29	430	241	1,101	38.0
Rick Barry, Miami (Fla.)	1965	26	340	293	973	37.4

Single-Game Scoring

Player, team (opponent)	Year	Pts	Player, Team (opponent)	Year	Pts
Selvy, Furman (Newberry)	1954	100	Floyd, Furman (Morehead St.)	1955	67
Mlkvy, Temple (Wilkes)	1951	73	Maravich, LSU (Tulane)	1969	66

| Maravich, LSU (Alabama) . . . . | 1970 | 69 | Handlan, W. & Lee (Furman) . . . . | 1951 | 66 |
| Murphy, Niagara (Syracuse) . . . . | 1969 | 68 | Zawoluk, St. John's (St. Peter's) . . . . | 1950 | 65 |

Individual Records, Season

Field goal percentage	Alcindor, UCLA, 1967	.667	**Rebounds per game**	Slack, Marshall, 1955 . . .	25.6
	Martens, Ab. Christian, 1972	.667	**Rebounds**	Dukes, Seton Hall, 1953	734
	Fleming, Arizona, 1974	.667	**Field goals attempted**	Maravich, LSU, 1970 . . .	1,168
Free throw percentage	Boyer, Arkansas, 1962	.993	**Free throws attempted**	Selvy, Furman, 1954 . . .	444

NCAA Division II Champions

Year Champion	Year Champion	Year Champion	Year Champion
1958—South Dakota	1963—South Dakota St.	1968—Kentucky Wesleyan	1973—Kentucky Wesleyan
1959—Evansville	1964—Evansville	1969—Kentucky Wesleyan	1974—Morgan State
1960—Evansville	1965—Evansville	1970—Philadelphia Textile	1975—Old Dominion
1961—Wittenberg	1966—Kentucky Wesleyan	1971—Evansville	1976—Puget Sound
1962—Mt. St. Mary's	1967—Winston-Salem	1972—Roanoke	1977—Tennessee-Chattanooga
			1978—Cheyney St. College

National Invitation Tournament Champions

Year Champion	Year Champion	Year Champion	Year Champion
1938—Temple	1948—St. Louis	1958—Xavier (Ohio)	1968—Dayton
1939—Long Island Univ.	1949—San Francisco	1959—St. John's	1969—Temple
1940—Colorado	1950—CCNY	1960—Bradley	1970—Marquette
1941—Long Island Univ.	1951—Brigham Young	1961—Providence	1971—North Carolina
1942—West Virginia	1952—LaSalle	1962—Dayton	1972—Maryland
1943—St. John's	1953—Seton Hall	1963—Providence	1973—Virginia Tech
1944—St. John's	1954—Holy Cross	1964—Bradley	1974—Purdue
1945—DePaul	1955—Duquesne	1965—St. John's	1975—Princeton
1946—Kentucky	1956—Louisville	1966—Brigham Young	1976—Kentucky
1947—Utah	1957—Bradley	1967—Southern Illinois	1977—St. Bonaventure
			1978—Texas

College Basketball Coach of the Year
(UNITED PRESS INTERNATIONAL)

Year Winner, College	Year Winner, College	Year Winner, College
1952—Dudley Moore, LaSalle	1961—Fred Taylor, Ohio State	1971—Al McGuire, Marquette
1953—Branch McCracken, Indiana	1962—Fred Taylor, Ohio State	1972—John Wooden, UCLA
1954—Dudley Moore, LaSalle	1963—Ed Jucker, Cincinnati	1973—John Wooden, UCLA
1955—Phil Woolpert, San Francisco	1964—John Wooden, UCLA	1974—Digger Phelps, Notre Dame
1956—Phil Woolpert, San Francisco	1965—Dave Strack, Michigan	1975—Bobby Knight, Indiana
1957—Frank McGuire, North Carolina	1966—Adolph Rupp, Kentucky	1976—Tom Young, Rutgers
1958—Tex Winter, Kansas State	1967—John Wooden, UCLA	1977—Bob Gaillard, San Francisco
1959—Adolph Rupp, Kentucky	1968—Guy Lewis, Houston	1978—Bill Foster, Duke; Abe Lemons, Texas
1960—Pete Newell, California	1969—John Wooden, UCLA	
	1970—John Wooden, UCLA	

UCLA's 88-Game All-Time Win Streak

1. UCLA 74, Cal.-Santa Barbara 61.
2. UCLA 64, S. California 60.
3. UCLA 69, Oregon 68.
4. UCLA 67, Oregon State 65.
5. UCLA 94, Oregon State 64.
6. UCLA 74, Oregon 67.
7. UCLA 57, Washington State 53.
8. UCLA 71, Washington 69.
9. UCLA 103, California 69.
10. UCLA 107, Stanford 72.
11. UCLA 73, S. California 62.
12. UCLA 91, Brigham Young 73.
13. UCLA 57, Long Beach 55.
14. UCLA 68, Kansas 60.
15. UCLA 68, Villanova 62.
16. UCLA 105, The Citadel 49.
17. UCLA 106, Iowa 72.
18. UCLA 110, Iowa State 81.
19. UCLA 117, Texas A&M 53.
20. UCLA 114, Notre Dame 56.
21. UCLA 119, Texas Christian 81.
22. UCLA 115, Texas 65.
23. UCLA 79, Ohio State 53.
24. UCLA 78, Oregon State 72.
25. UCLA 93, Oregon 68.
26. UCLA 118, Stanford 79.
27. UCLA 82, California 43.
28. UCLA 92, Santa Clara 57.
29. UCLA 108, Denver 61.
30. UCLA 92, Chicago Loyola 64.
31. UCLA 57, Notre Dame 32.
32. UCLA 81, S. California 56.
33. UCLA 89, Washington State 58.
34. UCLA 109, Washington 70.
35. UCLA 100, Washington 83.
36. UCLA 85, Washington State 55.
37. UCLA 92, Oregon 70.
38. UCLA 91, Oregon State 72.
39. UCLA 85, California 71.
40. UCLA 102, Stanford 73.
41. UCLA 79, S. California 66.
42. UCLA 90, Weber 58.
43. UCLA 73, Long Beach 57.
44. UCLA 96, Louisville 77.
45. UCLA 81, Florida State 76.
46. UCLA 94, Wisconsin 53.
47. UCLA 73, Bradley 38.
48. UCLA 81, Pacific 48.
49. UCLA 98, Cal.-Santa Barbara 67.
50. UCLA 89, Pittsburgh 73.
51. UCLA 82, Notre Dame 56.
52. UCLA 85, Drake 72.
53. UCLA 71, Illinois 64.
54. UCLA 64, Oregon 38.
55. UCLA 87, Oregon State 61.
56. UCLA 82, Stanford 67.
57. UCLA 69, California 50.
58. UCLA 92, San Francisco 64.
59. UCLA 101, Providence 77.
60. UCLA 87, Chicago Loyola 73.
61. UCLA 82, Notre Dame 63.
62. UCLA 79, S. California 56.
63. UCLA 84, Washington State 50.
64. UCLA 76, Washington 67.
65. UCLA 93, Washington 62.
66. UCLA 96, Washington State 64.
67. UCLA 72, Oregon 61.
68. UCLA 73, Oregon State 67.
69. UCLA 90, California 65.
70. UCLA 51, Stanford 45.
71. UCLA 76, S. California 56.
72. UCLA 98, Arizona State 81.
73. UCLA 54, San Francisco 39.
74. UCLA 70, Indiana 59.
75. UCLA 87, Memphis State 66.
76. UCLA 101, Arkansas 79.
77. UCLA 65, Maryland 64.
78. UCLA 77, SMU 60.
79. UCLA 84, N. C. State 66.
80. UCLA 110, Ohio U. 63.
81. UCLA 111, St. Bonaventure 59.
82. UCLA 86, Wyoming 58.
83. UCLA 90, Michigan 70.
84. UCLA 100, Washington 48.
85. UCLA 55, Washington State 45.
86. UCLA 92, California 56.
87. UCLA 66, Stanford 52.
88. UCLA 68, Iowa 44.

INDEX

Heitz, Kenny, 27, 204, 218
Helms, Joe, 116-17
Henson, Lou, 225
Herrerias, Rene, 83, 209
Heyman, Art, 173, 180
Hickman, Peck, 142, 145
Hill, Andy, 242
Hill, Bobby Joe, 197-98
Hiller, Buster, 72
Hillhouse, Art, 58
Hirsch, Jack, 183
Hitchcock, Ed, 34
Hobson, Howard, 64-65, 101, 164
Hogan, Frank, 94-96, 159
Hogue, Paul, 155-58, 167, 169-70, 173
Hollyfield, Larry, 242
Holman, Nat, 56, 58, 61, 89, 92, 96, 107
Hosket, Bill, 209
Houbregs, Bob, 104, 106
Howard, Terry, 260
Hoyt, Rickie, 155
Huband, Kim, 240
Hubbard, Phil, 271
Huffman, Marvin, 68
Hummer, Ed, 189
Hundley, Rod, 243
Hunter, Leslie, 174-75
Hurt, Bob, 100
Hyatt, Chuck, 60-61
Hyder, John "Whack," 116-17

Iba, Henry (Hank), 1, 20, 76, 101-2
Imhoff, Darrall, 144-45, 149, 152
Ireland, George, 173-76, 179, 205, 236, 242
Irish, Ned, 54, 78, 92, 94, 102
Irving, Julius, 18
Issel, Dan, 225, 260

Jackson, Keith, 70
Jacobs, Hirsch, 11
Jacobs, Michael Strauss, 77-78
Jacobson, Bob, 166
Jares, Joe, 233
Jarstad, John, 69-70
Johanson, Wally, 64
John, Maurice, 217
Johnson, Gus, 176
Johnson, Jerry, 218
Johnson, Marques, 259-60, 262, 266, 273
Johnson, Walter, 214
Jones, Clarence, 245
Jones, K. C., 12-16, 19, 114, 117, 119-20, 130
Jones, "Wah Wah," 82-83, 119
Jordan, Ed, 266-67
Jordan, Johnny, 53-54, 171
Jorgenson, Tom, 189
Jucker, Ed, 155, 157, 167-76
Julian, Doggie, 83

Kaftan, George, 80
Kalbaugh, Billy, 224
Kallenberg, H. F., 35
Keaney, Frank, 44
Kearns, Tommy, 127-28
Keller, Bill, 218
Kellogg, Junius, 95
Kenon, Karry, 245-46, 247
Keogan, George, 54, 72, 75-76
Kerford, Lloyd, 124
Kilpatrick, Gen. John Reed, 54-55
Kimmel, Bobby, 117
King, George, 142
King, Martin Luther, 244
King, Ron, 240-41
Kinsbrunner, Mac, 48
Kirvin, Billy, 152
Kladis, Nick, 173
Klos, Stan, 273
Knight, Bobby, 245, 257-58, 262-65, 267-70
Kotsores, Bill, 73, 75
Kotz, Johnny, 68
Kraak, Charlie, 103
Kraft, Jack, 201, 234-35
Kramer, Jerry, 26
Krause, Ed (Moose), 53-54
Krebs, Jim, 126
Kron, Tommy, 195-96, 198
Kuester, John, 274, 276
Kurland, Bob, 76-79

Lacey, Edgar, 192, 209
Lackey, Bob, 230, 233
LaGarde, Tommy, 274
Lamar, Dwight, 239
Lambert, Ward (Piggy), 41-42, 47, 60, 68
Lamson, Bob, 124-25
Lancaster, Harry, 168, 196
Lanier, Bob, 210, 224-26
Lapchick, Joe, 54, 56, 77, 80-82, 193, 199
Lardner, John, 23
Laskowski, John, 262
Lattin, Dave, 197
Lawhon, Mike, 240
Layne, Bobby, 154
Layne, Floyd, 89
Lear, Hal, 121
Lee, Alfred (Butch), 264, 272-73, 275-77
Lee, Bebe, 60
Lee, Greg, 236, 237, 238, 243, 247
Lee, James, 261
Lee, Jim, 281
Lee, Theodis, 211
Leggat, Harry, 75
Lemons, Abe, 234, 247, 257, 270, 282
Leonard, Bob, 103, 108
Levis, George, 41
Lewis, Bob, 74